THE GITA

IN THE VISION AND THE WORDS OF

SRI AUROBINDO

THE GITA

IN THE VISION AND THE WORDS OF

SRI AUROBINDO

First edition 2009
Fourth impression 2025

Rs 400
ISBN 978-81-7058-935-8

Published by Sri Aurobindo Ashram Publication Department
Pondicherry 605 002
Web https://www.sabda.in

Printed at Sri Aurobindo Ashram Press, Pondicherry
PRINTED IN INDIA

THE WHOLE OF THE GITA
THROUGH HIS OWN WORDS SLOKA AFTER SLOKA
IN THE VISION OF
SRI AUROBINDO*

* See "Postscript from the Editor", p. 337.

Sri Aurobindo c. 1918-1920

There are four very great events in history, the siege of Troy, the life and crucifixion of Christ, the exile of Krishna in Brindavan and the colloquy with Arjuna on the field of Kurukshetra. The siege of Troy created Hellas, the exile in Brindavan created devotional religion (for before there was only meditation and worship), Christ from his cross humanised Europe, the colloquy at Kurukshetra will yet liberate humanity. Yet it is said that none of these four events ever happened.

Sri Aurobindo
Thoughts and Aphorisms

Contents

N.B. All the titles here — of the six sections of the Introduction and of the eighteen chapters of the Gita and of their different parts (with the exception of chapter I, the title of which has been mentioned by the author on page nine of the Introduction) — are those of the chapters from *Essays on the Gita* where the subject matter of most of the concerned *slokas* has mainly been treated. The six sections of the Introduction consist of extracts from the first six chapters of *Essays on the Gita.*

Foreword

We are publishing here for the first time a near complete "translation" of the Bhagavad-Gita in the very words of Sri Aurobindo.

In the course of his research, the Editor found that nearly all 700 *slokas* of the Gita have actually been translated, or rather, rendered, by Sri Aurobindo, mostly in his *Essays on the Gita*, but in other books as well. Extracting them from their various sources, he succeeded in weaving them together, respecting the order of the Gita's *slokas*. Reading this book, we understand better why the Yoga of the Gita is an important part of Sri Aurobindo's Integral Yoga, and how it leads to a vaster, all-embracing vision of life and of man's spiritual evolution.

So this book offers to the reader not only a new translation and interpretation of this sacred Scripture, but something infinitely more precious to us: the secret of the Gita as it has been *seen* and experienced by Sri Aurobindo.

*Introduction**

I — OUR DEMAND AND NEED FROM THE GITA

First of all, there is undoubtedly a Truth one and eternal which we are seeking, from which all other truth derives, by the light of which all other truth finds its right place, explanation and relation to the scheme of knowledge. But precisely for that reason it cannot be shut up in a single trenchant formula, it is not likely to be found in its entirety or in all its bearings in any single philosophy or scripture or uttered altogether and for ever by any one teacher, thinker, prophet or Avatar. Secondly, this Truth, though it is one and eternal, expresses itself in Time and through the mind of man; therefore every Scripture must necessarily contain two elements, one temporary, perishable, belonging to the ideas of the period and country in which it was produced, the other eternal and imperishable and applicable in all ages and countries. What is of entirely permanent value is that which besides being universal has been experienced, lived and seen with a higher than the intellectual vision.

The truth of substance, the truth of living vision and experience on which the Gita's system was built is still sound and retains a permanent validity and significance. The Gita is a book that has worn extraordinarily well and it is almost as fresh and still in its real substance quite as new, because always renewable in experience, as when it first appeared in or was written into the frame of the Mahabharata.

What we can do with profit is to seek in the Gita for the actual living truths it contains, apart from their metaphysical form, to extract from it what can help us or the world at large and to put it in the most natural and vital form and expression we can find that will be suitable to the mentality and helpful to the spiritual needs of our present-day humanity. No doubt in this attempt we may mix a good deal of error born of our own individuality and of the ideas in which we live, as did greater men before us, but if we steep ourselves in the spirit of this great Scripture and, above all, if we have tried to live in that spirit, we may be sure of finding in it as much real truth as we are capable of receiving as well as the spiritual influence and actual help that, personally[1], we were intended to derive from it. And that is after all what Scriptures were written to give; the rest is academical disputation

* Editor's title.

1. "In the jail (*Alipur jail, where he was imprisoned from 5 May 1908 until 6 May 1909*) I had the Gita and the Upanishads with me, practised the Yoga of the Gita and meditated with the help of the Upanishads." Extract from a letter of the author, dated 13 September 1946. (*Editor's note*)

or theological dogma. Only those Scriptures, religions, philosophies which can be thus constantly renewed, relived, their stuff of permanent truth constantly reshaped and developed in the inner thought and spiritual experience of a developing humanity, continue to be of living importance to mankind. The rest remain as monuments of the past, but have no actual force or vital impulse for the future.

We of the coming day stand at the head of a new age of development which must lead to a new and larger synthesis. We are not called upon to be orthodox Vedantins of any of the three schools or Tantrics or to adhere to one of the theistic religions of the past or to entrench ourselves within the four corners of the teaching of the Gita. That would be to limit ourselves and to attempt to create our spiritual life out of the being, knowledge and nature of others, of the men of the past, instead of building it out of our own being and potentialities. We do not belong to the past dawns, but to the noons of the future. But just as the past syntheses have taken those which preceded them for their starting-point, so also must that of the future, to be on firm ground, proceed from what the great bodies of realised spiritual thought and experience in the past have given. Among them the Gita takes a most important place.

Our object, then, in studying the Gita will not be a scholastic or academical scrutiny of its thought, nor to place its philosophy in the history of metaphysical speculation, nor shall we deal with it in the manner of the analytical dialectician. We approach it for help and light and our aim must be to distinguish its essential and living message, that in it on which humanity has to seize for its perfection and its highest spiritual welfare.

II — THE DIVINE TEACHER

There are three things in the Gita which are spiritually significant, the divine personality of the Teacher, his characteristic relations with his disciple and the occasion of his teaching. The teacher is God himself descended into humanity; the disciple is the first, as we might say in modern language, the representative man of his age, closest friend and chosen instrument of the Avatar, his protagonist in an immense work and struggle the secret purpose of which is unknown to the actors in it, known only to the incarnate Godhead who guides it all from behind the veil of his unfathomable mind of knowledge; the occasion is the violent crisis of that work and struggle at the moment when the anguish and moral difficulty and blind violence of its apparent movements forces itself with the shock of a visible revelation on the mind of its representative man and raises the whole question of the meaning of God in the world and the goal and drift and sense of human life and conduct.

India has from ancient times held strongly a belief in the reality of the Avatara, the descent into form, the revelation of the Godhead in humanity. All existence is a manifestation of God because He is the only existence and nothing can be except as either a real figuring or else a figment of that one reality. Therefore every conscious being is in part or in some way a descent of the Infinite into the apparent finiteness of name and form. But when the divine Consciousness and Power, taking upon itself the human form and the human mode of action, possesses it not only by powers and magnitudes, by degrees and outward faces of itself but out of its eternal self-knowledge, when the Unborn knows itself and acts in the frame of the mental being and the appearance of birth, that is the height of the conditioned manifestation; it is the full and conscious descent of the Godhead, it is the Avatara.

When this eternal divine Consciousness always present in every human being, this God in man, takes possession partly or wholly of the human consciousness and becomes in visible human shape the guide, teacher, leader of the world, not as those who living in their humanity yet feel something of the power or light or love of the divine Gnosis informing and conducting them, but out of that divine gnosis itself, direct from its central force and plenitude, then we have the manifest Avatar. The inner Divinity is the eternal Avatar in man; the human manifestation is its sign and development in the external world. When we thus understand the conception of Avatarhood, we see that whether for the fundamental teaching of the Gita, our present subject, or for spiritual life generally the external aspect has only a secondary importance. So the Krishna who matters to us is the eternal incarnation of the Divine and not the historical teacher and leader of men. In seeking the kernel of the thought of the Gita we need, therefore, only concern ourselves with the spiritual significance of the human-divine Krishna of the Mahabharata who is presented to us as the teacher of Arjuna on the battle-field of Kurukshetra.

The historical Krishna, no doubt, existed. But we are concerned only with the figure of the divine Teacher as it is presented to us in the Gita and with the Power for which it there stands in the spiritual illumination of the human being. The Gita accepts the human Avatarhood; for the Lord speaks of the repeated, the constant[1] manifestation of the Divine in humanity, when He, the eternal Unborn assumes by His Maya, by the power of the infinite Consciousness to clothe itself apparently in finite forms, the conditions of becoming which we call birth. But it is not this upon which stress is laid, but on the transcendent, the cosmic and the internal Divine; it is on the Source of all things and the Master of all and on the Godhead secret in man. It is this

1. *babuni me vyatītānī janmāni... sambhavāmi yuge yuge.*

internal Divinity who is meant when the Gita speaks of the doer of violent asuric austerities troubling the God within or of the sin of those who despise the Divine lodged in the human body or of the same Godhead destroying our ignorance by the blazing lamp of knowledge. It is then the eternal Avatar, this God in man, the divine Consciousness always present in the human being who manifested in a visible form speaks to the human soul in the Gita, illumines the meaning of life and the secret of divine action and gives it the light of the divine knowledge and guidance and the assuring and fortifying word of the Master of existence in the hour when it comes face to face with the painful mystery of the world.

Thus the figure of Krishna becomes, as it were, the symbol of the divine dealings with humanity. And the action in which this divine figure moves is the whole wide action of man in life. This is the distinguishing feature of the Gita that it is the culmination of such an action which gives rise to its teaching and assigns that prominence and bold relief to the gospel of works which it enunciates with an emphasis and force we do not find in other Indian Scriptures. It is here that he reveals the secret of the necessity of action and the divinity behind our works. Here it is the action which leads to knowledge and in which the divine Knower figures himself. Arjuna and Krishna, this human and this divine, stand together not as seers in the peaceful hermitage of meditation, but as fighter and holder of the reins in the clamorous field, in the midst of the hurtling shafts, in the chariot of battle. The Teacher of the Gita is therefore not only the God in man who unveils himself in the word of knowledge, but the God in man who moves our whole world of action, by and for whom all our humanity exists and struggles and labours, towards whom all human life travels and progresses. He is the secret Master of works and sacrifice and the Friend of the human peoples.

III — THE HUMAN DISCIPLE

Such then is the divine Teacher of the Gita, the eternal Avatar, the Divine who has descended into the human consciousness, the Lord seated within the heart of all beings, He who guides from behind the veil all our thought and action and heart's seeking even as He directs from behind the veil of visible and sensible forms and forces and tendencies the great universal action of the world which He has manifested in His own being. All the strife of our upward endeavour and seeking finds its culmination and ceases in a satisfied fulfilment when we can rend the veil and get behind our apparent self to this real Self, can realise our whole being in this true Lord of our being, can give up our personality to and into this one real Person, merge our ever-dispersed and ever-converging mental activities into His plenary light, offer up our errant and struggling will and energies into His vast, luminous and undivided Will, at once renounce and satisfy all our dissipated outward-moving desires and emotions in the plenitude of His self-existent Bliss. This is the world-Teacher of whose eternal knowledge all other highest teaching is but the various reflection and partial word, this the Voice to which the hearing of our soul has to awaken.

Arjuna, the disciple who receives his initiation on the battlefield, is a counterpart of this conception; he is the type of the struggling human soul who has not yet received the knowledge, but has grown fit to receive it by action in the world in a close companionship and an increasing nearness to the higher and divine Self in humanity. Arjuna is the representative man of a great world-struggle and divinely-guided movement of men and nations; in the Gita he typifies the human soul of action brought face to face through that action in its highest and most violent crisis with the problem of human life and its apparent incompatibility with the spiritual state or even with a purely ethical ideal of perfection.

Arjuna is the fighter in the chariot with the divine Krishna as his charioteer. The Gita starts from action and Arjuna is the man of action and not of knowledge, the fighter, never the seer or the thinker. From the beginning of the Gita this characteristic temperament of the disciple is clearly indicated and it is maintained throughout. It becomes first evident in the manner in which he is awakened to the sense of what he is doing, the great slaughter of which he is to be the chief instrument, in the thoughts which immediately rise in him, in the standpoint and the psychological motives which make him recoil from the whole terrible catastrophe. They are not the thoughts, the standpoint, the motives of a philosophical or even of a deeply reflective mind or a spiritual temperament confronted with the same or a similar problem. They are those, as we might say, of the practical or the pragmatic man, the emotional, sensational, moral and intelligent human being not habituated to profound and original reflection or any sounding of the depths, accustomed rather to high but fixed standards of thought and action and a confident treading through all vicissitudes and difficulties, who now finds all his standards failing him and all the basis of his confidence in himself and his life shorn away from under him at a single stroke. That is the nature of the crisis which he undergoes. He has lived and guided himself by the Shastra, the moral and social code. The thought which preoccupies him, the standard which he obeys is the *dharma*[1], that collective Indian conception of the religious, social and moral

1. Dharma means literally that which one lays hold of and which holds things together, the law, the norm, the rule of nature, action and life.

rule of conduct, and especially the rule of the station and function to which he belongs, he the Kshatriya, the high-minded, self-governed, chivalrous prince and warrior and leader of Aryan men. Following always this rule, conscious of virtue and right dealing he has travelled so far and finds suddenly that it has led him to become the protagonist of a terrific and unparalleled slaughter, a monstrous civil war involving all the cultured Aryan nations which must lead to the complete destruction of the flower of their manhood and threatens their ordered civilisation with chaos and collapse.

To such a disciple the Teacher of the Gita gives his divine teaching. He has to lift him up out of this lower life into a higher consciousness, out of ignorant attachment to action into that which transcends, yet originates and orders action, out of ego into Self, out of life in mind, vitality and body into that higher nature beyond mind which is the status of the Divine. He has at the same time to give him that for which he asks and for which he is inspired to seek by the guidance within him, a new Law of life and action high above the insufficient rule of the ordinary human existence with its endless conflicts and oppositions, perplexities and illusory certainties, a higher Law by which the soul shall be free from this bondage of works and yet powerful to act and conquer in the vast liberty of its divine being. For the action must be performed, the world must fulfil its cycles and the soul of the human being must not turn back in ignorance from the work it is here to do. The whole course of the teaching of the Gita is determined and directed, even in its widest wheelings, towards the fulfilment of these three objects.

Dharma is a word which has an ethical and practical, a natural and philosophical and a religious and spiritual significance, and it may be used in any of these senses exclusive of the others, in a purely ethical, a purely philosophical or a purely religious sense. Ethically it means the law of righteousness, the moral rule of conduct, or in a still more outward and practical significance social and political justice, or even simply the observation of the social law.

We must take the idea of the Dharma in its fullest, deepest and largest conception, as the inner and the outer law by which the divine Will and Wisdom work out the spiritual evolution of mankind and its circumstances and results in the life of the race. Dharma in the Indian conception is not merely the good, the right, morality and justice, ethics; it is the whole government of all the relations of man with other beings, with Nature, with God, considered from the point of view of a divine principle working itself out in forms and laws of action, forms of the inner and the outer life, orderings of relations of every kind in the world. Dharma is both that which we hold to and that which holds together our inner and outer activities. In its primary sense it means a fundamental law of our nature which secretly conditions all our activities, and in this sense each being, type, species, individual, group has its own dharma. Secondly, there is the divine nature which has to develop and manifest in us, and in this sense dharma is the law of the inner workings by which that grows in our being. Thirdly, there is the law by which we govern our outgoing thought and action and our relations with each other so as to help best both our own growth and that of the human race towards the divine ideal.

Dharma is generally spoken of as something eternal and unchanging, and so it is in the fundamental principle, in the ideal, but in its forms it is continually changing and evolving, because man does not already possess the ideal or live in it, but aspires more or less perfectly towards it, is growing towards its knowledge and practice. And in this growth dharma is all that helps us to grow into the divine purity, largeness, light, freedom, power, strength, joy, love, good, unity, beauty, and against it stands its shadow and denial, all that resists its growth and has not undergone its law, all that has not yielded up and does not will to yield up its secret of divine values, but presents a front of perversion and contradiction, of impurity, narrowness, bondage, darkness, weakness, vileness, discord and suffering and division, and the hideous and the crude, all that man has to leave behind in his progress. This is the *adharma*, not-dharma, which strives with and seeks to overcome the dharma, to draw backward and downward, the reactionary force which makes for evil, ignorance and darkness. Between the two there is perpetual battle and struggle, oscillation of victory and defeat in which sometimes the upward and sometimes the downward forces prevail.

IV — THE CORE OF THE TEACHING

Undoubtedly, the Gita is a Gospel of Works, but of works which culminate in knowledge, that is, in spiritual realisation and quietude, and of works motived by devotion, that is, a conscious surrender of one's whole self first into the hands and then into the being of the Supreme, and not at all of works as they are understood by the modern mind, not at all an action dictated by egoistic and altruistic, by personal, social, humanitarian motives, principles, ideals. That which the Gita teaches is not a human, but a divine action; not the performance of social duties, but the abandonment of all other standards of duty or conduct for a selfless performance of the divine will working through our nature; not social service, but the action of the Best, the God-possessed, the Master-men done impersonally for the sake of the world and as a sacrifice to Him who stands behind man and Nature. In other words, the Gita is not a book of practical ethics, but of the spiritual life.

But the point here is that the modern mind has exiled from its practical motive-power the two essential things, God or the Eternal and spirituality or the God-state, which are the master conceptions of the Gita. It lives in humanity only, and the Gita would have us live in God, though for the world in God; in its life, heart and intellect only, and the Gita would have us live in the spirit; in the mutable Being who is "all creatures", and the Gita would have us live also in the Immutable and the Supreme; in the changing march of Time, and the Gita would have us live in the Eternal. Or if these higher things are now beginning to be vaguely envisaged, it is only to make them subservient to man and society; but God and spirituality exist in their own right and not as adjuncts. And in practice the lower in us must learn to exist for the higher, in order that the higher also may in us consciously exist for the lower, to draw it nearer to its own altitudes. Therefore it is a mistake to interpret the Gita from the standpoint of the mentality of today and force it to teach us the disinterested performance of duty as the highest and all-sufficient law. The Gita does not teach the disinterested performance of duties but the following of the divine life, the abandonment of all dharmas, to take refuge in the Supreme alone.

The Brahmic consciousness, the soul's freedom from works and the determination of works in the nature by the Lord within and above us, is the kernel of the Gita's teaching with regard to action. The equality which the Gita preaches is not disinterestedness, — the great command to Arjuna given *after* the foundation and main structure of the teaching have been laid and built, "Arise, slay thy enemies, enjoy a prosperous kingdom," has not the ring of an uncompromising altruism or of a white, dispassionate abnegation; it is a state of inner poise and wideness which is the foundation of spiritual freedom. With that poise, in that freedom we have to do the work "that is to be done".

The argument of the Gita resolves itself into three great steps by which action rises out of the human into the divine plane leaving the bondage of the lower for the liberty of a higher law. First, by the renunciation of desire and a perfect equality works have to be done as a sacrifice by man as the doer, a sacrifice to a deity who is the supreme and only Self though by him not yet realised in his own being. Secondly, not only the desire of the fruit, but the claim to be the doer of works has to be renounced in the realisation of the Self as the equal, the inactive, the immutable principle and of all works as simply the operation of universal Force, of the Nature-Soul, Prakriti, the unequal, active, mutable power. Lastly, the supreme Self has to be seen as the supreme Purusha governing this Prakriti, of whom the soul in Nature is a partial manifestation, by whom all works are directed, in a perfect transcendence, through Nature. To Him love and adoration and the sacrifice of works have to be offered; the whole being has to be surrendered to Him and the whole consciousness raised up to dwell in this divine consciousness so that the human soul may share in His divine transcendence of Nature and of His works and act in a perfect spiritual liberty.

The first step is Karmayoga, the selfless sacrifice of works, and here the Gita's insistence is on action. The second is Jnanayoga, the self-realisation and knowledge of the true nature of the self and the world; and here the insistence is on knowledge; but the sacrifice of works continues and the path of Works becomes one with but does not disappear into the path of Knowledge. The last step is Bhaktiyoga, adoration and seeking of the supreme Self as the Divine Being, and here the insistence is on devotion; but the knowledge is not subordinated, only raised, vitalised and fulfilled, and still the sacrifice of works continues; the double path becomes the triune way of knowledge, works and devotion. And the fruit of the sacrifice, the one fruit still placed before the seeker, is attained, union with the divine Being and oneness with the supreme divine nature.

V — KURUKSHETRA

The Gita is given as an episode in an epic history of nations and their wars and men and their deeds and arises out of a critical moment in the soul of one of its leading personages face to face with the crowning action of his life, a work terrible, violent and sanguinary, at the point when he must either recoil from it altogether or carry it through to its inexorable completion. The teaching of the Gita must therefore be regarded not merely in the light of a general spiritual philosophy or ethical doctrine, but as bearing upon a practical crisis in the application of ethics and spirituality to human life. For what that crisis stands, what is the significance of the battle of Kurukshetra and its effect on Arjuna's inner being, we have first to determine if we would grasp the central drift of the idea of the Gita.

What is it that makes the difficulty for the man who has to take the world as it is and act in it and yet would live, within, the spiritual life? What is this aspect of existence which appals his awakened mind and brings about what the title of the first chapter of the Gita calls significantly "The Yoga of the dejection of Arjuna", the dejection and discouragement felt by the human being when he is forced to face the spectacle of the universe as it really is with the veil of the ethical illusion, the illusion of self-righteousness torn from his eyes, before a higher reconciliation with himself is effected? It is that aspect which is figured outwardly in the carnage and massacre of Kurukshetra and spiritually by the vision of the Lord of all things as Time arising to devour and destroy the creatures whom it has made. This is the vision of the Lord of all existence as the universal Creator but also the universal Destroyer. It is one and the same truth seen first indirectly and obscurely in the facts of life and then directly and clearly in the soul's vision of that which manifests itself in life. The outward aspect is that of world-existence and human existence proceeding by struggle and slaughter; the inward aspect is that of the universal Being fulfilling himself in a vast creation and a vast destruction. Life a battle and a field of death, this is Kurukshetra; God the Terrible, this is the vision that Arjuna sees on that field of massacre.

From a clash of material or other forces everything in this world, if not the world itself, seems to be born; by a struggle of forces, tendencies, principles, beings it seems to proceed, ever creating new things, ever destroying the old, marching one knows not very well whither. However that may be, this is certain that there is not only no construction here without destruction, no harmony except by a poise of contending forces won out of many actual and potential discords, but also no continued existence of life except by a constant self-feeding and devouring of other life. The command seems to have gone out from the beginning, "Thou shalt not conquer except by battle with thy fellows and thy surroundings; thou shalt not even live except by battle and struggle and by absorbing into thyself other life. The first law of this world that I have made is creation and preservation by destruction."

Ancient thought accepted this starting-point so far as it could see it by scrutiny of the universe. The old Upanishads saw it very clearly and phrased it with an uncompromising thoroughness which will have nothing to do with any honeyed glosses or optimistic scuttlings of the truth. Hunger that is Death, they said, is the creator and master of this world, and they figured vital existence in the image of the Horse of the sacrifice. Matter they described by a name which means ordinarily food and they said, we call it food because it is devoured and devours creatures. The eater eating is eaten, this is the formula of the material world.

We must look existence in the face if our aim is to arrive at a right solution, whatever that solution may be. And to look existence in the face is to look God in the face; for the two cannot be separated, nor the responsibility for the laws of world-existence be shifted away from Him who created them or from That which constituted it. It is only a few religions which have had the courage to say without any reserve, like the Indian, that this enigmatic World-Power is one Deity, one Trinity, to lift up the image of the Force that acts in the world in the figure not only of the beneficent Durga, but of the terrible Kali in her blood-stained dance of destruction and to say, "This too is the Mother; this also know to be God; this too, if thou hast the strength, adore." And it is significant that the religion which has had this unflinching honesty and tremendous courage, has succeeded in creating a profound and wide-spread spirituality such as no other can parallel. For truth is the foundation of real spirituality and courage is its soul. *Tasyai satyam āyatanam.*

God is not only the Destroyer, but the Friend of creatures; not only the cosmic Trinity, but the Transcendent; the terrible Kali is also the loving and beneficent Mother; the Lord of Kurukshetra is the divine comrade and charioteer, the attracter of beings, incarnate Krishna. And whithersoever he is driving through all the strife and clash and confusion, to whatever goal or godhead he may be attracting us, it is — no doubt of that — to some transcendence of all these aspects upon which we have been so firmly insisting. But where, how, with what kind of transcendence, under what conditions, this we have to discover; and to discover it, the first necessity is to see the world as it is, to observe and value rightly his action as it reveals itself at the start and now; afterwards the way and the goal will better reveal themselves. We must acknowledge Kurukshetra; we must submit to the law of life by Death before we can find our way to the life immortal; we must open our eyes, with a less appalled gaze than Arjuna's, to the vision of our Lord of Time and Death and cease to deny, hate or recoil from the universal Destroyer.

VI — MAN AND THE BATTLE OF LIFE

The divine charioteer of Kurukshetra reveals Himself on one side as the Lord of all the worlds and the Friend and omniscient Guide of all creatures, on the other as Time the Destroyer "arisen for the destruction of these peoples." The Gita affirms this also as God; it does not attempt to evade the enigma of the world by escaping from it through a side-door. If we accept at all, as the Gita accepts, the existence of God, that is to say, of the omnipresent, omniscient, omnipotent, yet always transcendent Being who manifests the world and Himself in the world, who is not the slave but the lord of His creative Consciousness, Nature or Force (Maya, Prakriti or Shakti), who is not baffled or thwarted in His world-conception or design by His creatures, man or devil, who does not need to justify Himself by shifting the responsibility for any part of His creation or manifestation on that which is created or manifested, then the human being has to start from a great, a difficult act of faith. Finding himself in a world which is apparently a chaos of battling powers, a clash of vast and obscure forces, a life which subsists only by constant change and death, menaced from every side by pain, suffering, evil and destruction, he has to see the omnipresent Deity in it all and conscious that of this enigma there must be a solution and beyond this ignorance in which he dwells a Knowledge that reconciles, he has to take his stand upon this faith, "Though Thou slay me, yet will I trust in Thee." All human thought or faith that is active and affirmative, whether it be theistic, pantheistic or atheistic, does in fact involve more or less explicitly and completely such an attitude. It admits and it believes; admits the discords of the world, believes in some highest principle of God, universal Being or Nature which shall enable us to transcend, overcome or harmonise these discords, perhaps even to do all three at once, to harmonise by overcoming and transcending.

Then, as to human life in its actualities, we have to accept its aspect of a struggle and a battle mounting into supreme crises such as that of Kurukshetra. The Gita takes for its frame such a period of transition and crisis as humanity periodically experiences in its history, in which great forces clash together for a huge destruction and reconstruction, intellectual, social, moral, religious, political, and these in the actual psychological and social stage of human evolution culminate usually through a violent physical convulsion of strife, war or revolution. The Gita proceeds from the acceptance of the necessity in Nature for such vehement crises and it accepts not only the moral aspect, the struggle between righteousness and unrighteousness, between the self-affirming law of Good and the forces that oppose its progression, but also the physical aspect, the actual armed war or other vehement physical strife between the human beings who represent the antagonistic powers.

We must remember that the Gita was composed at a time when war was even more than it is now a necessary part of human activity and the idea of its elimination from the scheme of life would have been an absolute chimera. The gospel of universal peace and goodwill among men — for without a universal and entire mutual goodwill there can be no real and abiding peace — has never succeeded for a moment in possessing itself of human life during the historic cycle of our progress, because morally, socially, spiritually the race was not prepared and the poise of Nature in its evolution would not admit of its being immediately prepared for any such transcendence. Even now[1] we have not actually progressed beyond the feasibility of a system of accommodation between conflicting interests which may minimise the recurrence of the worst forms of strife. And towards this consummation the method, the approach which humanity has been forced by its own nature to adopt, is a monstrous mutual massacre unparalleled in history; a universal war full of bitterness and irreconcilable hatred, is the straight way and the triumphant means modern man has found for the establishment of universal peace. A day may come, must surely come, we will say, when humanity will be ready spiritually, morally, socially for the reign of universal peace; meanwhile the aspect of battle and the nature and function of man as a fighter have to be accepted and accounted for by any practical philosophy and religion. The Gita, taking life as it is and not only as it may be in some distant future, puts

1. This was written during the years of the First World War 1914-1918. (*Editor's note*)

the question how this aspect and function of life, which is really an aspect and function of human activity in general, can be harmonised with the spiritual existence.

The Gita is therefore addressed to a fighter, a man of action, one whose duty in life is that of war and protection, war as a part of government for the protection of those who are excused from that duty, debarred from protecting themselves and therefore at the mercy of the strong and the violent, war, secondly and by a moral extension of this idea, for the protection of the weak and the oppressed and for the maintenance of right and justice in the world. For all these ideas, the social and practical, the moral and the chivalrous enter into the Indian conception of the Kshatriya, the man who is a warrior and ruler by function and a knight and king in his nature. That system differed from the modern in its conception. To the modern mind man is a thinker, worker or producer and a fighter all in one, and the tendency of the social system is to lump all these activities and to demand from each individual his contribution to the intellectual, economical and military life and needs of the community without paying any heed to the demands of his individual nature and temperament. The ancient Indian civilisation laid peculiar stress on the individual nature, tendency, temperament and sought to determine by it the ethical type, function and place in the society. Nor did it consider man primarily as a social being or the fullness of his social existence as the highest ideal, but rather as a spiritual being in process of formation and development and his social life, ethical law, play of temperament and exercise of function as means and stages of spiritual formation. Thought and knowledge, war and government, production and distribution, labour and service were carefully differentiated functions of society [Brahmin, Kshatriya, Vaishya, Sudra], each assigned to those who were naturally called to it and providing the right means by which they could individually proceed towards their spiritual development and self-perfection.

The physical fact of war is only a special and outward manifestation of a general principle in life and the Kshatriya is only the outward manifestation and type of a general characteristic necessary to the completeness of human perfection. War typifies and embodies physically the aspect of battle and struggle which belongs to all life, both to our inner and our outer living, in a world whose method is a meeting and wrestling of forces which progress by mutual destruction towards a continually changing adjustment expressive of a progressive harmonising and hopeful of a perfect harmony based upon some yet ungrasped potentiality of oneness. The Kshatriya is the type and embodiment of the fighter in man who accepts this principle in life and faces it as a warrior striving towards mastery, not shrinking from the destruction of bodies and forms, but through it all aiming at the realisation of some principle of right, justice, law which shall be the basis of the harmony towards which the struggle tends. The Gita accepts this aspect of the world-energy and the physical fact of war which embodies it, and it addresses itself to the man of action, the striver and fighter, the Kshatriya, — war which is the extreme contradiction of the soul's high aspiration to peace within and harmlessness without, the striver and fighter whose necessary turmoil of struggle and action seems to be the very contradiction of the soul's high ideal of calm mastery and self-possession, — and it seeks for an issue from the contradiction, a point at which its terms meet and a poise which shall be the first essential basis of harmony and transcendence.

Man meets the battle of life in the manner most consonant with the essential quality most dominant in his nature. There are, according to the Sankhya philosophy accepted in this respect by the Gita, three essential qualities or modes of the world-energy and therefore also of human nature, *sattva*, the mode of poise, knowledge and satisfaction, *rajas*, the mode of passion, action and struggling emotion, *tamas*, the mode of ignorance and inertia. But there comes a stage in which the mind recoils from the whole problem and, dissatisfied with the solutions given by the threefold mode of Nature, *traiguṇya*, seeks for some higher solution outside of it or else above it. It looks for an escape either into something which is outside and void of all qualities and therefore of all activity or in something which is superior to the three qualities and master of them and therefore at once capable of action and unaffected, undominated by its own action, in the *nirguṇa* or the *triguṇātīta*. It aspires to an absolute peace and unconditioned existence or to a dominant calm and superior existence.

Arjuna is the Kshatriya, the rajasic man who governs his rajasic action by a high sattwic ideal. He advances to this gigantic struggle, to this Kurukshetra with the full acceptance of the joy of battle, as to "a holiday of fight", but with a proud confidence in the righteousness of his cause; he advances in his rapid chariot tearing the hearts of his enemies with the victorious clamour of his war-conch; for he wishes to look upon all these kings of men who have come here to champion against him the cause of unrighteousness and establish as a rule of life the disregard of law, justice and truth which they would replace by the rule of a selfish and arrogant egoism. When this confidence is shattered within him, when he is smitten down from his customary attitude and mental basis of life, it is by the uprush of the tamasic quality into the rajasic man, inducing a recoil of astonishment, grief, horror, dismay, dejection, bewilderment of the mind and the war of reason against itself, a collapse towards the principle of ignorance and inertia. As a result he turns towards renunciation.

Chapter One

The Yoga of the dejection of Arjuna

धृतराष्ट्र उवाच
धर्मक्षेत्रे कुरुक्षेत्रे समवेता युयुत्सवः ।
मामकाः पाण्डवाश्चैव किमकुर्वत सञ्जय ।।१।।

1. *Dhritarashtra* — **On the field of the Kurus, the field of the working out of the Dharma, the field of human action,** as we might symbolically translate the descriptive phrase, ***dharma-kṣetre kuru-kṣetre*****, assembled for the fight, what did my children, O Sanjaya, what did Pandu's sons?**[1]

सञ्जय उवाच
दृष्ट्वा तु पाण्डवानीकं व्यूढं दुर्योधनस्तदा ।
आचार्यमुपसङ्गम्य राजा वचनमब्रवीत् ।।२।।
पश्यैतां पाण्डुपुत्राणामाचार्य महतीं चमूम् ।
व्यूढां द्रुपदपुत्रेण तव शिष्येण धीमता ।।३।।
अत्र शूरा महेष्वासा भीमार्जुनसमा युधि ।
युयुधानो विराटश्च द्रुपदश्च महारथः ।।४।।
धृष्टकेतुश्चेकितानः काशिराजश्च वीर्यवान् ।
पुरुजित्कुन्तिभोजश्च शैब्यश्च नरपुङ्गवः ।।५।।
युधामन्युश्च विक्रान्त उत्तमौजाश्च वीर्यवान् ।
सौभद्रो द्रौपदेयाश्च सर्व एव महारथाः ।।६।।

2-6. *Sanjaya* — **Then the king, even Duryodhana, when he beheld the Pandavas army marshalled in battle array, approached the master [Drona] and spoke this word: — "Behold, O Master, this mighty host of the sons of Pandu by Drupad's son, thy wise disciple, marshalled in battle array. — There are their heroes and great bowmen, like unto Bhima and Arjuna in war, Yuyudhana and Virata and Drupada, the mighty warrior, — Dhrishtaketu and Cekitana and**

1. The portion set in bold corresponds more accurately to the Sanskrit text proper of the sloka. For a more detailed explanation see Postscript. (*Editor's note*)

Kashi's heroic king; and Purujit, Kuntibhoja and Shaibya, lion of men, — and Yudhamanyu of mighty deeds and hero Uttamaujas and Subhadra's son (Abhimanyu) and the sons of Draupadi, great warriors all.

अस्माकं तु विशिष्टा ये तान्निबोध द्विजोत्तम ।
नायका मम सैन्यस्य संज्ञार्थं तान्ब्रवीमि ते ॥७॥
भवान्भीष्मश्च कर्णश्च कृपश्च समितिञ्जयः ।
अश्वत्थामा विकर्णश्च सौमदत्तिस्तथैव च ॥८॥
अन्ये च बहवः शूरा मदर्थे त्यक्तजीविताः ।
नानाशस्त्रप्रहरणाः सर्वे युद्धविशारदाः ॥९॥
अपर्याप्तं तदस्माकं बलं भीष्माभिरक्षितम् ।
पर्याप्तं त्विदमेतेषां बलं भीमाभिरक्षितम् ॥१०॥
अयनेषु च सर्वेषु यथाभागमवस्थिताः ।
भीष्ममेवाभिरक्षन्तु भवन्तः सर्व एव हि ॥११॥

7-11. And they who are our chief and first, them also mark, O best of the twice-born, leaders of my army, for the reckoning let me speak their names, — thou and Bhishma and Karna, Kripa victorious in battle, Ashvatthama and Vikarna and Somdatta's son, — and many other courageous hearts that for me have cast their lives behind them, smiters with various weapons and many arms, and all are expert in war. — Weak to its task is this our strength but Bhishma guards the host; sufficient to its task is yonder strength of the foe and Bhima is their guard. Do ye then, each stationed to his work, stand up in all the gates of the war and Bhishma, ever Bhishma do ye guard, yes all guard him alone."

तस्य सञ्जनयन्हर्षं कुरुवृद्धः पितामहः ।
सिंहनादं विनद्योच्चैः शङ्खं दध्मौ प्रतापवान् ॥१२॥
ततः शङ्खाश्च भेर्यश्च पणवानकगोमुखाः ।
सहसैवाभ्यहन्यन्त स शब्दस्तुमुलोऽभवत् ॥१३॥

12-13. Then giving joy birth in Duryodhana's heart the Grandsire (Bhishma), elder of the Kurus, thundered loud his war-cry's lion roar, and blew his conchshell's blare, the man of might, — Then conchshell and bugle, trumpet and horn and drum, all suddenly were smitten and blown, and a huge rushing sound arose.

ततः श्वेतैर्हयैर्युक्ते महति स्यन्दने स्थितौ ।
माधवः पाण्डवश्चैव दिव्यौ शङ्खौ प्रदध्मतुः ॥१४॥

पाञ्चजन्यं हृषीकेशो देवदत्तं धनञ्जयः ।
पौण्ड्रं दध्मौ महाशङ्खं भीमकर्मा वृकोदरः ।।१५।।
अनन्तविजयं राजा कुन्तीपुत्रो युधिष्ठिरः ।
नकुलः सहदेवश्च सुघोषमणिपुष्पकौ ।।१६।।
काश्यश्च परमेष्वासः शिखण्डी च महारथः ।
धृष्टद्युम्नो विराटश्च सात्यकिश्चापराजितः ।।१७।।
द्रुपदो द्रौपदेयाश्च सर्वशः पृथिवीपते ।
सौभद्रश्च महाबाहुः शङ्खान्दध्मुः पृथक्पृथक् ।।१८।।
स घोषो धार्तराष्ट्राणां हृदयानि व्यदारयत् ।
नभश्च पृथिवीं चैव तुमुलो व्यनुनादयन् ।।१९।।

14-19. Then in their mighty car erect, their car with snow-white steeds, Madhava (Krishna) and Pandava (Arjuna) blew their divine shells, — Hrishikesha (Krishna) on Panchajanya, on Devadatta, god-given, Dhananjaya (Arjuna) blew, and on his great shell, Paundra, from far Bengal blew Vrikodara (Bhima), wolf-belly, the man of dreadful deeds, — and on Anantavijaya, boundless conquest, Yudhishthira the king, even Kunti's son, and Nakula and Sahadeva on Sughosha, far sounding, and Manipushpaka, jewel-flower. — And Kashi's king, that excellent bowman, and Shikhandi, that great fighter, and Dhrishtadyumna and Virata and Satyaki unconquered, — and Drupada and the children of Draupadi, and Subhadra's great-armed son, all these from all sides blew each his separate shell, O Lord of earth, — that the thunder of them tore the hearts of Dhritarashtra's sons and earth and heaven re-echoed with the clamour and the roar.

अथ व्यवस्थितान्दृष्ट्वा धार्तराष्ट्रान्कपिध्वजः ।
प्रवृत्ते शस्त्रसम्पाते धनुरुद्यम्य पाण्डवः ।।२०।।
हृषीकेशं तदा वाक्यमिदमाह महीपते ।

20-21[1]. Now as the ape-bannered, the Pandava (Arjuna), saw the Dhritarashtrians at their war-like posts, so heaved he up his bow and even as the shafts began to fall — spake to Hrishikesha this word, O king.

अर्जुन उवाच
सेनयोरुभयोर्मध्ये रथं स्थापय मेऽच्युत ।।२१।।
यावदेतान्निरीक्षेऽहं योद्धुकामानवस्थितान् ।
कैर्मया सह योद्धव्यमस्मिन्रणसमुद्यमे ।।२२।।
योत्स्यमानानवेक्षेऽहं य एतेऽत्र समागताः ।
धार्तराष्ट्रस्य दुर्बुद्धेर्युद्धे प्रियचिकीर्षवः ।।२३।।

21[2]-23. *Arjuna* — **Right in the midst between either host set thou my car, O Unfallen. — Let me scan these who stand arrayed and greedy for battle; let me know who must wage war with me in this great holiday of fight. — Fain would I see who are these that are here for combat to do in battle the will of Dhritarashtra's witless son.**

It is typical of the pragmatic man that it is through his sensations that he awakens to the meaning of his action. He has asked his friend and charioteer to place him between the two armies, not with any profounder idea, but with the proud intention of viewing and looking in the face these myriads of the champions of unrighteousness, a-dharma, whom he has to meet and conquer and slay "in this holiday of fight" so that the right may prevail.

सञ्जय उवाच
एवमुक्तो हृषीकेशो गुडाकेशेन भारत ।
सेनयोरुभयोर्मध्ये स्थापयित्वा रथोत्तमम् ।।२४।।
भीष्मद्रोणप्रमुखतः सर्वेषां च महीक्षिताम् ।
उवाच पार्थ पश्यैतान्समवेतान्कुरूनिति ।।२५।।

24-25. *Sanjaya* — **Thus, O Bharata, to Hrishikesha Gudakesha [Arjuna] said, who set in the midst between either army the noble car, — in front of Bhishma and Drona and all those kings of earth. "Lo, O Partha," he said, "all these Kurus met in one field!"**

तत्रापश्यत्स्थितान्पार्थः पितॄनथ पितामहान् ।
आचार्यान्मातुलान्भ्रातॄन् पुत्रान्पौत्रान्सखींस्तथा ।।२६।।
श्वशुरान्सुहृदश्चैव सेनयोरुभयोरपि ।
तान्समीक्ष्य स कौन्तेयः सर्वान्बन्धूनवस्थितान् ।।२७।।
कृपया परयाविष्टो विषीदन्निदमब्रवीत् ।

26-28[1]. There Partha saw fathers and grandsires stand, and teachers and uncles and brothers and sons and grandsons and dear comrades, — and fathers of wives and heart's friends, all in either battle opposed. And when the son of Kunti beheld all these dear friends and kindred facing each other in war, — his heart was besieged with utter pity and failed him, and he said:

It is as he gazes that the revelation of the meaning of a civil and domestic war comes home to him, a war in which not only men of the same race, the same nation, the same clan, but those of the same family and household stand upon opposite sides. All whom the social man holds most dear and sacred, he must meet as enemies and slay, — the worshipped teacher and preceptor, the old friend, comrade and companion in arms, grandsires, uncles, those who stood in the relation to him of father, of son, of grandson, connections by blood and connections by marriage, — all these social ties have to be cut asunder by the sword. It is not that he did not know these things before, but he has never realised it all; obsessed by his claims and wrongs and by the principles of his life, the struggle for the right, the duty of the Kshatriya to protect justice and the law and fight and beat down injustice and lawless violence, he has neither thought it out deeply nor felt it in his heart and at the core of his life. And now it is shown to his vision by the divine charioteer, placed sensationally before his eyes, and comes home to him like a blow delivered at the very centre of his sensational, vital and emotional being.

अर्जुन उवाच
दृष्ट्वेमं स्वजनं कृष्ण युयुत्सुं समुपस्थितम् ।।२८।।
सीदन्ति मम गात्राणि मुखं च परिशुष्यति ।
वेपथुश्च शरीरे मे रोमहर्षश्च जायते ।।२९।।
गाण्डीवं स्रंसते हस्तात्त्वक्चैव परिदह्यते ।
न च शक्नोम्यवस्थातुं भ्रमतीव च मे मनः ।।३०।।
निमित्तानि च पश्यामि विपरीतानि केशव ।
न च श्रेयोऽनुपश्यामि हत्वा स्वजनमाहवे ।।३१।।
न काङ्क्षे विजयं कृष्ण न च राज्यं सुखानि च ।
किं नो राज्येन गोविन्द किं भोगैर्जीवितेन वा ।।३२।।

28[2]-32. *Arjuna* — **O Krishna, I behold these kinsmen and friends arrayed in hostile armies — and my limbs sink beneath me and my face grows dry, and there are shudderings in my body, and my hair stands on end, — Gandiva falls from my hand and my very skin is on fire. Yea, I cannot stand and my brain whirls, — and evil omens, O Keshava, meet mine eyes. I can see no blessing for me, having slain my kin in fight. — I desire not victory, O Krishna, no, nor kingship nor delights. What shall we do with kingship, O Govinda, what with enjoyments, what with life?**

The first result is a violent sensational and physical crisis which produces a disgust of the action and its material objects and of life itself. He rejects the vital aim pursued by egoistic humanity in its action, — happiness and enjoyment; he rejects the vital aim of the Kshatriya, victory and rule and power and the government of men. What after all is this fight for justice when reduced to its practical terms, but just this, a fight for the interests of himself, his brothers and his party, for possession and enjoyment and rule? But at such a cost these things are not worth having. For they are of no value in themselves, but only as a means to the right maintenance of social and national life and it is these very aims that in the person of his kin and his race he is about to destroy.

येषामर्थे काङ्क्षितं नो राज्यं भोगाः सुखानि च ।
त इमेऽवस्थिता युद्धे प्राणांस्त्यक्त्वा धनानि च ।।३३।।
आचार्याः पितरः पुत्रास्तथैव च पितामहाः ।
मातुलाः श्वशुराः पौत्राः श्यालाः सम्बन्धिनस्तथा ।।३४।।
एतान्न हन्तुमिच्छामि घ्नतोऽपि मधुसूदन ।
अपि त्रैलोक्यराज्यस्य हेतोः किं नु महीकृते ।।३५।।

33-35. They for whose sake we desire kingship and enjoyments and delights, lo they all stand in battle against us casting behind them their riches and lives, — our teachers and our fathers and our sons, our grandsires and uncles and the fathers of our wives, and our grandsons and our wives' brothers and the kin of our beloved. — These, though they slay me, O Madhusudana, I would not slay, no, not for the empire of heaven and space and hell, much less for this poor earth of ours.

And then comes the cry of the emotions. These are they for whose sake life and happiness are desired, our "own people". Who would consent to slay these for the sake of all the earth, or even for the kingdom of the three worlds? What pleasure can there be in life, what happiness, what satisfaction in oneself after such a deed?

निहत्य धार्तराष्ट्रान्नः का प्रीतिः स्याज्जनार्दन।
पापमेवाश्रयेदस्मान्हत्वैतानाततायिनः ।।३६।।
तस्मान्नार्हा वयं हन्तुं धार्तराष्ट्रान्स्वबान्धवान् ।
स्वजनं हि कथं हत्वा सुखिनः स्याम माधव ।।३७।।

36-37. Slaying the sons of Dhritarashtra what joy would be left to us, O Janardana? Sin, sin alone would find lodging in us, if we slew these, though our adversaries and foes. — Therefore we do no right to slay the children of Dhritarashtra and their friends, for how can we be happy, O Madhava, if we slay our kin?

The whole thing is a dreadful sin, — for now the moral sense awakens to justify the revolt of the sensations and the emotions. It is a sin, there is no right nor justice in mutual slaughter; especially are those who are to be slain the natural objects of reverence and of love, those without whom one would not care to live, and to violate these sacred feelings can be no virtue, can be nothing but a heinous crime.

यद्यप्येते न पश्यन्ति लोभोपहतचेतसः ।
कुलक्षयकृतं दोषं मित्रद्रोहे च पातकम् ।।३८।।
कथं न ज्ञेयमस्माभिः पापादस्मान्निवर्तितुम् ।
कुलक्षयकृतं दोषं प्रपश्यद्भिर्जनार्दन ।।३९।।

38-39. Even so these see not; for their hearts are swept away by greed, error done in the ruin of our house and grievous sin in treachery to natural friends, — how shall we not understand and turn back from this sin, we who have eyes, O Janardana, for error done in the ruin of our house?

Granted that the offence, the aggression, the first sin, the crimes of greed and selfish passion which have brought things to such a pass came from the other side; yet armed resistance to wrong under such circumstances would be itself a sin and crime worse than theirs because they are blinded by passion and unconscious of guilt, while on this side it would be with a clear sense of guilt that the sin would be committed.

कुलक्षये प्रणश्यन्ति कुलधर्माः सनातनाः ।
धर्मे नष्टे कुलं कृत्स्नमधर्मोऽभिभवत्युत ।।४०।।
अधर्माभिभवात्कृष्ण प्रदुष्यन्ति कुलस्त्रियः ।
स्त्रीषु दुष्टासु वार्ष्णेय जायते वर्णसङ्करः ।।४१।।
सङ्करो नरकायैव कुलघ्नानां कुलस्य च ।
पतन्ति पितरो ह्येषां लुप्तपिण्डोदकक्रियाः ।।४२।।
दोषैरेतैः कुलघ्नानां वर्णसङ्करकारकैः ।
उत्साद्यन्ते जातिधर्माः कुलधर्माश्च शाश्वताः ।।४३।।
उत्सन्नकुलधर्माणां मनुष्याणां जनार्दन ।
नरकेऽनियतं वासो भवतीत्यनुशुश्रुम ।।४४।।
अहो बत महत्पापं कर्तुं व्यवसिता वयम् ।
यद्राज्यसुखलोभेन हन्तुं स्वजनमुद्यताः ।।४५।।

40-45. When the family dwindle, the eternal ideals of the race, *kula-dharmāḥ sanātanāḥ*, are lost, and when ideals are lost, unrighteousness, *a-dharmaḥ*, besets the whole race; — in the prevalence of unrighteousness, O Krishna, the women of the race go astray, and when women grow corrupt, bastard confusion, *varṇa-saṁkaraḥ*, is born again; — but confusion brings the slayers of the race and the race itself to very hell; for the long line of fathers perish and the food ceaseth and the water is given no more. — By these sins who

bring their race to perdition, fathers they of bastard confusion, the eternal ideals of the nation, *śāśvatāḥ jāti-dharmāḥ*, and the hearth, *kula-dharmāḥ*, are overthrown, — and for men who have lost the ancient righteousness of the race, in hell an eternal habitation is set apart, it is told. — Alas, a dreadful sin have we set ourselves to do, that we have made ready, from greed of lordship and pleasure, to slay our own kin.

And for what? For the maintenance of family morality, of the social law and the law of the nation? These are the very standards that will be destroyed by this civil war; the family itself will be brought to the point of annihilation, corruption of morals and loss of the purity of race will be engendered, the eternal laws of the race and moral law of the family will be destroyed. Ruin of the race, the collapse of its high traditions, ethical degradation and hell for the authors of such a crime, these are the only practical results possible of this monstrous civil strife.

यदि मामप्रतिकारमशस्त्रं शस्त्रपाणयः ।
धार्तराष्ट्रा रणे हन्युस्तन्मे क्षेमतरं भवेत् ।।४६।।

46. **Therefore it is more for my welfare that the sons of Dhritarashtra armed should slay me unarmed and unresisting. I will not fight.**

सञ्जय उवाच
एवमुक्त्वार्जुनः संख्ये रथोपस्थ उपाविशत् ।
विसृज्य सशरं चापं शोकोसंविग्नमानसः ।।४७।।

47. *Sanjaya* — **Thus spake Arjuna, and in the very battle's heart sat down upon his chariot seat, casting down the divine bow and inexhaustible quiver** given to him by the gods for that tremendous hour **when the arrow was on the string, for his soul was perplexed with grief.**

The character of this inner crisis is therefore not the questioning of the thinker; it is not a recoil from the appearances of life and a turning of the eye inward in search of the truth of things, the real meaning of existence and a solution or an escape from the dark riddle of the world. It is the sensational, emotional and moral revolt of the man hitherto satisfied with action and its current standards who finds himself cast by them into a hideous chaos where they are in violent conflict with each other and with themselves and there is no moral standing-ground left, nothing to lay hold of and walk by, no *dharma*. That for the soul of action in the mental being is the worst possible crisis, failure and overthrow.

CHAPTER II

I — The Creed of the Aryan Fighter

सञ्जय उवाच
तं तथा कृपयाविष्टमश्रुपूर्णाकुलेक्षणम् ।
विषीदन्तमिदं वाक्यमुवाच मधुसूदनः ।।१।।

1. *Sanjaya* — **Arjuna has thus lapsed into unheroic weakness, his eyes full and distressed with tears, his heart overcome by depression and discouragement, because he is invaded by pity.** The answer of the divine Teacher to the first flood of Arjuna's passionate self-questioning, his shrinking from slaughter, his sense of sorrow and sin, his grieving for an empty and desolate life, his forecast of evil results of an evil deed, is a strongly-worded rebuke.

श्रीभगवानुवाच
कुतस्त्वा कश्मलमिदं विषमे समुपस्थितम् ।
अनार्यजुष्टमस्वर्ग्यमकीर्तिकरमर्जुन ।।२।।

2. *Krishna* — **"Whence has come to thee this dejection, this stain and darkness of the soul in the hour of difficulty and peril?" asks Krishna of Arjuna. This is not the way cherished and followed by the Aryan man; this mood came not from heaven nor can it lead to heaven, and on earth it is the forfeiting of the glory that waits upon strength and heroism and noble works. Let him put from him this weak and self-indulgent pity, let him rise and smite his enemies!**

क्लैब्यं मा स्म गमः पार्थ नैतत्त्वय्युपपद्यते ।
क्षुद्रं हृदयदौर्बल्यं त्यक्त्वोत्तिष्ठ परन्तप ।।३।।

3. **All this is confusion of mind and delusion, a weakness of the heart, an unmanliness, a fall from the virility of the fighter and the hero. Not this was fitting in the son of Pritha, not thus should the champion and chief hope of a righteous cause abandon it in the hour of crisis and peril or suffer the sudden amazement of his heart and senses, the clouding of his reason and the downfall**

of his will to betray him into the casting away of his divine weapons and the refusal of his God-given work.

अर्जुन उवाच
कथं भीष्ममहं संख्ये द्रोणं च मधुसूदन ।
इषुभिः प्रतियोत्स्यामि पूजार्हावरिसूदन ॥४॥

4. *Arjuna* — **How shall I combat Bhishma in the fight and Drona, O Madhusudana, how shall I smite with arrows those venerable heads?** Arjuna attempts still to justify his refusal of the work and puts forward in its support the claim of his nervous and sensational being which shrinks from the slaughter, the claim of his heart which recoils from the sorrow and emptiness of life that will follow his act, the claim of his customary moral notions which are appalled by the necessity of slaying his gurus, Bhishma and Drona, the claim of his reason which sees no good but only evil results of the terrible and violent work assigned to him.

गुरूनहत्वा हि महानुभावान् श्रेयो भोक्तुं भैक्ष्यमपीह लोके ।
हत्वार्थकामांस्तु गुरूनिहैव भुञ्जीय भोगान्रुधिरप्रदिग्धान् ॥५॥

5. **Better the life of the mendicant living upon alms than this *dharma* of the Kshatriya, this battle and action culminating in undiscriminating massacre,** this principle of mastery and glory and power which can only be won by destruction and bloodshed, **this conquest of blood-stained enjoyments,** this vindication of justice and right by a means which contradicts all righteousness and this affirmation of the social law by a war which destroys in its process and result all that constitutes society.

न चैतद्विद्मः कतरन्नो गरीयो यद्वा जयेम यदि वा नो जयेयुः ।
यानेव हत्वा न जिजीविषामस्तेऽवस्थिताः प्रमुखे धार्तराष्ट्राः ॥६॥

6. **Therefore we know not which of these is better, that we should be victors or that we should be vanquished: for they whom slaying we should have no heart to live, lo, they Dhritarashtrians face us in the foeman's van.**

कार्पण्यदोषोपहतस्वभावः पृच्छामि त्वां धर्मसम्मूढचेताः ।
यच्छ्रेयः स्यान्निश्चितं ब्रूहि तन्मे शिष्यस्तेऽहं शाधि मां त्वां प्रपन्नम् ॥७॥

7. Arjuna in his reply to Krishna admits the rebuke even while he strives against and refuses the command. He is aware of his weakness and yet accepts subjection to it. **It is poorness of spirit, he owns, that has smitten away from him his true heroic nature; his whole consciousness is bewildered in its view of right and wrong and he accepts the divine Friend as his teacher;** but the emotional and intellectual props on which he had supported his sense of righteousness have been entirely cast down and he cannot accept a command which seems to appeal only to his old standpoint and gives him no new basis for action.

The whole upshot is that all-embracing inner bankruptcy which Arjuna expresses when he says that his whole conscious being, not the thought alone but heart and vital desires and all, are utterly bewildered and can find nowhere the *dharma*, nowhere any valid law of action. **For this alone he takes refuge as a disciple with Krishna; give me, he practically asks, that which I have lost, a true law, a clear rule of action, a path by which I can again confidently walk.** He does not ask for the secret of life or of the world, the meaning and purpose of it all, but for a *dharma*.

न हि प्रपश्यामि ममापनुद्याद् यच्छोकमुच्छोषणमिन्द्रियाणाम् ।
अवाप्य भूमावसपत्नमृद्धं राज्यं सुराणामपि चाधिपत्यम् ॥८॥

8. The compassion which actuates Arjuna in the rejection of his work and mission is not compassion but an impotence full of a weak self-pity, a recoil from the mental suffering which his act must entail on himself, — **I see not what shall thrust from me the sorrow that dries up the senses, though I win on earth rich kingship without rival and empire over the very gods in heaven;** — and of all things self-pity is among the most ignoble and un-Aryan of moods. Its pity for others is also a form of self-indulgence; it is the physical shrinking of the nerves from the act of slaughter, the egoistic emotional shrinking of the heart from the destruction of the Dhritarashtrians because they are "one's own people" and without them life will be empty. This pity is a weakness of the mind and senses. But this way is not for the developed Aryan man who has to grow not by weakness, but by an ascension from strength to strength. Arjuna is the divine man, the master-man in the making and as such he has been chosen by the gods. He has a work given to him, he has God beside him in his chariot, he has the heavenly bow Gandiva in his hand, he has the champions of unrighteousness, the opponents of the divine leading of the world in his front. Not his is the right to determine what he shall do or not do according to his emotions and his passions. He has to see only the work that must be done, *kartavyam karma*, to hear only the divine command.

सञ्जय उवाच
एवमुक्त्वा हृषीकेशं गुडाकेशः परन्तप ।
न योत्स्य इति गोविन्दमुक्त्वा तूष्णीं बभूव ह ।।९।।

9. *Sanjaya* — **Thus Gudakesha to Hrishikesha, the scourger of his foe said unto Govinda, "I will not fight", and ceased from words.**

तमुवाच हृषीकेशः प्रहसन्निव भारत ।
सेनयोरुभयोर्मध्ये विषीदन्तमिदं वचः ।।१०।।

10. He [Arjuna] is resolved that on the old basis of thought and motive he will not fight and he awaits in silence the answer to objections that seem to him unanswerable. It is these claims of Arjuna's egoistic being that Krishna sets out first to destroy in order to make place for the higher law which shall transcend all egoistic motives of action. **On him thus overcome with weakness in the midmost of either battle, Krishna smiled and said:**

श्रीभगवानुवाच
अशोच्यानन्वशोचस्त्वं प्रज्ञावादांश्च भाषसे ।
गतासूनगतासूंश्च नानुशोचन्ति पण्डिताः ।।११।।

11. *Krishna* — The answer of the Teacher proceeds upon two different lines, first, a brief reply (*11-38*) founded upon the highest ideas of the general Aryan culture in which Arjuna has been educated, secondly, another and larger (*39-72*) founded on a more intimate knowledge, opening into deeper truths of our being, which is the real starting-point of the teaching of the Gita. **Thou grievest for whom thou shouldst not grieve and yet speakest wise-seeming words.** Our sorrow for the death of men is an ignorant grieving for those for whom there is no cause to grieve, since they have neither gone out of existence nor suffered any painful or terrible change of condition, but are beyond death no less in being and no more unhappy in circumstance than in life. Arjuna has sought to justify his refusal on ethical and rational grounds, but he has merely cloaked by words of apparent rationality the revolt of his ignorant and unchastened emotions. He has spoken of the physical life and the death of the body as if these were the primary realities; but they have no such essential value to the sage and the thinker. **The enlightened man does not mourn either for the living or the dead,** for he knows that suffering and death are merely incidents in the history of the soul. The soul, not the body, is the reality.

न त्वेवाहं जातु नासं न त्वं नेमे जनाधिपाः ।
न चैव न भविष्यामः सर्वे वयमतः परम् ।।१२।।

12. **Neither is it that I was not before nor thou nor these kings nor that all we shall not be hereafter.** All these kings of men for whose approaching death he mourns, have lived before, they will live again in the human body.

देहिनोऽस्मिन्यथा देहे कौमारं यौवनं जरा ।
तथा देहान्तरप्राप्तिर्धीरस्तत्र न मुह्यति ।।१३।।

13. **For as the soul passes physically through childhood and youth and age, so it passes on to the changing of the body. The strong and wise soul is not perplexed, troubled or moved by them.** But still they are accepted only to be conquered. The calm and wise mind, the *dhīra*, the thinker who looks upon life steadily and does not allow himself to be disturbed and blinded by his sensations and emotions, is not deceived by material appearances.

मात्रास्पर्शास्तु कौन्तेय शीतोष्णसुखदुःखदाः ।
आगमापायिनोऽनित्यास्तांस्तितिक्षस्व भारत ।।१४।।

14. *titikṣā*, the will and power to endure, is the means. **The material touches which cause heat and cold, happiness and pain, things transient which come and go, these learn to endure.** Since the nature of suffering is a failure of the conscious-force in us to meet the shocks of existence and a consequent shrinking and contraction and its root is an inequality of that receptive and possessing force due to our self-limitation by egoism consequent on the ignorance of our true Self, the elimination of suffering must first proceed by the substitution of *titikṣā*, the facing, enduring and conquest of all shocks of existence for *jugupsā*, the shrinking and contraction: by this endurance and conquest we proceed to an equality which may be either an equal indifference to all contacts or an equal gladness in all contacts.

यं हि न व्यथयन्त्येते पुरुषं पुरुषर्षभ ।
समदुःखसुखं धीरं सोऽमृतत्वाय कल्पते ।।१५।।

15. **For the man whom these do not trouble nor pain, the leonine soul among men, the firm and wise who is equal in pleasure and suffering, makes himself apt for immortality.**

The equal-souled has to bear suffering and not hate, to receive pleasure and not rejoice. He looks beyond the apparent facts of the life of the body and senses to the real fact of his being and rises beyond the emotional and physical desires of the ignorant nature to the true and only aim of the human existence.

What is that real fact? that highest aim? This, that human life and death repeated through the aeons in the great cycles of the world are only a long progress by which the human being prepares and makes himself fit for immortality. And how shall he prepare himself? who is the man that is fit? The man who rises above the conception of himself as a life and a body, who knows himself and all as souls, learns himself to live in his soul and not in his body and deals with others too as souls and not as mere physical beings. For by immortality is meant not the survival of death, — that is already given to every creature born with a mind, — but the transcendence of life and death. It means that ascension by which man ceases to live as a mind-informed body and lives at last as a spirit and in the Spirit. To be disturbed by sorrow and horror as Arjuna has been disturbed, to be deflected by them from the path that has to be travelled, to be overcome by self-pity and intolerance of sorrow and recoil from the unavoidable and trivial circumstance of the death of the body, this is un-Aryan ignorance. It is not the way of the Aryan climbing in calm strength towards the immortal life.

नासतो विद्यते भावो नाभावो विद्यते सतः ।
उभयोरपि दृष्टोऽन्तस्त्वनयोस्तत्त्वदर्शिभिः ।।१६।।
अविनाशि तु तद्विद्धि येन सर्वमिदं ततम् ।
विनाशमव्ययस्यास्य न कश्चित्कर्तुमर्हति ।।१७।।

16-17. There is no such thing as death, for it is the body that dies and the body is not the man. **That which really is, cannot go out of existence,** though it may change the forms through which it appears, **just as that which is non-existent cannot come into being.** The soul is and cannot cease to be. **That we can learn from those who know, [who have *seen*] the true principles of existence, *tattvadarśibhiḥ*: this opposition of is and is not,** this balance of being and becoming which is the mind's view of existence, **finds its end in the realisation of the soul as the one imperishable self by whom all this universe has been extended. Who can slay the immortal spirit?**

अन्तवन्त इमे देहा नित्यस्योक्ताः शरीरिणः ।
अनाशिनोऽप्रमेयस्य तस्माद्युध्यस्व भारत ।।१८।।

18. Finite bodies have an end, but that which possesses and uses the body, is infinite, illimitable, eternal, indestructible. Therefore put away this vain sorrow and shrinking, fight, O son of Bharata!

This world, this manifestation of the Self in the material universe is not only a cycle of inner development, but a field in which the external circumstances of life have to be accepted as an environment and an occasion for that development. It is a world of mutual help and struggle; not a serene and peaceful gliding through easy joys is the progress it allows us, but every step has to be gained by heroic effort and through a clash of opposing forces.

य एनं वेत्ति हन्तारं यश्चैनं मन्यते हतम् ।
उभौ तौ न विजानीतो नायं हन्ति न हन्यते ॥१९॥

19. Who knows the Spirit as slayer and who deems Him to be slain, both of these discern not [have not the knowledge]. This slays not, neither is This slain. When we have known ourselves as this [the Absolute], then to speak of ourselves as slayer or slain is an absurdity. One thing only is the truth in which we have to live, the Eternal manifesting itself as the soul of man in the great cycle of its pilgrimage with birth and death for milestones, with worlds beyond as resting-places, with all the circumstances of life happy or unhappy as the means of our progress and battle and victory and with immortality as the home to which the soul travels.

न जायते म्रियते वा कदाचिन्नायं भूत्वा भविता वा न भूयः ।
अजो नित्यः शाश्वतोऽयं पुराणो न हन्यते हन्यमाने शरीरे ॥२०॥

20. This is not born, nor does it die, nor is it a thing that comes into being once and passing away will never come into being again. It is unborn, ancient, sempiternal; it is not slain with the slaying of the body.

वेदाविनाशिनं नित्यं य एनमजमव्ययम् ।
कथं स पुरुषः पार्थ कं घातयति हन्ति कम् ॥२१॥

21. He who knows Him to be imperishable, eternal, unborn and undecaying, whom does that man, O Partha, slay or cause to be slain?

वासांसि जीर्णानि यथा विहाय नवानि गृह्णाति नरोऽपराणि ।
तथा शरीराणि विहाय जीर्णान्यन्यानि संयाति नवानि देही ॥२२॥

22. It [the embodied soul] casts away old and takes up new bodies as a man changes worn-out raiment for new.

नैनं छिन्दन्ति शस्त्राणि नैनं दहति पावकः ।
न चैनं क्लेदयन्त्यापो न शोषयति मारुतः ।।२३।।

23. Weapons cannot cleave it, nor the fire burn, nor do the waters drench it, nor the wind dry.

अच्छेद्योऽयमदाह्योऽयमक्लेद्योऽशोष्य एव च ।
नित्यः सर्वगतः स्थाणुरचलोऽयं सनातनः ।।२४।।

24. Indivisible, unconsumable, unmergible, unwitherable is He. Eternally stable, immobile, all-pervading, it is for ever and for ever.

अव्यक्तोऽयमचिन्त्योऽयमविकार्योऽयमुच्यते ।
तस्मादेवं विदित्वैनं नानुशोचितुमर्हसि ।।२५।।

25. Not manifested like the body, but greater than all manifestation, not to be analysed by the thought, but greater than all mind, not capable of change and modification like the life and its organs and their objects, but beyond the changes of mind and life and body, it is yet the Reality which all these strive to figure. If thou knowest him as such, thou hast no cause to grieve.

अथ चैनं नित्यजातं नित्यं वा मन्यसे मृतम् ।
तथापि त्वं महाबाहो नैवं शोचितुमर्हसि ।।२६।।

26. Even if the truth of our being were a thing less sublime, vast, intangible by death and life, if the self were constantly subject to birth and death, still the death of beings ought not to be a cause of sorrow.

जातस्य हि ध्रुवो मृत्युर्ध्रुवं जन्म मृतस्य च ।
तस्मादपरिहार्येऽर्थे न त्वं शोचितुमर्हसि ।।२७।।

27. Certain is the death of that which is born and certain is the birth of that which dies; therefore in a thing inevitable thou oughtest not to grieve.

अव्यक्तादीनि भूतानि व्यक्तमध्यानि भारत ।
अव्यक्तनिधनान्येव तत्र का परिदेवना ।।२८।।

28. **For that is an inevitable circumstance of the soul's self-manifestation. Its birth is an appearing out of some state in which it is not non-existent but unmanifest to our mortal senses, its death is a return to that unmanifest world or condition and out of it it will again appear in the physical manifestation.** The to-do made by the physical mind and senses about death and the horror of death whether on the sick-bed or the battle-field, is the most ignorant of nervous clamours. **And what is there in this to grieve at and recoil and shrink?**

आश्चर्यवत्पश्यति कश्चिदेनमाश्चर्यवद्वदति तथैव चान्यः ।
आश्चर्यवच्चैनमन्यः शृणोति श्रुत्वाप्येनं वेद न चैव कश्चित् ।।२९।।

29. **One sees it as a mystery or one speaks of it or hears of it as a mystery, but none knows it.** In reality the higher truth is the real truth. All are that Self, that One, that Divine whom we look on and speak and hear of as the wonderful beyond our comprehension, for after all our seeking and declaring of knowledge and learning from those who have knowledge no human mind has ever known this Absolute.

देही नित्यमवध्योऽयं देहे सर्वस्य भारत ।
तस्मात्सर्वाणि भूतानि न त्वं शोचितुमर्हसि ।।३०।।

30. **The embodied One is for ever unslayable in the body of every man, O Bharata; and from Him are all creatures; therefore thou hast no cause for grief.** It is this which is here veiled by the world, the master of the body; all life is only its shadow; the coming of the soul into physical manifestation and our passing out of it by death is only one of its minor movements.

The Teacher then turns aside for a moment to give another answer to the cry of Arjuna over the sorrow of the death of kindred which will empty his life of the causes and objects of living. What is the true object of the Kshatriya's life and his true happiness? Not self-pleasing and domestic happiness, but to battle for the right is his true object of life and to find a cause for which he can lay down his life or by victory win the crown and glory of the hero's existence is his greatest happiness.

स्वधर्ममपि चावेक्ष्य न विकम्पितुमर्हसि ।
धर्म्याद्धि युद्धाच्छ्रेयोऽन्यत्क्षत्रियस्य न विद्यते ।।३१।।

31. Moreover if thou considerest the law of thy own being, thou oughtest not to tremble. There is no greater good for the Kshatriya than righteous battle. This is the action required of Arjuna in the path he has to travel; it has come inevitably in the performance of the function demanded of him by his *svadharma*, his social duty, the law of his life and the law of his being.

यदृच्छया चोपपन्नं स्वर्गद्वारमपावृतम् ।
सुखिनः क्षत्रियाः पार्थ लभन्ते युद्धमीदृशम् ।।३२।।

32. When such a battle comes to them of itself like the open gate of heaven, happy are the Kshatriyas then.

अथ चेत्त्वमिमं धर्म्यं संग्रामं न करिष्यसि ।
ततः स्वधर्मं कीर्तिं च हित्वा पापमवाप्स्यसि ।।३३।।

33. If thou doest not this battle for the right, then hast thou abandoned thy duty and virtue and thy glory, and sin shall be thy portion.

अकीर्तिं चापि भूतानि कथयिष्यन्ति तेऽव्ययाम् ।
सम्भावितस्य चाकीर्तिर्मरणादतिरिच्यते ।।३४।।
भयाद्रणादुपरतं मंस्यन्ते त्वां महारथाः ।
येषां च त्वं बहुमतो भूत्वा यास्यसि लाघवम् ।।३५।।
अवाच्यवादांश्च बहून्वदिष्यन्ति तवाहिताः ।
निन्दन्तस्तव सामर्थ्यं ततो दुःखतरं नु किम् ।।३६।।

34-36. He will by such a refusal incur disgrace and the reproach of fear and weakness and the loss of his Kshatriya honour. For what is worst grief for a Kshatriya? It is the loss of his honour, his fame, his noble station among the mighty men, the men of courage and power; that to him is much worse than death. Battle, courage, power, rule, the honour of the brave, the heaven of those who fall nobly, this is the warrior's ideal. To lower that ideal, to allow a smirch to fall on that honour, to give the example of a hero among heroes whose action lays itself open to the reproach of cowardice and weakness and thus to lower the moral standard of mankind, is to be false to himself and to the demand of the world on its leaders and kings.

हतो वा प्राप्स्यसि स्वर्गं जित्वा वा भोक्ष्यसे महीम् ।
तस्मादुत्तिष्ठ कौन्तेय युद्धाय कृतनिश्चयः ।।३७।।

37. Slain thou shalt win Heaven, victorious thou shalt enjoy the earth; therefore arise, O son of Kunti, resolved upon battle. This heroic appeal may seem to be on a lower level than the stoical spirituality which precedes and the deeper spirituality which follows; for in the next verse the Teacher bids him to

सुखदुःखे समे कृत्वा लाभालाभौ जयाजयौ ।
ततो युद्धाय युज्यस्व नैवं पापमवाप्स्यसि ।।३८।।

38. make grief and happiness, loss and gain, victory and defeat equal to his soul and then turn to the battle, — the real teaching of the Gita. But Indian ethics has always seen the practical necessity of graded ideals for the developing moral and spiritual life of man. The Kshatriya ideal, the ideal of the four orders is here placed in its social aspect, not as afterwards in its spiritual meaning. **So thou shalt not incur sin.** Thus Arjuna's plea of sorrow, his plea of the recoil from slaughter, his plea of the sense of sin, his plea of the unhappy results of his action, are answered according to the highest knowledge and ethical ideals to which his race and age had attained. It is the creed of the Aryan fighter.

II — THE YOGA OF THE INTELLIGENT WILL

We understand why the Gita follows the peculiar line of development it has taken, working out first a partial truth with only subdued hints of its deeper meaning, then returning upon its hints and bringing out their significance until it rises to its last great suggestion, its supreme mystery which it does not work out at all, but leaves to be lived out, as the later ages of Indian spirituality tried to live it out in great waves of love, of surrender, of ecstasy. Its eye is always on its synthesis and all its strains are the gradual preparation of the mind for its high closing note.

एषा तेऽभिहिता सांख्ये बुद्धिर्योगे त्विमां शृणु ।
बुद्ध्या युक्तो यया पार्थ कर्मबन्धं प्रहास्यसि ।।३९।।

39. Such is the intelligence, *buddhiḥ* (the intelligent knowledge of things and will), declared to thee in the Sankhya, hear now this in the Yoga, for if thou art in Yoga by this intelligence, O son of Pritha, thou shalt cast away the bondage of works.

In the moment of his turning from this first and summary answer to Arjuna's difficulties and in the very first words which strike the keynote of a spiritual solution, the Teacher makes at once a distinction which is of the utmost importance for the understanding of the Gita, — the distinction of Sankhya and Yoga.

The Gita is in its foundation a Vedantic work; it is one of the three recognised authorities for the Vedantic teaching. But still its Vedantic ideas are throughout and thoroughly coloured by the ideas of the Sankhya and the Yoga way of thinking and it derives from this colouring the peculiar synthetic character of its philosophy. It is in fact primarily a practical system of Yoga that it teaches and it brings in metaphysical ideas only as explanatory of its practical system; nor does it merely declare Vedantic knowledge, but it founds knowledge and devotion upon works, even as it uplifts works to knowledge, their culmination, and informs them with devotion as their very heart and kernel of their spirit. The Gita goes so far as to make works the distinctive characteristic of Yoga. In the Gita [action] is a permanent foundation; it is a means of the highest ascent and continues even after the complete liberation of the soul.

The Gita insists that Sankhya and Yoga are not two different, incompatible and discordant systems, but one in their principle and aim; they differ only in their method and starting-point. The Sankhya also is a Yoga, but it proceeds by knowledge; it starts, that is to say, by intellectual discrimination and analysis of the principles of our being and attains its aim through the vision and possession of the Truth. Yoga, on the other hand, proceeds by works; it is in its first principle Karmayoga; but it is evident from the whole teaching of the Gita and its later definitions that the word *karma* is used in a very wide sense and that by Yoga is meant the selfless devotion of all the inner as well as the outer activities as a sacrifice to the Lord of all works, offered to the Eternal as Master of all the soul's energies and austerities. Yoga is the practice of the Truth of which knowledge gives the vision, and its practice has for its motor-power a spirit of illumined devotion, of calm or fervent consecration to that which knowledge sees to be the Highest.

Such is the analysis by which the Gita founds its synthesis of Vedanta, Sankhya and Yoga, its synthesis of knowledge, works and devotion. By the pure Sankhya alone the combining of works and liberation is contradictory and impossible. By pure Monism alone the permanent continuation of works as a part of Yoga and the indulgence of devotion after perfect knowledge and liberation and union are attained, become impossible or at least irrational and otiose. The Sankhya knowledge of the Gita dissipates and the Yoga system of the Gita triumphs over all these obstacles.

The whole object of the first six chapters of the Gita is to synthetise in a large frame of Vedantic truth the two methods, ordinarily supposed to be diverse and even opposite, of the Sankhyas and the Yogins. The Sankhya is taken as the starting-point and the basis; but it is from the beginning and with a progressively increasing emphasis permeated with the ideas and methods of Yoga and remoulded in its spirit. The practical difference, as it seems to have presented itself to the religious minds of that day, lay first in this that Sankhya proceeded by knowledge and through the Yoga of the intelligence, while Yoga proceeded by works and the transformation of the active consciousness and, secondly, — a corollary of this first distinction, — that Sankhya led to entire passivity and the renunciation of works, *sannyāsa*, while Yoga held to be quite sufficient the inner renunciation of desire, the purification of the subjective principle which leads to action and the turning of works Godwards, towards the divine existence and towards liberation. Yet both had the same aim, the transcendence of birth and of this terrestrial existence and the union of the human soul with the Highest. This at least is the difference as it is presented to us by the Gita.

The practical difference [between the Sankhya and Yoga as developed by the Gita] is the same as that which now exists between the Vedantic Yogas of knowledge and of works, and the practical results of the difference are also the same. The Sankhya proceeded like the Vedantic Yoga of knowledge by the Buddhi, by the discriminating intelligence; ascetic renunciation of life and works is a necessary means of liberation. But for the Yoga of the Gita, as for the Vedantic Yoga of works, action is not only a preparation but itself the means of liberation; and it is the justice of this view which the Gita seeks to bring out with such an unceasing force and insistence, — an insistence, unfortunately, which could not prevail in India against the tremendous tide of Buddhism, was lost afterwards in the intensity of ascetic illusionism and the fervour of world-shunning saints and devotees and is only now beginning to exercise its real and salutary influence on the Indian mind. Renunciation is indispensable, but the true renunciation is the inner rejection of desire and egoism; without that the outer physical abandoning of works is a thing unreal and ineffective, with it it ceases even to be necessary, although it is not forbidden.

I have declared to you the poise of a self-liberating intelligence in Sankhya, says the divine Teacher to Arjuna. I will now declare to you another poise in Yoga. You are shrinking from the results of your works, you desire other results and turn from your right path in life because it does not lead you to them. But this idea of works and their result, desire of result as the motive, the work as a means for the satisfaction of desire, is the bondage of the ignorant who know not what works are, nor their true source, nor their real operation, nor their high utility. **My Yoga will free you from all bondage of the soul to its works, *karmabandhaṁ prahāsyasi*.**

नेहाभिक्रमनाशोऽस्ति प्रत्यवायो न विद्यते ।
स्वल्पमप्यस्य धर्मस्य त्रायते महतो भयात् ।।४०।।

40. You are afraid of many things, afraid of sin, afraid of suffering, afraid of hell and punishment, afraid of God, afraid of this world, afraid of the hereafter, afraid of yourself. What is it that you are not afraid of at this moment, you the Aryan fighter, the world's chief hero? But this is the great fear which besieges humanity, its fear of sin and suffering now and hereafter, its fear in a world of whose true nature it is ignorant, of a God whose true being also it has not seen and whose cosmic purpose it does not understand. **My Yoga will deliver you from the great fear and even a little of it, *alpam api asya dharmasya*, is a great step towards perfection and will bring deliverance. When you have once set out on this path, you will find that no step is lost; every least movement will be a gain; you will find there no obstacle that can baulk you of your advance.**

व्यवसायात्मिका बुद्धिरेकेह कुरुनन्दन ।
बहुशाखा ह्यनन्ताश्च बुद्धयोऽव्यवसायिनाम् ।।४१।।

41. Not the Friend and Lover of man speaks first, but the guide and teacher who has to remove from him his ignorance of his true self and of the nature of the world and of the springs of his own action. For it is because he acts ignorantly, with a wrong intelligence and therefore a wrong will in these matters, that man is or seems to be bound by his works; otherwise works are no bondage to the free soul. It is because of this wrong intelligence that he has hope and fear, wrath and grief and transient joy; otherwise works are possible with a perfect serenity and freedom. Therefore it is the Yoga of the buddhi, the intelligence, that is first enjoined on Arjuna. To act with right intelligence and, therefore, a right will, fixed in the One, aware of the one self in all and acting out of its equal serenity, not running about in different directions under the thousand impulses of our superficial mental self, is the Yoga of the intelligent will.

There are, says the Gita, two types of intelligence in the human being. The first is concentrated, poised, one, homogeneous, directed singly towards the Truth; unity is its characteristic, concentrated fixity is its very being. In the other there is no single will, no unified intelligence, but only an endless number of ideas many-branching, coursing about, that is to say, in this or that direction in pursuit of the desires which are offered to it by life and by the environment.

Buddhi, the word used, means, properly speaking, the mental power of understanding but it is evidently used by the Gita in a large philosophic sense for the whole action of the discriminating and deciding mind which determines both the direction and use of our thoughts and the direction and use of our acts; thought, intelligence, judgment, perceptive choice and aim are all included in its functioning: for the characteristic of the unified intelligence is not only concentration of the mind that knows, but especially concentration of the mind that decides and persists in the decision, *vyavasāya*, while the sign of the dissipated intelligence is not so much even discursiveness of the ideas and perceptions as discursiveness of the aims and desires, therefore of the will. Will, then, and knowledge are the two functions of the Buddhi. The unified intelligent will is fixed in the enlightened soul, it is concentrated in inner self-knowledge; the many-branching and multifarious, busied with many things, careless of the one thing needful is on the contrary subject to the restless and discursive action of the mind, dispersed in outward life and works and their fruits.

यामिमां पुष्पितां वाचं प्रवदन्त्यविपश्चितः ।
वेदवादरताः पार्थ नान्यदस्तीति वादिनः ।।४२।।
कामात्मानः स्वर्गपरा जन्मकर्मफलप्रदाम् ।
क्रियाविशेषबहुलां भोगैश्वर्यगतिं प्रति ।।४३।।

42-43. Almost the first word of the synthesis of works and knowledge is a strong, almost a violent censure and repudiation of the Vedavada.

For the pragmatic mind of the Vedavadins [those who dwelt in the tradition of the Vedic hymns and the Vedic sacrifice] the Aryan religion of the Rishis meant the strict performance of the Vedic sacrifices and the use of the sacred Vedic mantras in order to possess all human desires in this world, wealth, progeny, victory, every kind of good fortune, and the joys of immortality in Paradise beyond. **This flowery word which they declare who have not clear discernment, devoted to the creed of the Veda, whose creed is that there is nothing else, souls of desire, seekers of Paradise, — it gives the fruits of the works of birth, it is multifarious with specialities of rites, it is directed to enjoyment and lordship as its goal.** (*see also II-52/53*)

भोगैश्वर्यप्रसक्तानां तयापहृतचेतसाम् ।
व्यवसायात्मिका बुद्धिः समाधौ न विधीयते ।।४४।।

44. Those who like the Vedavadins make sense-enjoyment the object of action and its fulfilment the highest aim of the soul, are misleading guides. The inner subjective self-delight independent of objects is our true aim and the

high and wide poise of our peace and liberation. Therefore, it is the upward and inward orientation of the intelligent will that we must resolutely choose with a settled concentration and perseverance, *vyavasāya*; we must fix it firmly in the calm self-knowledge of the Purusha.

त्रैगुण्यविषया वेदा निस्त्रैगुण्यो भवार्जुन ।
निर्द्वन्द्वो नित्यसत्त्वस्थो निर्योगक्षेम आत्मवान् ।।४५।।

45. The Gita even seems to go on to attack the Veda itself which, though it has been practically cast aside, is still to Indian sentiment intangible, inviolable, the sacred origin and authority for all its philosophy and religion. **The action of the three gunas is the subject-matter of the Veda, *traiguṇya-visayā vedāḥ*; but do thou become free from the triple guna, O Arjuna, *nistraiguṇyo bhavārjuna*, without the dualities, *nirdvandvaḥ*, ever based in thy true being, *nitya-sattva-sthaḥ*, without getting or having, *niryogakṣemaḥ*, possessed of thy self, *ātmavān*.** For what gettings and havings has the free soul? Once we are possessed of the Self, we are in possession of all things. And yet he does not cease from work and action. — Be free from obscuration and bewilderment by the three *guṇas* and action can continue, as it must continue, and even the largest, richest or most enormous and violent action; it does not matter.

यावानर्थ उदपाने सर्वतः संप्लुतोदके ।
तावान्सर्वेषु वेदेषु ब्राह्मणस्य विजानतः ।।४६।।

46. The Vedas in the widest terms, "all the Vedas", — which might well include the Upanishads also and seems to include them, for the general term *Śruti* is used later on, — are declared to be unnecessary for the man who knows. **As much use as there is in a well with water in flood on every side, so much is there in all the Vedas, *sarveṣu vedeṣu*, for the Brahmin who has the knowledge, *brāhmaṇasya vijānataḥ*.**

कर्मण्येवाधिकारस्ते मा फलेषु कदाचन ।
मा कर्मफलहेतुर्भूर्मा ते सङ्गोऽस्त्वकर्मणि ।।४७।।

47. There is the originality and power of the Gita, that having affirmed this static condition, this superiority to nature, this emptiness even of all that constitutes ordinarily the action of Nature for the liberated soul,

it is still able to vindicate for it, to enjoin on it even the continuance of works and thus avoid the great defect of the merely quietistic and ascetic philosophies. **Thou hast a right to action, but only to action, never to its fruits; let not the fruits of thy works be thy motive, neither let there be in thee any attachment to inactivity, *saṅgo'karmaṇi*.**

The Gita can only be understood, like any other great work of the kind, by studying it in its entirety and as a developing argument. But the modern interpreters, starting from the great writer Bankim Chandra Chatterji who first gave to the Gita this new sense of a Gospel of Duty, had laid an almost exclusive stress on the first three or four chapters and in those on the idea of equality (*see Introduction — 4*), on the expression *kartavyaṁ karma*, the work that is to be done, which they render by duty, and on the phrase, "Thou hast a right to action, but none to the fruits of action", which is now popularly quoted as the great word, *mahāvākya*, of the Gita. The rest of the eighteen chapters with their high philosophy are given a secondary importance. But it is the wrong way to handle this Scripture. "The work that is to be done", a phrase which the Gita uses with the greatest wideness including in it all works, *sarva-karmāṇi*, far exceeds though it may include social duties or ethical obligations. What is the work to be done is not to be determined by the individual choice; nor is the right to the action and the rejection of claim to the fruit the great word of the Gita, but only a preliminary word governing the first state of the disciple when he begins ascending the hill of Yoga.

योगस्थः कुरु कर्माणि सङ्गं त्यक्त्वा धनञ्जय ।
सिद्ध्यसिद्ध्योः समो भूत्वा समत्वं योग उच्यते ।।४८।।

48. Therefore it is not the works practised with desire by the Vedavadins, it is not the claim for the satisfaction of the restless and energetic mind by a constant activity, the claim made by the practical or the kinetic man, which is here enjoined. **Fixed in Yoga do thy actions, *yoga-sthaḥ kuru karmāṇi*, having abandoned attachment, *saṅgaṁ tyaktvā*, having become equal, *samo bhūtvā*, in failure and success; for it is equality that is meant by Yoga, *samatvaṁ yoga ucyate*.**

The self, spirit or Brahman is one in all and therefore one to all; it is the equal Brahman, *samaṁ brahma*; the Gita even goes so far [*in this passage*] as to identify equality and Yoga. That is to say, equality is the sign of unity with the Brahman, of becoming Brahman, of growing into an undisturbed spiritual poise of being in the Infinite. Its importance can hardly be exaggerated; for it is the sign of our having passed beyond the egoistic determinations of our nature, of our having conquered our enslaved response to the dualities, of our having transcended the shifting turmoil of the gunas, of our having entered into the calm and peace of liberation. Equality is a term of consciousness which brings into the whole of our being and nature the eternal tranquillity of the Infinite. Moreover, it is the condition of a securely and perfectly divine action.

Knowledge is the consciousness of unity with the One; and in relation with the many different beings and existences of the universe it must show itself by an equal oneness with all.

दूरेण ह्यवरं कर्म बुद्धियोगाद्धनञ्जय ।
बुद्धौ शरणमन्विच्छ कृपणाः फलहेतवः ।।४९।।

49. Works are far inferior to Yoga of the intelligence; desire rather refuge in the intelligence; poor and wretched souls are they who make the fruit of their works the object of their thoughts and activities.

बुद्धियुक्तो जहातीह उभे सुकृतदुष्कृते ।
तस्माद्योगाय युज्यस्व योगः कर्मसु कौशलम् ।।५०।।

50. Action is distressed by the choice between a relative good and evil, the fear of sin and the difficult endeavour towards virtue? **But the liberated who has united his reason and will with the Divine, *buddhi-yuktaḥ*, casts away from him even here in this world of dualities both good doing and evil doing, *sukṛita-duṣkṛite*;** for he rises to a higher law beyond good and evil, founded in the liberty of self-knowledge. Such desireless action can have no decisiveness, no effectiveness, no efficient motive, no large or vigorous creative power? Not so; action done in Yoga is not only the highest but the wisest, the most potent and efficient even for the affairs of the world; for it is informed by the knowledge and will of the Master of works: **therefore to Yoga gird thy soul; Yoga is skill in works, *yogaḥ karmasu kauśalam*,** the skill that comes by unity with the eternal spirit we are in the measure of our light labouring to express.

कर्मजं बुद्धियुक्ता हि फलं त्यक्त्वा मनीषिणः ।
जन्मबन्धविनिर्मुक्ताः पदं गच्छन्त्यनामयम् ।।५१।।

51. But all action directed towards life leads away from the universal aim of the Yogin which is by common consent to escape from bondage to this distressed and sorrowful human birth? Not so, either; **the sages who do works without desire for fruits and in Yoga with the Divine are liberated from the bondage of birth and reach that other perfect status in which there are none of the maladies which afflict the mind and life of a suffering humanity.**

यदा ते मोहकलिलं बुद्धिर्व्यतितरिष्यति ।
तदा गन्तासि निर्वेदं श्रोतव्यस्य श्रुतस्य च ।।५२।।
श्रुतिविप्रतिपन्ना ते यदा स्थास्यति निश्चला ।
समाधावचला बुद्धिस्तदा योगमवाप्स्यसि ।।५३।।

52-53. The Scriptures are even a stumbling-block; for the letter of the Word — perhaps because of its conflict of texts and its various and mutually dissentient interpretations — bewilders the understanding, which can only find certainty and concentration by the light within. **When thy intelligence shall cross beyond the whorl of delusion, then shalt thou become indifferent to Scripture heard or that which thou hast yet to hear. When thy intelligence which is bewildered by the Sruti, shall stand unmoving and stable in Samadhi, then shalt thou attain to Yoga.** So offensive is all this to conventional religious sentiment that attempts are naturally made by the convenient and indispensable human faculty of text-twisting to put a different sense on some of these verses, but the meaning is plain and hangs together from beginning to end. It is not surprising at all that with the conflict of so many philosophical schools all founding themselves on the texts of the Veda and Upanishads, the Gita should describe the understanding as being perplexed and confused, led in different directions by the Sruti, *śruti-vipratipannā*. The understanding may well get disgusted and indifferent, *gantāsi nirvedam*, refuse to hear any more texts new or old, and go into itself to discover the truth in the light of a deeper and inner and direct experience.

The Gita in later chapters (*see, IX-17, X-22, XV-15*) speaks highly of the Veda and the Upanishads. They are divine Scriptures, they are the Word. The Lord himself is the knower of Veda and the author of Vedanta, *vedavid vedānta-kṛit* (*XV-15*); the Lord is the one object of knowledge in all the Vedas, *sarvair vedair aham eva vedyaḥ* (*XV-15*), a language which implies that the word Veda means the book of knowledge and that these Scriptures deserve their appellation. The Purushottama from his high supremacy above the Immutable and the mutable has extended himself in the world and in the Veda, *loke veda ca* (*XV-18*). Still the letter of the Scripture binds and confuses, as the apostle of Christianity warned his disciples when he said that the letter killeth and it is the spirit that saves; and there is a point beyond which the utility of the Scripture itself ceases. The real source of knowledge is the

Lord in the heart; "I am seated in the heart of every man and from me is knowledge," says the Gita (*XV-15*); the Scripture is only a verbal form of that inner Veda, of that self-luminous Reality, it is *śabda-brahma* (*VI-44*): the mantra, says the Veda, has risen from the heart, from the secret place where is the seat of the Truth, *sadanād ṛitasya, guhāyām*. That origin is its sanction; but still the infinite Truth is greater than its word. Nor shall you say of any Scripture that it alone is all-sufficient and no other truth can be admitted, as the Vedavadins said of the Veda, *nānyad astīti vādinaḥ* (*II-42*). This is a saving and liberating word which must be applied to all the Scriptures of the world. Take all the Scriptures that are or have been, still you shall not say that there is nothing else or that the truth your intellect cannot find there is not true because you cannot find it there. That is the limited thought of the sectarian or the composite thought of the eclectic religionist, not the untrammelled truth-seeking of the free and illumined mind and God-experienced soul. Heard or unheard before, that always is the truth which is seen by the heart of man in its illumined depths or heard within from the Master of all knowledge, the knower of the eternal Veda.

But in the end the sadhaka of the integral Yoga must take his station, or better still, if he can, always and from the beginning he must live in his own soul beyond the written Truth, — *śabda-brahmātivartate*, — beyond all that he has heard and all that he has yet to hear, — *śrotavyasya śrutasya ca*. For he is not the sadhaka of a book or of many books; he is a sadhaka of the Infinite.

अर्जुन उवाच
स्थितप्रज्ञस्य का भाषा समाधिस्थस्य केशव ।
स्थितधीः किं प्रभाषेत किमासीत व्रजेत किम् ।।५४।।

54. *Arjuna* — Arjuna is not satisfied: he wishes to know how the change to this state will affect the outward action of the man, what result it will have on his speech, his movements, his state, what difference it will make in this acting, living human being. **Voicing the average human mind, he asks for some outward, physical, practically discernible sign of this great Samadhi; how does such a man speak, how sit, how walk?**

श्रीभगवानुवाच
प्रजहाति यदा कामान्सर्वान्पार्थ मनोगतान् ।
आत्मन्येवात्मना तुष्टः स्थितप्रज्ञस्तदोच्यते ।।५५।।

55. *Krishna* — Krishna persists merely in enlarging upon the ideas he has already brought forward, on the soul-state behind the action, not on

the action itself. **It is the fixed anchoring of the intelligence in a state of desireless equality that is the one thing needed.**

The sign of the man in Samadhi is not that he loses consciousness of objects and surroundings and of his mental and physical self and cannot be recalled to it even by burning or torture of the body, — the ordinary idea of the matter; trance is a particular intensity, not the essential sign. **The test is the expulsion of all desires, their inability to get at the mind, and it is the inner state from which this freedom arises, the delight of the soul gathered within itself, *ātmani-eva-ātmanā tuṣṭaḥ*, with the mind equal and still and high-poised above the attractions and repulsions,** the alternations of sunshine and storm and stress of the external life. It is drawn inward even when acting outwardly; it is concentrated in self even when gazing out upon things; it is directed wholly to the Divine even when to the outward vision of others busy and preoccupied with the affairs of the world. The only possible test of its possession is inward.

दुःखेष्वनुद्विग्नमनाः सुखेषु विगतस्पृहः ।
वीतरागभयक्रोधः स्थितधीर्मुनिरुच्यते ।।५६।।

56. Equality is the great stamp of the liberated soul and of that equality even the most discernible signs are still subjective. **A man with mind untroubled by sorrows, who has done with desire for pleasures, from whom liking and wrath and fear have passed away, such is the sage whose understanding has become founded in stability.**

यः सर्वत्रानभिस्नेहस्तत्तत्प्राप्य शुभाशुभम् ।
नाभिनन्दति न द्वेष्टि तस्य प्रज्ञा प्रतिष्ठिता ।।५७।।

57. **Who in all things is without affection though visited by this good or that evil and neither hates nor rejoices, his intelligence sits firmly founded in wisdom.**

यदा संहरते चायं कूर्मोऽङ्गानीव सर्वशः ।
इन्द्रियाणीन्द्रियार्थेभ्यस्तस्य प्रज्ञा प्रतिष्ठिता ।।५८।।

58. The first movement must be obviously to get rid of desire which is the whole root of the evil and suffering; and in order to get rid of desire, we must put an end to the cause of desire, the rushing out of the senses to seize and enjoy their objects. **We must draw them back when they**

are inclined thus to rush out, draw them away from their objects, — as the tortoise draws in his limbs into the shell, so these into their source, quiescent in the mind, the mind quiescent in intelligence, the intelligence quiescent in the soul and its self-knowledge, observing the action of Nature, but not subject to it, not desiring anything that the objective life can give, [**firmly founded in knowledge.**]

विषया विनिवर्तन्ते निराहारस्य देहिनः ।
रसवर्जं रसोऽप्यस्य परं दृष्ट्वा निवर्तते ।।५९।।

59. **If one abstains from food, the object of sense ceases to affect, but the affection itself of the sense, the *rasa*, remains; it is only when, even in the exercise of the sense, it can keep back from seeking its sensuous aim in the object, *artha*, and abandon the affection, the desire for the pleasure of taste, that the highest level of the soul is reached.**

It is not an external asceticism, the physical renunciation of the objects of sense that I am teaching, suggests Krishna immediately to avoid a misunderstanding which is likely at once to arise. Not the renunciation of the Sankhyas or the austerities of the rigid ascetic with his fasts, his maceration of the body, his attempt to abstain even from food; that is not the self-discipline or the abstinence which I mean, for I speak of an inner withdrawal, a renunciation of desire. The embodied soul, having a body, has to support it normally by food for its normal physical action; by abstention from food it simply removes from itself the physical contact with the object of sense, but does not get rid of the inner relation which makes that contact hurtful. It retains the pleasure of the sense in the object, the *rasa*, the liking and disliking, — for *rasa* has two sides; the soul must, on the contrary, be capable of enduring the physical contact without suffering inwardly this sensuous reaction. Otherwise there is *nivṛitti*, cessation of the object, *viṣayā vinivartante* but no subjective cessation, no *nivṛitti* of the mind; but the senses are of the mind, subjective, and subjective cessation of the *rasa* is the only real sign of mastery. But how is this desireless contact with objects, this unsensuous use of the senses possible? **It is possible, *paraṁ dṛiṣṭvā*, by the vision of the supreme,** — *param*, the Soul, the Purusha, — and by living in the Yoga, in union or oneness of the whole subjective being with that, through the Yoga of the intelligence. — The Teacher points the disciple towards an inner renunciation which is the real issue from his crisis and the way towards the soul's superiority to the world-Nature and yet its calm and self-possessed action in the world. Not a physical asceticism, but an inner askesis is the teaching of the Gita.

यततो ह्यपि कौन्तेय पुरुषस्य विपश्चितः ।
इन्द्रियाणि प्रमाथीनि हरन्ति प्रसभं मनः ॥६०॥

60. **Even the mind of the sage, the man of clear, wise and discerning soul who really labours to acquire complete self-mastery and perfection finds itself hurried and carried away by the vehement insistence of the senses.**

तानि सर्वाणि संयम्य युक्त आसीत मत्परः ।
वशे हि यस्येन्द्रियाणि तस्य प्रज्ञा प्रतिष्ठिता ॥६१॥

61. **All the senses must be brought utterly under control; for only by an absolute control of the senses can the wise and calm intelligence be firmly established in its proper seat.** This cannot be done perfectly by the act of the intelligence itself, by a merely mental self-discipline; it can only be done by Yoga with something which is higher than itself and in which calm and self-mastery are inherent. And this Yoga can only arrive at its success **by devoting, by consecrating, by giving up the whole self to the Divine, "to Me", says Krishna;** for the Liberator is within us, but it is not our mind, nor our intelligence, nor our personal will, — they are only instruments. It is the Lord in whom, as we are told in the end, we have utterly to take refuge. And for that we must at first **make him the object of our whole being and keep in soul-contact with him. This is the sense of the phrase "he must sit firm in Yoga, wholly given up to Me";** but as yet it is the merest passing hint after the manner of the Gita, three words only which contain in seed the whole gist of the highest secret yet to be developed. *Yukta āsīta matparaḥ.*

ध्यायतो विषयान्पुंसः सङ्गस्तेषूपजायते ।
सङ्गात्सञ्जायते कामः कामात्क्रोधोभिजायते ॥६२॥
क्रोधाद् भवति सम्मोहः सम्मोहात् स्मृतिविभ्रमः ।
स्मृतिभ्रंशाद् बुद्धिनाशो बुद्धिनाशात्प्रणश्यति ॥६३॥

62-63. **The mind naturally lends itself to the senses; it observes the objects of sense with an inner interest, settles upon them and makes them the object of absorbing thought for the intelligence and of strong interest for the will. By that attachment comes, by attachment desire, by desire distress, passion and anger when the desire is not satisfied or is thwarted or opposed, and by passion the soul is obscured, the intelligence and will forget to see and be seated in the calm observing soul; there is a fall from the memory of one's true self, and by that lapse the intelligent will is also obscured, destroyed even. For, for the time being,** it no longer exists to our memory of ourselves, it disappears in a cloud of passion; we become passion, wrath, grief and cease to be self and intelligence and will.

रागद्वेषवियुक्तैस्तु विषयानिन्द्रियैश्चरन् ।
आत्मवश्यैर्विधेयात्मा प्रसादमधिगच्छति ।।६४।।
प्रसादे सर्वदुःखानां हानिरस्योपजायते ।
प्रसन्नचेतसो ह्याशु बुद्धिः पर्यवतिष्ठते ।।६५।।

64-65. *yukta āsīta matparaḥ*. If this is done, then it becomes possible to move among the objects of sense, ranging over them with the senses, in contact with them, acting on them, but with the senses entirely under the control of the subjective self, — not at the mercy of the objects and their contacts and reactions, — and that self again obedient to the highest self, the Purusha. Then, free from reactions, the senses will be delivered from the affections of liking and disliking, escape the duality of positive and negative desire, and calm, peace, large and sweet clearness of soul and temperament, happy tranquillity, *ātmaprasāda*, will settle upon the man. That clear tranquillity is the source of the soul's felicity; all grief begins to lose its power of touching the tranquil soul; the intelligence is rapidly established in the peace of the self; suffering is destroyed. It is this calm, desireless, griefless fixity of the *buddhi* in self-poise and self-knowledge to which the Gita gives the name of Samadhi.

नास्ति बुद्धिरयुक्तस्य न चायुक्तस्य भावना ।
न चाभावयतः शान्तिरशान्तस्य कुतः सुखम् ।।६६।।

66. Who is not in Yoga has not understanding, who is not in Yoga has not infinite and inward contemplation, who thinks not infinitely and inwardly has not peace of soul, and how shall he be happy whose soul is not at peace?

इन्द्रियाणां हि चरतां यन्मनोऽनुविधीयते ।
तदस्य हरति प्रज्ञां वायुर्नावमिवाम्भसि ।।६७।।

67. The senses excited by their objects create a restless or often violent disturbance, a strong or even headlong outward movement towards the seizure of these objects and their enjoyment, and they carry away the sense-mind, as the winds carry away a ship upon the sea; the mind subjected to the emotions, passions, longings, impulsions awakened by this outward movement

of the senses carries away similarly the intelligent will, which loses therefore its power of calm discrimination and mastery.

तस्माद्यस्य महाबाहो निगृहीतानि सर्वशः ।
इन्द्रियाणीन्द्रियार्थेभ्यस्तस्य प्रज्ञा प्रतिष्ठिता ।।६८।।

68. Therefore it is that his Reason is firmly based whose senses are reined in on all sides from the things of their desire.

या निशा सर्वभूतानां तस्यां जागर्ति संयमी ।
यस्यां जाग्रति भूतानि सा निशा पश्यतो मुनेः ।।६९।।

69. This life of the dualities which is to earth-bound creatures their day, their waking, their consciousness, their bright condition of activity and knowledge, is to him a night, a troubled sleep and darkness of the soul; that higher being which is to them a night, a sleep in which all knowledge and will cease, is to the self-mastering sage his waking, his luminous day of true being, knowledge and power.

आपूर्यमाणमचलप्रतिष्ठं समुद्रमापः प्रविशन्ति यद्वत् ।
तद्वत्कामा यं प्रविशन्ति सर्वे स शान्तिमाप्नोति न कामकामी ।।७०।।

70. They are troubled and muddy waters disturbed by every little inrush of desire; he is an ocean of wide being and consciousness which is ever being filled, yet ever motionless in its large poise of his soul; all the desires of the world enter into him as waters into the sea, yet he has no desire nor is troubled.

विहाय कामान्यः सर्वान्पुमांश्चरति निःस्पृहः ।
निर्ममो निरहङ्कारः स शान्तिमधिगच्छति ।।७१।।

71. For while they are filled with the troubling sense of ego and mine and thine, he is one with the one Self in all and has no "I" or "mine", *nirmamo nirahaṁkāraḥ*. He acts as others, but he has abandoned all desires and their longings. He attains to the great peace.

एषा ब्राह्मी स्थितिः पार्थ नैनां प्राप्य विमुह्यति ।
स्थित्वास्यामन्तकालेऽपि ब्रह्मनिर्वाणमृच्छति ।।७२।।

72. The status he reaches is the Brahmic condition; he gets to firm standing in the Brahman, *eṣā brāhmī sthitiḥ*. It is a reversal of the whole view, experience, knowledge, values, seeings of earth-bound creatures. He is not bewildered by the shows of things; he has extinguished his individual ego in the One, lives in that unity and, fixed in that status at his end, can attain to extinction in the Brahman, Nirvana, *brahma-nirvāṇam*, — not the negative self-annihilation of the Buddhists, but the great immergence of the separate personal self into the vast reality of the one infinite impersonal Existence.

It is not enough for the sadhaks of the integral Yoga to have the utter realisation only in the trance of Samadhi or in a motionless quietude, but he must in trance or in waking, in passive reflection or energy of action be able to remain in the constant Samadhi of the firmly founded Brahmic consciousness.

Such, subtly unifying Sankhya, Yoga and Vedanta, is the first foundation of the teaching of the Gita. It is far from being all, but it is the first indispensable practical unity of knowledge and works with a hint already of the third crowning intensest element in the soul's completeness, divine love and devotion.

Chapter III

I — Works and Sacrifice

The Yoga of the intelligent will and its culmination in the Brahmic status, which occupies all the close of the second chapter, contains the seed of much of the teaching of the Gita, — its doctrine of desireless works, of equality, of the rejection of outward renunciation, of devotion to the Divine; but as yet all this is slight and obscure. What is most strongly emphasised as yet is the withdrawal of the will from the ordinary motive of human activities, desire, from man's normal temperament of the sense-seeking thought and will with its passions and ignorance, and from its customary habit of troubled many-branching ideas and wishes to the desireless calm unity and passionless serenity of the Brahmic poise. So much Arjuna has understood. Krishna seems quite to admit the orthodox philosophical doctrine when he says that works are far inferior to the Yoga of the intelligence. And yet works are insisted upon as part of the Yoga; so that there seems to be in this teaching a radical inconsistency. Not only so; for some kind of work no doubt may persist for a while, the minimum, the most inoffensive; but here is a work wholly inconsistent with knowledge, with serenity and with the motionless peace of the self-delighted soul, — a work terrible, even monstrous, a bloody strife, a ruthless battle, a giant massacre. Yet it is this that is enjoined, this that it is sought to justify by the teaching of inner peace and desireless equality and status in the Brahman! Here then is an unreconciled contradiction.

अर्जुन उवाच
ज्यायसी चेत्कर्मणस्ते मता बुद्धिर्जनार्दन ।
तत्किं कर्मणि घोरे मां नियोजयसि केशव ।।१।।
व्यामिश्रेणेव वाक्येन बुद्धिं मोहयसीव मे ।
तदेकं वद निश्चित्य येन श्रेयोऽहमाप्नुयाम् ।।२।।

1-2. *Arjuna* — Arjuna breaks out impatiently, — for here is no rule of conduct such as he sought, but rather, as it seems to him, the negation of all action, — **If thou holdest the intelligence to be greater than action, *jyāyasī karmaṇo buddhiḥ*, why then dost thou appoint me to an action terrible in its** nature, ***kiṁ karmaṇi ghore māṁ niyojayasi*? Thou bewilderest my understanding with a mingled word: speak one thing decisively by which I can attain to what is the best.** It is always the pragmatic man who has no value for metaphysical thought or for the inner life except when they help him to his one demand, a *dharma*, a law of life in the world or, if need be, of leaving the world; for that too is a decisive action which he can understand. But to live and act in the world, yet be above it, this is a mingled and confusing word the sense of which he has no patience to grasp.

श्रीभगवानुवाच
लोकेऽस्मिन्द्विविधा निष्ठा पुरा प्रोक्ता मयानघ ।
ज्ञानयोगेन साङ्ख्यानां कर्मयोगेन योगिनाम् ।।३।।

3. *Krishna* — **Twofold is the self-application of the soul by which it enters into the Brahmic condition: that of the Sankhyas by the Yoga of knowledge, that of the Yogins by the Yoga of works.** The Teacher first makes a distinction between the two means of salvation on which in this world men can concentrate separately, the Yoga of knowledge, the Yoga of works, the one implying, it is usually supposed, renunciation of works as an obstacle to salvation, the other accepting works as a means of salvation.

न कर्मणामनारम्भान्नैष्कर्म्यं पुरुषोऽश्नुते ।
न च संन्यसनादेव सिद्धिं समधिगच्छति ।।४।।

4. The Teacher begins by showing that the renunciation of the Sankhyas, the physical renunciation, Sannyasa, is neither the only way, nor at all the better way. *Naiṣkarmya*, a calm voidness from works, is no doubt that to which the soul, the Purusha has to attain; for it is Prakriti which does the work and the soul has to rise above involution in the activities of the being and attain to a free serenity and poise watching over the operations of Prakriti, but not affected by them. That, and not cessation of the works of Prakriti, is what is really meant by the soul's *naiṣkarmya*. Therefore it is an error to think that by not engaging in any kind of action, *karmaṇām anārambhāt*, this actionless state of the soul, *naiṣkarmyam*, can be attained and enjoyed. Mere renunciation of works is not a sufficient, not even quite a proper means for salvation. **Not by abstention from works does a man enjoy actionlessness, nor by mere renunciation (of works) does he attain to his perfection,** — to *siddhi*, the accomplishment of the aims of his self-discipline by Yoga.

न हि कश्चित्क्षणमपि जातु तिष्ठत्यकर्मकृत् ।
कार्यते ह्यवशः कर्म सर्वः प्रकृतिजैर्गुणैः ॥५॥

5. **For none stands even for a moment not doing work; everyone is made to do action helplessly by the modes born of Prakriti.** The strong perception of the great cosmic action and the eternal activity and power of the cosmic energy is a very remarkable feature of the Gita. Man embodied in the natural world cannot cease from action, not for a moment, not for a second; his very existence here is an action; the whole universe is an act of God, mere living even is His movement.

कर्मेन्द्रियाणि संयम्य य आस्ते मनसा स्मरन् ।
इन्द्रियार्थान्विमूढात्मा मिथ्याचारः स उच्यते ॥६॥

6. It is not our physical movements and activities alone which are meant by works, by *karma*; our mental existence also is a great complex action, it is even the greater and more important part of the works of the unresting energy, — subjective cause and determinant of the physical. We have gained nothing if we repress the effect but retain the activity of the subjective cause. The objects of sense are only an occasion for our bondage, the mind's insistence on them is the means, the instrumental cause. **A man may control, *saṁyamya*, his organs of action and refuse to give them their natural play, but he has gained nothing if his mind continues to remember and dwell upon the objects of sense. Such a man has bewildered himself with false notions of self-discipline, a false and self-deceiving line of action, *mithyācāra*;** he has not understood its object or its truth, nor the first principles of his subjective existence; therefore all his methods of self-discipline are false and null.

यस्त्विन्द्रियाणि मनसा नियम्यारभतेऽर्जुन ।
कर्मेन्द्रियैः कर्मयोगमसक्तः स विशिष्यते ॥७॥

7. Since the mind is the instrumental cause, since inaction is impossible, what is rational, necessary, the right way is a controlled action of the subjective and objective organism. The mind must bring the senses under its control as an instrument of the intelligent will and then the organs of action must be used for their proper office, for action, but for action done as Yoga. But what is the essence of this self-control, what is meant by action done as Yoga, *Karmayoga*? **It is non-attachment, it is to do works without clinging with the mind to the objects of sense and the fruit of the works.** Not

complete inaction, which is an error, a confusion, a self-delusion, an impossibility, but action full and free done without subjection to sense and passion, desireless and unattached works, are the first secret of perfection. Krishna makes a statement, **he who controlling the senses by the mind engages with the organs of action in Yoga of action, he excels, *indriyāṇi manasā niyamya-ārabhate karmayogam.***

नियतं कुरु कर्म त्वं कर्म ज्यायो ह्यकर्मणः ।
शरीरयात्रापि च ते न प्रसिद्ध्येदकर्मणः ॥८॥

8. And Krishna immediately goes on to draw from the statement an injunction, to sum it up and convert it into a rule. **Do thou do controlled action, *niyataṁ kuru karma tvam*:** *niyatam* takes up the *niyamya*, *kuru karma* takes up the *ārabhate karmayogam*. Not formal works fixed by an external rule, but desireless works controlled by the liberated *buddhi*, is the Gita's teaching. **I have said that knowledge, the intelligence, is greater than works, *jyāyasī karmaṇo buddhiḥ*, but I did not mean that inaction is greater than action; the contrary is the truth, *karma jyāyo akarmaṇaḥ*.** For knowledge does not mean renunciation of works, it means equality and non-attachment to desire and the objects of sense; and it means the poise of the intelligent will in the Soul free and high-uplifted above the lower instrumentation of Prakriti and controlling the works of the mind and the senses and body in the power of self-knowledge and the pure objectless self-delight of spiritual realisation, *niyataṁ karma*. *Buddhiyoga* is fulfilled by *karmayoga*; the Yoga of the self-liberating intelligent will finds its full meaning by the Yoga of desireless works. Thus the Gita founds its teaching of the necessity of desireless works, *niṣkāma karma*, and unites the subjective practice of the Sankhyas — rejecting their merely physical rule — with the practice of Yoga. Our physical life, its maintenance, its continuance is a journey, a pilgrimage of the body, *śarīra-yātrā*, and that cannot be effected without action.

यज्ञार्थात्कर्मणोऽन्यत्र लोकोऽयं कर्मबन्धनः ।
तदर्थं कर्म कौन्तेय मुक्तसङ्गः समाचर ॥९॥

9. The difficulty is this, how, our nature being what it is and desire the common principle of its action, is it possible to institute a really desireless action? For what we call ordinarily disinterested action is not really desireless; it is simply a replacement of certain smaller personal interests by other larger desires which have only the appearance of being impersonal,

virtue, country, mankind. We cannot become impersonal by obeying something outside ourselves, for we cannot so get outside ourselves; we can only do it by rising to the highest in ourselves, into our free Soul and Self which is the same and one in all and has therefore no personal interests, to the Divine in our being who possesses Himself transcendent of cosmos and is therefore not bound by His cosmic works or His individual action. That is what the Gita teaches and desirelessness is only a means to this end, not an aim in itself. Yes, but how is it to be brought about? By doing all works with sacrifice as the only object, is the reply of the divine Teacher. **By doing works otherwise than for sacrifice, this world of men is in bondage to works; for sacrifice practise works, O son of Kunti, becoming free from all attachment.** It is evident that all works and not merely sacrifice and social duties can be done in this spirit; any action may be done either from the ego-sense narrow or enlarged or for the sake of the Divine. All being and all action of Prakriti exist only for the sake of the Divine; from that it proceeds, by that it endures, to that it is directed. But so long as we are dominated by the ego-sense we cannot perceive or act in the spirit of this truth, but act for the satisfaction of the ego and in the spirit of the ego, otherwise than for sacrifice. Egoism is the knot of the bondage. By acting Godwards, without any thought of ego, we loosen this knot and finally arrive at freedom.

II — THE SIGNIFICANCE OF SACRIFICE

In the first six chapters the Gita lays a large foundation for its synthesis of works and knowledge, its synthesis of Sankhya, Yoga and Vedanta. But first it finds that *karma*, works, has a particular sense in the language of the Vedantins; it means the Vedic sacrifices and ceremonies. By works the Vedantins understood these religious works, the sacrificial system, the *yajña*, full of a careful order, *vidhi*, of exact and complicated rites. But in Yoga works had a much wider significance. The Gita insists on this wider significance; in our conception of spiritual activity all works have to be included, *sarva-karmāṇi*. At the same time it does not, like Buddhism, reject the idea of the sacrifice, it prefers to uplift and enlarge it. Yes, it says in effect, not only is sacrifice, *yajña*, the most important part of life, but all life, all works should be regarded as sacrifice, are *yajña*, though by the ignorant they are performed without the higher knowledge and by the most ignorant not in the true order, *avidhi-pūrvakam*. Sacrifice is the very condition of life; "With sacrifice as their eternal companion the Father of creatures created the peoples". But the sacrifices of the Vedavadins are offerings of desire directed towards material rewards, desire eager for the result of works, desire looking to a larger enjoyment in Paradise as immortality and highest salvation. This the system of the Gita cannot admit; for that in its very inception starts with the renunciation of desire, with its rejection and destruction as the enemy of the soul. The Gita does not deny the validity even of the Vedic sacrificial works; it admits them, it admits that by these means one may get enjoyment here and Paradise beyond; "It is I myself, says the divine Teacher, who accept these sacrifices and to whom they are offered, I who give these fruits in the form of the gods since so men choose to approach me (*IX-23/25*)". But this is not the true road, nor is the enjoyment of Paradise the liberation and fulfilment which man has to seek. It is the ignorant who worship the gods, not knowing whom they are worshipping ignorantly in these divine forms; for they are worshipping, though in ignorance, the One, the Lord, the only Deva, and it is he who accepts their offering. To that Lord must the sacrifice be offered, the true sacrifice of all the life's energies and activities, with devotion, without desire, for His sake and for the welfare of the peoples.

The Gita's theory of sacrifice is stated in two separate passages; one we find in the third chapter (*10-16*), another in the fourth (*24-35*); the first gives it in language which might, taken by itself, seem to be speaking only of the ceremonial sacrifice; the second interpreting that into the sense of a large philosophical symbolism, transforms at once its whole significance and raises it to a plane of high psychological and spiritual truth.

सहयज्ञाः प्रजाः सृष्ट्वा पुरोवाच प्रजापतिः ।
अनेन प्रसविष्यध्वमेष वोऽस्त्विष्टकामधुक् ॥१०॥

10. With sacrifice the Lord of creatures of old created creatures and said, "By this shall you bring forth (fruits or offspring), let this be your milker of desires. All truth of works must depend upon the truth of being. All active existence must be in its inmost reality a sacrifice of works offered by Prakriti to Purusha, Nature offering to the supreme and infinite Soul the desire of the multiple finite Soul within her. Life is an altar to which she brings her workings and the fruits of her workings and lays them before whatever aspect of the Divinity the consciousness in her has reached for whatever result of the sacrifice the desire of the living soul can seize on as its immediate or its highest good. According to the grade of consciousness and being which the soul has reached in Nature, will be the Divinity it worships, the delight which it seeks and the hope for which it sacrifices. And in the movement of the mutable Purusha in Nature all is and must be interchange; for existence is one and its divisions must found themselves on some law of mutual dependence, each growing by each and living by all. Where sacrifice is not willingly given, Nature exacts it by force, she satisfies the law of her living. A mutual giving and receiving is the law of Life without which it cannot for one moment endure, and this fact is the stamp of the divine creative Will on the world it has manifested in its being, the proof that **with sacrifice as their eternal companion the Lord of creatures has created all these existences.** The universal law of sacrifice is the sign that the world is of God and belongs to God and that life is his dominion and house of worship and not a field for the self-satisfaction of the independent ego; not the fulfilment of the ego, — that is only our crude and obscure beginning, — but the discovery of God, the worship and seeking of the Divine and the Infinite through a constantly enlarging sacrifice culminating in a perfect self-giving founded on a perfect self-knowledge, is that to which the experience of life is at last intended to lead.

देवान्भावयतानेन ते देवा भावयन्तु वः ।
परस्परं भावयन्तः श्रेयः परमवाप्स्यथ ।।११।।

11. **Foster by this the gods and let the gods foster you; fostering each other, you shall attain to the supreme good,** ***śreyaḥ param avāpsyatha.*** The Divine may be known in an inferior action through the *devas*, the gods, the powers of the divine Soul in Nature and in the eternal interaction of these powers and the soul of man, mutually giving and receiving, mutually helping, increasing, raising each others' workings and satisfaction, a commerce in which man rises towards a growing fitness for the supreme good. He recognises that his life is a part of this divine action in Nature and not a thing separate and to be held and pursued for its own sake.

इष्टान्भोगान्हि वो देवा दास्यन्ते यज्ञभाविताः ।
तैर्दत्तानप्रदायैभ्यो यो भुङ्क्ते स्तेन एव सः ।।१२।।

12. **Fostered by sacrifice the gods shall give you desired enjoyments; who enjoys their given enjoyments and has not given to them, he is a thief.** He regards his enjoyments and the satisfaction of his desires as the fruit of sacrifice and the gift of the gods in their divine universal workings and he ceases to pursue them in the false and evil spirit of sinful egoistic selfishness as if they were a good to be seized from life by his own unaided strength without return and without thankfulness. Because of this ignorance whose seal is egoism, the creature ignores the law of sacrifice and seeks to take all he can for himself and gives only what Nature by her internal and external compulsion forces him to give. He can really take nothing except what she

allows him to receive as his portion, what the divine Powers within her yield to his desire. The egoistic soul in a world of sacrifice is as if a thief or robber who takes what these Powers bring to him and has no mind to give in return.

यज्ञशिष्टाशिनः सन्तो मुच्यन्ते सर्वकिल्बिषैः ।
भुञ्जते ते त्वघं पापा ये पचन्त्यात्मकारणात् ।।१३।।

13. The good who eat what is left from the sacrifice, are released from all sin; but evil are they and enjoy sin who cook (the food) for their own sake. As this spirit increases in him, he subordinates his desires, becomes satisfied with sacrifice as the law of life and works and is content with whatever remains over from the sacrifice, giving up all the rest freely as an offering in the great and beneficent interchange between his life and the world-life.

अन्नाद् भवन्ति भूतानि पर्जन्यादन्नसम्भवः ।
यज्ञाद् भवति पर्जन्यो यज्ञः कर्मसमुद्भवः ।।१४।।
कर्म ब्रह्मोद्भवं विद्धि ब्रह्माक्षरसमुद्भवम् ।
तस्मात्सर्वगतं ब्रह्म नित्यं यज्ञे प्रतिष्ठितम् ।।१५।।

14-15. From food creatures come into being, from rain is the birth of food, from sacrifice comes into being the rain, sacrifice is born of work; work know to be born of Brahman, Brahman is born of the Immutable; therefore is the all-pervading Brahman established in the sacrifice. Even in the passage itself, without the illumining interpretation afterwards given to it in the fourth chapter, we have already an indication of a wider sense when it is said that **sacrifice is born from work, work from *brahman*, *brahman* from the Akshara, and therefore the all-pervading Brahman, *sarvagataṁ brahma*, is established in the sacrifice.** The connecting logic of the "therefore" and the repetition of the word *brahma* are significant; for it shows clearly that the *brahman* from which all work is born has to be understood with an eye not so much to the current Vedic teaching in which it means the Veda as to a symbolical sense in which the creative Word is identical with the all-pervading Brahman, the Eternal, the one Self present in all existences, *sarvabhūteṣu*, and present in all the workings of existence. The Veda is the knowledge of the Divine, the Eternal; but it is the knowledge of him [the Divine] in the workings of Prakriti, in the workings of the three *guṇas*, first qualities or modes of Nature, *traiguṇya-viṣayā vedāḥ*. This Brahman or Divine in the workings of Nature is born, as we may say, out of the Akshara, the immutable Purusha, the Self who stands above all the modes or qualities or workings of Nature, *nistraiguṇya*. The Brahman is one but self-displayed in two aspects, the immutable Being and the creator and originator of works in the mutable becoming, *ātman*, *sarvabhūtāni*; it is the immobile omnipresent Soul of things and it is the spiritual principle of the mobile working of things, Purusha poised in himself and Purusha active in Prakriti; it is *akṣara* and *kṣara*. In both of these aspects the Divine Being, Purushottama, manifests himself in the universe; the immutable above all qualities is His poise of peace, self-possession, equality, *samaṁ brahma*; from that proceeds His manifestation in the qualities of Prakriti and their universal workings; from the Purusha in Prakriti, from this Brahman with qualities, proceed all the works[1] of the universal energy, Karma, in man and in all existences; from that work proceeds the principle of sacrifice. Even the material interchange between gods and men proceeds upon this principle, as typified in the dependence of rain and its product food on this working and on them the physical birth of creatures. For all the working of Prakriti is in its true nature a sacrifice, *yajña*, with the Divine Being as the enjoyer of all energisms and works and sacrifice and the great Lord of all existences, *bhoktāraṁ yajña-tapasāṁ sarvaloka-maheśvaram*, and to know this Divine all-pervading and established in sacrifice, *sarvagataṁ [brahma nityaṁ] yajñe pratiṣṭhitam*, is the true, the Vedic knowledge.

एवं प्रवर्तितं चक्रं नानुवर्तयतीह यः ।
अघायुरिन्द्रियारामो मोघं पार्थ स जीवति ॥१६॥

16. He who follows not here the wheel thus set in movement, evil is his being, sensual is his delight, in vain, O Partha, that man lives, *moghaṁ pārtha sa jīvati*. Whoever goes contrary to this law of action and pursues works and enjoyment for his own isolated personal self-interest, lives in vain; he misses the true meaning and aim and utility of living and the upward growth of the soul; he is not on the path which leads to the highest good.

1. That this is the right interpretation results also from the opening of the eighth chapter where the universal principles are enumerated, *akṣara (brahma)*, *svabhāva*, *karma*, *kṣara bhāva*, *puruṣa*, *adhiyajña*. Akshara is the immutable Brahman, spirit or self, Atman; swabhava is the principle of the self, *adhyātma*, operative as the original nature of the being, "own way of becoming", and this proceeds out of the self, the Akshara; Karma proceeds from that and is the creative movement, *visarga*, which brings all natural beings and all changing subjective and objective shapes of being into existence; the result of Karma therefore is all this mutable becoming, the changes of nature developed out of the original self-nature, *kṣara bhāva* out of *svabhāva*; Purusha is the soul, the divine element in the becoming, *adhidaivata*, by whose presence the workings of Karma become a sacrifice, *yajña*, to the Divine within; *adhiyajña* is this secret Divine who receives the sacrifice.

III — THE PRINCIPLE OF DIVINE WORKS

यस्त्वात्मरतिरेव स्यादात्मतृप्तश्च मानवः ।
आत्मन्येव च सन्तुष्टस्तस्य कार्यं न विद्यते ॥१७॥
नैव तस्य कृतेनार्थो नाकृतेनेह कश्चन।
न चास्य सर्वभूतेषु कश्चिदर्थव्यपाश्रयः ॥१८॥

17-18. Having thus stated the necessity of sacrifice, — we shall see hereafter in what sense we may understand a passage which seems at first sight to convey only a traditional theory of ritualism and the necessity of the ceremonial offering, — Krishna proceeds to state the superiority of the spiritual man to works. **But the man whose delight is in the Self, *ātma-ratiḥ*, and who is satisfied with the enjoyment of the Self, *ātma-tṛiptaḥ*, and in the Self he is content, *ātmani saṅtuṣṭaḥ*, for him there exists no work that needs to be done, *tasya kāryaṁ na vidyate*. He has no object here to be gained by action done and none to be gained by action undone; he has no dependence on all these existences for any object to be gained.**

Here then are the two ideals, Vedist and Vedantist, standing as if in all their sharp original separation and opposition, on one side the active ideal of acquiring enjoyments here and the highest good beyond by sacrifice and the mutual dependence of the human being and the divine powers and on the other, facing it, the austerer ideal of the liberated man who, independent in the Spirit, has nothing to do with enjoyment or works or the human or the divine worlds, but exists only in the peace of the supreme Self, joys only in the calm joy of the Brahman. In that Self and not in any personal enjoyment he finds now his sole satisfaction, complete content, pure delight; he has nothing to gain by action or inaction, depends neither on gods nor men for anything, seeks no profit from any, for the self-delight is all-sufficient to him, but does works for the sake of the Divine only, as a pure sacrifice, without attachment or desire.

तस्मादसक्तः सततं कार्यं कर्म समाचर ।
असक्तो ह्याचरन्कर्म परमाप्नोति पूरुषः ॥१९॥

19. The next verses create a ground for the reconciliation between the two extremes; the secret is not inaction as soon as one turns towards the higher truth, but desireless action both before and after it is reached. The liberated man has nothing to gain by action, but nothing also to gain by inaction, and it is not at all for any personal object that he has to make his choice. **Therefore without attachment perform ever the work that is to be done**

(done for the sake of the world, *lokasaṅgraha*, as is made clear immediately afterward); **for by doing work without attachment man attains to the highest, *param āpnoti pūruṣaḥ*.**

कर्मणैव हि संसिद्धिमास्थिता जनकादयः ।
लोकसंग्रहमेवापि सम्पश्यन्कर्तुमर्हसि ॥२०॥

20. **For it was even by works that Janaka and the rest attained to perfection.** The works of sacrifice are thus vindicated as a means of liberation and absolute spiritual perfection, *saṁsiddhi*. So Janaka and other great Karmayogins of the mighty ancient Yoga attained to perfection, by equal and desireless works done as a sacrifice, without the least egoistic aim or attachment. So too and with the same desirelessness, after liberation and perfection, works can and have to be continued by us in a large divine spirit, with the calm high nature of a spiritual royalty. **Thou shouldst do works regarding also the holding together of the peoples, *lokasaṅgraham*,** the maintaining of all in their dharma and the Dharma, the maintenance of their growth in all its stages and in all its paths towards the Divine.

यद्यदाचरति श्रेष्ठस्तत्तदेवेतरो जनः ।
स यत्प्रमाणं कुरुते लोकस्तदनुवर्तते ॥२१॥

21. **Whatsoever the Best doeth, that the lower kind of man puts into practice; the standard he creates, the people follows.** To exceed himself was the goal of the ancient Vedic sages for the individual, not by losing all his personal aims in the aims of an organised human society, but by enlarging, heightening, aggrandising himself into the consciousness of the Godhead. The rule given here by the Gita is the rule for the master-man, the superman, the divinised human being, the Best, *śreṣṭhaḥ*, not in the sense of any Nietzschean, any one-sided and lopsided, any Olympian, Apollonian or Dionysian, any angelic or demoniac supermanhood, but in that of the man whose whole personality has been offered up into the being, nature and consciousness of the one transcendent and universal Divinity and by loss of the smaller self has found its greater self, has been divinised.

The best, the individuals who are in advance of the general line and above the general level of the collectivity, are the natural leaders of mankind, for it is they who can point to the race both the way they must follow and the standard or ideal they have to keep to or to attain. But the divinised man is the Best in no ordinary sense of the word and his influence, his example must have a power which that of no ordinarily superior man can exercise. What example then shall he give? What rule or standard shall he uphold?

न मे पार्थास्ति कर्तव्यं त्रिषु लोकेषु किञ्चन ।
नानवाप्तमवाप्तव्यं वर्त एव च कर्मणि ॥२२॥

22. O son of Pritha, I have no work that I need to do in all the three worlds, I have nothing that I have not gained and have yet to gain, and I abide verily in the paths of action, *varta eva ca karmaṇi*, — *eva* implying, I abide in it and do not leave it as the Sannyasin thinks himself bound to abandon works. The divine Teacher, the Avatar gives his own example, his own standard to Arjuna. "I abide in the path of action, he seems to say, the path that all men follow; thou too must abide in action. In the way I act, in that way thou too must act. I am above the necessity of works, for I have nothing to gain by them; I am the Divine who possess all things and all beings in the world and I am myself beyond the world as well as in it and I do not depend upon anything or anyone in all the three worlds for any object; yet I act. This too must be thy manner and spirit of working. I, the Divine, am the rule and the standard; it is I who make the path in which men tread; I am the way and the goal. But I do all this largely, universally, visibly in part, but far more invisibly; and men do not really know the way of my workings."

यदि ह्यहं न वर्तेयं जातु कर्मण्यतन्द्रितः ।
मम वर्त्मानुवर्तन्ते मनुष्याः पार्थ सर्वशः ॥२३॥
उत्सीदेयुरिमे लोका न कुर्यां कर्म चेदहम् ।
सङ्करस्य च कर्ता स्यामुपहन्यामिमाः प्रजाः ॥२४॥

23-24. For if I did not abide sleeplessly in the paths of action, men follow in every way my path, these peoples would sink to destruction if I did not works and I should be the creator of confusion and slay these creatures.

सक्ताः कर्मण्यविद्वांसो यथा कुर्वन्ति भारत ।
कुर्याद्विद्वांस्तथासक्तश्चिकीर्षुर्लोकसंग्रहम् ॥२५॥

25. As those who know not act with attachment to the action, he who knows should act without attachment, having for his motive to hold together the peoples, *lokasaṅgraham*. This great march of the peoples towards a far-off divine ideal has to be held together, prevented from falling into the bewilderment, confusion and utter discord of the understanding which would lead to dissolution and destruction and to which the world moving forward in the night or dark twilight of ignorance would be too easily prone if it were not held together, conducted, kept to the great lines of its discipline by the illumination, by the strength, by the rule and example, by the visible standard and the invisible influence of its Best.

न बुद्धिभेदं जनयेदज्ञानां कर्मसङ्गिनाम् ।
जोषयेत्सर्वकर्माणि विद्वान्युक्तः समाचरन् ।।२६।।

26. **He should not create a division of their understanding in the ignorant who are attached to their works; he should set them to all actions, doing them himself with knowledge and in Yoga.** "Thou, the Teacher seems to say, when thou knowest and seest, when thou hast become the divinised man, must be the individual power of God, the human yet divine example, even as I am in my avatars. Most men dwell in the ignorance, the God-seer dwells in the knowledge; but let him not confuse the minds of men by a dangerous example, rejecting in his superiority the works of the world; let him not cut short the thread of action before it is spun out, let him not perplex and falsify the stages and gradations of the ways I have hewn. The whole range of human action has been decreed by me with a view to the progress of man from the lower to the higher nature, from the apparent undivine to the conscious Divine. The whole range of human works must be that in which the God-knower shall move. All individual, all social action, all the works of the intellect, the heart and the body are still his, not any longer for his own separate sake, but for the sake of God in the world, of God in all beings and that all those beings may move forward, as he has moved, by the path of works towards the discovery of the Divine in themselves. Outwardly his actions may not seem to differ essentially from theirs; battle and rule as well as teaching and thought, all the various commerce of man with man may fall in his range; but the spirit in which he does them must be very different, and it is that spirit which by its influence shall be the great attraction drawing men upwards to his own level, the great lever lifting the mass of men higher in their ascent."

There are few more important passages in the Gita than these seven striking couplets (*20-26*). But they must not be interpreted as no more than a philosophical and religious justification of social service, patriotic, cosmopolitan and humanitarian effort and attachment to the hundred eager social schemes and dreams which attract the modern intellect. It is not the rule of a large moral and intellectual altruism which is here announced, but that of a spiritual unity with God and with this world of beings who dwell in him and in whom he dwells. It is not an injunction to subordinate the individual to society and humanity or immolate egoism on the altar of the human collectivity, but to fulfil the individual in God and to sacrifice the ego on the one true altar of the all-embracing Divinity. Patriotism, cosmopolitanism, service of society, collectivism, humanitarianism, the ideal or religion of humanity are admirable aids towards our escape from our primary condition of individual, family, social, national egoism into a secondary stage in which the individual realises, as far as it can be done on the intellectual, moral and emotional level, the oneness of his existence with the existence of other beings. But the thought of the Gita reaches beyond to a tertiary condition of our developing self-consciousness towards which the secondary is only a partial stage of advance.

IV — THE DETERMINISM OF NATURE

There are, in fact, different planes of our conscious existence, and what is practical truth on one plane ceases to be true, because it assumes a quite different appearance, as soon as we rise to a higher level from which we can see things more in the whole. What we now call in our ordinary mentality our free will and have a certain limited justification for so calling it, yet appears to the Yogin who has climbed beyond and to whom our night is day and our day night, not free will at all, but a subjection to the modes of Nature. He regards the same facts, but from the higher outlook of the whole-knower, *kṛitsna-vit*, while we view it altogether from the more limited mentality of our partial knowledge, *akṛitsna-vidaḥ*, which is an ignorance. What we vaunt of as our freedom is to him bondage.

प्रकृतेः क्रियमाणानि गुणैः कर्माणि सर्वशः ।
अहङ्कारविमूढात्मा कर्ताहमिति मन्यते ।।२७।।

27. While the actions are being entirely done by the modes of Nature, he whose self is bewildered by egoism thinks that it is his "I" which is doing them.

तत्त्ववित्तु महाबाहो गुणकर्मविभागयोः ।
गुणा गुणेषु वर्तन्त इति मत्वा न सज्जते ।।२८।।

28. But one who knows the true principles of the divisions of the modes and of works, *guṇa-karma-vibhāgayoḥ*, realises that it is the modes which are acting and reacting on each other, *guṇā guṇeṣu vartante*, and is not caught in them by attachment. Here there is the clear distinction between two levels of consciousness, two standpoints of action, that of the soul caught in the web of its egoistic nature and doing works with the idea, but not the reality of free will, under the impulsion of Nature, and that of the soul delivered from its identification with the ego, observing, sanctioning and governing the works of Nature from above her.

What then is this self that is bewildered by Nature, this soul that is subject to her? The answer is that we are speaking of the apparent self, of the apparent soul, not of the real self, not of the true Purusha. It is really the ego which is subject to Nature, inevitably, because it is itself part of Nature, one functioning of her machinery; but when the self-awareness in the mind-consciousness identifies itself with the ego, it creates the appearance of a lower self, an ego-self. And so too what we think of ordinarily as the soul is really the natural personality, not the true Person, the Purusha, but the desire-soul in us which is a reflection of the consciousness of the Purusha in the workings of Prakriti: it is, in fact, itself only an action of the three modes and therefore a part of Nature. Thus there are, we may say, two souls in us, the apparent or desire-soul, which changes with the mutations of the gunas and is entirely constituted and determined by them, and the free and eternal Purusha not limited by Nature and her gunas. We have two selves, the apparent self, which is only the ego, that mental centre in us which takes up this mutable action of Prakriti, this mutable personality, and which says "I am this personality, I am this natural being who am doing these works," — but the natural being is simply Nature, a composite of the gunas, — and the true self which is, indeed, the upholder, the possessor and the lord of Nature and figured in her, but is not itself the mutable natural personality.

प्रकृतेर्गुणसंमूढाः सज्जन्ते गुणकर्मसु ।
तानकृत्स्नविदो मन्दान्कृत्स्नविन्न विचालयेत् ।।२९।।

29. Those who are bewildered by the modes, not knowers of the whole, let not the knower of the whole disturb them in their mental standpoint. The Gita makes a distinction between those who have not the knowledge of the whole, *a-kṛitsnavidaḥ*, and are misled by the partial truths of existence, and the Yogin who has the synthetic knowledge of the totality, *kṛitsna-vit*. To see all existence steadily and see it whole and not be misled by its conflicting truths, is the first necessity for the calm and complete wisdom to which the

Yogin is called upon to rise. A certain absolute freedom is one aspect of the soul's relations with Nature at one pole of our complex being; a certain absolute determinism by Nature is the opposite aspect at its opposite pole; and there is also a partial and apparent, therefore an unreal eidolon of liberty which the soul receives by a contorted reflection of these two opposite truths in the developing mentality. It is the latter to which we ordinarily give, more or less inaccurately, the name of free will; but the Gita regards nothing as freedom which is not a complete liberation and mastery.

The fundamental error of the Mind is this fall from self-knowledge by which the individual soul conceives of its individuality as a separate fact instead of as a form of Oneness and makes itself the centre of its own universe instead of knowing itself as one concentration of the universal. It is conscious of things and knows them only as they present themselves to its individuality and therefore it falls into an ignorance of the rest and thereby into an erroneous conception even of that which it seems to know: for since all being is interdependent, the knowledge either of the whole or of the essence is necessary for the right knowledge of the part. — An eternal portion of the Divine, *aṁśaḥ sanātanaḥ*, this part is by the law of the Infinite inseparable from its Divine Whole, this part is indeed itself that Whole, except in its frontal appearance, its frontal separative self-experience.

We can only understand entirely if we get to some sense of the Absolute and yet look at its workings in all the relativities which are being manifested, — look not only at each by itself, but each in relation to all and to that which exceeds and reconciles them all. In fact we can only know by getting to the divine view and purpose in things and not merely looking at our own. For behind all relativities there is this Absolute which gives them their being and their justification.

मयि सर्वाणि कर्माणि संन्यस्याध्यात्मचेतसा ।
निराशीर्निर्ममो भूत्वा युध्यस्व विगतज्वरः ॥३०॥

30. It is not in the end Nature which mechanically determines its own action; it is the will of the Supreme which inspires her; he who has already slain the Dhritarashtrians, he of whom Arjuna is only the human instrument, a universal Soul, a transcendent Godhead is the master of her labour. The reposing of works in the Impersonal is a means of getting rid of the personal egoism of the doer, but the end is to give up all our actions to that great Lord of all, *sarva-loka-maheśvara*. **With a consciousness identified with the Self, *adhyātma-cetasā*, renouncing all thy actions into Me, *mayi sarvāṇi karmāṇi sannyasya*, freed from personal hopes and desires, from the thought of**

"I" and "mine", *nirāśīr-nirmamo bhūtvā*, delivered from the fever of the soul, fight, work, do my will in the world. The Divine motives, inspires, determines the entire action; the human soul impersonal in the Brahman is the pure and silent channel of his power; that power in the Nature executes the divine movement. Such only are the works of the liberated soul, *muktasya karma*, for in nothing does he act from a personal inception; such are the actions of the accomplished Karmayogin. They rise from a free spirit and disappear without modifying it, like waves that rise and disappear on the surface of conscious, immutable depths, *karma samagraṁ pravilīyate.*

ये मे मतमिदं नित्यमनुतिष्ठन्ति मानवाः ।
श्रद्धावन्तोऽनसूयन्तो मुच्यन्ते तेऽपि कर्मभिः ॥३१॥
ये त्वेतदभ्यसूयन्तो नानुतिष्ठन्ति मे मतम् ।
सर्वज्ञानविमूढांस्तान्विद्धि नष्टानचेतसः ॥३२॥

31-32. **For men who with faith and without carping follow this my Word are released, they also, from bondage to their works; but they who will find fault with and follow not this higher teaching, know of them that all their knowledge is a delusion; their intellect is nought, they are lost men.** In fact, these higher truths can only be helpful, because there only they are true to experience and can be lived, on a higher and vaster plane of consciousness and being. To view these truths from below is to mis-see, misunderstand and probably to misuse them. It is a higher truth that the distinction of good and evil is indeed a practical fact and law valid for the egoistic human life which is the stage of transition from the animal to the divine, but on a higher plane we rise beyond good and evil, are above their duality even as the Godhead is above it. But the unripe mind, seizing on this truth without rising from the lower consciousness where it is not practically valid, will simply make it a convenient excuse for indulging its Asuric propensities, denying the distinction between good and evil altogether and falling by self-indulgence deeper into the morass of perdition.

सदृशं चेष्टते स्वस्याः प्रकृतेर्ज्ञानवानपि ।
प्रकृतिं यान्ति भूतानि निग्रहः किं करिष्यति ॥३३॥

33. So too with the truth of the determinism of Nature; it will be mis-seen and misused, as those misuse it who declare that a man is what his nature has made him and cannot do otherwise than as his nature compels him. It is true in a sense, but not in the sense which is attached to it, not in the

sense that the ego-self can claim irresponsibility and impunity for itself in its works; for it has will and it has desire and so long as it acts according to its will and desire, even though that be its nature, it must bear the reactions of its Karma. It is in a net, if you will, a snare which may well seem perplexing, illogical, unjust, terrible to its present experience, to its limited self-knowledge, but a snare of its own choice, a net of its own weaving. The Gita says, indeed, **All existences follow their nature and what shall coercing it avail, *nigrahaḥ kiṁ kariṣyati*?** which seems, if we take it by itself, a hopelessly absolute assertion of the omnipotence of Nature over the soul; **even the man of knowledge acts according to his own nature.**

The tiger can be no more blamed for killing and devouring than the atom for its blind movements, the fire for burning and consuming or the storm for its destructions. But we can see clearly enough that it is not really the tiger, but Nature in the tiger that kills, it is Nature in the tiger that devours; and if it refrains from killing or devouring, it is from satiety, from fear or from indolence, from another principle of Nature in it. As it was Nature in the animal that killed, so it is Nature in the animal that refrained from killing. Whatever soul is in it, sanctions passively the action of Nature, is as much passive in its passion and activity as in its indolence or inaction. The animal like the atom acts according to the mechanism of its Nature, and not otherwise, *sadṛiśaṁ ceṣṭate svasyāḥ prakṛiteḥ*, as if mounted on a machine, *yantrārūḍho māyayā*.

Well, but in man at least there is another action, a free soul, a free will, a sense of responsibility, a real doer other than Nature, other than the mechanism of Maya? So it seems, because in man there is a conscious intelligent will; *buddhi* is full of the light of the observing Purusha, who through it, it seems, observes, understands, approves or disapproves, gives or withholds the sanction, seems indeed at last to begin to be the lord of his nature. Man is not like the tiger or the fire or the storm; he cannot kill and say as a sufficient justification, "I am acting according to my nature", and he cannot do it, because he has not the nature and not, therefore, the law of action, *svadharma*, of the tiger, storm or fire. He has a conscious intelligent will, a *buddhi*, and to that he must refer his actions. If he does not do so, if he acts blindly according to his impulses and passions, then the law of his being is not rightly worked out, *svadharmaḥ su-anuṣṭhitaḥ*, he has not acted according to the full measure of his humanity, but even as might the animal.

According to its nature each creature must act and it cannot act by anything else. Ego and personal will and desire are nothing more than vividly conscious forms and limited natural workings of a universal Force that is itself formless and infinite and far exceeds them; reason and intelligence and mind and sense and life and body, all that we vaunt or take for our own, are

Nature's instruments and creations. But the impersonal Self does not act and is not part of Nature: it observes the action from behind and above and remains lord of itself and a free and impassive knower and witness. The soul that lives in this impersonality is not affected by the actions of which our nature is an instrument; Nature works out her action and the soul impersonal and universal supports her but is not involved, is not attached, is not entangled, is not troubled, is not bewildered.

इन्द्रियस्येन्द्रियस्यार्थे रागद्वेषौ व्यवस्थितौ ।
तयोर्न वशमागच्छेत्तौ ह्यस्य परिपन्थिनौ ।।३४।।

34. **In the object of this or that sense liking and disliking are set in ambush; fall not into their power, for they are the besetters of the soul in its path.**

श्रेयान्स्वधर्मो विगुणः परधर्मात्स्वनुष्ठितात् ।
स्वधर्मे निधनं श्रेयः परधर्मो भयावहः ।।३५।।

35. And on this (*sl. 33*) the Gita founds the injunction to follow faithfully in our action the law of our nature. **Better is one's own law of works, *svadharma*, though in itself faulty than an alien law well wrought out, *śreyān svadharmo viguṇaḥ paradharmāt svanuṣṭhitāt*; death in one's own law of being is better, perilous is it to follow an alien law** (*see also XVIII-47*). This *svadharma* certainly does not mean that we are to follow any impulse, even though evil, which what we call our nature dictates to us. One's own nature, rule, function, should be observed and followed, — even if defective, it is better than the well-performed rule of another's nature. Death in one's own law of nature is better for a man than victory in an alien movement. To follow the law of another's nature is dangerous to the soul, contradictory, as we may say, to the natural way of his evolution, a thing mechanically imposed and therefore imported, artificial and sterilising to one's growth towards the true stature of the spirit. What comes out of the being is the right and healthful thing, the authentic movement, not what is imposed on it from outside or laid on it by life's compulsions or the mind's error.

It is not, certainly, the superficial temperament or the character or habitual impulses that are meant, but in the literal sense of the Sanskrit word our "own being", our essential nature, the divine stuff of our souls. Whatever springs from this root or flows from these sources is profound, essential, right; the rest — opinions, impulses, habits, desires — may be merely surface formations or casual vagaries of the being or impositions from outside. They shift and change, but this remains constant. It is not the executive forms taken by Nature in us that are ourselves or the abidingly constant and expressive shape of ourselves; it is the spiritual being in us — and this includes the soul-becoming of it — that persists through time in the universe.

अर्जुन उवाच
अथ केन प्रयुक्तोऽयं पापं चरति पूरुषः ।
अनिच्छन्नपि वार्ष्णेय बलादिव नियोजितः ॥३६॥

36. *Arjuna* — **If there is no fault in following our nature, what are we then to say of that in us which drives a man to sin, as if by force, even against his own struggling will?** It is the phenomenon expressed sententiously by Horace, "*Video meliora proboque, deteriora sequor*" (I see the better and approve of it, I follow the worse).

श्रीभगवानुवाच
काम एष क्रोध एष रजोगुणसमुद्भवः ।
महाशनो महापाप्मा विद्ध्येनमिह वैरिणम् ॥३७॥

37. *Krishna* — **This is desire and its companion wrath, children of rajas, the restless all-devouring principle of passion, a mighty sinner, and this desire is the soul's great enemy and has to be slain.** Abstention from evil-doing [is declared] to be the first condition for liberation, and always [is enjoined] self-mastery, self-control, *saṁyama*, control of the mind, senses, all the lower being. There is therefore a distinction to be made between what is essential in the nature, its native and inevitable action, which it avails not at all to repress, suppress, coerce, and what is accidental to it, its wanderings, confusions, perversions, over which we must certainly get control. There is a distinction implied too between coercion and suppression, *nigraha*, and control with right use and right guidance, *saṁyama*. The former is a violence done to the nature by the will, which in the end depresses the natural powers of the being, *ātmānam avasādayet*; the latter is the control of the lower by the higher self, which successfully gives to those powers their right action and their maximum efficiency, — *yogaḥ karmasu kauśalam*.

धूमेनाव्रियते वह्निर्यथादर्शो मलेन च ।
यथोल्बेनावृतो गर्भस्तथा तेनेदमावृतम् ॥३८॥
आवृतं ज्ञानमेतेन ज्ञानिनो नित्यवैरिणा ।
कामरूपेण कौन्तेय दुष्पूरेणानलेन च ॥३९॥

38-39. **Desire, the insatiable fire which besieges your worldly action, the eternal enemy of knowledge by which it is covered over here in your nature as is a fire by smoke or a mirror by dust or the unborn child with the caul,**

इन्द्रियाणि मनो बुद्धिरस्याधिष्ठानमुच्यते ।
एतैर्विमोहयत्येष ज्ञानमावृत्य देहिनम् ।।४०।।
तस्मात्त्वमिन्द्रियाण्यादौ नियम्य भरतर्षभ ।
पाप्मानं प्रजहि ह्येनं ज्ञानविज्ञाननाशनम् ।।४१।।

40-41. **and which you must slay** in order to live in the calm, clear, luminous truth of the spirit. **The senses, mind and intellect are the seat of this eternal cause of imperfection** and yet it is within this sense, mind and intellect, this play of the lower nature that you would limit your search for perfection! **Therefore in the beginning constrain the senses; with these Desire cloudeth over knowledge and bewildereth the embodied spirit.**

इन्द्रियाणि पराण्याहुरिन्द्रियेभ्यः परं मनः ।
मनसस्तु परा बुद्धिर्यो बुद्धेः परतस्तु सः ।।४२।।

42. The Gita following and almost quoting the Upanishads states the ascending order of our subjective powers. **Supreme beyond their objects are the senses, supreme over the senses the mind, supreme over the mind the intelligent will: that which is supreme over the intelligent will, is he,** — is the conscious self, the Purusha.

एवं बुद्धेः परं बुद्ध्वा संस्तभ्यात्मानमात्मना ।
जहि शत्रुं महाबाहो कामरूपं दुरासदम् ।।४३।।

43. Therefore it is this Purusha, this supreme cause of our subjective life which we have to understand and become aware of by the intelligence; in that we have to fix our will. So holding our lower subjective self in Nature firmly poised and stilled by means of the greater really conscient self, we can destroy the restless ever-active enemy of our peace and self-mastery, the mind's desire. **Awakening by the understanding to the Highest which is beyond even the discerning mind, put force on the self by the self to make it firm and still, and slay this enemy who is so hard to assail, Desire.** Both the tamasic recoil of escape and the rajasic movement of struggle and victory are only justified when they look beyond themselves through the sattwic principle to the self-knowledge which legitimises both the recoil and the struggle.

Is the condition of the predominantly sattwic nature freedom and is this will in man a free will? That the Gita from the standpoint of a higher consciousness in which alone is true freedom, denies. The buddhi or conscious intelligent will is still an instrument of Nature and when it acts, even in the most sattwic sense, it is still Nature which acts and the soul which is carried on the wheel by Maya. At any rate, at least nine-tenths of our freedom of will is a palpable fiction; that will is created and determined not by its own self-existent action at a given moment, but by our past, our heredity, our training, our environment, the whole tremendous complex thing we call Karma, which is, behind us, the whole past action of Nature on us and the world converging in the individual, determining what he is, determining what his will shall be at a given moment and determining, as far as analysis can see, even its action at that moment. The ego associates itself always with its Karma and it says "I did" and "I will" and "I suffer", but if it looks at itself and sees how it was made, it is obliged to say of man as of the animal, "Nature did this in me, Nature wills in me", and if it qualifies by saying "my Nature", that only means "Nature as self-determined in this individual creature".

Freedom, highest self-mastery begin when above the natural self we see and hold the supreme Self of which the ego is an obstructing veil and a blinding shadow. And that can only be when we see the one Self in us seated above Nature and make our individual being one with it in being and consciousness and in its individual nature of action only an instrument of a supreme Will, the one Will that is really free. For that we must rise high above the three gunas, become *triguṇātīta*; for that Self is beyond even the sattwic principle. We have to climb to it through the sattwa, but we attain to it only when we get beyond sattwa; we reach out to it from the ego, but only reach it by leaving the ego. We have at a certain stage to liberate ourselves even from the desire of our liberation.

So far then extends the determinism of Nature, and what it amounts to is this that the ego from which we act is itself an instrument of the action of Prakriti and cannot therefore be free from the control of Prakriti; the will of the ego is a will determined by Prakriti, it is a part of the nature as it has been formed in us. Certainly, the will in us has always to choose between a certain number of possibilities, for that is the way in which Nature always acts; even our passivity, our refusal to will, is itself a choice, itself an act of the will of Nature in us; even in the atom there is a will always at its work. The whole difference is the extent to which we associate our idea of self with the action of the will in Nature; when we so associate ourselves, we think of it as our will and say that it is a free will and that it is we who are acting. And error or not, illusion or not, this idea of our will, of our action is not a thing of no consequence, of no utility; everything in Nature has a consequence and a utility. It is rather that process of our conscious being by which Nature in us becomes more and more aware of and responsive to the presence of the secret Purusha within her and opens by that increase of knowledge to a greater possibility of action; it is by the aid of the ego-idea and the personal will that she raises herself to her own higher possibilities. The sense of free will, illusion or not, is a necessary machinery of the action of Nature, necessary for man during his progress, and it would be disastrous for him to lose it before he is ready for a higher truth.

But it is not a sheer delusion, it is only an error of standpoint and an error of placement. The ego thinks that it is the real self and acts as if it were the true centre of action and as if all existed for its sake, and there it commits an error of standpoint and placement. It is not wrong in thinking that there is something or someone within ourselves, within this action of our nature, who is the true centre of its action and for whom all exists; but this is not the ego, it is the Lord secret within our hearts, the divine Purusha, and the Jiva, other than ego, who is a portion of his being. The self-assertion of ego-sense is the broken and distorted shadow in our minds of the truth that there is a real Self within us which is the master of all and for whom and at whose behest Nature goes about her works. So too the ego's idea of free will is a distorted and misplaced sense of the truth that there is a free Self within us and that the will in Nature is only a modified and partial reflection of its Will.

CHAPTER IV

I — The Possibility and Purpose of Avatarhood

श्रीभगवानुवाच
इमं विवस्वते योगं प्रोक्तवानहमव्ययम् ।
विवस्वान्मनवे प्राह मनुरिक्ष्वाकवेऽब्रवीत् ।।१।।

1. *Krishna* — In speaking of this Yoga in which action and knowledge become one, the Yoga of the sacrifice of works with knowledge, in which works are fulfilled in knowledge, knowledge supports, changes and enlightens works, and both are offered to the Purushottama, the supreme Divinity who becomes manifest within us as Narayana, Lord of all our being and action seated secret in our hearts for ever, who becomes manifest even in the human form as the Avatar, the divine birth taking possession of our humanity, Krishna has declared in passing that **this was the ancient and original Yoga which he gave to Vivasvan, the Sun-God, Vivasvan gave it to Manu, the father of men, Manu gave it to Ikshvaku, head of the Solar line,**

एवं परम्पराप्राप्तमिमं राजर्षयो विदुः ।
स कालेनेह महता योगो नष्टः परन्तप ।।२।।

2. **and so it came down from royal sage to royal sage till it was lost in the great lapse of Time,**

स एवायं मया तेऽद्य योगः प्रोक्तः पुरातनः ।
भक्तोऽसि मे सखा चेति रहस्यं ह्येतदुत्तमम् ।।३।।

3. **and is now renewed for Arjuna, because he is the lover and devotee, friend and comrade of the Avatar. For this, he says, is the highest secret, *rahasyaṁ hyetad uttamam*,** — thus claiming for it a superiority to all other forms of Yoga, because this gives the highest secret and the whole secret; it unites into itself all the Yogic paths as the highest being of the Divine reconciles and makes one in itself all the different and even contrary powers and principles of its manifested being.

अर्जुन उवाच
अपरं भवतो जन्म परं जन्म विवस्वतः ।
कथमेतद्विजानीयां त्वमादौ प्रोक्तवानिति ।।४।।

4. *Arjuna* — Arjuna takes the declaration about the transmission of the Yoga in its most physical sense and asks **how the Sun-God, one of the first-born of beings, ancestor of the Solar dynasty, can have received the Yoga from the man Krishna who is only now born into the world.**

श्रीभगवानुवाच
बहूनि मे व्यतीतानि जन्मानि तव चार्जुन ।
तान्यहं वेद सर्वाणि न त्वं वेत्थ परन्तप ।।५।।

5. *Krishna* — [Krishna accepts] the opportunity which Arjuna gives him of declaring his concealed Godhead, a declaration for which he had prepared when he gave himself as the divine example for the worker who is not bound by his works. He now openly announces himself as the incarnate Godhead, the Avatar. We must look a little more closely at this Avatarhood and at the significance of the divine Birth of which it is the outward expression. **Many are my lives that are past, *bahūni me vyatītāni janmāni*, and thine also, O Arjuna; all of them I know, but thou knowest not, O scourge of the foe.**

अजोऽपि सन्नव्ययात्मा भूतानामीश्वरोऽपि सन् ।
प्रकृतिं स्वामधिष्ठाय सम्भवाम्यात्ममायया ।।६।।

6. **Though I am the unborn, *ajaḥ*, though I am imperishable in my self-existence, *avyaya-ātmā*, though I am the Lord of all existences, *bhūtānām īśvaraḥ*, yet I stand upon my own Nature, *prakritiṁ svām adhiṣṭhāya*, and I come into birth by my self-Maya, *sambhavāmi-ātma-māyayā.***

It is notable that with a slight but important variation of language the Gita describes in the same way both the action of the Divine in bringing about the ordinary birth of creatures and his action in his birth as the Avatar. **Leaning upon my own Nature, *prakṛitiṁ svām avaṣṭabhya,* it will say later** [in **IX-8], I loose forth variously, *visṛijāmi*, this multitude of creatures helplessly subject owing to the control of Prakriti, *avaśaṁ prakṛiter vaśāt.* Standing upon my own Nature, it says here** [in IV-6], **I am born by my self-Maya, *prakṛitiṁ svām adhiṣṭhāya... ātma-māyayā*, I loose forth myself, *ātmānaṁ sṛijāmi.*** The action implied in the word *avaṣṭabhya* is a forceful downward pressure by which the object controlled is overcome, oppressed, blocked or limited in its movement or working and becomes helplessly subject to the controlling power, *avaśaṁ vaśāt*; Nature in this action becomes mechanical and its multitude of creatures are held helpless in the mechanism, not lords of their own action. On the contrary the action implied in the word *adhiṣṭhāya* is a dwelling in, but also a standing upon and over the Nature, a conscious control and government by the indwelling Godhead, *adhiṣṭhātrī devatā*, in which the Purusha is not helplessly driven by the Prakriti through ignorance, but rather the Prakriti is full of the light and the will of the Purusha. Therefore in the normal birth that which is loosed forth, — created, as we say, — is the multitude of creatures or becomings, *bhūta-grāmam*; in the divine birth that which is loosed forth, self-created, is the self-conscious self-existent being, *ātmānam*; for the Vedantic distinction between *ātmā* and *bhūtāni* is that which is made in European philosophy between the Being and its becomings. In both cases Maya is the means of the creation or manifestation, but in the divine birth it is by self-Maya, *ātma-māyayā*, not the involution in the lower Maya of the ignorance, but the conscious action of the self-existent Godhead in its phenomenal self-representation, well aware of its operation and its purpose, — that which the Gita calls elsewhere Yogamaya. In the ordinary birth Yogamaya is used by the Divine to envelop and conceal itself from the lower consciousness, so it becomes for us the means of the ignorance, *avidyā-māyā*; but it is by this same Yogamaya that self-knowledge also is made manifest in the return of our consciousness to the Divine, it is the means of the knowledge, *vidyā-māyā*; and in the divine birth it so operates — as the knowledge controlling and enlightening the works which are ordinarily done in the Ignorance.

The language of the Gita shows therefore that the divine birth is that of the conscious Godhead in our humanity and essentially the opposite of the ordinary birth even though the same means are used, because it is not the birth into the Ignorance, but the birth of the knowledge, not a physical phenomenon, but a soul-birth. It is the Soul's coming into birth as the self-existent Being controlling consciously its becoming and not lost to self-knowledge in the cloud of the ignorance. It is the Soul born into the body as Lord of Nature, standing above and operating in her freely by its will, not entangled and helplessly driven round and round in the mechanism; for it works in the knowledge and not, as most do, in the ignorance. It is the secret Soul in all coming forward from its governing secrecy behind the veil to possess wholly in a human type, but as the Divine, the birth which ordinarily it possesses only from behind the veil as the Ishwara while the outward consciousness in front of the veil is rather possessed than in possession because there it is a partially conscious being, the Jiva lost to self-knowledge and bound in its works through a phenomenal subjection to Nature. The

Avatar[1] therefore is a direct manifestation in humanity by Krishna the divine Soul of that divine condition of being to which Arjuna, the human soul, the type of a highest human being, a Vibhuti, is called upon by the Teacher to arise, and to which he can only arise by climbing out of the ignorance and limitation of his ordinary humanity. It is the manifestation from above of that which we have to develop from below; it is the descent of God into that divine birth of the human being into which we mortal creatures must climb; it is the attracting divine example given by God to man in the very type and form and perfected model of our human existence.

We see that the mystery of the divine Incarnation in man, the assumption by the Godhead of the human type and the human nature, is in the view of the Gita only the other side of the eternal mystery of human birth itself which is always in its essence, though not in its phenomenal appearance, even such a miraculous assumption. The eternal and universal self of every human being is God; even his personal self is a part of the Godhead, *mamaivāṁśaḥ*, — not a fraction or fragment, surely, since we cannot think of God as broken up into little pieces, but a partial consciousness of the one Consciousness, a partial power of the one Power, a partial enjoyment of world-being by the one and universal Delight of being, and therefore in manifestation or, as we say, in Nature a limited and finite being of the one infinite and illimitable Being. The stamp of that limitation is an ignorance by which he forgets, not only the Godhead from which he came forth, but the Godhead which is always within him, there living in the secret heart of his own nature, there burning like a veiled Fire on the inner altar in his own temple-house of human consciousness.

The Gita speaks clearly of the Lord himself being born; Krishna speaks of his many births that are past and makes it clear by his language that it is not merely the receptive human being but the Divine of whom he makes this affirmation, because he uses the very language of the Creator, the same language which he will employ when he has to describe his creation of the world. **Although I am the unborn Lord of creatures, I create (loose forth) my *self* by my Maya,** presiding over the actions of my Prakriti. Here there is no question of the Lord and the human Jiva or of the Father and the Son, the divine Man, but only of the Lord and his Prakriti. The Divine descends by his own Prakriti into birth in its human form and type and brings into it the divine Consciousness and the divine Power, though consenting, though willing to act in the form, type, mould of humanity, and he governs its actions in the body as the indwelling and over-dwelling Soul, *adhiṣṭhāya*. From above he governs

1. The word Avatara means a descent; it is a coming down of the Divine below the line which divides the divine from the human world or status.

always, indeed, for so he governs all nature, the human included; from within also he governs all nature, always, but hidden; the difference here is that he is manifest, that the nature is conscious of the divine Presence as the Lord, the Inhabitant, and it is not by his secret will from above, "the will of the Father which is in heaven," but by his quite direct and apparent will that he moves the nature. And here there seems to be no room for the human intermediary; for it is by resort to his own nature, *prakṛtiṁ svām*, and not the special nature of the Jiva that the Lord of all existence thus takes upon himself the human birth.

This doctrine is a hard saying, a difficult thing for the human reason to accept; and for an obvious reason, because of the evident humanity of the Avatar. The Avatar is always a dual phenomenon of divinity and humanity; the Divine takes upon himself the human nature with all its outward limitations and makes them the circumstances, means, instruments of the divine consciousness and the divine power, a vessel of the divine birth and the divine works. But so surely it must be, since otherwise the object of the Avatar's descent is not fulfilled; for that object is precisely to show that the human birth with all its limitations can be made such a means and instrument of the divine birth and divine works, precisely to show that the human type of consciousness can be compatible with the divine essence of consciousness made manifest, can be converted into its vessel, drawn into nearer conformity with it by a change of its mould and a heightening of its powers of light and love and strength and purity; and to show also how it can be done. If the Avatar were to act in an entirely supernormal fashion, this object would not be fulfilled. A merely supernormal or miraculous Avatar would be a meaningless absurdity; not that there need be an entire absence of the use of supernormal powers such as Christ's so-called miracles of healing, for the use of supernormal powers is quite a possibility of human nature; but there need not be that at all, nor in any case is it the root of the matter, nor would it at all do if the life were nothing else but a display of supernormal fireworks. The Avatar does not come as a thaumaturgic magician, but as the divine leader of humanity and the exemplar of a divine humanity. Even human sorrow and physical suffering he must assume and use so as to show, first, how that suffering may be a means of redemption, — as did Christ, — secondly, to show how, having been assumed by the divine soul in the human nature, it can also be overcome in the same nature, — as did Buddha. The rationalist who would have cried to Christ, "If thou art the Son of God, come down from the cross," or points out sagely that the Avatar was not divine because he died and died too by disease, — as a dog dieth, — knows not what he is saying: for he has missed the root of the whole matter. Even, the Avatar of sorrow and suffering must come before there can be the Avatar of divine joy; the human limitation must be assumed in order to show how it can be overcome; and the way and the extent of the overcoming, whether internal only or external also, depends upon the stage of the human advance; it must not be done by a non-human miracle.

यदा यदा हि धर्मस्य ग्लानिर्भवति भारत ।
अभ्युत्थानमधर्मस्य तदात्मानं सृजाम्यहम् ।।७।।

7. For whensoever there is the fading of the Dharma and the uprising of unrighteousness, then I loose myself forth into birth, *ātmānaṁ sṛijāmi.*

All here is God, is the Spirit or Self-existence, is Brahman, *ekamevādvitīyam*, — there is nothing else, nothing other and different from it and there can be nothing else, can be nothing other and different from it; Nature is and can be nothing else than a power of the divine consciousness; all beings are and can be nothing else than inner and outer, subjective and objective soul-forms and bodily forms of the divine being which exist in or result from the power of its consciousness. Far from the Infinite being unable to take on finiteness, the whole universe is nothing else but that; we can see, look as we may, nothing else at all in the whole wide world we inhabit. Far from the Spirit being incapable of form or disdaining to connect itself with form of matter or mind and to assume a limited nature or a body, all here is nothing but that, the world exists only by that connection, that assumption. Far from the world being a mechanism of law with no soul or spirit intervening in the movement of its forces or the action of its minds and bodies, the whole world and every particle of it is on the contrary nothing but the divine force in action and that divine force determines and governs its every movement, inhabits its every form, possesses here every soul and mind; all is in God and in him moves and has its being, in all he is, acts and displays his being; every creature is the disguised Narayana.

Far from the unborn being unable to assume birth, all beings are even in their individuality unborn spirits, eternal without beginning or end, and in their essential existence and the universality all are the one unborn Spirit of whom birth and death are only a phenomenon of the assumption and change of forms. The assumption of imperfection by the perfect is the whole mystic phenomenon of the universe; but the imperfection appears in the form and action of the mind or body assumed, subsists in the phenomenon, — in that which assumes it there is no imperfection, even as in the Sun which illumines all there is no defect of light or of vision, but only in the capacities of the individual organ of vision. God's rule is not an absentee, foreign and external government; he governs all because he exceeds all, but also because he dwells within all movements and is their absolute soul and spirit.

The finite is indeed nothing but a definition, a face value of the Infinite's self-representations to its own variations of consciousness; the real value of each finite phenomenon is an infinite value, is indeed the very Infinite. Each being is infinite in its self-existence, whatever it may be in the action of its phenomenal nature, its temporal self-representation. The man is not himself alone, a rigidly separate self-existent individual, but humanity in a mind and body of itself; and humanity too is no rigidly separate self-existent species or genus, it is the All-existence, the universal Godhead figuring itself in the type of humanity; there it works out certain possibilities, develops, evolves, as we now say, certain powers of its manifestations. What it evolves, is itself, is the Spirit.

For what we mean by Spirit is self-existent being with an infinite power of consciousness and unconditioned delight in its being; it is either that or nothing, or at least nothing which has anything to do with man and the world or with which, therefore, man or the world has anything to do. Matter, body is only a massed motion of force of conscious being employed as a starting-point for the variable relations of consciousness working through its power of sense; nor is Matter anywhere really void of consciousness, for even in the atom, the cell there is a power of will, an intelligence at work; but that power is the power of will and intelligence of the Self, Spirit or Godhead within it, it is not the separate, self-derived will or idea of the mechanical cell or atom.

परित्राणाय साधूनां विनाशाय च दुष्कृताम् ।
धर्मसंस्थापनार्थाय सम्भवामि युगे युगे ।।८।।

8. For the deliverance of the good, ***sādhūnām,*** to relieve the seekers of the Dharma who are oppressed by the reign of the reactionary darkness, **for the destruction of the evil-doers,** to destroy the wrong-doers who seek to maintain the denial of the Dharma, **for the enthroning of the Right I am born from age to age,** ***sambhavāmi yuge yuge.***

We have to remark carefully that the upholding of Dharma in the world is not the only object of the descent of the Avatar, that great mystery of the Divine manifest in humanity; for the upholding of the Dharma is not an all-sufficient object in itself, not the supreme possible aim for the manifestation of a Christ, a Krishna, a Buddha, but is only the general condition of a higher aim and a more supreme and divine utility. For there are two aspects of the divine birth; one is a descent, the birth of God in humanity, the Godhead manifesting itself in the human form and nature, the eternal Avatar; the other is an ascent, the birth of man into the Godhead, man rising into the divine nature and consciousness, *madbhāvam āgataḥ*; it is the being born anew in a second birth of the soul. It is that new birth which Avatarhood and the upholding of the Dharma are intended to serve.

If there were not this rising of man into the Godhead to be helped by the descent of God into humanity, Avatarhood for the sake of the Dharma would be an otiose phenomenon, since mere Right, mere justice or standards of virtue can always be upheld by the divine omnipotence through its ordinary means, by great men or great movements, by the life and work of sages and kings and religious teachers, without any actual incarnation. The Avatar comes as the manifestation of the divine nature in the human nature, the apocalypse of its Christhood, Krishnahood, Buddhahood, in order that the human nature may by moulding its principle, thought, feeling, action, being on the lines of that Christhood, Krishnahood, Buddhahood transfigure itself into the divine. The law, the Dharma which the Avatar establishes is given for that purpose chiefly; the Christ, Krishna, Buddha stands in its centre as the gate, he makes through himself the way men shall follow. That is why each Incarnation holds before men his own example and declares of himself that he is the way and the gate; he declares too the oneness of his humanity with the divine being, declares that the Son of Man and the Father above from whom he has descended are one, that Krishna in the human body, *mānuṣīṁ tanum āśritam*, and the supreme Lord and Friend of all creatures are but two revelations of the same divine Purushottama, revealed there in his own being, revealed here in the type of humanity.

[The human being] is ignorant because there is upon the eyes of his soul and all its organs the seal of that Nature, Prakriti, Maya, by which he has been put forth into manifestation out of God's eternal being; she has minted him like a coin out of the precious metal of the divine substance, but overlaid with a strong coating of the alloy of her phenomenal qualities, stamped with her own stamp and mark of animal humanity, and although the secret sign of the Godhead is there, it is at first indistinguishable and always with difficulty decipherable, not to be really discovered except by that initiation into the mystery of our own being which distinguishes a Godward from an earthward humanity. In the Avatar, the divinely-born Man, the real substance shines through the coating; the mark of the seal is there only for form, the vision is that of the secret Godhead, the power of the life is that of the secret Godhead, and it breaks through the seals of the assumed human nature; the sign of the Godhead, an inner soul-sign, not outward, not physical, stands out legible for all to read who care to see or who can see; for the Asuric nature is always blind to these things, it sees the body and not the soul, the external being and not the internal, the mask and not the Person. In the ordinary human birth the Nature-aspect of the universal Divine assuming humanity prevails; in the incarnation the God-aspect of the same phenomenon takes its place. In the one he allows the human nature to take possession of his partial being and to dominate it; in the other he takes possession of his partial type of being and its nature and divinely dominates it. Not by evolution or ascent like the ordinary man, the Gita seems to tell us, not by a growing into the divine birth, but by a direct descent into the stuff of humanity and a taking up of its moulds. But it is to assist that ascent or evolution the descent is made or accepted; it is to prepare even, however far off, the kingdom of God, **the victory of the seekers of light and perfection, *sādhūnām*, and the overthrow of those who fight for the continuance of the evil and the darkness.**

This external Avatarhood is a sign, in the symbol of a human life, of the eternal inner Godhead making himself manifest in the field of [our] own human mentality and corporeality so that [we] can grow into unity with that and be possessed by it. The divine manifestation of a Christ, Krishna, Buddha in external humanity has for its inner truth the same manifestation of the eternal Avatar within in our own inner humanity. That which has been done in the outer human life of earth, may be repeated in the inner life of all human beings.

जन्म कर्म च मे दिव्यमेवं यो वेत्ति तत्त्वतः ।
त्यक्त्वा देहं पुनर्जन्म नैति मामेति सोऽर्जुन ।।९।।

9. He who knoweth thus in its right principles my divine birth and my divine work, when he abandons his body, comes not to rebirth, he comes to Me, O Arjuna.

वीतरागभयक्रोधा मन्मया मामुपाश्रिताः ।
बहवो ज्ञानतपसा पूता मद्भावमागताः ।।१०।।

10. Delivered from liking and fear and wrath, full of me, taking refuge in me, many purified by austerity of knowledge have arrived at my nature of being (*madbhāvam*, the divine nature of the Purushottama).

The Divine is at work in man in the ignorance and at work in man in the knowledge. To know Him is our soul's highest welfare and the condition of its perfection, but to know and realise Him as a transcendent peace and silence is not all; the secret that has to be learned is at once the secret of the eternal and unborn Divine and the secret of the divine birth and works, *janma karma ca me divyam*. The action which proceeds from that knowledge, will be free from all bondage; **he who so knoweth me, says the Teacher, is not bound by works.** Through the knowledge and possession of the divine birth he comes to the unborn and imperishable Divine who is the self of all beings, *ajo avyaya ātmā*; through the knowledge and execution of divine works to the Master of works, the lord of all beings, *bhūtānām īśvara*. He lives in that unborn being; his works are those of that universal Mastery.

The Avatar comes to bring nearer the kingdom of heaven on earth in the collectivity as well as to build the kingdom of heaven within in the individual human soul. The inner fruit of the Avatar's coming is gained by those who learn from it the true nature of the divine birth and the divine works and who, growing full of him in their consciousness and taking refuge in him with their whole being, *manmayā mām upāśritāḥ*. purified by the realising force of their knowledge and delivered from the lower nature, attain to the divine being and divine nature, *madbhāvam āgatāḥ*. The Avatar comes to reveal the divine nature in man above this lower nature and to show what are the divine works, free, unegoistic, disinterested, impersonal, universal, full of the divine light, the divine power and the divine love. To attain to the divine birth, — a divinising new birth of the soul into a higher consciousness, — and to do divine works both as a means towards that before it is attained and as an expression of it after it is attained, is then all the Karmayoga of the Gita.

No doubt, the descent of the Avatar, like the divine birth from the other side, is essentially a spiritual phenomenon, as is shown by the Gita's *ātmānaṁ sṛijāmi*, it is a soul-birth; but still there is here an attendant physical birth. There the Gita's doctrine of Avatarhood stands. It is true that the physical Avatarhood does not fill a large space in the Gita, but still it does occupy a definite place in the chain of its teachings and is implied in the whole scheme, the very framework being the Avatar leading the *vibhūti*, the man who has risen to the greatest heights of mere manhood, to the divine birth and divine works. No doubt, too, the inner descent of the Godhead to raise the human soul into himself is the main thing, — it is the inner Christ, Krishna or Buddha that matters. But just as the outer life is of immense importance for the inner development, so the external Avatarhood is of no mean importance for this great spiritual manifestation. The consummation in the mental and physical symbol assists the growth of the inner reality; afterwards the inner reality expresses itself with greater power in a more perfect symbolisation of itself through the outer life. Between these two, spiritual reality and mental and physical expression, acting and returning upon each other constantly the manifestation of the Divine in humanity has elected to move always in the cycles of its concealment and its revelation.

ये यथा मां प्रपद्यन्ते तांस्तथैव भजाम्यहम् ।
मम वर्त्मानुवर्तन्ते मनुष्याः पार्थ सर्वशः ।।११।।

11. As men approach me, so I accept them to my love, *bhajāmi*; men follow in every way my path, O son of Pritha.

[It does not] matter essentially in what form and name or putting forward what aspect of the Divine he comes; for in all ways, varying with their nature, men are following the path set to them by the Divine which will in the end lead them to him and the aspect of him which suits their nature is that which they can best follow when he comes to lead them; in whatever way men accept, love and take joy in God, in that way God accepts, loves and takes joy in man. ***Ye yathā māṁ prapadyante tān-tathaiva bhajāmi-aham.***

But it is by directing [all the emotions] in growing knowledge towards him that we enter into more intimate relations with him, and all that is false and ignorant in them will fall away as we draw nearer towards unity. To all of them he answers, taking us in the stage of progress in which we are, for if we met no kind of response or help to our imperfect approach, the more perfect relations could never be established.

काङ्क्षन्तः कर्मणां सिद्धिं यजन्त इह देवताः ।
क्षिप्रं हि मानुषे लोके सिद्धिर्भवति कर्मजा ।।१२।।

12. But most men, desiring the fulfilment of their works, sacrifice to the gods, to various forms and personalities of the one Godhead, **because the fulfilment *(siddhi)* that is born of works,** — of works without knowledge, — **is very swift and easy in the human world;** it belongs indeed to that world alone. The other, the divine self-fulfilment in man by the sacrifice with knowledge to the supreme Godhead, is much more difficult; its results belong to a higher plane of existence and they are less easily grasped. Men therefore have to follow the fourfold law of their nature and works and on this plane of mundane action they seek the Godhead through his various qualities.

चातुर्वर्ण्यं मया सृष्टं गुणकर्मविभागशः ।
तस्य कर्तारमपि मां विद्ध्यकर्तारमव्ययम् ।।१३।।

13. But, says Krishna, though I am the doer of the fourfold works and creator of its fourfold law, *cāturvarṇyam* (see also XVIII-41), **yet I must be known also as the non-doer, the imperishable, the immutable Self.** He is not the doer of works in the personal sense of our action involved in Prakriti; for

God works through his power, conscious nature, effective force, — Shakti, Maya, Prakriti, — but yet above it, not involved in it, not subject to it, not unable to lift himself beyond the laws, workings, habits of action it creates, not affected or bound by them, not unable to distinguish himself, as we are unable, from the workings of life, mind and body. He is the doer of works who acts not, *kartāram akartāram*. **Know me for the doer of this (the fourfold law of human workings, according to the divisions of quality and active function, *guṇa-karma-vibhāgaśaḥ*,) who am yet the imperishable non-doer.** He is in the action of the divine consciousness the creator of the fourfold Law and the doer of the works of the world and at the same time in the silence of the divine consciousness the impartial witness of the works of his own Nature, — for he is always, beyond both the silence and the action, the supreme Purushottama.

न मां कर्माणि लिम्पन्ति न मे कर्मफले स्पृहा ।
इति मां योऽभिजानाति कर्मभिर्न स बद्ध्यते ।।१४।।

14. **Works fix not themselves on me, *na limpanti*, nor have I desire for the fruits of action.** But neither is he the inactive, impassive, unpuissant Witness and nothing else; for it is he who works in the steps and measures of his power; every movement of it, every particle of the world of beings it forms is instinct with his presence, full of his consciousness, impelled by his will, shaped by his knowledge. For God is the impersonal beyond this egoistic personality and this strife of the modes of Nature, and as the Purushottama also, the impersonal Personality, he possesses this supreme freedom even in works. Therefore the doer of divine works even while following the fourfold law has to know and live in that which is beyond, in the impersonal Self and so in the supreme Godhead. **He who thus knows me is not bound by his works.**

एवं ज्ञात्वा कृतं कर्म पूर्वैरपि मुमुक्षुभिः ।
कुरु कर्मैव तस्मात्त्वं पूर्वैः पूर्वतरं कृतम् ।।१५।।

15. **So knowing was work done by the men of old who sought liberation; do therefore, thou also, work of that more ancient kind done by ancient men.**

II — THE DIVINE WORKER (1)

किं कर्म किमकर्मेति कवयोऽप्यत्र मोहिताः ।
तत्ते कर्म प्रवक्ष्यामि यज्ज्ञात्वा मोक्ष्यसेऽशुभात् ।।१६।।

16. The Gita does not try to define works by any outward signs. The signs by which it distinguishes divine works are all profoundly intimate and subjective; the stamp by which they are known is invisible, spiritual, supra-ethical. They are recognisable only by the light of the soul from which they come. For, it says, **what is action and what is inaction, as to this even the sages are perplexed and deluded,** because, judging by practical, social, ethical, intellectual standards, they discriminate by accidentals and do not go to the root of the matter; **I will declare to thee that action by the knowledge of which thou shalt be released from all ills.**

कर्मणो ह्यपि बोद्धव्यं बोद्धव्यं च विकर्मणः ।
अकर्मणश्च बोद्धव्यं गहना कर्मणो गतिः ।।१७।।

17. **One has to understand about action as well as to understand about wrong action and about inaction one has to understand; thick and tangled is the way of works.** Action in the world is like a deep forest, *gahana*, through which man goes stumbling as best he can, by the light of the ideas of his time, the standards of his personality, his environment, or rather of many times, many personalities, layers of thought and ethics from many social stages all inextricably confused together, temporal and conventional amidst all their claim to absoluteness and immutable truth, empirical and irrational in spite of their aping of right reason. And finally the sage seeking in the midst of it all a highest foundation of fixed law and an original truth finds himself obliged to raise the last supreme question, whether all action and life itself are not a delusion and a snare and whether cessation from action, *akarma*, is not the last resort of the tired and disillusioned human soul. But, says Krishna, by action, by works, not by inaction comes the knowledge and the release.

कर्मण्यकर्म यः पश्येदकर्मणि च कर्म यः ।
स बुद्धिमान्मनुष्येषु स युक्तः कृत्स्नकर्मकृत् ।।१८।।

18. What then is the solution? what is that type of works by which we shall be released from the ills of life, from this doubt, this error, this grief, from this mixed, impure and baffling result even of our purest and best-

intentioned acts, from these million forms of evil and suffering? No outward distinctions need be made, is the reply; no work the world needs, be shunned; no limit or hedge set round our human activities; on the contrary, **All action should be done, but from a soul in Yoga with the Divine, *yuktaḥ kṛitsna-karma-kṛit.*** *Akarma*, cessation from action is not the way; the man who has attained to the insight of the highest reason, perceives that such inaction is itself a constant action, a state subject to the workings of Nature and her qualities. The mind that takes refuge in physical inactivity, is still under the delusion that it and not Nature is the doer of works; it has mistaken inertia for liberation; it does not see that even in what seems absolute inertia greater than that of the stone or clod, Nature is at work, keeps unimpaired her hold. On the contrary in the full flood of action the soul is free from its works, is not the doer, not bound by what is done, and he who lives in the freedom of the soul, not in the bondage of the modes of Nature, alone has release from works. **He who in action can see inaction and can see action still continuing in cessation from works, is the man of true reason and discernment among men, *sa buddhi-mān manuṣyeṣu.* Therefore the liberated man is not afraid of action, he is a large and universal doer of all works, poised in the silent calm of the soul, tranquilly in Yoga with the Divine.** The perfect Yogin is no solitary musing on the Self in his ivory tower of spiritual isolation, but **yuktaḥ-kṛitsna-karma-kṛit, a many-sided universal worker for the good of the world, for God in the world.** The Divine is the lord of his works, he is only their channel through the instrumentality of his nature conscious of and subject to her Lord. **By the flaming intensity and purity of this knowledge all his works are burned up as in a fire** and his mind remains without any stain or disfiguring mark from them, calm, silent, unperturbed, white and clean and pure. To do all in this liberating knowledge, without the personal egoism of the doer, is the first sign of the divine worker.

यस्य सर्वे समारम्भाः कामसङ्कल्पवर्जिताः ।
ज्ञानाग्निदग्धकर्माणं तमाहुः पण्डितं बुधाः ।।१९।।
त्यक्त्वा कर्मफलासङ्गं नित्यतृप्तो निराश्रयः ।
कर्मण्यभिप्रवृत्तोऽपि नैव किञ्चित्करोति सः ।।२०।।

19-20. The second sign is freedom from desire; for where there is not the personal egoism of the doer, desire becomes impossible; it is starved out, sinks for want of a support, dies of inanition. Outwardly the liberated man seems to undertake works of all kinds like other men, but **from all his inceptions and undertakings the inferior concept and nether will of desire is entirely banished, *sarve samārambhāḥ kāma-saṅkalpa-varjitāḥ.* He has abandoned all attachment to the fruits of his works,** and where one does not work for the fruit, but solely as an impersonal instrument of the Master of works, desire can find no place, — not even the desire to serve successfully, for the fruit is the Lord's and determined by him and not by the personal will and effort, or to serve with credit and to the Master's satisfaction, for the real doer is the Lord himself and all glory belongs to a form of his Shakti missioned in the nature and not to the limited human personality. **Ever satisfied without any kind of dependence, *nitya-tṛipto nirāśrayaḥ*, the human mind and soul of the liberated man does nothing, *na kiñcit karoti*; even though through his nature he engages in action,** it is the Nature, the executive Shakti, it is the conscious Goddess governed by the divine Inhabitant who does the work.

The result may be success, as the ordinary mind understands it, or it may seem to that mind to be defeat and failure; but to him it is always the success intended, not by him, but by the all-wise manipulator of action and result, because he does not seek for victory, but only for the fulfilment of the divine will and wisdom which works out its ends through apparent failure as well as and often with greater force than through apparent triumph.

Afterwards Krishna declares that **the sacrifice of knowledge is the highest, all work finds its consummation in knowledge, by the fire of knowledge all works are burnt up; therefore by Yoga works are renounced and their bondage overcome for the man who is in possession of his Self.**

निराशीर्यतचित्तात्मा त्यक्तसर्वपरिग्रहः ।
शारीरं केवलं कर्म कुर्वन्नाप्नोति किल्बिषम् ।।२१।।

21. **The liberated man has no personal hopes; he does not seize on things as his personal possessions; he receives what the divine Will brings him, covets nothing, is jealous of none:** what comes to him he takes without repulsion and without attachment; what goes from him he allows to depart into the whirl of things without repining or grief or sense of loss. **His heart and self are under perfect control;** they are free from reaction and passion, they make no turbulent response to the touches of outward things. **His action is indeed a purely physical action, *śārīraṁ kevalaṁ karma*;** for all else comes from above, is not generated on the human plane, is only a reflection of the will, knowledge, joy of the divine Purushottama. Therefore **he does not by a stress on doing and its objects bring about in his mind and heart any of those reactions which we call passion and sin.** For sin consists not at all in the outward deed, but in an impure reaction of the personal will, mind and heart which accompanies it or causes it; the impersonal, the spiritual is always pure, *apāpaviddham*, and gives to all that it does its own inalienable purity. This spiritual impersonality is a third sign of the divine worker.

यदृच्छालाभसन्तुष्टो द्वन्द्वातीतो विमत्सरः ।
समः सिद्धावसिद्धौ च कृत्वापि न निबद्ध्यते ।।२२।।

22. **He who is satisfied with whatever gain comes to him and equal in failure and success, is not bound even when he acts.** The result of this knowledge, this desirelessness and this impersonality is a perfect equality in the soul and the nature. Equality is the fourth sign of the divine worker. **He has passed beyond the dualities, he is *dvandvātīta*.** We have seen that he regards with equal eyes, without any disturbance of feeling, failure and success, victory and defeat; but not only these, all dualities are in him surpassed and reconciled. The outward distinctions by which men determine their psychological attitude towards the happenings of the world, have for him only a subordinate and instrumental meaning. He does not ignore them, but he is above them. Good happening and evil happening, so all-important to the human soul subject to desire, are to the desireless divine soul equally welcome since by their mingled strand are worked out the developing forms of the eternal good. He cannot be defeated, since all for him is moving towards the divine victory in the Kurukshetra of Nature, *dharmakṣetre kurukṣetre*, the field of doings which is the field of the evolving Dharma, and every turn of the conflict has been designed and mapped by the foreseeing eye of the Master of the battle, the Lord of works and Guide of the dharma. Honour and dishonour from men cannot move him, nor their praise nor their blame. Arjuna the Kshatriya prizes naturally honour and reputation and is right in shunning disgrace and the name of coward as worse than death; but Arjuna the liberated soul need care for none of these things, he has only to know the *kartavyaṁ karma*, the work which the supreme Self demands from him, and to do that and leave the result to the Lord of his actions.

गतसङ्गस्य मुक्तस्य ज्ञानावस्थितचेतसः ।
यज्ञायाचरतः कर्म समग्रं प्रविलीयते ।।२३।।

23. **When a man liberated, free from attachment, acts for sacrifice, all his action is dissolved,** leaves, that is to say, no result of bondage or after-impression [or after-effects or consequences] on his free, pure, perfect and equal soul. **The liberated man is able to do works as a sacrifice because he is freed from attachment through his mind, heart and spirit being firmly founded in self-knowledge, *gata-saṅgasya muktasya jñāna-avasthita-cetasaḥ*. All his work disappears completely as soon as done, *pravilīyate*,** suffers *laya*, as one might say, in the being of the Brahman; it has no reactionary consequence on the soul of the apparent doer. The work is done by the Lord through his Nature,

it is no longer personal to the human instrument. The work itself becomes but power of the nature and substance of the being of the Brahman.

Again, the sign of the divine worker is that which is central to the divine consciousness itself, a perfect inner joy and peace which depends upon nothing in the world for its source or its continuance; it is innate, it is the very stuff of the soul's consciousness, it is the very nature of divine being. The ordinary man depends upon outward things for his happiness; therefore he has desire; therefore he has anger and passion, pleasure and pain, joy and grief; therefore he measures all things in the balance of good fortune and evil fortune. None of these things can affect the divine soul. That equality, impersonality, peace, joy, freedom do not depend on so outward a thing as doing or not doing works. The Gita insists repeatedly on the difference between the inward and the outward renunciation, *tyāga* and *sannyāsa*. The latter, it says, is valueless without the former, hardly possible even to attain without it, and unnecessary when there is the inward freedom. In fact *tyāga* itself is the real and sufficient Sannyasa.

III — THE LORD OF THE SACRIFICE

The whole of the Gita's gospel of works rests upon its idea of sacrifice and contains in fact the eternal connecting truth of God and the world and works. The gospel of the Gita reposes upon this fundamental Vedantic truth that all being is the one Brahman and all existence the wheel of Brahman, a divine movement opening out from God and returning to God. All is the expressive activity of Nature and Nature a power of the Divine which works out the consciousness and will of the divine Soul master of her works and inhabitant of her forms. It is for his satisfaction that she descends into the absorption of the forms of things and the works of life and mind and returns again through mind and self-knowledge to the conscious possession of the Soul that dwells within her. There is first an involving of self and all it is or means in an evolution of phenomena; there is afterwards an evolution of self, a revelation of all it is and means, all that is hidden and yet suggested by the phenomenal creation. This cycle of Nature could not be what it is but for the Purusha assuming and maintaining simultaneously three eternal poises each of which is necessary to the totality of this action. It must manifest itself in the mutable, and there we see it as the finite, the many, all existences, *sarvabhūtāni*. It appears to us as the finite personality of these million creatures with their infinite diversities and various relations and it appears to us behind these as the soul and force of the action of the gods, — that is to say, the cosmic powers and qualities of the Divine which preside over the workings of the life of the universe and constitute to our perception different universal forms of the one Existence, or, it may be, various self-statements of personality of the one supreme Person. Then, secret behind and within all forms and existences, we perceive too an immutable, an infinite, a timeless, an impersonal, a one unchanging spirit of existence, an indivisible Self of all that is, in which all these may find themselves to be really one. And therefore by returning to that the active, finite personality of the individual being discovers that it can release itself into a silent largeness of universality and the peace and poise of an immutable and unattached unity with all that proceeds from and is supported by this indivisible Infinite. But the highest secret of all, *uttamaṁ rahasyam*, is the Purushottama. This is the supreme Divine, God, who possesses both the infinite and the finite and in whom the personal and the impersonal, the one Self and the many existences, being and becoming, the world-action and the supracosmic peace, *pravṛitti* and *nivṛitti*, meet, are united, are possessed together and in each other. In God all things find their secret truth and their absolute reconciliation.

These passages (*slokas 22-23*) are followed by a perfectly explicit and detailed interpretation of the meaning of *yajña* in the language of the Gita which leaves no doubt at all about the symbolic use of the words and the psychological character of the sacrifice enjoined by this teaching. This elaborate Vedantic explanation of the Yajna sets out with a vast and comprehensive definition in which it is declared that the act and energy and materials of the sacrifice, the giver and receiver of the sacrifice, the goal and object of the sacrifice are all the one Brahman.

ब्रह्मार्पणं ब्रह्म हविर्ब्रह्माग्नौ ब्रह्मणा हुतम् ।
ब्रह्मैव तेन गन्तव्यं ब्रह्मकर्मसमाधिना ।।२४।।

24. Brahman is the giving, Brahman is the food-offering, by Brahman it is offered into the Brahman-fire, Brahman is that which is to be attained by samadhi in Brahman-action.

This then is the knowledge in which the liberated man has to do works of sacrifice. It is the knowledge declared of old in the great Vedantic utterances, "I am He," "All this verily is the Brahman, Brahman is this Self." It is the knowledge of the entire unity; it is the One manifest as the doer and the deed and the object of works, knower and knowledge and the object of knowledge. The universal energy into which the action is poured is the Divine; the consecrated energy of the giving is the Divine; whatever is offered is only some form of the Divine; the giver of the offering is the Divine himself in man; the action, the work, the sacrifice is itself the Divine in movement, in activity; the goal to be reached by sacrifice is the Divine. For the man who has this knowledge and lives and acts in it, there can be no binding works, no personal and egoistically appropriated action; there is only the divine Purusha acting by the divine Prakriti in His own being, offering everything into the fire of His self-conscious cosmic energy, while the knowledge and the possession of His divine existence and consciousness by the soul unified with Him is the goal of all this God-directed movement and activity. To know that and to live and act in this unifying consciousness is to be free.

In the light of a larger knowledge, Matter also can be seen to be the Brahman, a self-energy put forth by the Brahman, a form and substance of Brahman. A certain reverence for Matter and a sacramental attitude in all dealings with it is possible. The act of the taking of food is spoken of as a material sacrament, a sacrifice, an offering of Brahman to Brahman by Brahman. The Spirit has made itself Matter in order to place itself there as an instrument for the well-being and joy, *yogakṣema*, of created beings, for a self-offering of universal physical utility and service.

दैवमेवापरे यज्ञं योगिनः पर्युपासते ।
ब्रह्माग्नावपरे यज्ञं यज्ञेनैवोपजुह्वति ।।२५।।

25. But all even of the Yogins have not attained to this knowledge. **Some Yogins follow after the sacrifice which is of the gods; others offer the sacrifice by the sacrifice itself into the Brahman-fire.** The former conceive of the Divine in various forms and powers and seek him by various means, ordinances, *dharmas*, laws or, as we might say, settled rites of action, self-discipline, consecrated works; for the latter, those who already know, the simple fact of sacrifice, of offering whatever work to the Divine itself, of casting all their activities into the unified divine consciousness and energy, is their one means, their one *dharma*.

श्रोत्रादीनीन्द्रियाण्यन्ये संयमाग्निषु जुह्वति ।
शब्दादीन्विषयानन्य इन्द्रियाग्निषु जुह्वति ।।२६।।
सर्वाणीन्द्रियकर्माणि प्राणकर्माणि चापरे ।
आत्मसंयमयोगाग्नौ जुह्वति ज्ञानदीपिते ।।२७।।

26-27. The means of sacrifice are various; the offerings are of many kinds. There is the psychological sacrifice of self-control and self-discipline. **Some offer the hearing and all their senses into the fires of control, others**

offer [sound and the other] objects of sense into the fires of sense, and others offer all the actions of the sense and all the actions of the vital force into the fire of the Yoga of self-control kindled by knowledge.

द्रव्ययज्ञास्तपोयज्ञा योगयज्ञास्तथापरे ।
स्वाध्यायज्ञानयज्ञाश्च यतयः संशितव्रताः ।।२८।।

28. The offering of the striver after perfection may be material and physical, ***dravya-yajña,*** like that consecrated in worship by the devotee to his deity, **or it may be the austerity of his self-discipline and energy of his soul** directed to some high aim, ***tapo-yajña,*** **or it may be some form of Yoga** like the Pranayama of the Rajayogins and Hathayogins, or any other *yoga-yajña*, **or the knowledge of the Vedas.** All these tend to the purification of the being; all sacrifice is a way towards the attainment of the highest.

अपाने जुह्वति प्राणं प्राणेऽपानं तथापरे ।
प्राणापानगती रुद्ध्वा प्राणायामपरायणाः ।।२९।।

29. Some offer the upper breath into the lower and the lower breath into the upper, stopping the passages of the inbreath and outbreath, absorbed in government of the breath that is life;

अपरे नियताहाराः प्राणान्प्राणेषु जुह्वति ।
सर्वेऽप्येते यज्ञविदो यज्ञक्षपितकल्मषाः ।।३०।।

30. others, eating temperately, offer up the breaths into the breaths as into a sacrificial fire. And all these, yea all, are wise in sacrifice, and by sacrifice the obscuration of sin fades away from them.

यज्ञशिष्टामृतभुजो यान्ति ब्रह्म सनातनम् ।
नायं लोकोऽस्त्ययज्ञस्य कुतोऽन्यः कुरुसत्तम ।।३१।।

31. They who enjoy the nectar of immortality left over from the sacrifice attain to the eternal Brahman. Sacrifice is the law of the world and nothing can be gained without it, neither mastery here, nor the possession of heavens beyond, nor the supreme possession of all; **this world is not for him who doeth not sacrifice, how then any other world?**

एवं बहुविधा यज्ञा वितता ब्रह्मणो मुखे ।
कर्मजान्विद्धि तान्सर्वानेवं ज्ञात्वा विमोक्ष्यसे ।।३२।।

32. **Therefore all these and many other forms of sacrifice have been extended in the mouth of the Brahman,** the mouth of that Fire which receives all offerings; they are all means and forms of the one great Existence in activity, means by which the action of the human being can be offered up to That of which his outward existence is a part and with which his inmost self is one. **They are all born of work;** all proceed from and are ordained by the one vast energy of the Divine which manifests itself in the universal *karma* and makes all the cosmic activity a progressive offering to the one Self and Lord and of which the last stage for the human being is self-knowledge and the possession of the divine or Brahmic consciousness. **So knowing thou shalt become free.**

श्रेयान्द्रव्यमयाद्यज्ञाज्ज्ञानयज्ञः परन्तप ।
सर्वं कर्माखिलं पार्थ ज्ञाने परिसमाप्यते ।।३३।।

33. But there are gradations in the range of these various forms of sacrifice, the physical offering the lowest, the sacrifice of knowledge the highest. **The sacrifice of knowledge is greater than any material sacrifice. All works in their totality find their culmination and completeness in the knowledge of the Divine, *sarvaṁ karmākhilaṁ jñāne parisamāpyate.*** They are not an obstacle, but the way to the supreme knowledge. Knowledge is that in which all this action culminates, not any lower knowledge, but the highest, self-knowledge and God-knowledge.

Action is the first power of life. Nature begins with force and its works which, once conscious in man, become will and its achievements; therefore it is that by turning his action Godwards the life of man best and most surely begins to become divine. When the will in him is made one with the divine will and the whole action of the being proceeds from the Divine and is directed towards the Divine, the union in works is perfectly accomplished. But works fulfil themselves in knowledge. By union in will and works we become one in the omnipresent conscious being from whom all our will and works have their rise and draw their power and in whom they fulfil the round of their energies. By knowledge [we arrive] at conscious oneness with that which we know, — for by identity alone can complete and real knowledge exist. But knowledge is not complete without works; for the Will in being also is God and not the being or its self-aware silent existence alone, and if works find their culmination in knowledge, knowledge also finds its fulfilment in works.

तद्विद्धि प्रणिपातेन परिप्रश्नेन सेवया ।
उपदेक्ष्यन्ति ते ज्ञानं ज्ञानिनस्तत्त्वदर्शिनः ।।३४।।

34. **This wisdom [we] must learn by prostration and questioning and service; we get first initiation into it from the men of knowledge who have** ***seen,*** not those who know merely by the intellect, **its essential truths,** ***tattva-darśinaḥ.***

यज्ज्ञात्वा न पुनर्मोहमेवं यास्यसि पाण्डव ।
येन भूतान्यशेषेण द्रक्ष्यस्यात्मन्यथो मयि ।।३५।।

35. **Knowledge is that by possessing which we shall not fall again into the bewilderment of the mind's ignorance** and into its bondage to mere sense-knowledge and to the inferior activity of the desires and passions. **The knowledge in which all culminates is that by which thou shalt see all existences (becomings,** ***bhūtāni*****) without exception in the Self, then in Me.** For the Self is that one, immutable, all-pervading, all-containing, self-existent reality or Brahman hidden behind our mental being into which our consciousness widens out when it is liberated from the ego; we come to see all beings as becomings, *bhūtāni*, within that one self-existence. But this Self or immutable Brahman we see too to be the self-presentation to our essential psychological consciousness of a supreme Being who is the source of our existence and of whom all that is mutable or immutable is the manifestation. He is God, the Divine, the Purushottama.

Atmani atho mayi. The demand is to see all things in the Self and then in "Me" the Ishwara, to renounce all action into the Self, Spirit, Brahman and thence into the supreme Person, the Purushottama. There is here a still greater and profounder complex of spiritual experience, a larger transmutation of the significance of human life, a more mystic and heart-felt sweep of the return of the stream to the ocean, the restoration of personal works and the cosmic action to the Eternal Worker.

Man's way to liberation and perfection lies through an increasing impersonality. It is his ancient and constant experience that the more he opens himself to the impersonal and infinite, to that which is pure and high and one and common in all things and beings, the impersonal and infinite in Nature, the impersonal and infinite in life, the impersonal and infinite in his own subjectivity, the less he is bound by his ego and by the circle of the finite, the more he feels a sense of largeness, peace, pure happiness. The pleasure, joy, satisfaction which the finite by itself can give or the ego in its own right attain, is transitory, petty and insecure. To dwell entirely in the ego-sense and its finite conceptions, powers, satisfactions is to find this world for ever full of transience and suffering, *anityam asukham*; the finite life is always troubled by a certain sense of vanity for this fundamental reason that the finite is not the whole or the highest truth of life; life is not entirely real until it opens into the sense of the infinite. It is for this reason that the Gita opens its gospel of works by insisting on the Brahmic consciousness, the impersonal life, that great object of the discipline of the ancient sages. For the impersonal, the infinite, the One in which all the impermanent, mutable, multiple activity of the world finds above itself its base of permanence, security and peace, is the immobile Self, the Akshara, the Brahman. If we see this, we shall see that to raise one's consciousness and the poise of one's being out of limited personality into this infinite and impersonal Brahman is the first spiritual necessity. To see all beings in this one Self is the knowledge which raises the soul out of egoistic ignorance and its works and results; to live in it is to acquire peace and firm spiritual foundation.

The ego, the limited and troubled personality is then quieted and merged in the consciousness of the one impersonal Self, while the works of Nature continue to our vision to operate through all these "becomings" or existences who are now seen by us as living and acting and moving, under her impulsion entirely, in this one infinite Being; our own finite existence is seen and felt to be only one of these and its workings are seen and felt to be those of Nature, not of our real self which is the silent, impersonal unity. The ego claimed them as its own doings and therefore we thought them ours; but the ego is now dead and henceforth they are no longer ours, but Nature's. We have achieved by the slaying of ego impersonality in our being and consciousness; we have achieved by the renunciation of desire impersonality in the works of our nature. We are free not only in inaction, but in action. The liberation given by this perfect impersonality is real, is complete, is indispensable; but is it the last word, the end of the whole matter? All life, all world-existence, we have said, is the sacrifice offered by Nature to the Purusha, the one and secret soul in Nature, in whom all her workings take place. We have risen out of ego and desire and limited personality and by impersonality, its great corrective, we have found the impersonal Godhead; we have identified our being with the one self and soul in whom all exist. The sacrifice of works continues, conducted not by ourselves any longer, but by Nature, — Nature operating through the finite part of our being, mind, senses, body, — but in our infinite being. But to whom then is this sacrifice offered and with what object? For the impersonal has no activity and no desires, no object to be gained, no dependence for anything on all this world of creatures; it exists for itself, in its own self-delight, in its own immutable eternal being.

There is still, after the ego has been conquered, a divine Lord and enjoyer of the sacrifice, *bhoktāraṁ yajña tapasām*, and there is still an object in the sacrifice. The impersonal Brahman is not the very last word, not the utterly highest secret of our being; for impersonal and personal, finite and infinite turn out to be only two opposite, yet concomitant aspects of a divine Being unlimited by these distinctions who is both these things at once. God is an ever unmanifest Infinite ever self-impelled to manifest himself in the finite; he is the great impersonal Person of whom all personalities are partial appearances; he is the Divine who reveals himself in the human being, the Lord seated in the heart of man. Knowledge teaches us to see all beings in the one impersonal self, for so we are liberated from the separative ego-sense, and then through this delivering impersonality to see them in this God, "*ātmani atho mayi*, in the Self and then in Me". We have to arrive at him not through our lower personality, but through the high, infinite and impersonal part of our being, and that we find by becoming this self one in all in whose existence the whole world is comprised. Therefore it is to the Impersonal that we have first to attain. But the silent immobility of the impersonal Self [is not] the whole all-revealing all-satisfying truth of the Divine. To see that we have to look through its silence to the Purushottama, and he in his divine greatness possesses both the Akshara and the Kshara; he is seated in the immobility, but he manifests himself in the movement and in all the action of cosmic Nature; to him even after liberation the sacrifice of works in Nature continues to be offered. For he remains to the end the master of works and the soul of sacrifice.

This then is the sense of the Gita's doctrine of sacrifice. Its full significance depends on the idea of the Purushottama which as yet is not developed, and therefore we have had to anticipate that central teaching. At present the Teacher simply gives a hint, merely adumbrates this supreme presence of the Purushottama and his relation to the immobile Self in whom it is our first business, our pressing spiritual need to find our poise of perfect peace and equality by attainment to the Brahmic condition. He speaks as yet not at all in set terms of the Purushottama, but of himself, — "I", Krishna, Narayana, the Avatar, the God in man who is also the Lord in the universe incarnated in the figure of the divine charioteer of Kurukshetra. "In the Self, then in Me," is the formula he gives, implying that the transcendence of the individual personality by seeing it as a "becoming" in the impersonal self-existent Being is simply a means of arriving at that great secret impersonal Personality, which is thus silent, calm and uplifted above Nature in the impersonal Being, but also present and active in Nature in all these million becomings. The idea of the Purushottama, seen here as the incarnate Narayana, Krishna, is therefore the key. Without it the withdrawal from the lower nature to the Brahmic condition leads necessarily to inaction of the liberated man, his indifference to the works of the world; with it the same withdrawal becomes a step by which the works of the world are taken up in the spirit, with the nature and in the freedom of the Divine. See the silent Brahman as the goal and the world with all its activities has to be forsaken; see God, the Divine, the Purushottama as the goal, superior to action yet its inner spiritual cause and object and original will, and the world with all its activities is conquered and possessed in a divine transcendence of the world.

IV — EQUALITY AND KNOWLEDGE

अपि चेदसि पापेभ्यः सर्वेभ्यः पापकृत्तमः ।
सर्वं ज्ञानप्लवेनैव वृजिनं सन्तरिष्यसि ।।३६।।

36. Yoga and knowledge are, in this early part of the Gita's teaching, the two wings of the soul's ascent. By Yoga is meant union through divine works done without desire, with equality of soul to all things and all men, as a sacrifice to the Supreme, while knowledge is that on which this desirelessness, this equality, this power of sacrifice is founded. **Even if thou art the greatest doer of sin beyond all sinners, thou shalt cross over all the crookedness of evil in the ship of knowledge.**

यथैधांसि समिद्धोऽग्निर्भस्मसात्कुरुतेऽर्जुन ।
ज्ञानाग्निः सर्वकर्माणि भस्मसात्कुरुते तथा ।।३७।।

37. **As a fire kindled turns to ashes its fuel, so the fire of knowledge turns all works to ashes.** By this it is not at all meant that when knowledge is complete, there is cessation from works.

न हि ज्ञानेन सदृशं पवित्रमिह विद्यते ।
तत्स्वयं योगसंसिद्धः कालेनात्मनि विन्दति ।।३८।।

38. **There is nothing in the world equal in purity to knowledge.** By knowledge desire and its first-born child, sin, are destroyed. But the actuality of it [knowledge] comes from within ourselves: **the man who is perfected by Yoga, finds it of himself in the self by the course of Time,** it grows within him, that is to say, and he grows into it as he goes on increasing in desirelessness, in equality, in devotion to the Divine.

श्रद्धावाँल्लभते ज्ञानं तत्परः संयतेन्द्रियः ।
ज्ञानं लब्ध्वा परां शान्तिमचिरेणाधिगच्छति ।।३९।।

39. It is only of the supreme knowledge that this can altogether be said; the knowledge which the intellect of man amasses, is gathered laboriously by the senses and the reason from outside. **To get this other knowledge,** self-existent, intuitive, self-experiencing, self-revealing, **we must have conquered and controlled our mind and senses, *saṁ-yatendriyaḥ*,** so that we are no longer subject to their delusions, but rather the mind and senses become its pure mirror; **we must have fixed our whole conscious being on the truth of that supreme reality in which all exists, *tat-paraḥ*,** so that it may display in us its luminous self-existence. Finally, **we must have a faith which no intellectual doubt can be allowed to disturb, *śraddhāvān labhate jñānam*. And when a man has got the Knowledge, he attains very quickly to the high and perfect peace.**

अज्ञश्चाश्रद्दधानश्च संशयात्मा विनश्यति ।
नायं लोकोऽस्ति न परो न सुखं संशयात्मनः ।।४०।।

40. The ignorant who has not faith, the soul of doubt goeth to perdition; neither this world, nor the supreme world, nor any happiness is for the soul full of doubts.

योगसन्न्यस्तकर्माणं ज्ञानसंछिन्नसंशयम् ।
आत्मवन्तं न कर्माणि निबध्नन्ति धनञ्जय ।।४१।।

41. He who has destroyed all doubt by knowledge and has by Yoga given up all works and is in possession of the Self is not bound by his works. But still in the lower knowledge doubt and scepticism have their temporary uses; in the higher they are stumbling-blocks: for there the whole secret is not the balancing of truth and error, but a constantly progressing realisation of revealed truth. In intellectual knowledge there is always a mixture of falsehood or incompleteness which has to be got rid of by subjecting the truth itself to sceptical enquiry; but in the higher knowledge falsehood cannot enter and that which intellect contributes by attaching itself to this or that opinion, cannot be got rid of by mere questioning, but will fall away of itself by persistence in realisation, by proceeding to further and more complete realisation through a deeper, higher and wider living in the Spirit. And what is not yet realised must be prepared for by faith, not by sceptical questioning, because this truth is not a truth which has to be proved, but a truth which has to be lived inwardly, a greater reality into which we have to grow. Finally, it is in itself a self-existent truth.

तस्मादज्ञानसम्भूतं हृत्स्थं ज्ञानासिनात्मनः ।
छित्त्वैनं संशयं योगमातिष्ठोत्तिष्ठ भारत ।।४२।।

42. **The doubts,** the perplexities which prevent us from accepting and following it, **arise from [the] ignorance, from the sense-bewildered, opinion-perplexed heart and mind,** living as they do in a lower and phenomenal truth and therefore questioning the higher realities. **They have to be cut away by the sword of knowledge,** by the knowledge that realises, **by resorting constantly to Yoga,** that is, by living out the union with the Supreme whose truth being known all is known, *yasmin vijñāte sarvaṁ vijñātam.*

Our present state is an Ignorance and a many-sided seeking; it seeks for the truth of all things but, — as is evident from the insistence and the variety of the human mind's speculations as to the fundamental Truth which explains all others, the Reality at the basis of all things, — the fundamental truth of things, their basic reality must be found in some at once fundamental and universal Real; it is that which, once discovered, must embrace and explain all, — for "that being known, all will be known"[1]: the fundamental Real must necessarily be and contain the truth of all existence, the truth of the individual, the truth of the universe, the truth of all that is beyond the universe.

1. This was what was meant by the Upanishad when it spoke of the Brahman as "that which being known all is known".

CHAPTER V

I — *The Divine Worker (2)*

अर्जुन उवाच
सन्न्यासं कर्मणां कृष्ण पुनर्योगं च शंससि ।
यच्छ्रेय एतयोरेकं तन्मे ब्रूहि सुनिश्चितम् ॥१॥

1. *Arjuna* — Again Arjuna is perplexed; here are desireless works, the principle of Yoga, and renunciation of works, the principle of Sankhya, put together side by side as if part of one method, yet there is no evident reconciliation between them. For the kind of reconciliation which the Teacher has already given, — in outward inaction to see action still persisting and in apparent action to see a real inaction since the soul has renounced its illusion of the worker and given up works into the hands of the Master of sacrifice, — is for the practical mind of Arjuna too slight, too subtle and expressed almost in riddling words; he has not caught their sense or at least not penetrated into their spirit and reality. Therefore he asks again,

Thou declarest to me the renunciation of works, O Krishna, and again thou declarest to me Yoga; which one of these is the better way, that tell me with a clear decisiveness.

श्रीभगवानुवाच
सन्न्यासः कर्मयोगश्च निःश्रेयसकरावुभौ ।
तयोस्तु कर्मसन्न्यासात्कर्मयोगो विशिष्यते ॥२॥

2. *Krishna* — The answer is important, for it puts the whole distinction very clearly and indicates though it does not develop entirely the line of reconciliation. **Renunciation and Yoga of works both bring about the soul's salvation, but of the two the Yoga of works is distinguished above the renunciation of works.**

ज्ञेयः स नित्यसन्न्यासी यो न द्वेष्टि न काङ्क्षति ।
निर्द्वन्द्वो हि महाबाहो सुखं बन्धात्प्रमुच्यते ॥३॥

3. **He should be known as always a Sannyasin** even when he is doing action **who neither dislikes nor desires; for free from the dualities he is released easily and happily from the bondage.**

साङ्ख्ययोगौ पृथग्बालाः प्रवदन्ति न पण्डिताः ।
एकमप्यास्थितः सम्यगुभयोर्विन्दते फलम् ।।४।।

4. **Children speak of Sankhya and Yoga apart from each other, not the wise; if a man applies himself integrally to one, he gets the fruit of both,** because in their integrality each contains the other.

यत्साङ्ख्यैः प्राप्यते स्थानं तद्योगैरपि गम्यते ।
एकं साङ्ख्यं च योगं च यः पश्यति स पश्यति ।।५।।

5. **The status which is attained by the Sankhya, to that the men of the Yoga also arrive; who sees Sankhya and Yoga as one, he sees.**

सन्न्यासस्तु महाबाहो दुःखमाप्तुमयोगतः ।
योगयुक्तो मुनिर्ब्रह्म नचिरेणाधिगच्छति ।।६।।

6. **But renunciation is difficult to attain without Yoga; the sage who has Yoga attains soon to the Brahman.** The painful process of outward Sannyasa, *duḥkham āptum*, is an unnecessary process. While Sannyasa is difficult for embodied beings who must do works so long as they are in the body, Yoga of works is entirely sufficient and it rapidly and easily brings the soul to Brahman.

योगयुक्तो विशुद्धात्मा विजितात्मा जितेन्द्रियः ।
सर्वभूतात्मभूतात्मा कुर्वन्नपि न लिप्यते ।।७।।

7. **When a man has Yoga, the Self of him is purified from obscuration, he is master of the Self and victor over the senses. His self becomes the self of all existences (of all things that have become), and even though he does works, he is not involved in them.** He knows that the actions are not his, but Nature's and by that very knowledge he is free; he has renounced works, does no actions, though actions are done through him; he becomes the Self, the Brahman, *brahma-bhūta*, he sees all existences as becomings, *bhūtāni*, of that self-existent Being, his own only one of them, all their actions as only the development

of cosmic Nature working through their individual nature and his own actions also as a part of the same cosmic activity. **He whose self has become the self of all existences, *sarva-bhūtātma-bhūtātmā*, acts and yet is not affected by his works, is not caught in them, receives from them no soul-ensnaring reaction, *kurvann api na lipyate*.**

नैव किञ्चित्करोमीति युक्तो मन्येत तत्त्ववित् ।
पश्यञ्शृण्वन्स्पृशञ्जिघ्रन्नश्नन्गच्छन्स्वपञ्श्वसन् ।।८।।
प्रलपन्विसृजन्गृह्णन्नुन्मिषन्निमिषन्नपि ।
इन्द्रियाणीन्द्रियार्थेषु वर्तन्त इति धारयन् ।।९।।

8-9. **The man who knows the principles of things thinks, his mind in Yoga** with the inactive Impersonal, **"I am doing nothing"; when he sees, hears, touches, smells, eats, moves, sleeps, breathes, speaks, ejects, takes, opens his eyes or closes them, he holds that it is only the senses acting upon the objects of the senses.**

ब्रह्मण्याधाय कर्माणि सङ्गं त्यक्त्वा करोति यः ।
लिप्यते न स पापेन पद्मपत्रमिवाम्भसा ।।१०।।

10. It is perfectly true that all actions, as well as the fruit of action, have to be given up, to be renounced, but inwardly, not outwardly, not into the inertia of Nature, but to the Lord in sacrifice, into the calm and joy of the Impersonal from whom all action proceeds without disturbing his peace. The true Sannyasa of action is the reposing of all works on the Brahman. **He who, having abandoned attachment, acts reposing (or founding) his works on the Brahman, *brahmaṇi-ādhāya karmāṇi*, is not stained by sin even as water clings not to the lotus-leaf.** That Yoga of works is, we have seen, the offering of all action to the Lord, which induces as its culmination an inner and not an outer, a spiritual, not a physical giving up of works into the Brahman, into the being of the Lord. When works are thus "reposed on the Brahman," the personality of the instrumental doer ceases; though he acts, he does nothing; for he has given up not only the fruits of his works, but the works themselves and the doing of them to the Lord. The Divine then takes the burden of works from him; the Supreme becomes the doer and the act and the result.

The Gita insists on the giving up of actions, *sarva-karmāṇi sannyasya*, but inwardly to the Brahman. Brahman in the Kshara supports wholly the action of Prakriti, Brahman in the Akshara, even while supporting, dissociates itself from the action, preserves its freedom; the individual soul, unified with the Brahman in the Akshara, is free and dissociated, yet, unified with the Brahman in the Kshara, supports but is not affected. This it can do best when it sees that both are aspects of the one Purushottama. The individual soul makes the divinised natural being an instrument of the divine Will, *nimitta-mātram*. He remains even in action *triguṇātīta*, beyond the gunas, free from the gunas, *nistraiguṇya*, he fulfils entirely at last the early injunction of the Gita, *nistraiguṇyo bhavārjuna*. He is indeed still "the enjoyer of the gunas", as is the Brahman, "though not limited by them", "unattached, yet all-supporting", even as is that Brahman (*see also XIII-15*). But the action of the gunas within him is quite changed. This change is the final evolution of the nature and the consummation of the divine birth. When it is accomplished, the soul is aware of itself as the master of its nature and, grown a light of the divine Light and will of the divine Will, is able to change its natural workings into a divine action.

कायेन मनसा बुद्ध्या केवलैरिन्द्रियैरपि ।
योगिनः कर्म कुर्वन्ति सङ्गं त्यक्त्वात्मशुद्धये ।।११।।

11. **Therefore, the Yogins first do works with the body, mind, understanding, or even merely with the organs of action, abandoning attachment, for self-purification, *saṅgaṁ tyaktvā-ātma-śuddhaye*.**

युक्तः कर्मफलं त्यक्त्वा शान्तिमाप्नोति नैष्ठिकीम् ।
अयुक्तः कामकारेण फले सक्तो निबद्ध्यते ।।१२।।

12. **By abandoning attachment to the fruits of works the soul in union with Brahman attains to peace of rapt foundation in Brahman, but the soul not in union is attached to the fruit and bound by the action of desire.**

सर्वकर्माणि मनसा सन्न्यस्यास्ते सुखं वशी ।
नवद्वारे पुरे देही नैव कुर्वन्न कारयन् ।।१३।।

13. The foundation, the purity, the peace once attained, **the embodied soul perfectly controlling its nature, having renounced all its actions by the mind, inwardly, not outwardly, sits at ease in its nine-gated city neither doing nor causing to be done.**

न कर्तृत्वं न कर्माणि लोकस्य सृजति प्रभुः ।
न कर्मफलसंयोगं स्वभावस्तु प्रवर्तते ।।१४।।

14. For this soul is the one impersonal Soul in all, the all-pervading Lord, *prabhu, vibhu,* who, as the impersonal, neither creates the works of the world, nor the mind's idea of being the doer, *na kartṛitvaṁ na karmāṇi lokasya sṛijati prabhuḥ,* nor the coupling of works to their fruits, *na karma-phala-saṁyogam,* the chain of cause and effect. **All that is worked out by the Nature in the man, *svabhāvas-tu pravartate, svabhāva*,** his principle of self-becoming, as the word literally means. Nature here is Kshara, a constant movement and mutation in Time, a constant becoming. But this Nature is simply the executive power of the Soul itself; for only by what he is, can she become, only according to the possibilities of his becoming, can she act; she works out the becoming of his being. Her Karma is determined by Swabhava, the own-nature, the law of self-becoming of the soul, even though, because it is the agent and executive of the becoming, the action rather seems often to determine the nature. According to what we are, we act, and by our action we develop, we work out what we are. Nature is the action, the mutation, the becoming, and it is the Power that executes all these; but the Soul is the conscious Being from which that Power proceeds, from whose luminous stuff of consciousness she has drawn the variable will that changes and expresses its changes in her actions. (*see also VIII-3/4*)

There is a Consciousness — or a Conscient — behind, that is the lord, witness, knower, enjoyer, upholder and source of sanction for her works; this consciousness is Soul or Purusha. Prakriti shapes the action in us; Purusha in her or behind her witnesses, assents, bears and upholds it. Prakriti forms the thought in our minds; Purusha in her or behind her knows the thought and the truth in it. Prakriti determines the result of the action; Purusha in her or behind her enjoys or suffers the consequence. Prakriti forms mind and body, labours over them, develops them; Purusha upholds the formation and evolution and sanctions each step of her works. Prakriti applies the Will-force which works in things and men; Purusha sets that Will-force to work by his vision of that which should be done. This Purusha or supporting Consciousness is therefore the cause, recipient and support of all Nature's works, but he is not himself the doer. Prakriti, Nature-Force, in front and Shakti, Conscious-Force, Soul-Force behind her, — for these two are the inner and outer faces of the universal Mother, — account for all that is done in the universe. The universal Mother, Prakriti-Shakti, is the one and only worker.

नादत्ते कस्यचित्पापं न चैव सुकृतं विभुः ।
अज्ञानेनावृतं ज्ञानं तेन मुह्यन्ति जन्तवः ।।१५।।

15. The all-pervading Impersonal accepts neither the sin nor the virtue of any: these are things created by the ignorance in the creature, by his egoism of the doer, by his ignorance of his highest self, by his involution in the operation of Nature; **because knowledge is veiled by Ignorance, mortal men are deluded.**

ज्ञानेन तु तदज्ञानं येषां नाशितमात्मनः ।
तेषामादित्यवज्ज्ञानं प्रकाशयति तत्परम् ।।१६।।

16. When the self-knowledge within him is released from this dark envelope, that knowledge lights up like a sun the real self within him; he knows himself then to be the soul supreme above the instruments of Nature. Pure, infinite, inviolable, immutable, he is no longer affected; no longer does he imagine himself to be modified by her workings. By complete identification with the Impersonal **he can, too, release himself from the necessity of returning by birth into her movement** (*sl. 17*). This knowledge of which the Gita speaks, is not an intellectual activity of the mind; it is a luminous growth into the highest state of being by the outshining of the light of the divine sun of Truth, "That Truth, the Sun lying concealed in the darkness" of our ignorance of which the Rig-Veda speaks, *tat satyaṁ sūryaṁ tamasi kṣiyantam*. The immutable Brahman is there in the spirit's skies above this troubled lower nature of the dualities, untouched either by its virtue or by its sin, accepting neither our sense of sin nor our self-righteousness, untouched by its joy and its sorrow, indifferent to our joy in success and our grief in failure, master of all, supreme, all-pervading, *prabhu vibhu*, calm, strong, pure, equal in all things, the source of Nature, not the direct doer of our works, but the witness of Nature and her works, not imposing on us either the illusion of being the doer, for that illusion is the result of the ignorance of this lower Nature. But this freedom, mastery, purity we cannot see; we are bewildered by the natural ignorance which hides from us the eternal self-knowledge of the Brahman secret within our being. But knowledge comes to its persistent seeker and removes the natural self-ignorance; **it shines out like a long-hidden sun and lights up to our vision that self-being supreme beyond the dualities of this lower existence, *ādityavat prakāśayati tat param*.**

तद्बुद्धयस्तदात्मानस्तन्निष्ठास्तत्परायणाः ।
गच्छन्त्यपुनरावृत्तिं ज्ञाननिर्धूतकल्मषाः ।।१७।।

17. By a long whole-hearted endeavour, by directing our whole conscious being to That, by making That our whole aim, *tan-niṣṭhās tat-*

***parāyaṇāḥ*, by turning It into the whole object of our discerning mind and so seeing It not only in ourselves but everywhere, we become one thought and self with That, *tad-buddhayas tad-ātmānaḥ*, we are washed clean of all the darkness and suffering of the lower man by the waters of knowledge,[1] *jñāna-nirdhūta-kalmaṣāḥ*.**

विद्याविनयसम्पन्ने ब्राह्मणे गवि हस्तिनि ।
शुनि चैव श्वपाके च पण्डिताः समदर्शिनः ॥१८॥

18. In all he [the liberated soul] sees two things, the Divine inhabiting every being equally, the varying manifestation unequal only in its temporary circumstances. **In the animal and man, in the dog, the unclean outcaste and the learned and virtuous Brahmin,** in the saint and the sinner, in the indifferent and the friendly and the hostile, in those who love him and benefit and those who hate him and afflict, **he sees himself, he sees God and has at heart for all the same equal kindliness, the same divine affection.** Circumstances may determine the outward clasp or the outward conflict, **but can never affect his equal eye, his open heart,** his inner embrace of all. And in all his actions there will be the same principle of soul, a perfect equality, and the same principle of work, the will of the Divine in him active for the need of the race in its gradually developing advance towards the Godhead.

इहैव तैर्जितः सर्गो येषां साम्ये स्थितं मनः ।
निर्दोषं हि समं ब्रह्म तस्माद् ब्रह्मणि ते स्थिताः ॥१९॥

19. The result is a perfect equality to all things and all persons; and then only can we repose our works completely in the Brahman. **For the Brahman is equal, *samaṁ brahma*, and it is only when we have [here in the body] this perfect equality, *sāmye sthitaṁ manaḥ*, seeing with an equal eye the learned and cultured Brahmin, the cow, the elephant, the dog, the outcaste** and knowing all as one Brahman, that we can, living in that oneness, see like the Brahman our works proceeding from the nature freely without any fear of attachment, sin or bondage. Sin and stain then cannot be; **for we have overcome, [conquered] that creation** full of desire and its works and reactions which belongs to the ignorance, ***ihaiva tair jitaḥ sargaḥ*,** and living in the supreme and divine Nature there is no longer fault or defect in our works;

1. The Rig-Veda so speaks of the streams of the Truth, the waters that have perfect knowledge, the waters that are full of the divine sunlight, *ṛitasya dhārāḥ, āpo vicetasaḥ, svarvatīr apaḥ*. What are here metaphors, are there concrete symbols.

for these are created by the inequalities of the ignorance. **The equal Brahman is faultless, *nirdoṣaṁ hi samaṁ brahma,*** beyond the confusion of good and evil, **and living in the Brahman, *brahmaṇi sthitāḥ*,** we too rise beyond good and evil.

When we look upon the world with dispassionate and curious eyes that search only for the Truth, our first result is the perception of a boundless energy of infinite existence, infinite movement, infinite activity pouring itself out in limitless Space, in eternal Time; we perceive that it exists for itself, not for us. This boundless Movement does not regard us as unimportant to it. This mighty Energy is an equal and impartial mother, *samam brahma*, and its intensity and force of movement is the same in the formation and upholding of a system of suns and the organisation of the life of an ant-hill. This Brahman dwells equally in all existences. Equally partaken of by all in its being, we are tempted to say, equally distributed to all in its energy. But Brahman dwells in all, indivisible, yet as if divided and distributed. The consciousness of this infinite Energy is other than our mental consciousness, it is indivisible and gives, not an equal part of itself, but its whole self at one and the same time to the solar system and to the ant-hill. To Brahman there are no whole and parts, but each thing is all itself and benefits by the whole of Brahman. Quality and quantity differ, the self is equal. The form and manner and result of the force of action vary infinitely, but the eternal, primal, infinite energy is the same in all.

न प्रहृष्येत्प्रियं प्राप्य नोद्विजेत्प्राप्य चाप्रियम् ।
स्थिरबुद्धिरसम्मूढो ब्रह्मविद् ब्रह्मणि स्थितः ।।२०।।

20. **It [the divine soul] does not rejoice in the touches of the pleasant or feel anguish in the touches of the unpleasant.** Neither the wounds of things, nor the wounds of friends, nor the wounds of enemies can disturb **the firmness of its outgazing mind or bewilder its receiving heart;** this soul is in its nature, as the Upanishad puts it, *avraṇam*, without wound or scar. In all things it has the same imperishable Ananda. **The higher knowledge we then get is that which is to the knower of Brahman his constant vision of things when he lives uninterruptedly in the Brahman, *brahmavid brahmaṇi sthitaḥ*.** That is not a vision or knowledge or consciousness of Brahman to the exclusion of all else, but a seeing of all in Brahman and as the Self. For, it is said, **the knowledge by which we rise beyond all relapse back into the bewilderment of our mental nature, is that by which thou shalt see all existences without exception in the Self, then in Me.**

II — NIRVANA AND WORKS IN THE WORLD (1)

The union of the soul with the Purushottama by a Yoga of the whole being is the complete teaching of the Gita and not only the union with the immutable Self as in the narrower doctrine which follows the exclusive way of knowledge. That is why the Gita subsequently, after it has effected the reconciliation of knowledge and works, is able to develop the idea of love and devotion, unified with both works and knowledge, as the highest height of the way to the supreme secret. For if the union with the immutable Self were the sole secret or the highest secret, that would not at all be possible; for then at a given point our inner basis for love and devotion, no less than our inner foundation of works, would crumble away and collapse. Union by Yoga with the Purushottama means the knowledge and enjoyment of our oneness with him in our self-existent being and of a certain differentiation in our active being. It is the vision of the Divine in the world harmonised with a realisation of the Divine in the self which makes action and devotion possible to the liberated man, and not only possible but inevitable in the perfect mode of his being.

But the direct way to union lies through the firm realisation of the immutable Self, and it is the Gita's insistence on this as a first necessity, after which alone works and devotion can acquire their whole divine meaning, that makes it possible for us to mistake its drift. It is in the close of the fifth and throughout the sixth chapter that this insistence is strongest and most comprehensive. There we get the description of a Yoga which would seem at first sight to be incompatible with works and we get the repeated use of the word Nirvana to describe the status to which the Yogin arrives.

The mark of this status is the supreme peace of a calm self-extinction, *śāntiṁ nirvāṇa-paramām*, and, as if to make it quite clear that it is not the Buddhist's Nirvana in a blissful negation of being, but the Vedantic loss of a partial in a perfect being that it intends, the Gita uses always the phrase *brahma-nirvāṇa*, extinction in the Brahman; and the Brahman here certainly seems to mean the Immutable, to denote primarily at least the inner timeless Self withdrawn from active participation even though immanent in the externality of Nature. We are accustomed indeed to regard Nirvana and any kind of existence and action in the world as incompatible. If we look closely at the Gita, we shall see that it [the incompatibility] does not form part of this supreme Vedantic teaching.

The Gita after speaking of the perfect equality of the Brahman-knower who has risen into the Brahman-consciousness, *brahmavid brahmaṇi sthitaḥ*, develops in nine verses that follow its idea of Brahma-Yoga and of Nirvana in the Brahman.

बाह्यस्पर्शेष्वसक्तात्मा विन्दत्यात्मनि यत्सुखम् ।
स ब्रह्मयोगयुक्तात्मा सुखमक्षयमश्नुते ।।२१।।

21. **When the soul is no longer attached to the touches of outward things, *bāhya-sparśeṣu-asakta-ātmā*, then one finds the happiness that exists in the Self, *ātmani yat sukham*; such a one enjoys an imperishable happiness, *sukham akṣayam aśnute*, because his self is in Yoga, *yukta*, by Yoga with the Brahman, *brahma-yoga-yukta-ātmā*.**

The non-attachment is essential in order to be free from the attacks of desire and wrath and passion, a freedom without which true happiness is not possible. It [the divine soul] is without attachment to [the] outward touches [of things], but finds everywhere the same joy that it finds in itself, because its self is theirs, has become one self with the self of all beings, because it is united with the one and equal Brahman in them through all their differences, *brahma-yoga-yuktātmā, sarva-bhūtātma-bhūtātmā*.

ये हि संस्पर्शजा भोगा दुःखयोनय एव ते ।
आद्यन्तवन्तः कौन्तेय न तेषु रमते बुधः ।।२२।।

22. **The enjoyments born of the touches of things are causes of sorrow, they have a beginning and an end; therefore the sage, the man of awakened understanding, *budhaḥ*, does not place his delight in these.**

शक्नोतीहैव यः सोढुं प्राक्शरीरविमोक्षणात् ।
कामक्रोधोद्भवं वेगं स युक्तः स सुखी नरः ।।२३।।

23. To be freed from wrath and passion and fear and attraction is repeatedly stressed as a necessary condition of the liberated status, and for this we must learn to bear their shocks, which cannot be done without exposing ourselves to their causes. **He who can bear here in the body the velocity of wrath and desire, is the Yogin, the happy man.** That happiness and that equality are to be gained entirely by man in the body: he is not to suffer any least remnant of the subjection to the troubled lower nature to remain in the idea that the perfect release will come by a putting off of the body; a perfect spiritual freedom is to be won here upon earth, *ihaiva*, and possessed and enjoyed in the human life, *prāk śarīra-vimokṣaṇāt*.

योऽन्तःसुखोऽन्तरारामस्तथान्तर्ज्योतिरेव यः ।
स योगी ब्रह्मनिर्वाणं ब्रह्मभूतोऽधिगच्छति ।।२४।।

24. He who has the inner happiness and the inner ease and repose and the inner light, that Yogin becomes the Brahman and reaches self-extinction in the Brahman, *brahma-nirvāṇam*. Here, very clearly, Nirvana means the extinction of the ego in the higher spiritual, inner Self, that which is for ever timeless, spaceless, not bound by the chain of cause and effect and the changes of the world-mutation, self-blissful, self-illumined and for ever at peace. The Yogin ceases to be the ego, the little person limited by the mind and the body; he becomes the Brahman; he is unified in consciousness with the immutable divinity of the eternal Self which is immanent in his natural being. For the delight [of the divine soul], its divine ease, its happiness, its glad light are eternal within, ingrained in itself, *ātma-ratiḥ, antaḥ-sukho'ntar-ārāmas tathā-antar-jyotir eva*. What joy it takes in outward things is not for their sake, not for things which it seeks in them and can miss, but for the self in them, for their expression of the Divine, for that which is eternal in them and which it cannot miss.

लभन्ते ब्रह्मनिर्वाणमृषयः क्षीणकल्मषाः ।
छिन्नद्वैधा यतात्मानः सर्वभूतहिते रताः ।।२५।।

25. But is this a going in into some deep sleep of samadhi away from all world-consciousness, or is it the preparatory movement for a dissolution of the natural being and the individual soul into some absolute Self who is utterly and for ever beyond Nature and her works, *laya*, *mokṣa*? Is that withdrawal necessary before we can enter into Nirvana, or is Nirvana, as the context seems to suggest, a state which can exist simultaneoulsy with world-consciousness and even in its own way include it? Apparently the latter, for in the succeeding verse the Gita goes on to say, **Sages win Nirvana in the Brahman, they in whom the stains of sin are effaced and the knot of doubt is cut asunder, masters of their selves, who are occupied in doing good to all creatures, *sarva-bhūta-hite ratāḥ*.** That would almost seem to mean that to be thus is to be in Nirvana. But the next verse is quite clear and decisive.

कामक्रोधवियुक्तानां यतीनां यतचेतसाम् ।
अभितो ब्रह्मनिर्वाणं वर्तते विदितात्मनाम् ।।२६।।

26. ***Yatis* (those who practise self-mastery by Yoga and austerity) who are delivered from desire and wrath and have gained self-mastery, for them Nirvana in the Brahman exists all about them, encompasses them, they already live in it because they have knowledge of the Self.** That is to say, to have knowledge and possession of the self is to exist in Nirvana. This is

clearly a large extension of the idea of Nirvana. Freedom from all stain of the passions, the self-mastery of the equal mind on which that freedom is founded, equality to all beings, *sarva-bhūteṣu*, and beneficial love for all, final destruction of that doubt and obscurity of the ignorance which keeps us divided from the all-unifying Divine and the knowledge of the One Self within us and in all are evidently the conditions of Nirvana which are laid down in these verses of the Gita, go to constitute it and are its spiritual substance.

Thus Nirvana is clearly compatible with world-consciousness and with action in the world. This action in the world is not inconsistent with living in Brahman, it is rather its inevitable condition and outward result because the Brahman in whom we find Nirvana, the spiritual consciousness in which we lose the separative ego-consciousness, is not only within us but within all these existences, exists not only above and apart from all these universal happenings, but pervades them, contains them and is extended in them. Therefore by Nirvana in the Brahman must be meant a destruction or extinction of the limited separative consciousness, falsifying and dividing, which is brought into being on the surface of existence by the lower Maya of the three gunas, and entry into Nirvana is a passage into this other true unifying consciousness which is the heart of existence and its continent and its whole containing and supporting, its whole original and eternal and final truth. Nirvana when we gain it, enter into it, is not only within us, but all around, *abhito vartate*, because this is not only the Brahman-consciousness which lives secret within us, but the Brahman-consciousness in which we live. It is the Self which we are within, the supreme Self of our individual being but also the Self which we are without, the supreme Self of the universe, the self of all existences. By living in that self we live in all, and no longer in our egoistic being alone; by oneness with that self a steadfast oneness with all in the universe becomes the very nature of our being and the root status of our active consciousness and root motive of all our action.

स्पर्शान्कृत्वा बहिर्बाह्यांश्चक्षुश्चैवान्तरे भ्रुवोः ।
प्राणापानौ समौ कृत्वा नासाभ्यन्तरचारिणौ ।।२७।।
यतेन्द्रियमनोबुद्धिर्मुनिर्मोक्षपरायणः ।
विगतेच्छाभयक्रोधो यः सदा मुक्त एव सः ।।२८।।

27-28. But again we get immediately afterwards two verses which might seem to lead away from this conclusion. **Having put outside of himself all outward touches, *sparśān bāhyān*, and concentrated the vision between the eyebrows and made equal the *prāṇa* and the *apāna* moving within the nostrils,**

having controlled the senses, the mind and the understanding, the sage devoted to liberation, from whom desire and wrath and fear have passed away is ever free. Here we have a process of Yoga that brings in an element which seems quite other than the Yoga of works and other even than the pure Yoga of knowledge by discrimination and contemplation. Are we to suppose that the Gita gives this process as the last movement of a release by dissolution or only as a special means and a strong aid to overcome the outward-going mind? Is this the finale, the climax, the last word? We shall find reason to regard it as both a special means, an aid, and at least one gate of a final departure, not by dissolution, but by an uplifting to the supracosmic existence. For even here in this passage this is not the last word; the last word, the finale, the climax comes in a verse that follows and is the last couplet of the chapter.

भोक्तारं यज्ञतपसां सर्वलोकमहेश्वरम् ।
सुहृदं सर्वभूतानां ज्ञात्वा मां शान्तिमृच्छति ।।२९।।

29. **When a man has known Me as the Enjoyer of sacrifice and tapasya (of all askesis and energisms), *bhoktāraṁ yajña-tapasāṁ*, the mighty lord of all the worlds, *sarva-loka-maheśvaraṁ*, the friend of all creatures, *suhṛidaṁ sarva-bhūtānāṁ*, he comes by the peace, *jñātvā māṁ śāntim ṛicchati*.** The power of the Karmayoga comes in again; the knowledge of the active Brahman, the cosmic supersoul, is insisted on among the conditions of the peace of Nirvana.

We get back to the great idea of the Gita, the idea of the Purushottama; it is always that which Krishna means by his "I" and "Me", the Divine who is there as the one self in our timeless immutable being, who is present too in the world, in all existences, in all activities, the master of the silence and the peace, the master of the power and the action, who is here incarnate as the divine charioteer of the stupendous conflict, the Transcendent, the Self, the All, the master of every individual being. He is the enjoyer of all sacrifice and of all tapasya, therefore shall the seeker of liberation do works as a sacrifice and as a tapasya; he is the lord of all the worlds, manifested in Nature and in these beings, therefore shall the liberated man still do works for the right government and leading on the peoples in these worlds, *lokasaṅgraha*; he is the friend of all existences, therefore is the sage who has found Nirvana within him and all around, still and always occupied with the good of all creatures. Therefore too, even when he has found oneness with the Divine in his timeless and immutable self, is he still capable, since he embraces the relations also of the play of Nature, of divine love for man and of love for the Divine, of bhakti.

Chapter VI

Nirvana and Works in the World (2)

The sixth chapter is a large comment on and a full development of the idea of these closing verses of the fifth, — that shows the importance which the Gita attaches to them. We shall therefore run as briefly as possible through the substance of this sixth chapter.

श्रीभगवानुवाच
अनाश्रितः कर्मफलं कार्यं कर्म करोति यः ।
स संन्यासी च योगी च न निरग्निर्न चाक्रियः ।।१।।

1. *Krishna* — First the Teacher emphasises — and this is very significant — his often repeated asseveration about the real essence of Sannyasa, that it is an inward, not an outward renunciation. **Whoever does the work to be done, *kāryam karma*, without resort to its fruits, he is the Sannyasin and the Yogin, not the man who lights not the sacrificial fire and does not the works.**

यं संन्यासमिति प्राहुर्योगं तं विद्धि पाण्डव ।
न ह्यसंन्यस्तसङ्कल्पो योगी भवति कश्चन ।।२।।

2. **What they have called renunciation (Sannyasa), know to be in truth Yoga; for none becomes a Yogin who has not renounced the desire-will in the mind, *saṅkalpa*.**

आरुरुक्षोर्मुनेर्योगं कर्म कारणमुच्यते ।
योगारूढस्य तस्यैव शमः कारणमुच्यते ।।३।।

3. Works are to be done, but with what purpose and in what order? **They are first to be done while ascending the hill of Yoga, for then works are the cause, *kāraṇam*.** The cause of what? The cause of self-perfection, of liberation, of nirvana in the Brahman; for by doing works with a steady

practice of the inner renunciation this perfection, this liberation, this conquest of the desire-mind and the ego-self and the lower nature are easily accomplished. **But when one has got to the top?** Then works are no longer the cause; **the calm of self-mastery and self-possession, *śamaḥ*, gained by works becomes the cause.** Again, the cause of what? Of fixity in the Self, in the Brahman-consciousness and of the perfect equality in which the divine works of the liberated man are done.

यदा हि नेन्द्रियार्थेषु न कर्मस्वनुषज्जते ।
सर्वसङ्कल्पसंन्यासी योगारूढस्तदोच्यते ॥४॥

4. For when one does not get attached to the objects of sense or to works and has renounced all will of desire in the mind, then is he said to have ascended to the top of Yoga.

उद्धरेदात्मनात्मानं नात्मानमवसादयेत् ।
आत्मैव ह्यात्मनो बन्धुरात्मैव रिपुरात्मनः ॥५॥

5. By the self thou shouldst deliver the self, thou shouldst not depress and cast down the self whether by self-indulgence or suppression; **for the self is the friend of the self and the self is the enemy.**

बन्धुरात्मात्मनस्तस्य येनात्मैवात्मना जितः ।
अनात्मनस्तु शत्रुत्वे वर्तेतात्मैव शत्रुवत् ॥६॥

6. To the man is his self a friend in whom the (lower) self has been conquered by the (higher) self, but to him who is not in possession of his (higher) self, the (lower) self is as if an enemy and it acts as an enemy.

जितात्मनः प्रशान्तस्य परमात्मा समाहितः ।
शीतोष्णसुखदुःखेषु तथा मानापमानयोः ॥७॥

7. When one has conquered one's self and attained to the calm of a perfect self-mastery and self-possession, then is the supreme self in a man founded and poised even in his outwardly conscious human being, *samāhita*. In other words, to master the lower self by the higher, the natural self by the spiritual is the way of man's perfection and liberation. He has conquered his lower self, reached the perfect calm in which his highest self is manifest to him, that highest self always concentrated in its own being, *samāhita*, in Samadhi, not only in the trance of the inward-drawn consciousness, but always, in the waking state of the mind as well, in exposure to the causes of desire and of the disturbance of calm, **to grief and pleasure, heat and cold, honour and disgrace,** all the dualities.

ज्ञानविज्ञानतृप्तात्मा कूटस्थो विजितेन्द्रियः ।
युक्त इत्युच्यते योगी समलोष्टाश्मकाञ्चनः ।।८।।

8. **He becomes satisfied with knowledge, master of his senses, a Yogin** by sattwic equality, — for equality is Yoga, *samatvaṁ yoga ucyate*, — **regarding alike clod and stone and gold, tranquil and self-poised.** This higher self is the Akshara, *kūṭastha*, which stands above the changes and the perturbations of the natural being; **and the Yogin is said to be in Yoga with it** when he also is like it, *kūṭastha*, when he is superior to all appearances and mutations, **when he is satisfied with self-knowledge, when he is equal-minded to all things and happenings and persons.**

सुहृन्मित्रार्युदासीनमध्यस्थद्वेष्यबन्धुषु ।
साधुष्वपि च पापेषु समबुद्धिर्विशिष्यते ।।९।।

9. **He is equal in soul to friend and enemy and to neutral and indifferent,** because he sees that these are transitory relations born of the changing conditions of life. Even by the pretensions of learning and purity and virtue and the claims to superiority which men base upon these things, he is not led away. **He is equal-souled to all men, to the sinner and the saint, to the virtuous, learned and cultured Brahmin and the fallen outcaste.** All these are the Gita's descriptions of the sattwic equality, and they sum up well enough what is familiar to the world as the calm philosophic equality of the sage. Where then is the difference between this and the larger equality taught by the Gita? It lies in the difference between the intellectual and philosophic discernment and the spiritual, the Vedantic knowledge of unity on which the Gita founds its teaching.

योगी युञ्जीत सततमात्मानं रहसि स्थितः ।
एकाकी यतचित्तात्मा निराशीरपरिग्रहः ।।१०।।

10. The Gita proceeds to give us in addition to its general method of knowledge and works a special process of Rajayogic meditation also, a

powerful method of practice, *abhyāsa*, a strong way to the complete control of the mind and all its workings. In this process **the Yogin is directed to practise continually union with the Self so that that may become his normal consciousness. He is to sit apart and alone, with all desire and idea of possession banished from his mind, self-controlled in his whole being and consciousness.**

शुचौ देशे प्रतिष्ठाप्य स्थिरमासनमात्मनः ।
नात्युच्छ्रितं नातिनीचं चैलाजिनकुशोत्तरम् ।।११।।
तत्रैकाग्रं मनः कृत्वा यतचित्तेन्द्रियक्रियः ।
उपविश्यासने युञ्ज्याद्योगमात्मविशुद्धये ।।१२।।

11-12. He should set in a pure spot his firm seat, neither too high, nor yet too low, covered with a cloth, with a deer-skin, with sacred grass, and there seated with a concentrated mind and with the workings of the mental consciousness and the senses under control he should practise Yoga for self-purification, *ātma-viśuddhaye.*

समं कायशिरोग्रीवं धारयन्नचलं स्थिरः ।
संप्रेक्ष्य नासिकाग्रं स्वं दिशश्चानवलोकयन् ।।१३।।
प्रशान्तात्मा विगतभीर्ब्रह्मचारिव्रते स्थितः ।
मनः संयम्य मच्चित्तो युक्त आसीत मत्परः ।।१४।।

13-14. The posture he takes must be the motionless erect posture proper to the practice of Rajayoga; the vision should be drawn in and fixed between the eyebrows, not regarding the regions. The mind is to be kept calm and free from fear and the vow of Brahmacharya observed; the whole controlled mentality must be devoted and turned to the Divine (to Me), *manaḥ saṁyamya maccittaḥ*, so that the lower action of the consciousness shall be merged in the higher peace. For the object to be attained is the still peace of Nirvana. **He must sit firm in Yoga. wholly given up to Me, *yukta āsīta matparaḥ*** (*see also II-61*).

युञ्जन्नेवं सदात्मानं योगी नियतमानसः ।
शान्तिं निर्वाणपरमां मत्संस्थामधिगच्छति ।।१५।।

15. Thus always putting himself in Yoga by control of his mind the Yogin attains to the supreme peace of Nirvana which has its foundation in Me, *śāntiṁ nirvāṇa-paramāṁ mat-saṁsthām-adhigacchati.*

नात्यश्नतस्तु योगोऽस्ति न चैकान्तमनश्नतः ।
न चाति स्वप्नशीलस्य जाग्रतो नैव चार्जुन ।।१६।।

16. And yet the result is not, while one yet lives, a Nirvana which puts away every possibility of action in the world, every relation with beings in the world. It would seem at first that it ought to be so. No doubt, the Yogin for a time still remains in the body, but the cave, the forest, the mountain-top seem now the fittest, the only possible scene of his continued living and constant trance of Samadhi his sole joy and occupation. But, first, while this solitary Yoga is being pursued, the renunciation of all other action is not recommended by the Gita. **This Yoga, it says, is not for the man who gives up sleep and food and play and action, even as it is not for those who indulge too much in these things of the life and the body.**

युक्ताहारविहारस्य युक्तचेष्टस्य कर्मसु ।
युक्तस्वप्नावबोधस्य योगो भवति दुःखहा ।।१७।।

17. **But the sleep and waking, the food, the play, the putting forth of effort in works should all be *yukta*.** In all states, in waking and in sleeping, in food and play and action, the Yogin will then be in Yoga with the Divine, and all will be done by him in the consciousness of the Divine as the self and as the All and as that which supports and contains his own life and his action. **Yoga slayeth his sorrows.**

यदा विनियतं चित्तमात्मन्येवावतिष्ठते ।
निःस्पृहः सर्वकामेभ्यो युक्त इत्युच्यते तदा ।।१८।।

18. **This peace of Nirvana is reached [and the Yogin is said to be in Yoga] when all the mental consciousness is perfectly controlled and liberated from desire and remains still in the Self,**

यथा दीपो निवातस्थो नेङ्गते सोपमा स्मृता ।
योगिनो यतचित्तस्य युञ्जतो योगमात्मनः ।।१९।।

19. **when, motionless like the light of a lamp in a windless place, it [the consciousness of the Yogin who practises union with the Self] ceases from its restless action, shut in from its outward motion,**

यत्रोपरमते चित्तं निरुद्धं योगसेवया ।
यत्र चैवात्मनात्मानं पश्यन्नात्मनि तुष्यति ।।२०।।

20. and by the silence and stillness of the mind, [by the practice of Yoga] the Self is seen within, not disfigured as in the mind, but in the Self, seen, not as it is mistranslated falsely or partially by the mind and represented to us through the ego, but **self-perceived by the Self, *svaprakāśa*. Then the soul is satisfied, *ātmanā-ātmānaṁ paśyannātmani tuṣyati*,**

सुखमात्यन्तिकं यत्तद्बुद्धिग्राह्यमतीन्द्रियम् ।
वेत्ति यत्र न चैवायं स्थितश्चलति तत्त्वतः ।।२१।।

21. and knows its own true and exceeding bliss, not that untranquil happiness which is the portion of the mind and the senses, but an inner and serene felicity **in which it is safe from the mind's perturbations and can no longer fall away from the spiritual truth of its being, a truth which is beyond perception by the sense but seizable by the perceptions of the reason, *buddhi-grāhyam atīndriyam*.**

यं लब्ध्वा चापरं लाभं मन्यते नाधिकं ततः ।
यस्मिन्स्थितो न दुःखेन गुरुणापि विचाल्यते।।२२।।
तं विद्याद्दुःखसंयोगवियोगं योगसंज्ञितम् ।
स निश्चयेन योक्तव्यो योगोऽनिर्विण्णचेतसा ।।२३।।

22-23. Not even the fieriest assault of mental grief can disturb it; for mental grief comes to us from outside, is a reaction to external touches, and this is the inner, the self-existent happiness of those who no longer accept the slavery of the unstable mental reactions to external touches. **It is the putting away of the contact with pain, the divorce of the mind's marriage with grief, *duḥkha-saṁyoga-viyogam*.** The **firm winning of this inalienable spiritual bliss is Yoga, it is the divine union; it is the greatest of all gains and the treasure beside which all others lose their value. Therefore is this Yoga to be resolutely practised without yielding to any discouragement by difficulty or failure,** *anirviṇṇa-cetasā*, until the release, until the bliss of Nirvana is secured as an eternal possession.

Practice unfalteringly with a heart free from despondency, the Yoga; for even though in the earlier stage of the path we drink deep of the bitter poison of internal discord and suffering, the last taste of this cup is the sweetness of the nectar of immortality and the honey-wine of an eternal Ananda.

सङ्कल्पप्रभवान्कामांस्त्यक्त्वा सर्वानशेषतः ।
मनसैवेन्द्रियग्रामं विनियम्य समन्ततः ।।२४।।

24. The main stress here has fallen on the stilling of the emotive mind, the mind of desire and the senses which are the recipients of outward touches and reply to them with our customary emotional reactions; but even the mental thought has to be stilled in the silence of the self-existent being. **First, all the desires born of the desire-will have to be wholly abandoned without any exception or residue and the senses have to be held in by the mind so that they shall not run out to all sides** after their usual disorderly and restless habit.

शनैः शनैरुपरमेद् बुद्ध्या धृतिगृहीतया ।
आत्मसंस्थं मनः कृत्वा न किञ्चिदपि चिन्तयेत् ।।२५।।

25. But next the mind itself has to be seized by the buddhi and drawn inward. **One should slowly cease from mental action by a buddhi held in the grasp of fixity and having fixed the mind in the higher self one should not think of anything at all.**

यतो यतो निश्चरति मनश्चञ्चलमस्थिरम् ।
ततस्ततो नियम्यैतदात्मन्येव वशं नयेत् ।।२६।।

26. **Whenever the restless and unquiet mind goes forth, it should be controlled and brought into subjection in the Self.**

प्रशान्तमनसं ह्येनं योगिनं सुखमुत्तमम् ।
उपैति शान्तरजसं ब्रह्मभूतमकल्मषम् ।।२७।।

27. **When the mind is thoroughly quieted, then there comes upon the Yogin the highest, stainless, passionless bliss of the soul that has become the Brahman.**

युञ्जन्नेवं सदात्मानं योगी विगतकल्मषः ।
सुखेन ब्रह्मसंस्पर्शमत्यन्तं सुखमश्नुते ।।२८।।

28. **Thus freed from stain of passion and putting himself constantly into Yoga, the Yogin easily and happily enjoys the touch of the Brahman which is an exceeding bliss.** Thus comes an all-pervading power of wide tranquillity

and peace, a bliss of release from the siege of our imposed fantastic self-torturing nature, the deep undisturbed exceeding happiness of the touch of the eternal and infinite replacing by its permanence the strife and turmoil of impermanent things, ***sukhena brahma-saṁsparśam atyantaṁ sukham aśnute.*** The soul is fixed in the delight of the self, *ātma-ratiḥ*, in the single and infinite Ananda of the spirit and hunts no more after outward touches and their griefs and pleasures.

सर्वभूतस्थमात्मानं सर्वभूतानि चात्मनि ।
ईक्षते योगयुक्तात्मा सर्वत्र समदर्शनः ।।२९।।

29. **The man whose self is in Yoga, sees the self in all beings and all beings in the self, he sees all with an equal vision (or, he is equal-visioned everywhere).** All that he sees is to him the Self, all is his self, all is the Divine. But is there no danger, if he dwells at all in the mutability of the Kshara, of his losing all the results of this difficult Yoga, losing the Self and falling back into the mind, of the Divine losing him and the world getting him, of his losing the Divine and getting back in its place the ego and the lower nature? No, says the Gita.

यो मां पश्यति सर्वत्र सर्वं च मयि पश्यति ।
तस्याहं न प्रणश्यामि स च मे न प्रणश्यति ।।३०।।

30. **He who sees Me everywhere and sees all in Me, to him I do not get lost, nor does he get lost to Me.** For this peace of Nirvana, though it is gained through the Akshara, is founded upon the being of the Purushottama, *mat-saṁsthām*, and that is extended, the Divine, the Brahman is extended too in the world of beings and, though transcendent of it, not imprisoned in its own transcendence. One has to see all things as He and live and act wholly in that vision; that is the perfect fruit of the Yoga.

सर्वभूतस्थितं यो मां भजत्येकत्वमास्थितः ।
सर्वथा वर्तमानोऽपि स योगी मयि वर्तते ।।३१।।

31. But why act? Is it not safer to sit in one's solitude looking out upon the world, if you will, seeing it in Brahman, in the Divine, but not taking part in it, not moving in it, not living in it, not acting in it, living rather ordinarily in the inner Samadhi? Should not that be the law, the rule, the dharma of this highest spiritual condition? No, again; for the liberated Yogin

there is no other law, rule, dharma than simply this, to live in the Divine and love the Divine and be one with all beings; his freedom is an absolute and not a contingent freedom, self-existent and not dependent any longer on any rule of conduct, law of life or limitation of any kind. He has no longer any need of a process of Yoga, because he is now perpetually in Yoga.

The Yogin who has taken his stand upon oneness and loves Me in all beings, however and in all ways he lives and acts, lives and acts in Me. The love of the world spiritualised, changed from a sense-experience to a soul-experience, is founded on the love of God and in that love there is no peril and no shortcoming. Fear and disgust of the world may often be necessary for the recoil from the lower nature, for it is really the fear and disgust of our own ego which reflects itself in the world. But to see God in the world is to fear nothing, it is to embrace all in the being of God; to see all as the Divine is to hate and loathe nothing, but love God in the world and the world in God. (*see also IX-9/10*)

The Gita brings in here as always bhakti as the climax of the Yoga, ***sarva-bhūta-sthitaṁ yo māṁ bhajati-ekatvam āsthitaḥ***; that may almost be said to sum up the whole final result of the Gita's teaching — **whoever loves God in all and his soul is founded upon the divine oneness, however he lives and acts, lives and acts in God. —** Whatever he does and however he lives, the free soul lives in the Divine; he is the privileged child of the mansion, *bālavat*, who cannot err or fall because all he is and does is full of the Perfect, the All-blissful, the All-loving, the All-beautiful. The kingdom which he enjoys, *rājyaṁ samṛiddham*, is a sweet and happy dominion of which it may be said, in the pregnant phrase of the Greek thinker, "The kingdom is of the child."

The spiritual seeing of God and world is not ideative only, not even mainly or primarily ideative. It is direct experience and as real, vivid, near, constant, effective, intimate as to the mind its sensuous seeing and feeling of images, objects and persons. It is only the physical mind that thinks of God and spirit as an abstract conception which it cannot visualise or represent to itself except by words and names and symbolic images and fictions. Spirit sees spirit, the divinised consciousness sees God as directly and more directly, as intimately and more intimately than bodily consciousness sees matter. It sees, feels, thinks, senses the Divine. For to the spiritual consciousness all manifest existence appears as a world of spirit and not a world of matter, not a world of life, not a world even of mind; these other things are to its view only God-thought, God-force, God-form. That is what the Gita means by **living and acting in Vasudeva, *sarvathā vartamāno'pi sa yogī mayi vartate.***

आत्मौपम्येन सर्वत्र समं पश्यति योऽर्जुन ।
सुखं वा यदि वा दुःखं स योगी परमो मतः ।।३२।।

32. But at least the things of the lower nature will be shunned and feared, the things which the Yogin has taken so much trouble to surmount? Not this either; all is embraced in the equality of the self-vision. **He, O Arjuna, who sees with equality everything in the image of the Self, whether it be grief or it be happiness, him I hold to be the supreme Yogin.** Seeing in others the play of the dualities which he himself has left and surmounted, he shall still see all as himself, his self in all, God in all and, not disturbed or bewildered by the appearances of these things, moved only by them to help and heal, to occupy himself with the good of all beings, to lead men to the spiritual bliss, to work for the progress of the world Godwards, he shall live the divine life, so long as days upon earth are his portion.

That is the old Vedantic knowledge of the Upanishads which the Gita holds up constantly before us; but it is its superiority to other later formulations of it that it turns persistently this knowledge into a great practical philosophy of divine living. Always it insists on the relation between this knowledge of oneness and Karmayoga, and therefore on the knowledge of oneness as the basis of a liberated action in the world. Whenever it speaks of knowledge, it turns at once to speak of equality which is its result; whenever it speaks of equality, it turns to speak too of the knowledge which is its basis. The equality it enjoins does not begin and end in a static condition of the soul useful only for self-liberation; it is always a basis of works. The peace of the Brahman in the liberated soul is the foundation; the large, free, equal, world-wide action of the Lord in the liberated nature radiates the power which proceeds from that peace; these two made one synthesise divine works and God-knowledge.

अर्जुन उवाच
योऽयं योगस्त्वया प्रोक्तः साम्येन मधुसूदन ।
एतस्याहं न पश्यामि चञ्चलत्वात्स्थितिं स्थिराम् ।।३३।।
चञ्चलं हि मनः कृष्ण प्रमाथि बलवद् दृढम् ।
तस्याहं निग्रहं मन्ये वायोरिव सुदुष्करम् ।।३४।।

33-34. *Arjuna* — But this Yoga is after all no easy thing to acquire, as Arjuna indeed suggests, for the restless mind is always liable to be pulled down from these heights by the attacks of outward things and to fall back into the strong control of grief and passion and inequality. **Nay, Madhusudan, for the restlessness of man's mind I can see no sure abiding in this Yoga of one-heartedness of which thou hast spoken. For very restless is the mind, O Krishna, and turbulent and strong and hard, and to rein it in I hold as difficult as to put a bridle upon the wind.**

श्रीभगवानुवाच
असंशयं महाबाहो मनो दुर्निग्रहं चलम् ।
अभ्यासेन तु कौन्तेय वैराग्येण च गृह्यते ॥३५॥
असंयतात्मना योगो दुष्प्राप इति मे मतिः ।
वश्यात्मना तु यतता शक्योऽवाप्तुमुपायतः ॥३६॥

35-36. *Krishna* — **Surely the mind is restless and hard to bridle, but by askesis, *abhyāsa*, O son of Kunti, and by turning away the heart from its affections, *vairāgya*, it can be caught and controlled. Very difficult of attainment is Yoga to the ungoverned spirit, so I hold; but when a man governeth himself and striveth by the right means, Yoga is not impossible to attain.**

अर्जुन उवाच
अयतिः श्रद्धयोपेतो योगाच्चलितमानसः ।
अप्राप्य योगसंसिद्धिं कां गतिं कृष्ण गच्छति ॥३७॥
कच्चिन्नोभयविभ्रष्टश्छिन्नाभ्रमिव नश्यति ।
अप्रतिष्ठो महाबाहो विमूढो ब्रह्मणः पथि ॥३८॥
एतन्मे संशयं कृष्ण छेत्तुमर्हस्यशेषतः ।
त्वदन्यः संशयस्यास्य छेत्ता न ह्युपपद्यते ॥३९॥

37-39. *Arjuna* — When he realises fully the nature of the Yoga which he is bidden to embrace, his pragmatic nature accustomed to act from mental will and preference and desire is appalled by its difficulty and he asks what is the end of the soul which attempts and fails. **When a man hath faith but cannot strive aright and his mind swerveth from Yoga, and he attaineth not to success in Yoga, what is the last state of such a man, O Krishna? Whether it does not lose both this life of human activity and thought and emotion which it has left behind and the Brahmic consciousness to which it aspires and falling from both perish like a dissolving cloud? — This doubt of mine must thou solve to its very heart, O Krishna, for I shall not find any other who can destroy this doubt, but only Thee.**

श्रीभगवानुवाच
पार्थ नैवेह नामुत्र विनाशस्तस्य विद्यते ।
न हि कल्याणकृत्कश्चिद् दुर्गतिं तात गच्छति ॥४०॥
प्राप्य पुण्यकृतां लोकानुषित्वा शाश्वतीः समाः ।
शुचीनां श्रीमतां गेहे योगभ्रष्टोऽभिजायते ॥४१॥

अथवा योगिनामेव कुले भवति धीमताम् ।
एतद्धि दुर्लभतरं लोके जन्म यदीदृशम् ।।४२।।
तत्र तं बुद्धिसंयोगं लभते पौर्वदेहिकम् ।
यतते च ततो भूयः संसिद्धौ कुरुनन्दन ।।४३।।

40-43. *Krishna* — **Neither in this world nor in the other, Partha, is there for that man any perdition. None who doeth good can come to an evil end, O beloved. But to the world of the righteous he goeth and there dwelleth for endless seasons and then is born again, the man fallen from Yoga, in a house of pure and fortunate men. Or else he even cometh to being in the house of the wise, in a land of Yogins, for such a birth as this in this world is one of the hardest to win. There he getteth touch again with the mind he had in his former body, and with that to start him he striveth yet harder after perfection.**

पूर्वाभ्यासेन तेनैव ह्रियते ह्यवशोऽपि सः ।
जिज्ञासुरपि योगस्य शब्दब्रह्मातिवर्तते ।।४४।।

44. **For he is seized and hurried forward even by that former habit and askesis of his, though it be without his own will. Even if a man's mind is curious after Yoga, he overpasseth the outer Brahman in the Word (*or,* the knowledge of the knower is passing beyond the range of Veda and Upanishad), *śabda-brahma-ativartate.*** (*see also II-52/53*)

प्रयत्नाद्यतमानस्तु योगी संशुद्धकिल्बिषः ।
अनेकजन्मसंसिद्धस्ततो याति परां गतिम् ।।४५।।

45. **The Yogin earnestly striving is purified of sin; perfected by toil of many births he arriveth at his highest salvation.**

तपस्विभ्योऽधिको योगी ज्ञानिभ्योऽपि मतोऽधिकः ।
कर्मिभ्यश्चाधिको योगी तस्माद्योगी भवार्जुन ।।४६।।

46. The divine Teacher returns to this idea (*of sl. 31*) and makes it his culminating utterance. **The Yogin is greater than the doers of askesis, greater than the men of knowledge, greater than the men of works; become then the Yogin, O Arjuna,** the Yogin, one who seeks for and attains, by works and knowledge and askesis or by whatever other means, not even spiritual knowledge or power or anything else for their own sake, but the union with God alone; for in that all else is contained and in that lifted beyond itself to a

divinest significance. But even among Yogins the greatest is the Bhakta.

योगिनामपि सर्वेषां मद्गतेनान्तरात्मना।
श्रद्धावान्भजते यो मां स मे युक्ततमो मतः ।।४७।।

47. **Of all Yogins he who with all his inner self given up to Me, *mad-gatena-antarātmanā*, for Me has love and faith, *śraddhāvān bhajate yo mām*, him I hold to be the most united with Me in Yoga, *sa me yuktatamo mataḥ*.**

It is this that is the closing word of these first six chapters and contains in itself the seed of the rest, of that which still remains unspoken and is nowhere entirely spoken; for it is always and remains something of a mystery and a secret, *rahasyam*, the highest spiritual mystery and the divine secret.

The Gita [presents] the Supreme as something greater even than the immutable Self, more comprehensive, one who is at once this Self and the Master of works in Nature. But he directs the works of Nature with the eternal calm, the equality, the superiority to works and personality which belong to the immutable. This, we may say, is the poise of being from which he directs works, and by growing into this we are growing into his being and into the poise of divine works. From this he goes forth as the Will and Power of his being in Nature, manifests himself in all existences, is born as Man in the world, is there in the heart of all men, reveals himself as the Avatar, the divine birth in man; and as man grows into his being, it is into the divine birth that he grows. Works must be done as a sacrifice to this Lord of our works, and we must by growing into the Self realise our oneness with him in our being and see our personality as a partial manifestation of him in Nature. One with him in being, we grow one with all beings in the universe and do divine works, not as ours, but as his workings through us for the maintenance and leading of the peoples.

This is the essential thing to be done, and once this is done, the difficulties which present themselves to Arjuna will disappear. The problem is no longer one of our personal action, for that which makes our personality becomes a thing temporal and subordinate, the question is then only one of the workings of the divine Will through us in the universe. To understand that we must know what this supreme Being is in himself and in Nature, what the workings of Nature are and what they lead to, and the intimate relation between the soul in Nature and this supreme Soul, of which bhakti with knowledge is the foundation. The elucidation of these questions is the subject of the rest of the Gita.

Chapter VII

I — The Two Natures

The first six chapters of the Gita have been treated as a single block of teachings, its primary basis of practice and knowledge; the remaining twelve may be similarly treated as two closely connected blocks which develop the rest of the doctrine from this primary basis. The seventh to the twelfth chapters lay down a large metaphysical statement of the nature of the Divine Being and on that foundation closely relate and synthetise knowledge and devotion, just as the first part of the Gita related and synthetised works and knowledge. The vision of the World-Purusha intervenes in the eleventh chapter, gives a dynamic turn to this stage of the synthesis and relates it vividly to works and life. Thus again all is brought powerfully back to the original question of Arjuna round which the whole exposition revolves and completes its cycle. Afterwards (*chap. 13-18*) the Gita proceeds by the differentiation of the Purusha and Prakriti to work out its ideas of the action of the gunas, of the ascension beyond the gunas and of the culmination of desireless works with knowledge where that coalesces with Bhakti, — knowledge, works and love made one, — and it rises thence to its great finale, the supreme secret of self-surrender to the Master of Existence.

It has not yet been stated who is this Supreme, incarnate here in the divine teacher and charioteer of works, or what are his relations to the Self and to the individual being in Nature. Nor is it clear how the Will to works coming from him can be other than the will in the nature of the three gunas. Will seems to be an aspect of the executive part of being, to be power and active force of nature, Shakti, Prakriti. Is there then a higher Nature than that of the three gunas? Is there a power of pragmatic creation, will, action other than that of ego, desire, mind, sense, reason, and the vital impulse?

श्रीभगवानुवाच
मय्यासक्तमनाः पार्थ योगं युञ्जन्मदाश्रयः ।
असंशयं समग्रं मां यथा ज्ञास्यसि तच्छृणु ।।१।।

1. *Krishna* — Therefore, in this uncertainty, what has now to be done is to give more completely the knowledge on which divine works are to be founded. And this can only be the complete, the integral knowledge of the Divine who is the source of works and in whose being the worker becomes by knowledge free; for he knows the free Spirit from whom all works proceed and participates in his freedom. Moreover this knowledge must bring a light that justifies the assertion with which the first part of the Gita closes. It must ground the supremacy of bhakti over all other motives and powers of spiritual consciousness and action; it must be a knowledge of the supreme Lord of all creatures to whom alone the soul can offer itself in the perfect self-surrender which is the highest height of all love and devotion. This is what the Teacher proposes to give in the opening verses of the seventh chapter which initiate the development that occupies all the rest of the book. **Hear, he says, how by practising Yoga with a mind attached to Me and with Me as *āśraya* (the whole basis, lodgment, point of resort of the conscious being and action) thou shalt know Me without any remainder of doubt, integrally, *samagraṁ mām*.**

ज्ञानं तेऽहं सविज्ञानमिदं वक्ष्याम्यशेषतः ।
यज्ज्ञात्वा नेह भूयोऽन्यज्ज्ञातव्यमवशिष्यते ।।२।।

2. **I will speak to thee without omission or remainder, *aśeṣataḥ,*** for otherwise a ground of doubt may remain, **the essential knowledge, attended with all the comprehensive knowledge, by knowing which there shall be no other thing here left to be known.** The implication of the phrase is that the Divine Being is all, *vāsudevaḥ sarvam*, and therefore if he is known integrally in all his powers and principles, then all is known, not only the pure Self, but the world and action and Nature. There is then nothing else here left to be known, because all is that Divine Existence. It is only because our view here is not thus integral, because it rests on the dividing mind and reason and the separative idea of the ego, that our mental perception of things is an ignorance. We have to get away from this mental and egoistic view to the true unifying knowledge, and that has two aspects, the essential, *jñāna*, and the comprehensive, *vijñāna*, the direct spiritual awareness of the supreme Being and the right intimate knowledge of the principles of his existence, Prakriti, Purusha and the rest, by which all that is can be known in its divine origin and in the supreme truth of its nature. (*see also IX-1*)

मनुष्याणां सहस्रेषु कश्चिद्यतति सिद्धये ।
यततामपि सिद्धानां कश्चिन्मां वेत्ति तत्त्वतः ।।३।।

3. That integral knowledge, says the Gita, is a rare and difficult thing; **among thousands of men one here and there strives after perfection, and of those who strive and attain to perfection one here and there knows me in all the principles of my existence, *tattvataḥ*.**

भूमिरापोऽनलो वायुः खं मनो बुद्धिरेव च ।
अहङ्कार इतीयं मे भिन्ना प्रकृतिरष्टधा ।।४।।
अपरेयमितस्त्वन्यां प्रकृतिं विद्धि मे पराम् ।
जीवभूतां महाबाहो ययेदं धार्यते जगत् ।।५।।

4-5. Then, to start with and in order to found this integral knowledge, the Gita makes that deep and momentous distinction which is the practical basis of all its Yoga, the distinction between the two Natures, the phenomenal and the spiritual Nature. **The five elements** [conditions of material being], **mind, reason, ego, this is my eightfold divided Nature. — But know my other Nature different from this, the supreme which becomes the Jiva and by which this world is upheld.** Here is the first new metaphysical idea of the Gita which helps it to start from the notions of the Sankhya philosophy and yet exceed them and give to their terms, which it keeps and extends, a Vedantic significance. **An eightfold Nature constituted of the five *bhūtas*,** — elements, as it is rendered, but rather elemental or essential conditions of material being to which are given the concrete names of earth, water, fire, air and ether, — **the mind with its various senses and organs, the reason-will and the ego,** is the Sankhya description of Prakriti. The Sankhya stops there, and because it stops there, it has to set up an unbridgeable division between the soul and Nature; it has to posit them as two quite distinct primary entities. The Gita also, if it stopped there, would have to make the same incurable antinomy between the Self and cosmic Nature which would then be only the Maya of the three gunas and all this cosmic existence would be simply the result of this Maya; it could be nothing else. But there is something else, there is a higher principle, a nature of spirit, *parā prakṛitir me*. There is a supreme nature of the Divine which is the real source of cosmic existence and its fundamental creative force and effective energy and of which the other lower and ignorant Nature is only a derivation and a dark shadow. In this highest dynamis Purusha and Prakriti are one. Prakriti there is only the will and the executive power of the Purusha, his activity of being, — not a separate entity, but himself in Power.

[*It is not sufficient to say*] that this supreme Nature is the power involved and inherent in unmanifest Spirit or Self out of which cosmos comes and into which it returns. It is that, but it is much more; for that is only one of its spiritual states. It is the integral conscious-power of the supreme Being, *cit-śakti*, which is behind the self and cosmos. In the immutable Self it is involved in the Spirit; it is there, but in *nivṛitti* or a holding back from action; in the mutable self and the cosmos it comes out into action, *pravṛitti*. There by its dynamic presence it evolves in the Spirit all existences and appears in them as their essential spiritual nature, the persistent truth behind their play of subjective and objective phenomena. It is the essential quality and force, *svabhāva*, the self-principle of all their becoming, the inherent principle and divine power behind their phenomenal existence. The real truth [of our active existence] is this spiritual power, this divine force of being, this essential quality of the spirit in things or rather of the spirit in which things are and from which they draw all their potencies and the seeds of their movements.

एतद्योनीनि भूतानि सर्वाणीत्युपधारय ।
अहं कृत्स्नस्य जगतः प्रभवः प्रलयस्तथा ॥६॥
मत्तः परतरं नान्यत्किञ्चिदस्ति धनञ्जय ।
मयि सर्वमिदं प्रोतं सूत्रे मणिगणा इव ॥७॥

6-7. **This other higher Prakriti is, says Krishna, my supreme nature, *prakṛitiṁ me parām*.** And this "I" here is the Purushottama, the supreme Being, the supreme Soul, the transcendent and universal Spirit. The original and eternal nature of the Spirit and its transcendent and originating Shakti is what is meant by the Para Prakriti. For speaking first of the origin of the world from the point of view of the active power of his Nature, Krishna assevers, **This is the womb of all beings, *etad yonīni bhūtāni*.** And in the next line of the couplet, again stating the same fact from the point of view of the originating Soul, he continues, **I am the birth of the whole world and so too its dissolution; there is nothing else supreme beyond Me.** Here then the supreme Soul, Purushottama, and the supreme Nature, Para Prakriti, are identified: they are put as two ways of looking at one and the same reality. For when Krishna declares, I am the birth of the world and its dissolution, it is evident that it is this Para Prakriti, supreme Nature, of his being which is both these things. The Spirit is the supreme Being in his infinite consciousness and the supreme Nature is the infinity of power or will of being of the Spirit, — it is his infinite consciousness in its inherent divine energy and its supernal divine action. The birth is the movement of evolution of this conscious Energy out of the Spirit, *parā prakṛitir jīvabhūtā*, its activity in the mutable universe; the dissolution is the withdrawing of that activity by involution of the Energy into the immutable existence and self-gathered power of the Spirit. That then is what is initially meant by the supreme Nature.

The supreme Nature, *parā prakṛitiḥ*, is then the infinite timeless conscious power of the self-existent Being out of which all existences in the cosmos are manifested and come out of timelessness into Time. But in order to provide a spiritual basis for this manifold universal becoming in the cosmos the supreme Nature formulates itself as the Jiva. To put it otherwise, the eternal multiple soul of the Purushottama appears as individual spiritual existence in all the forms of the cosmos. All existences are instinct with the life of the one indivisible Spirit; all are supported in their personality, actions and forms by the eternal multiplicity of the one Purusha. The Gita does not say that the supreme Prakriti is in its essence the Jiva, *jīvātmikām*, but that it has become the Jiva, *jīva-bhūtām*; and it is implied in that expression that behind its manifestation as the Jiva here it is originally something else and higher, it is nature of the one supreme spirit. The Jiva, as we are told later on, is the Lord, *īśvara*, but in his partial manifestation, *mamaivāṁśaḥ*; even all the multiplicity of beings in the universe or in numberless universes could not be in their becoming the integral Divine, but only a partial manifestation of the infinite One. In them Brahman the one indivisible existence resides as if divided, *avibhaktaṁ ca bhūteṣu vibhaktam iva ca sthitam*. The unity is the greater truth, the multiplicity is the lesser truth, though both are a truth and neither of them is an illusion.

It is by the unity of this spiritual nature that the world is sustained, *yayedaṁ dhāryate jagat*, even as it is that from which it is born with all its becomings, *etad-yonīni bhūtāni sarvāṇi*, and that also which withdraws the whole world and its existences into itself in the hour of dissolution, *ahaṁ kṛitsnasya jagataḥ prabhavaḥ pralayas tathā*. But in the manifestation which is thus put forth in the Spirit, upheld in its action, withdrawn in its periodical rest from action, the Jiva is the basis of the multiple existence; it is the multiple soul, if we may so call it, or, if we prefer, the soul of the multiplicity we experience here. It is one always with the Divine in its being, different from it only in the power of its being, — different not in the sense that it is not at all the same power, but in this sense that it only supports the one power in a partial multiply individualised action. Therefore all things are initially, ultimately and in the principle of their continuance too the Spirit. The fundamental nature of all is nature of the Spirit, and only in their lower differential phenomena do they seem to be something else, to be nature of body, life, mind, reason, ego and the senses. But these are phenomenal derivatives, they are not the essential truth of our nature and our existence.

The supreme nature of spiritual being gives us then both an original truth and power of existence beyond cosmos and a first basis of spiritual truth for the manifestation in the cosmos. But where is the link between this supreme nature and the lower phenomenal nature? **On me, says Krishna, all**

this, all that is here — *sarvam idam,* the common phrase in the Upanishads for the totality of phenomena in the mobility of the universe — is strung like pearls upon a thread. But this is only an image which we cannot press very far; for the pearls are only kept in relation to each other by the thread and have no other oneness or relation with the pearl-string except their dependence on it for this mutual connection. Let us go then from the image to that which it images. It is the supreme nature of Spirit, the infinite conscious power of its being, self-conscient, all-conscient, all-wise, which maintains these phenomenal existences in relation to each other, penetrates them, abides in and supports them and weaves them into the system of its manifestation. This one supreme power manifests not only in all as the One, but in each as the Jiva, the individual spiritual presence; it manifests also as the essence of all quality of Nature.

रसोऽहमप्सु कौन्तेय प्रभास्मि शशिसूर्ययोः ।
प्रणवः सर्ववेदेषु शब्दः खे पौरुषं नृषु ।।८।।
पुण्यो गन्धः पृथिव्यां च तेजश्चास्मि विभावसौ ।
जीवनं सर्वभूतेषु तपश्चास्मि तपस्विषु ।।९।।
बीजं मां सर्वभूतानां विद्धि पार्थ सनातनम् ।
बुद्धिर्बुद्धिमतामस्मि तेजस्तेजस्विनामहम् ।।१०।।
बलं बलवतां चाहं कामरागविवर्जितम् ।
धर्माविरुद्धो भूतेषु कामोऽस्मि भरतर्षभ ।।११।।

8-11. [*In the immediately subsequent passage*] the Gita gives a number of instances to show how the Divine in the power of his supreme nature manifests and acts within the animate and so-called inanimate existences of the universe. *We may disentangle them from the loose and free order which the exigence of the poetical form imposes and put them in their proper philosophical series.*[1] First, the divine Power and Presence works within the five elemental conditions of matter. **I am taste in the waters, sound in ether, scent in earth, energy of light in fire, and,** it may be added for more completeness, **touch or contact in air.** That is to say, the Divine himself in his Para Prakriti is the energy at the basis of the various sensory relations of which, according to the ancient Sankhya system, the ethereal, the radiant, electric and gaseous, the liquid and the other elemental conditions of matter are the physical medium. The five elemental conditions of matter are the quantitative or material element in the lower nature and are the basis of material forms. The five Tanmatras — taste, touch, scent and the others — are the

1. Editor's italics.

qualitative element. From the material point of view matter is the reality and the sensory relations are derivative; but from the spiritual point of view the truth is the opposite. Matter and the material media are themselves derivative powers and at bottom are only concrete ways or conditions in which the workings of the quality of Nature in things manifest themselves to the sensory consciousness of the Jiva. The one original and eternal fact is the energy of Nature, the power and quality of being which so manifests itself to the soul through the senses. But energy or power of being in Nature is the Divine himself in his Prakriti; each sense in its purity is therefore that Prakriti, each sense is the Divine in his dynamic conscious force.

This we gather better from the other terms of the series. **I am the light of sun and moon, the manhood in man, the intelligence of the intelligent, the energy of the energetic, the strength of the strong, the ascetic force of those who do askesis, *tapasyā*. I am life in all existences.** In each case it is the energy of the essential quality on which each of these becomings depends for what it has become, that is given as the characteristic sign indicating the presence of the divine Power in their nature. Again, **I am pranava in all the Vedas,** that is to say, the basic syllable OM, which is the foundation of all the potent creative sounds of the revealed word; OM is the one universal formulation of the energy of sound and speech, that which contains and sums up, synthetises and releases all the spiritual power and all the potentiality of Vak and Shabda and of which the other sounds, out of whose stuff words of speech are woven, are supposed to be the developed evolutions. Force, light, power, is the eternal seed from which all other things are the developments and derivations and variabilities and plastic circumstances. Therefore the Gita throws in as the most general statement in the series, **Know me to be the eternal seed of all existences, O son of Pritha.** This eternal seed is the power of spiritual being, the conscious will in the being, the seed which, as it is said elsewhere, (*XIV- 3/4*) the Divine casts into the great Brahman, into the supramental vastness, and from that all are born into phenomenal existence. It is that seed of spirit which manifests itself as the essential quality in all becomings and constitutes their swabhava.

The practical distinction between this original power of essential quality and the phenomenal derivations of the lower nature, between the thing itself in its purity and the thing in its lower appearances, is indicated very clearly at the close of the series. **I am the strength of the strong devoid of desire and liking,** stripped of all attachment to the phenomenal pleasure of things. **I am in beings the desire which is not contrary to their dharma.**

ये चैव सात्त्विका भावा राजसास्तामसाश्च ये ।
मत्त एवेति तान्विद्धि न त्वहं तेषु ते मयि ।।१२।।

12. **And as for the secondary subjective becomings of Nature, *bhāvāḥ*** (states of mind, affections of desire, movements of passion, the reactions of the senses), the limited and dual play of reason, the turns of the feeling and moral sense, **which are sattwic, rajasic and tamasic,** as for the working of the three gunas, they are, says the Gita, not themselves the pure action of the supreme spiritual nature, but are derivations from it, **they are verily from me, *matta eva*, they have no other origin, but I am not in them, it is they that are in me.** Here is indeed a strong and yet subtle distinction. "I am, says the Divine, the essential light, strength, desire, power, intelligence, but these derivations from them I am not in my essence, nor am I in them, yet are they all of them from me and they are all in my being." It is then upon the basis of these statements that we have to view the transition of things from the higher to the lower and again from the lower back to the higher nature.

But how can the Divine be desire, *kāma*? for this desire, this *kāma* has been declared to be our one great enemy who has to be slain. But that desire was the desire of the lower nature of the gunas which has its native point of origin in the rajasic being; for this is what we usually mean when we speak of desire. This other, the spiritual, is a will not contrary to the dharma. Dharma in the spiritual sense is not morality or ethics. Dharma, says the Gita elsewhere, is action governed by the swabhava, the essential law of one's nature. And this swabhava is at its core the pure quality of the spirit in its inherent power of conscious will and in its characteristic force of action. The desire meant here is therefore the purposeful will of the Divine in us searching for and discovering not the pleasure of the lower Prakriti, but the Ananda of its own play and self-fulfilling; it is the desire of the divine Delight of existence unrolling its own conscious force of action in accordance with the law of the swabhava.

But what again is meant by saying that the Divine is not in the becomings, the forms and affections of the lower nature, even the sattwic, though they all are in his being? In a sense he must evidently be in them, otherwise they could not exist. But what is meant is that the true and supreme spiritual nature of the Divine is not imprisoned there; they are only phenomena in his being created out of it by the action of the ego and the ignorance. The ignorance presents everything to us in an inverted vision and at least a partially falsified experience. We imagine that the soul is in the body, almost a result and derivation from the body; even we so feel it: but it is the body that is in the soul and a result and derivation from the soul. We think of the spirit as a small part of us — the Purusha who is no bigger than the thumb — in this great mass of material and mental phenomena: in reality, the latter for all its imposing appearance is a very small thing in the infinity of the being of the spirit. So it is here; in much the same sense these things are in the Divine rather than the Divine in these things.

त्रिभिर्गुणमयैर्भावैरेभिः सर्वमिदं जगत् ।
मोहितं नाभिजानाति मामेभ्यः परमव्ययम् ।।१३।।

13. This lower nature of the three gunas which creates so false a view of things and imparts to them an inferior character is a Maya, a power of illusion, by which it is not meant that it is all non-existent or deals with unrealities, but that it bewilders our knowledge, creates false values, envelops us in ego, mentality, sense, physicality, limited intelligence and there conceals from us the supreme truth of our existence. This illusive Maya hides from us the Divine that we are, the infinite and imperishable spirit. **By these three kinds of becoming which are of the nature of the gunas, this whole world is bewildered and does not recognise Me supreme beyond them and imperishable.**

दैवी ह्येषा गुणमयी मम माया दुरत्यया ।
मामेव ये प्रपद्यन्ते मायामेतां तरन्ति ते ।।१४।।

14. But why then, since the Divine is there after all and the divine nature at the root even of these bewildering derivations, since we are the Jiva and the Jiva is that, is **this Maya so hard to overcome, *māyā duratyayā*?** Because it is still the Maya of the Divine, ***daivī hyeṣā guṇamayī mama māyā*, this is my divine Maya of the gunas.** It is itself divine and a development from the nature of the Divine, but the Divine in the nature of the gods; it is *daivī*, of the godheads or, if you will, of the Godhead, but of the Godhead in its divided subjective and lower cosmic aspects, sattwic, rajasic and tamasic. It is a cosmic veil which the Godhead has spun around our understanding. We have to work out this web in ourselves and turn through it and from it leaving it behind us when its use is finished, turn from the gods to the original and supreme Godhead in whom we shall discover at the same time the last sense of the gods and their works and the inmost spiritual verities of our own imperishable existence. **To Me who turn and come, they alone cross over beyond this Maya.**

All this world, says the Gita, because it is bewildered by the three states of being determined by the modes of Nature, fail to recognise me, for this my divine Maya of the modes of Nature is hard to get beyond; those cross beyond it who approach Me; but those who dwell in the Asuric nature of being, have their

knowledge reft from them by Maya. In other words, there is the inherent consciousness of the divine in all, for in all the Divine dwells; but he dwells there covered by his Maya and the essential self-knowledge of beings is reft from them, turned into the error of egoism by the action of Maya, the action of the mechanism of Prakriti. Still by drawing back from the mechanism of Nature to her inner and secret Master man can become conscious of the indwelling Divinity.

II — THE SYNTHESIS OF DEVOTION AND KNOWLEDGE

After giving us in the first fourteen verses of this chapter a leading philosophical truth of which we stand in need, the Gita hastens in the next sixteen verses to make an immediate application of it. It turns it into a first starting-point for the unification of works, knowledge and devotion, — for the preliminary synthesis of works and knowledge by themselves has already been accomplished.

We have before us three powers, the Purushottama as the supreme truth of that into which we have to grow, the Self and the Jiva. Or, as we may put it, there is the Supreme, there is the impersonal spirit, and there is the multiple soul, timeless foundation of our spiritual personality, the true and eternal individual, *mamaivāṁśaḥ sanātanaḥ*. All these three are divine, all three are the Divine. The supreme spiritual nature of being, the Para Prakriti free from any limitation by the conditioning Ignorance, is the nature of the Purushottama. In the impersonal Self there is the same divine nature, but here it is in its state of eternal rest, equilibrium, inactivity, nivritti. Finally, for activity, for pravritti, the Para Prakriti becomes the multiple spiritual personality, the Jiva. But the intrinsic activity of this supreme Nature is always a spiritual, a divine working. It is force of the supreme divine Nature, it is the conscious will of the being of the Supreme that throws itself out in various essential and spiritual power of quality in the Jiva: that essential power is the swabhava of the Jiva. All act and becoming which proceed directly from this spiritual force are a divine becoming and a pure and spiritual action. Therefore it follows that in action the effort of the human individual must be to get back to his true spiritual personality and to make all his works flow from the power of its supernal Shakti, to develop action through the soul and the inmost intrinsic being, not through the mental idea and vital desire, and to turn all his acts into a pure outflowing of the will of the Supreme, all his life into a dynamic symbol of the Divine Nature.

But there is also this lower nature of the three gunas whose character is the character of the ignorance and whose action is the action of the ignorance, mixed, confused, perverted; it is the action of the lower personality, of the ego, of the natural and not of the spiritual individual. It is in order to recede from that false personality that we have to resort to the impersonal Self and make ourselves one with it. Then, freed so from the ego personality, we can find the relation of the true individual to the Purushottama. It is one with him in being, even though necessarily partial and determinative, because individual, in action and temporal manifestation of nature. Freed too from the lower nature we can realise the higher, the divine, the spiritual.

The Gita has laid it down from the beginning that the very first precondition of the divine birth, the higher existence is the slaying of rajasic desire and its children, and that means the exclusion of sin. Sin is the working of the lower nature. And in order to get rid of this crude compulsion of the being by the lower Prakriti in its inferior modes we must have recourse to the highest mode of that Prakriti, the sattwic, which is seeking always for a harmonious light of knowledge and for a right rule of action. We cannot get beyond the three gunas if we do not first develop within ourselves the rule of the highest guna, sattwa.

न मां दुष्कृतिनो मूढाः प्रपद्यन्ते नराधमाः ।
माययापहृतज्ञाना आसुरं भावमाश्रिताः ।।१५।।

15. The evil-doers, *duṣkṛitinaḥ*, attain not to me, says the Purushottama, souls bewildered, low in the human scale; for their knowledge is reft away from them by Maya and they resort to the nature of being of the Asura. A first necessary step upward is to aspire to a higher nature and a higher law, to become a right thinker and a right doer. This too is not in itself enough; for even the sattwic man is subject to the bewilderment of the gunas. Still by the constant upward aspiration in his ethical aim he in the end gets rid of the obscuration of sin which is the obscuration of rajasic desire and passion and acquires a purified nature capable of deliverance from the rule of the triple Maya. By virtue alone man cannot attain to the highest, but by virtue (the true inner *puṇya*, a sattwic clarity in thought, feeling, temperament, motive and conduct, not a merely conventional or social virtue) he can develop a first capacity for attaining to it, *adhikāra*. Man, therefore, has first of all to become ethical, *sukṛitī*, and then to rise to heights beyond any mere ethical rule of living, to the light, largeness and power of the spiritual nature, where he gets beyond the grasp of the dualities and its delusion, *dvandva-moha*.

**चतुर्विधा भजन्ते मां जनाः सुकृतिनोऽर्जुन ।
आर्तो जिज्ञासुरर्थार्थी ज्ञानी च भरतर्षभ ।।१६।।**

16. The Gita now lays down another and greater necessity for the Karmayogin who has unified his Yoga of works with the Yoga of knowledge. Not knowledge and works alone are demanded of him now, but *bhakti* also, devotion to the Divine, love and adoration and the soul's desire of the Highest. This demand, not expressly made until now, had yet been prepared when the Teacher laid down as the necessary turn of his Yoga the conversion of all works into a sacrifice to the Lord of our being and fixed as its culmination the giving up of all works, not only into our impersonal Self, but through impersonality into the Being from whom all our will and power originate. What was there implied is now brought out and we begin to see more fully the Gita's purpose. It is this bhakti of an integral knowledge and integral self-giving which the Gita now begins to develop. For note that it is bhakti with knowledge which the Gita demands from the disciple and it regards all other forms of devotion as good in themselves but still inferior; they may do well by the way, but they are not the thing at which it aims in the soul's culmination.

Among those who have put away the sin of the rajasic egoism and are moving towards the Divine, the Gita distinguishes between four kinds of *bhaktas*. There are those who turn to him as a refuge from sorrow and suffering in the world, *ārta*. There are those who seek him as the giver of good in the world, *arthārthī*. There are those who come to him in the desire for knowledge, *jijñāsu*. And lastly there are those who adore him with knowledge, *jñānī*. All are approved by the Gita, but only on the last does it lay the seal of its complete sanction. **All these movements without exception are high and good, *udārāḥ sarva evaite* (*sl. 18*), but the bhakti with knowledge excels them all, *viśiṣyate* (*sl. 17*).** We may say that these forms are successively the bhakti of the vital-emotional and affective nature,[1] that of the practical and dynamic nature, that of the reasoning intellectual nature, and that of the highest intuitive being which takes up all the rest of the nature into unity with the Divine.

**तेषां ज्ञानी नित्ययुक्त एकभक्तिर्विशिष्यते ।
प्रियो हि ज्ञानिनोऽत्यर्थमहं स च मम प्रियः ।।१७।।**

1. The later *bhakti* of ecstatic love is at its roots psychic in nature; it is vital-emotional only in its inferior forms or in some of its more outward manifestations.

17. Thus by spiritual development devotion becomes one with knowledge. The Jiva comes to delight in the one Godhead, — in the Divine known as all being and consciousness and delight and as all things and beings and happenings, known in Nature, known in the self, known for that which exceeds self and Nature. **He is ever in constant union with him, *nitya-yuktaḥ*;** his whole life and being are an eternal Yoga with the Transcendent than whom there is nothing higher, with the Universal besides whom there is none else and nothing else. **On him is concentrated all his bhakti, *ekabhaktiḥ*,** not on any partial godhead, rule or cult. This single devotion is his whole law of living and he has gone beyond all creeds of religious belief, rules of conduct, personal aims of life. He has no griefs to be healed, for he is in possession of the All-blissful. He has no desires to hunger after, for he possesses the Highest and the All and is close to the All-Power that brings all fulfilment. He has no doubts or baffled seekings left, for all knowledge streams upon him from the Light in which he lives. **He loves perfectly the Divine and is his beloved;** for as he takes joy in the Divine, so too the Divine takes joy in him. **This is the God-lover who has the knowledge, *jñānī bhakta*.**

उदाराः सर्व एवैते ज्ञानी त्वात्मैव मे मतम् ।
आस्थितः स हि युक्तात्मा मामेवानुत्तमां गतिम् ।।१८।।

18. And this knower, says the Godhead in the Gita, is my self, *jñānī tvātmaiva me*; the others seize only motives and aspects in Nature, **but he the very self-being and all-being of the Purushottama with which he is in union.** His is the divine birth in the supreme Nature, integral in being, completed in will, absolute in love, perfected in knowledge. In him the Jiva's cosmic existence is justified because it has exceeded itself and so **found its own whole and highest truth of being.**

बहूनां जन्मनामन्ते ज्ञानवान्मां प्रपद्यते ।
वासुदेवः सर्वमिति स महात्मा सुदुर्लभः ।।१९।।

19. Practically, however, the others may be regarded as preparatory movements. For the Gita itself here says that **it is only at the end of many existences that one can, after possession of the integral knowledge** and after working that out in oneself through many lives, **attain at the long last to the Transcendent. For the knowledge of the Divine as all things that are is difficult to attain and rare on earth is the great soul, *mahātmā*, who is capable of fully so seeing him** and of entering into him with his whole being, in every way of his nature, by the wide power of this all-embracing knowledge, *sarva-vit sarvabhāvena.* (*see also* X-6)

All is then to us a divine Reality manifesting himself in us and in the cosmos. If this [revealing spiritual] experience is exclusive, we get the pantheistic identity, the One that is all: but the pantheistic vision is only a partial seeing. This extended universe is not all that the Spirit is, there is an Eternal greater than it by which alone its existence is possible. Cosmos is not the Divine in all his utter reality, but a single self-expression, a true but minor motion of his being. The divine Reality is something greater than the universal existence, but yet — all universal and particular things are that Divine and nothing else, — significative of him, we might say, and not entirely That in any part or sum of their appearance, but still they could not be significative of him if they were something else and not term and stuff of the divine existence. That is the Real; but they are its expressive realities.

This is what is intended by the phrase, ***vāsudevaḥ sarvam iti*****; the Godhead is all that is universe and all that is in the universe and all that is more than the universe.** The Gita lays stress first on his supracosmic existence. For otherwise the mind would miss its highest goal and remain turned towards the cosmic only or else attached to some partial experience of the Divine in the cosmos. It lays stress next on his universal existence in which all moves and acts. For that is the justification of the cosmic effort and that is the vast spiritual self-awareness in which the Godhead self-seen as the Time-Spirit does his universal works. Next it insists with a certain austere emphasis on the acceptance of the Godhead as the divine inhabitant in the human body. For he is the Immanent in all existences, and if the indwelling divinity is not recognised, not only will the divine meaning of individual existence be missed, the urge to our supreme spiritual possibilities deprived of its greatest force, but the relations of soul with soul in humanity will be left petty, limited and egoistic. Finally, it insists at great length on the divine manifestation in all things in the universe and affirms the derivation of all that is from the nature, power and light of the one Godhead. For that seeing too is essential to the God-knowledge.

कामैस्तैस्तैर्हृतज्ञानाः प्रपद्यन्तेऽन्यदेवताः ।
तं तं नियममास्थाय प्रकृत्या नियताः स्वया ।।२०।।

20. It may be asked how is that devotion high and noble, *udāra*, which seeks God only for the worldly boons he can give or as a refuge in sorrow and suffering, and not the Divine for its own sake? Do not egoism, weakness, desire reign in such an adoration and does it not belong to the lower nature? Moreover, where there is not knowledge, the devotee does not approach the Divine in his integral all-embracing truth, *vāsudevaḥ sarvam iti*, but constructs imperfect names and images of the Godhead which are only reflections of his own need, temperament and nature, and he worships them to help or appease his natural longings. He constructs for the Godhead the name and form of Indra or Agni, of Vishnu or Shiva, of a divinised Christ or Buddha, or else some composite of natural qualities, an indulgent God of love and mercy, or a severe God of righteousness and justice, or an awe-inspiring God of wrath and terror and flaming punishments, or some amalgam of any of these, and to that he raises his altars without and in his heart and mind and falls down before it to demand from it worldly good and joy or healing of his wounds or a sectarian sanction for an erring, dogmatic, intellectual, intolerant knowledge. All this up to a certain point is true enough. **Very rare is the great soul who knows that Vasudeva the omnipresent Being is all that is, *vāsudevaḥ sarvam iti sa mahātmā sudurlabhaḥ*. — Men are led away by various outer desires which take from them the working of the inner knowledge, *kāmais tais tair hṛita-jñānāḥ*. Ignorant, they resort to other godheads,** imperfect forms of the deity which correspond to their desires, ***prapadyante 'nya-devatāḥ*. Limited, they set up this or that rule and cult, *taṁ taṁ niyamam āsthāya*, which satisfies the need of their nature, *prakṛityā niyatāḥ svayā*.** And in all this it is a compelling personal determination, it is this narrow need of their own nature that they follow and take for the highest truth, — incapable yet of the infinite and its largeness.

**यो यो यां यां तनुं भक्तः श्रद्धयार्चितुमिच्छति ।
तस्य तस्याचलां श्रद्धां तामेव विदधाम्यहम् ।।२१।।
स तया श्रद्धया युक्तस्तस्याराधनमीहते ।
लभते च ततः कामान्मयैव विहितान्हि तान् ।।२२।।
अन्तवत्तु फलं तेषां तद्भवत्यल्पमेधसाम् ।
देवान्देवयजो यान्ति मद्भक्ता यान्ति मामपि ।।२३।।**

21-23. The Godhead in these forms gives them their desires if their faith is whole; but these fruits and gratifications are temporary and it is a petty intelligence and unformed reason which make the pursuit of them its principle of religion and life. And so far as there is a spiritual attainment by this way, it is only to the gods; it is only the Divine in formations of mutable nature and as the giver of her results that they realise. **But those who adore the transcendent and integral Godhead embrace all this** and transform it all, exalt the gods to their highest, Nature to her summits, **and go beyond them to the very Godhead,**

realise and attain to the Transcendent. ***Devān deva-yajo yānti mad-bhaktā yānti mām api.***

According to their nature, as they approach him, he accepts their bhakti and answers to it with the reply of divine love and compassion. These forms are after all a certain kind of manifestation through which the imperfect human intelligence can touch him, these desires are first means by which our souls turn towards him: nor is any devotion worthless or ineffective, whatever its limitations. It has the one grand necessity, faith. **Whatever form of me any devotee with faith desires to worship, I make that faith of his firm and undeviating. — By the force of that faith in his cult and worship he gets his desire and the spiritual realisation for which he is at the moment fitted.** By seeking all his good from the Divine, he shall come in the end to seek in the Divine all his good. By depending for his joys on the Divine, he shall learn to fix in the Divine all his joy. By knowing the Divine in his forms and qualities, he shall come to know him as the All and the Transcendent who is the source of all things.

Even as men approach him, so he accepts them and responds too by the divine Love to their bhakti, ***tathaiva bhajate.*** **Whatever form of being, whatever qualities they lend to him, through that form and those qualities he helps them to develop, encourages or governs their advance and in their straight way or their crooked draws them towards him.** What they see of him is a truth, but a truth represented to them in the terms of their own being and consciousness, partially, distortedly, not in the terms of its own higher reality, not in the aspect which it assumes when we become aware of the complete Divinity. This is the justification of the cruder and more primitive elements of religion and also their sentence of transience and passing. They are justified because there is a truth of the Divine behind them and only so could that truth of the Divine be approached in that stage of the developing human consciousness and be helped forward; they are condemned, because to persist always in these crude conceptions and relations with the Divine is to miss that closer union towards which these crude beginnings are the first steps, however faltering. (*see also IX-23/25*)

अव्यक्तं व्यक्तिमापन्नं मन्यन्ते मामबुद्धयः ।
परं भावमजानन्तो ममाव्ययमनुत्तमम् ।।२४।।
नाहं प्रकाशः सर्वस्य योगमायासमावृतः ।
मूढोऽयं नाभिजानाति लोको मामजमव्ययम् ।।२५।।
वेदाहं समतीतानि वर्तमानानि चार्जुन ।
भविष्याणि च भूतानि मां तु वेद न कश्चन ।।२६।।

24-26. Still the supreme Godhead does not at all reject these devotees because of their imperfect vision. **For the Divine in his supreme transcendent being, unborn, imminuable and superior to all these partial manifestations, cannot be easily known to any living creature. He is self-enveloped in this immense cloak of Maya, that Maya of his Yoga,** by which he is one with the world and yet beyond it, immanent but hidden, seated in all hearts but **not revealed to any and every being. Man in Nature thinks that these manifestations in Nature are all the Divine,** when they are only his works and his powers and his veils. **He knows all past and all present and future existences, but him none yet knoweth. If then after thus bewildering them with his workings in Nature,** he were not to meet them in these at all, there would be no divine hope for man or for any soul in Maya.

इच्छाद्वेषसमुत्थेन द्वन्द्वमोहेन भारत ।
सर्वभूतानि सम्मोहं सर्गे यान्ति परन्तप ।।२७।।
येषां त्वन्तगतं पापं जनानां पुण्यकर्मणाम् ।
ते द्वन्द्वमोहनिर्मुक्ता भजन्ते मां दृढव्रताः ।।२८।।

27-28. **By the delusion of the dualities, *dvandva-moha*, which arises from wish and disliking, *icchā-dveṣa*, all existences in the creation are led into bewilderment.** That is the ignorance, the egoism which fails to see and lay hold on the Divine everywhere, because it sees only the dualities of Nature and is constantly occupied with its own separate personality and its seekings and shrinkings. **For escape from this circle the first necessity in our works is to get clear of the sin of the vital ego,** the fire of passion, the tumult of desire of the rajasic nature, **and this has to be done by the steadying sattwic impulse of the ethical being. When that is done, *yeṣāṁ tvantagataṁ pāpaṁ janānāṁ puṇya-karmaṇām*, it is necessary to rise above the dualities** and to become impersonal, equal, one self with the Immutable, one self with all existences. Equality and vision of unity once perfectly gained, ***te dvandva-moha-nirmuktāḥ*, a supreme bhakti, an all-embracing devotion to the Divine, becomes the whole and the sole law of the being.** All other law of conduct merges into that surrender, *sarva-dharmān parityajya.* **The soul then becomes firm in this bhakti and in the vow of self-consecration** of all its being, knowledge, works; for it has now for its sure base, its absolute foundation of existence and action the perfect, the integral, the unifying knowledge of the all-originating Godhead, ***te bhajante māṁ dṛḍha-vratāḥ.***

III — THE SUPREME DIVINE (1)

Already what has been said in the seventh chapter provides us with the starting-point of our new and fuller position and fixes it with sufficient precision. Substantially it comes to this that we are to move inwardly towards a greater consciousness and a supreme existence, not by a total exclusion of our cosmic nature, but by a higher, a spiritual fulfilment of all that we now essentially are. Only there is to be a change from our mortal imperfection to a divine perfection of being.

Our first experience of what is beyond our normal status, concealed behind the egoistic being in which we live, is still for the Gita the calm of a vast impersonal immutable self in whose equality and oneness we lose our petty egoistic personality and cast off in its tranquil purity all our narrow motives of desire and passion. But our second completer vision reveals to us a living Infinite, a divine immeasurable Being from whom all that we are proceeds and to which all that we are belongs, self and nature, world and spirit. When we are one with him in self and spirit, we do not lose ourselves but rather recover our true selves in him poised in the supremacy of this Infinite. And this is done at one and the same time by three simultaneous movements, — an integral self-finding through works founded in his and our spiritual nature, an integral self-becoming through knowledge of the Divine Being in whom all exists and who is all, and — most sovereign and decisive movement of all — an integral self-giving through love and devotion of our whole being to this All and this Supreme, attracted to the Master of our works, to the Inhabitant of our hearts, to the continent of all our conscious existence. To him who is the source of all that we are, we give all that we are. Our persistent consecration turns into knowledge of him all our knowing and into light of his power all our action. The passion of love in our self-giving carries us up to him and opens the mystery of his deepest heart of being. Love completes the triple cord of the sacrifice, perfects the triune key of the highest secret, *uttamaṁ rahasyam*.

An integral knowledge in our self-giving is the first condition of its effective force. And therefore we have first of all to know this Purusha in all the powers and principles of his divine existence, *tattvataḥ*, in the whole harmony of it, in its eternal essence and living process. But to the ancient thought all the value of this knowledge, *tattva-jñāna*, lay in its power for release out of our mortal birth into the immortality of a supreme existence. The Gita therefore proceeds next to show how this liberation too in the highest degree is a final outcome of its own movement of spiritual self-fulfilment. The knowledge of the Purushottama, it says in effect, is the perfect knowledge of the Brahman.

जरामरणमोक्षाय मामाश्रित्य यतन्ति ये ।
ते ब्रह्म तद्विदुः कृत्स्नमध्यात्मं कर्म चाखिलम् ।।२९।।

29. **Those who have resort to Me as their refuge, *mām āśritya*,** their divine light, their deliverer, receiver and harbourer of their souls, — **those who turn to Me in their spiritual effort towards release from age and death,** from the mortal being and its limitations, says Krishna, **come to know that Brahman, *tad brahma*, and all the integrality of the spiritual nature, *adhyātmam*, and the entirety of Karma.**

साधिभूताधिदैवं मां साधियज्ञं च ये विदुः ।
प्रयाणकालेऽपि च मां ते विदुर्युक्तचेतसः ।।३०।।

30. **And because they know Me and know at the same time the material and the divine nature of being, *adhibhūta-adhidaivam*, and the truth of the Master of sacrifice, *adhiyajñam*, they keep knowledge of Me also in the critical moment of their departure from physical existence and have at that moment their whole consciousness in union with Me. Therefore they attain to Me.** No longer bound to the mortal existence, they reach the very highest status of the Divine quite as effectively as those who lose their separate personality in the impersonal and immutable Brahman. Thus the Gita closes this important and decisive seventh chapter.

CHAPTER VIII

The Supreme Divine (2)

अर्जुन उवाच
किं तद्ब्रह्म किमध्यात्मं किं कर्म पुरुषोत्तम ।
अधिभूतं च किं प्रोक्तमधिदैवं किमुच्यते ॥१॥
अधियज्ञः कथं कोऽत्र देहेऽस्मिन्मधुसूदन ।
प्रयाणकाले च कथं ज्ञेयोऽसि नियतात्मभिः ॥२॥

1-2. *Arjuna* — Here we have certain expressions which give us in their brief sum the chief essential truths of the manifestation of the supreme Divine in the cosmos. All the originative and effective aspects of it are there, all that concerns the soul in its return to integral self-knowledge. **First there is That Brahman, *tad brahma*; *adhyātma*, second, the principle of the self in Nature; *adhibhūta* and *adhidaiva* next, the objective phenomenon and subjective phenomenon of being; *adhiyajña* last, the secret of the cosmic principle of works and sacrifice.** I, the Purushottama, *māṁ viduḥ*, says in effect Krishna, I who am above all these things, must yet be sought and known through all together and by means of their relations, — that is the only complete way for the human consciousness which is seeking its path back towards Me. But these terms in themselves are not at first quite clear or at least they are open to different interpretations, they have to be made precise in their connotation, and Arjuna the disciple at once asks for their elucidation.

श्रीभगवानुवाच
अक्षरं ब्रह्म परमं स्वभावोऽध्यात्ममुच्यते ।
भूतभावोद्भवकरो विसर्गः कर्मसंज्ञितः ॥३॥
अधिभूतं क्षरो भावः पुरुषश्चाधिदैवतम् ।
अधियज्ञोऽहमेवात्र देहे देहभृतां वर ॥४॥

3-4. *Krishna* — Krishna answers very briefly. **By That Brahman,** a phrase which in the Upanishads is more than once used for the self-existent as opposed to the phenomenal being, the Gita intends, it appears, **the immutable self-existence** which is the highest self-expression of the Divine and on whose unalterable eternity all the rest, all that moves and evolves, is founded, ***akṣaraṁ paramam*. By *adhyātma* it means *svabhāva*,** the spiritual way and law of being of the soul in the supreme Nature. **Karma, it says, is the name given to the creative impulse and energy, *visargaḥ*,** which looses out things from this first essential self-becoming, this Swabhava, and effects, creates, works out under its influence the cosmic becoming of existences in Prakriti. **By *adhibhūta* is to be understood all the result of mutable becoming, *kṣaro bhāvaḥ*. By *adhidaiva* is intended the Purusha, the soul in Nature,** the subjective being who observes and enjoys as the object of his consciousness all that is this mutable becoming of his essential existence worked out here by Karma in Nature. **By *adhiyajña*, the Lord of works and sacrifice, I mean, says Krishna, myself, the Divine, the Godhead, the Purushottama** here secret in the body of all these embodied existences. All that is, therefore, falls within this formula. (*see III-14/15 footnote*)

Here is indicated the Gita's idea of the process of the cosmos. First there is the Brahman, the highest immutable self-existent being which all existences are behind the play of cosmic Nature in time and space and causality, *deśa-kāla-nimitta*. For by that self-existence alone time and space and causality are able to exist, and without that unchanging support omnipresent, yet indivisible they could not proceed to their divisions and results and measures. But of itself the immutable Brahman does nothing, causes nothing, determines nothing; it is impartial, equal, all-supporting, but does not select or originate. What then originates, what determines, what gives the divine impulsion of the Supreme? what is it that governs Karma and actively unrolls the cosmic becoming in Time out of the eternal being? It is Nature as Swabhava. The Supreme, the Godhead, the Purushottama is there and supports on his eternal immutability the action of his higher spiritual Shakti. He displays the divine Being, Consciousness, Will or Power, *yayedaṁ dhāryate jagat*: that is the Para Prakriti. The self-awareness of the Spirit in this supreme Nature perceives in the light of self-knowledge the dynamic idea, the authentic truth of whatever he separates in his own being and expresses it in the Swabhava, the spiritual nature of the Jiva. The inherent truth and principle of the self of each Jiva, that which works itself out in manifestation, the essential divine nature in all which remains constant behind all conversions, perversions, reversions, that is the Swabhava. All that is in the Swabhava is loosed out into cosmic Nature for her to do what she can with it under the inner eye of the Purushottama. Out of the constant *svabhāva*, out of the essential nature and self-principle of being of each becoming, she creates the varied mutations by which she strives to express it, unrolls all her changes in name and form, in time and space and those successions of condition developed one out of the other in time and space which we call causality, *nimitta*.

All this bringing out and continual change from state to state is Karma, is action of Nature, is the energy of Prakriti, the worker, the goddess of processes. It is first a loosing forth of the *svabhāva* into its creative action, *visargaḥ*. The creation is of existences in the becoming, *bhūta-karaḥ*, and of all that they subjectively or otherwise become, *bhāva-karaḥ*. All taken together, it is a constant birth of things in Time, *udbhava*, of which the creative energy of Karma is the principle. All this mutable becoming emerges by a combination of the powers and energies of Nature, *adhibhūta*, which constitutes the world and is the object of the soul's consciousness. In it all the soul is the enjoying and observing Deity in Nature; the divine powers of mind and will and sense, all the powers of its conscious being by which it reflects this working of Prakriti are its godheads, *adhidaiva*. This soul in Nature is therefore the *kṣara puruṣa*, it is the mutable soul, the eternal activity of the Godhead: the same soul in the Brahman drawn back from her is the *akṣara puruṣa*, the immutable self, the eternal silence of the Godhead. But in the form and body of the mutable being inhabits the supreme Godhead. Possessing at once the calm of the immutable existence and the enjoyment of the mutable action there dwells in man the Purushottama. He is not only remote from us in some supreme status beyond, but he is here too in the body of every being, in the heart of man and in Nature. There he receives the works of Nature as a sacrifice and awaits the conscious self-giving of the human soul: but always even in the human creature's ignorance and egoism he is the Lord of his swabhava and the Master of all his works, who presides over the law of Prakriti and Karma. From him the soul came forth into the play of Nature's mutations; to him the soul returns through immutable self-existence to the highest status of the Divine, *paraṁ dhāma*.

अन्तकाले च मामेव स्मरन्मुक्त्वा कलेवरम् ।
यः प्रयाति स मद्भावं याति नास्त्यत्र संशयः ।।५।।
यं यं वाऽपि स्मरन्भावं त्यजत्यन्ते कलेवरम् ।
तं तमेवैति कौन्तेय सदा तद्भावभावितः ।।६।।

5-6. Man, born into the world, revolves between world and world in the action of Prakriti and Karma. Purusha in Prakriti is his formula: what the soul in him thinks, contemplates and acts, that always he becomes. All that he had been, determined his present birth; and all that he is, thinks, does in this life up to the moment of his death, determines what he will become in the worlds beyond and in lives yet to be. If birth is a becoming, death also is a becoming, not by any means a cessation. **The body is abandoned, but the soul goes on its way, *tyaktvā kalevaram*.** Much then depends on what he is

at the critical moment of his departure. For whatever form of becoming his consciousness is fixed on at the time of death and has been full of that always in his mind and thought before death, to that form he must attain, since the Prakriti by Karma works out the soul's thoughts and energies and that is in real fact her whole business. Therefore, if the soul in the human being desires to attain to the status of the Purushottama, there are two necessities, two conditions which must be satisfied before that can be possible. He must have moulded towards that ideal his whole inner life in his earthly living; and he must be faithful to his aspiration and will in his departing. **Whoever leaves his body and departs, says Krishna, remembering me at his time of end, comes to my *bhāva*, that of the Purushottama, my status of being.** He is united with the original being of the Divine and that is the ultimate becoming of the soul, *paro bhāvaḥ,* the last result of Karma in its return upon itself and towards its source. The soul which has followed the play of cosmic evolution that veils here its essential spiritual nature, its original form of becoming, *svabhāva*, and has passed through all these other ways of becoming of its consciousness which are only its phenomena, *taṁ taṁ bhāvam*, returns to that essential nature and, finding through this return its true self and spirit, comes to the original status of being which is from the point of view of the return a highest becoming, *mad-bhāvam.* In a certain sense we may say that it becomes God, since it unites itself with nature of the Divine in a last transformation of its own phenomenal nature and existence.

तस्मात्सर्वेषु कालेषु मामनुस्मर युद्ध्य च ।
मय्यर्पितमनोबुद्धिर्मामेवैष्यस्यसंशयम् ॥७॥
अभ्यासयोगयुक्तेन चेतसा नान्यगामिना ।
परमं पुरुषं दिव्यं याति पार्थानुचिन्तयन् ॥८॥

7-8. The Gita here lays a great stress on the thought and state of mind at the time of death, a stress which will with difficulty be understood if we do not recognise what may be called the self-creative power of the consciousness. What the thought, the inner regard, the faith, *śraddhā*, settles itself upon with a complete and definite insistence, into that our inner being tends to change. This tendency becomes a decisive force when we go to those higher spiritual and self-evolved experiences which are less dependent on external things than is our ordinary psychology, enslaved as that is to outward Nature. There we can see ourselves steadily becoming that on which we keep our minds fixed and to which we constantly aspire. Therefore there any lapse of the thought, any infidelity of the memory means always a retardation of the change or some fall in its process and a going back towards what we were before, — at least so long as we have not substantially and irrevocably fixed our new becoming. When we have done that, when we have made it normal to our experience, the memory of it remains self-existently because that now is the natural form of our consciousness. In the critical moment of passing from the mortal plane of living, the importance of our then state of consciousness becomes evident. **The divine subjective becoming on which the mind has to be fixed firmly in the moment of the physical death, *yaṁ smaran bhāvaṁ tyajati-ante kalevaram*, must have been one into which the soul was at each moment growing inwardly during the physical life, *sadā tad-bhāva-bhāvitaḥ*** (*sl.* 6). **Therefore, says the divine Teacher, at all times remember me and fight, *tasmāt sarveṣu kāleṣu mām anusmara yudhya ca*; for if thy mind and thy understanding are always fixed on and given up to Me, *mayi-arpita-mano-buddhiḥ*, to Me thou shalt surely come. For it is by thinking always of him with a consciousness united with him in an undeviating Yoga of constant practice that one comes to the divine and supreme Purusha, *paramaṁ puruṣaṁ divyaṁ*.**

कविं पुराणमनुशासितारमणोरणीयांसमनुस्मरेद्यः ।
सर्वस्य धातारमचिन्त्यरूपमादित्यवर्णं तमसः परस्तात् ।।९।।
प्रयाणकाले मनसाऽचलेन भक्त्या युक्तो योगबलेन चैव ।
भ्रुवोर्मध्ये प्राणमावेश्य सम्यक् स तं परं पुरुषमुपैति दिव्यम् ।।१०।।
यदक्षरं वेदविदो वदन्ति विशन्ति यद्यतयो वीतरागाः ।
यदिच्छन्तो ब्रह्मचर्यं चरन्ति तत्ते पदं संग्रहेण प्रवक्ष्ये ।।११।।

9-11. We arrive here at the first description of this supreme Purusha, — the Godhead who is even more and greater than the Immutable and to whom the Gita gives subsequently the name of Purushottama. He too in his timeless eternity is immutable and far beyond all this manifestation and here in Time there dawn on us only faint glimpses of his being conveyed through many varied symbols and disguises, *avyakto-akṣaraḥ*. Still he is not merely a featureless or indiscernible existence, *anirdeśyam*; or he is indiscernible only because **he is subtler than the last subtlety** of which the mind is aware and because **the form of the Divine is beyond our thought, *aṇor aṇīyāṁsam acintya-rūpam*. This supreme Soul and Self is the Seer, the Ancient of Days** and in his eternal self-vision and wisdom **the Master and Ruler of all existence who sets in their place in his being all things that are, *kaviṁ purāṇam anuśāsitāraṁ sarvasya dhātāram*.**

Beyond the [unmanifest,] *avyaktam*, **[beyond the darkness,] *tamasaḥ parastāt*, is the Supreme, the Purushottama of the Gita**, the Para Purusha of the

Upanishads. **It is *ādityavarna*[1] in contrast to the darkness of the Unmanifest;** it is a metaphor, but not a mere metaphor, for it is a symbol also, and not merely a symbol, but a fact of spiritual experience. The sun in the yoga is the symbol of the supermind. It is that Light of which the Vedic mystics got a glimpse. For the supermind is all light and no darkness.

This supreme Soul is the immutable self-existent Brahman of whom the Veda-knowers speak, and this is that into which the doers of askesis enter when they have passed beyond the affections of the mind of mortality and for the desire of which they practise the control of the bodily passions. That eternal reality is the highest step, place, foothold of being, *padam*; therefore is it the supreme goal of the soul's movement in Time, itself no movement but a status original, sempiternal and supreme, *paraṁ sthānam ādyam* (*sl. 28*).

The Gita describes the last state of the mind of the Yogin in which he passes from life through death to this supreme divine existence, *paraṁ puruṣam divyam*. A motionless mind, a soul armed with the strength of Yoga, a union with God in bhakti, — the union by love is not here superseded by the featureless unification through knowledge, it remains to the end a part of the supreme force of the Yoga, — **and the life-force entirely drawn up and set between the brows in the seat of mystic vision.**

सर्वद्वाराणि संयम्य मनो हृदि निरुध्य च ।
मूर्ध्न्याधायात्मनः प्राणमास्थितो योगधारणाम् ।।१२।।
ओमित्येकाक्षरं ब्रह्म व्याहरन्मामनुस्मरन् ।
यः प्रयाति त्यजन्देहं स याति परमां गतिम् ।।१३।।

12-13. All the doors of the sense are closed, the mind is shut in into the heart, the life-force taken up out of its diffused movement into the head, the intelligence concentrated in the utterance of the sacred syllable OM and its conceptive thought in the remembrance of the supreme Godhead [of OM], *mām anusmaran*.

अनन्यचेताः सततं यो मां स्मरति नित्यशः ।
तस्याहं सुलभः पार्थ नित्ययुक्तस्य योगिनः ।।१४।।
मामुपेत्य पुनर्जन्म दुःखालयमशाश्वतम् ।
नाप्नुवन्ति महात्मानः संसिद्धिं परमां गताः ।।१५।।

1. *ādityavarna*: of the splendour of the sun. (*Editor's note*)

14-15. That is the established Yogic way of going, a last offering up of the whole being to the Eternal, the Transcendent. But still that is only a process; the essential condition is **the constant undeviating memory of the Divine in life, even in action and battle — *mām anusmara yudhya ca* — and the turning of the whole act of living into an uninterrupted Yoga, *nitya-yoga*. Whoever does that, finds Me easy to attain, says the Godhead; he is the great soul who reaches the supreme perfection.**

आब्रह्मभुवनाल्लोकाः पुनरावर्तिनोऽर्जुन ।
मामुपेत्य तु कौन्तेय पुनर्जन्म न विद्यते ।।१६।।

16. The condition to which the soul arrives when it thus departs from life is supracosmic. **The highest heavens of the cosmic plan are subject to a return to rebirth; but there is no rebirth imposed on the soul that departs to Me (the Purushottama).** Therefore whatever fruit can be had from the aspiration of knowledge to the indefinable Brahman, is acquired also by this other and comprehensive aspiration through knowledge, works and love to the self-existent Godhead who is the Master of works and the Friend of mankind and of all beings. **To know him so and so to seek him does not bind to rebirth or to the chain of Karma; the soul can satisfy its desire to escape permanently from the transient and painful condition of our mortal being** (*sl. 15*).

सहस्रयुगपर्यन्तमहर्यद् ब्रह्मणो विदुः ।
रात्रिं युगसहस्रान्तां तेऽहोरात्रविदो जनाः ।।१७।।

17. And the Gita here, in order to make more precise to the mind this circling round of births and the escape from it, adopts the ancient theory of the cosmic cycles which became a fixed part of Indian cosmological notions. There is an eternal cycle of alternating periods of cosmic manifestation and non-manifestation, each period called respectively **a day and a night of the creator Brahma, each of equal length in Time, the long aeon of his working which endures for a thousand ages, the long aeon of his sleep of another thousand silent ages.** Whether we entertain or we dismiss this cosmological notion depends on the value we are inclined to assign to the knowledge of **the knowers of day and night.**

अव्यक्ताद्व्यक्तयः सर्वाः प्रभवन्त्यहरागमे ।
रात्र्यागमे प्रलीयन्ते तत्रैवाव्यक्तसंज्ञके ।।१८।।

18. **At the coming of the Day all manifestations are born into being out of the unmanifest, at the coming of the Night all vanish or are dissolved into it.**

भूतग्रामः स एवायं भूत्वा भूत्वा प्रलीयते ।
रात्र्यागमेऽवशः पार्थ प्रभवत्यहरागमे ।।१९।।

19. **Thus all these existences alternate helplessly in the cycle of becoming and non-becoming; they come into the becoming again and again, *bhūtvā bhūtvā*, and they go back constantly into the unmanifest.**

परस्तस्मात्तु भावोऽन्योऽव्यक्तोऽव्यक्तात्सनातनः ।
यः स सर्वेषु भूतेषु नश्यत्सु न विनश्यति ।।२०।।

20. But this unmanifest is not the original divinity of the Being; **there is another status of his existence, *bhāvo 'nyo*, a supracosmic unmanifest beyond this cosmic non-manifestation,** which is eternally self-seated, is not an opposite of this cosmic status of manifestation but far above and unlike it, **changeless, eternal, not forced to perish with the perishing of all these existences.**

अव्यक्तोऽक्षर इत्युक्तस्तमाहुः परमां गतिम् ।
यं प्राप्य न निवर्तन्ते तद्धाम परमं मम ।।२१।।

21. **He is called the unmanifest immutable, him they speak of as the supreme soul and status, and those who attain to him return not; that is my supreme place of being, *paramaṁ dhāma*.** For the soul attaining to it has escaped out of the cycle of cosmic manifestation and non-manifestation.

पुरुषः स परः पार्थ भक्त्या लभ्यस्त्वनन्यया ।
यस्यान्तःस्थानि भूतानि येन सर्वमिदं ततम् ।।२२।।

22. **But,** — although this condition is supracosmic and although it is eternally unmanifest, — still **that supreme Purusha has to be won by a bhakti which turns to him alone in whom all beings exist and by whom all this world has been extended in space.** In other words, the supreme Purusha is not an entirely relationless Absolute aloof from our illusions, but he is the Seer, Creator and Ruler of the worlds, *kavim anuśāsitāram, dhātāram*, and it is by knowing and by loving Him as the One and the All, *vāsudevaḥ sarvam iti*,

that we ought by a union with him of our whole conscious being in all things, all energies, all actions to seek the supreme consummation, the perfect perfection, the absolute release.

यत्र काले त्वनावृत्तिमावृत्तिं चैव योगिनः ।
प्रयाता यान्ति तं कालं वक्ष्यामि भरतर्षभ ।।२३।।
अग्निर्ज्योतिरहः शुक्लः षण्मासा उत्तरायणम् ।
तत्र प्रयाता गच्छन्ति ब्रह्म ब्रह्मविदो जनाः ।।२४।।
धूमो रात्रिस्तथा कृष्णः षण्मासा दक्षिणायनम् ।
तत्र चान्द्रमसं ज्योतिर्योगी प्राप्य निवर्तते ।।२५।।

23-25. Then there comes a more curious thought which the Gita has adopted from the mystics of the early Vedanta. It gives **the different times at which the Yogin has to leave his body according as he wills to seek rebirth or to avoid it. Fire and light and smoke or mist, the day and the night, the bright fortnight of the lunar month and the dark, the northern solstice and the southern, these are the opposites. By the first in each pair the knowers of the Brahman go to the Brahman; but by the second the Yogin reaches the "lunar light" and returns subsequently to human birth.**

शुक्लकृष्णे गती ह्येते जगतः शाश्वते मते ।
एकया यात्यनावृत्तिमन्ययावर्तते पुनः ।।२६।।
नैते सृती पार्थ जानन्योगी मुह्यति कश्चन ।
तस्मात्सर्वेषु कालेषु योगयुक्तो भवार्जुन ।।२७।।

26-27. **These are the bright and the dark paths, called the path of the gods and the path of the fathers in the Upanishads, and the Yogin who knows them is not misled into any error. Therefore at all times be in Yoga.**

For that is after all the essential, to make the whole being one with the Divine, so entirely and in all ways as to be naturally and constantly fixed in union, and thus to make all living, not only thought and meditation, but action, labour, battle, a remembering of God. "Remember me and fight", means not to lose the ever-present thought of the Eternal for one single moment in the clash of the temporal which normally absorbs our minds, and that seems sufficiently difficult, almost impossible. It is entirely possible indeed only if the other conditions are satisfied. If we have become in our consciousness one self with all, one self which is always to our thought the Divine, and even our eyes and our other senses see and sense the Divine Being everywhere so that it is impossible for us at any time at all to feel or think of anything as that merely which the unenlightened sense perceives, but only as the Godhead at once concealed and manifested in that form, and if our will is one in consciousness with a supreme will and every act of will, of mind, of body is felt to come from it, to be its movement, instinct with it or identical, then what the Gita demands can be integrally done. The remembrance of the Divine Being becomes no longer an intermittent act of the mind, but the natural condition of our activities and in a way the very substance of the consciousness. The Jiva has become possessed of its right and natural, its spiritual relation to the Purushottama and all our life is a Yoga, an accomplished and yet an eternally self-accomplishing oneness.

वेदेषु यज्ञेषु तपःसु चैव दानेषु यत्पुण्यफलं प्रदिष्टम् ।
अत्येति तत्सर्वमिदं विदित्वा योगी परं स्थानमुपैति चाद्यम् ।।२८।।

28. (*Untranslated — see sl. 9/11*)

Chapter IX

I — The Secret of Secrets

The Teacher is going to open the mind of Arjuna to the knowledge and sight of the integral Divinity and lead up to the vision of the eleventh book, by which the warrior of Kurukshetra becomes conscious of the author and upholder of his being and action and mission, the Godhead in man and the world, whom nothing in man and in the world limits or binds, because all proceeds from him, is a movement in his infinite being, continues and is supported by his will, is justified in his divine self-knowledge, has him always for its origin, substance and end. Arjuna is to become aware of himself as existing only in God and as acting only by the power within him, his workings only an instrumentality of the divine action, his egoistic consciousness only a veil and to his ignorance a misrepresentation of the real being within him which is an immortal spark and portion of the supreme Godhead.

Now the world Being appears to him as the body of God ensouled by the eternal Time-spirit and with its majestic and dreadful voice missions him to the crash of the battle. He is called by it to the liberation of his spirit, to the fulfilment of his action in the cosmic mystery, and the two — liberation and action — are to be one movement. His intellectual doubts are clearing away as a greater light of self-knowledge and the knowledge of God and Nature is being unfolded before him. But intellectual clarity is not enough; he must see with the inner sight illumining his blind outward human vision, so that he may act with the consent of his whole being, with a perfect faith in all his members, *śraddhā*, with a perfect devotion to the Self of his self and the Master of his being and to the same Self of the world and Master of all being in the universe. In substance the integral knowledge of the Being who is speaking to him is to be now unveiled to his eyes so that he cannot choose but see.

Throughout Krishna, the Avatar, the Teacher, the charioteer of the human soul in the world-action, has been preparing the revelation of the secret of himself, Nature's deepest secret. He has kept one note always sounding across his preparatory strain and insistently coming in as a warning and prelude of the larger ultimate harmony of his integral Truth. That note was the idea of a supreme Godhead which dwells within man and Nature, but is greater than man and Nature, is found by impersonality of the self, but of which impersonal self is not the whole significance. We now see the meaning of that strong recurring insistence. It was this one Godhead, the same in universal self and man and Nature who through the voice of the Teacher in the chariot was preparing for his absolute claim to the whole being of the awakened seer of things and doer of works. "I who am within thee," he was saying, "I who am here in this human body, I for whom all exists, acts, strives, am at once the secret of the self-existent spirit and of the cosmic action. This 'I' is the greater I of whom the largest human personality is only a partial and fragmentary manifestation, Nature itself only an inferior working. Master of the soul, master of all the works of the cosmos, I am the one Light, the sole Power, the only Being. This Godhead within thee is the Teacher, the Sun, the lifter of the clear blaze of knowledge in which thou becomest aware of the difference between thy immutable self and thy mutable nature. But look beyond the light itself to its source; then shalt thou know the supreme Soul in which is recovered the spiritual truth of personality and Nature. See then the one self in all beings that thou mayst see me in all beings; see all beings in one spiritual self and reality, because that is the way to see all beings in me; know one Brahman in all that thou mayst see God who is the supreme Brahman. Know thyself, be thyself that thou mayst be united with me of whom this timeless self is the clear light or the transparent curtain. I the Godhead am the highest truth of self and spirit."

Arjuna has to see that the same Godhead is the higher truth too not only of self and spirit but of Nature and his own personality, the secret at once of the individual and the universe. Here is the place of bhakti in the scheme of the Yoga of an integral self-liberation. It is an adoration and aspiration towards that which is greater than imperishable self or changing Nature. All knowledge then becomes an adoration and aspiration, but all works too become an adoration and aspiration. Works of Nature and freedom of soul are unified in this adoration and become one self-uplifting to the one Godhead.

श्रीभगवानुवाच
इदं तु ते गुह्यतमं प्रवक्ष्याम्यनसूयवे ।
ज्ञानं विज्ञानसहितं यज्ज्ञात्वा मोक्ष्यसेऽशुभात् ।।१।।

1. *Krishna* — This truth is the secret of being which the Gita is now going to apply in its amplitude of result for our inner life and our outer works. **What it is going to say is the most secret thing of all. It is the knowledge of the whole Godhead, *samagraṁ mām*,** which the Master of his being has promised to Arjuna, **that essential knowledge attended with the complete**

knowledge of it in all its principles, *jñānam and vijñānam*, which will leave nothing yet to be known. The whole knot of the ignorance which has bewildered his human mind and has made his will recoil from his divinely appointed work, will have been cut entirely asunder. (*see also VII-2*)

राजविद्या राजगुह्यं पवित्रमिदमुत्तमम् ।
प्रत्यक्षावगमं धर्म्यं सुसुखं कर्तुमव्ययम् ।।२।।

2. **This is the wisdom of all wisdoms, the secret of all secrets, the king-knowledge, the king-secret. It is a pure and supreme light which one can verify by direct spiritual experience and see in oneself as the truth: it is the right and just knowledge, the very law of being. It is easy to practise** when one gets hold of it, sees it, tries faithfully to live in it.

अश्रद्दधानाः पुरुषा धर्मस्यास्य परन्तप ।
अप्राप्य मां निवर्तन्ते मृत्युसंसारवर्त्मनि ।।३।।

3. But faith is necessary; if faith is absent, **if one trusts to the critical intelligence which goes by outward facts and jealously questions the revelatory knowledge** (*sl. 1*) because that does not square with the divisions and imperfections of the apparent nature and seems to exceed it and state something which carries us beyond the first practical facts of our present existence, its grief, its pain, evil, defect, undivine error and stumbling, *aśubham*, then there is no possibility of living out that greater knowledge. **The soul that fails to get faith in the higher truth and law, must return into the path of ordinary mortal living subject to death and error and evil: it cannot grow into the Godhead which it denies.** For this is a truth which has to be lived, — and lived in the soul's growing light, not argued out in the mind's darkness. One has to grow into it, one has to become it, — that is the only way to verify it. It is only by an exceeding of the lower self that one can become the real divine self and live the truth of our spiritual existence. All the apparent truths one can oppose to it are appearances of the lower Nature. **The release from the evil and the defect of the lower Nature, *aśubham*,** (*sl. 1*) **can only come by accepting a higher knowledge** in which all this apparent evil becomes convinced of ultimate unreality, is shown to be a creation of our darkness.

But to grow thus into the freedom of the divine Nature one must accept and believe in the Godhead secret within our present limited nature. For the reason why the practice of this Yoga becomes possible and easy is that in doing it we give up the whole working of all that we naturally are into the hands of that inner divine Purusha. The Godhead works out the divine birth in us progressively, simply, infallibly, by taking up our being into his and by filling it with his own knowledge and power, *jñāna-dīpena bhāsvatā*; he lays hands on our obscure ignorant nature and transforms it into his own light and wideness. What with entire faith and without egoism we believe in and impelled by him will to be, the God within will surely accomplish. But the egoistic mind and life we now and apparently are, must first surrender itself for transmutation into the hands of that inmost secret Divinity within us.

II — THE DIVINE TRUTH AND WAY

The Gita then proceeds to unveil the supreme and integral secret, the one thought and truth in which the seeker of perfection and liberation must learn to live and the one law of perfection of his spiritual members and of all their movements. This supreme secret is the mystery of the transcendent Godhead who is all and everywhere, yet so much greater and other than the universe and all its forms that nothing here contains him, nothing expresses him really, and no language which is borrowed from the appearances of things in space and time and their relations can suggest the truth of his unimaginable being. The consequent law of our perfection is an adoration by our whole nature and its self-surrender to its divine source and possessor. Our one ultimate way is the turning of our entire existence in the world, and not merely of this or that in it, into a single movement towards the Eternal. By the power and mystery of a divine Yoga we have come out of his inexpressible secrecies into this bounded nature of phenomenal things. By a reverse movement of the same Yoga we must transcend the limits of phenomenal nature and recover the greater consciousness by which we can live in the Divine and the Eternal.

मया ततमिदं सर्वं जगदव्यक्तमूर्तिना ।
मत्स्थानि सर्वभूतानि न चाहं तेष्ववस्थितः ।।४।।

4. The supreme being of the Divine is beyond manifestation: the true sempiternal image of him is not revealed in matter, nor is it seized by life, nor is it cognisable by mind, *acintya-rūpa, avyakta-mūrti*. What we see is only a self-created form, *rūpa*, not the eternal form of the Divinity, *svarūpa*. There is someone or there is something that is other than the universe, inexpressible, unimaginable, an ineffably infinite Godhead beyond anything that our largest or subtlest conceptions of infinity can shadow. **All this weft of things to which we give the name of universe,** all this immense sum of motion

to which we can fix no limits and vainly seek in its forms and movements for any stable reality, any status, level and point of cosmic leverage, **has been spun out, shaped, extended by this highest Infinite, founded upon this ineffable supracosmic Mystery.** It is founded upon a self-formulation which is itself unmanifest and unthinkable. All this mass of becomings always changing and in motion, **all these creatures, existences, things, breathing and living forms cannot contain him** either in their sum or in their separate existence. **He is not in them;** it is not in them or by them that he lives, moves or has his being, — God is not the Becoming. **It is they that are in him,** it is they that live and move in him and draw their truth from him; **they are his becomings, he is their being, *mat-sthāni sarvabhūtāni na cāhaṁ teṣvavasthitaḥ*.** In the unthinkable timeless and spaceless infinity of his existence he has extended this minor phenomenon of a boundless universe in an endless space and time.

न च मत्स्थानि भूतानि पश्य मे योगमैश्वरम् ।
भूतभृन्न च भूतस्थो ममात्मा भूतभावनः ।।५।।

5. And even to say of him that all exists in him is not the whole truth of the matter, not the entirely real relation: for it is to speak of him with the idea of space, and the Divine is spaceless and timeless. Space and time, immanence and pervasion and exceeding are all of them terms and images of his consciousness. **There is a Yoga of divine Power, *me yoga aiśvaraḥ*,** by which the Supreme creates phenomena of himself in a spiritual, not a material, self-formulation of his own extended infinity, an extension of which the material is only an image. He sees himself as one with that, is identified with that and all it harbours. In that infinite self-seeing, which is not his whole seeing, — the pantheist's identity of God and universe is a still more limited view, — he is at once one with all that is and yet exceeds it; but he is other also than this self or extended infinity of spiritual being which contains and exceeds the universe. All exists here in his world-conscious infinite, but that again is upheld as a self-conception by the supracosmic reality of the Godhead which exceeds all our terms of world and being and consciousness. This is the mystery of his being that he is supracosmic, yet not in any exclusive sense extracosmic. For he pervades it all as its self; **there is a luminous uninvolved presence of the self-being of God, *mama-ātmā*, which is in constant relation with the becoming and brings all its existences into manifestation by his simple presence, *bhūta-bhṛin na ca bhūta-stho mama-ātmā bhūta-bhāvanaḥ*.** Therefore it is that we have these terms of Being and becoming, existence in itself, *ātman*, and existences dependent upon it, *bhūtāni*, mutable beings and immutable being. But the highest truth of these two relations and the resolution of their antinomy must be found in that which exceeds it; it is the supreme Godhead who manifests both containing self and its contained phenomena by the power of his spiritual consciousness, *yogamāyā*. And it is only through union with him in our spiritual consciousness that we can arrive at our real relations with his being.

Thus the Gita begins by affirming that **the Supreme contains all things in himself, but is not in any, *mat-sthāni sarva-bhūtāni*, all are situated in Me, not I in them,** and yet it proceeds immediately to say, **and yet all existences are not situated in Me, my self is the bearer of all existences and it is not situated in existences.** And yet again it insists with an apparent self-contradiction that **the Divine has lodged himself, has taken up his abode in the human body, *mānuṣīṁ tanum āśritam*, and that the recognition of this truth is necessary for the soul's release by the integral way of works and love and knowledge.** These statements are only in appearance inconsistent with each other. It is as the supracosmic Godhead that he is not in existences, nor even they in him; for the distinction we make between Being and becoming applies only to the manifestation in the phenomenal universe. In the supracosmic existence all is eternal Being and all, if there too there is any multiplicity, are eternal beings; nor can the spatial idea of indwelling come in, since a supracosmic absolute being is not affected by the concepts of time and space which are created here by the Lord's Yogamaya. There a spiritual, not a spatial or temporal coexistence, a spiritual identity and coincidence must be the foundation. But on the other hand in the cosmic manifestation there is an extension of universe in space and time by the supreme unmanifest supracosmic Being, and in that extension he appears first as **a self who supports all these existences; *bhūta-bhṛit*, he bears them in his all-pervading self-existence.** And, even, through this omnipresent self the supreme Self too, the Paramatman, can be said to bear the universe; he is its invisible spiritual foundation and the hidden spiritual cause of the becoming of all existences. He bears the universe as the secret spirit in us bears our thoughts, works, movements. He seems to pervade and to contain mind, life and body, to support them by his presence: but this pervasion is itself an act of consciousness, not material; the body itself is only a constant act of consciousness of the spirit.

यथाकाशस्थितो नित्यं वायुः सर्वत्रगो महान् ।
तथा सर्वाणि भूतानि मत्स्थानीत्युपधारय ।।६।।

6. This divine Self contains all existences; all are situated in him, not materially in essence, but in that extended spiritual conception of self-being of which our too rigid notion of a material and etheric space is only a rendering in the terms of the physical mind and senses. In reality all even here is spiritual coexistence, identity and coincidence; but that is a fundamental truth which we cannot apply until we get back to the supreme consciousness. We have to say, then, using these terms of relation in space and time, that the universe and all its beings exist in the divine Self-existent as everything else exists in the spatial primacy of ether. **It is as the great, the all-pervading aerial principle dwells in the etheric that all existences dwell in Me, that is how you have to conceive of it.**

सर्वभूतानि कौन्तेय प्रकृतिं यान्ति मामिकाम् ।
कल्पक्षये पुनस्तानि कल्पादौ विसृजाम्यहम्।।७।।
प्रकृतिं स्वामवष्टभ्य विसृजामि पुनः पुनः ।
भूतग्राममिमं कृत्स्नमवशं प्रकृतेर्वशात्।।८।।

7-8. **The Supreme from above cosmic existence leans or presses down upon his Nature to loose from it in an eternal cyclic recurrence all that it contains in it,** all that was once manifest and has become latent. **All existences act in the universe in subjection to this impelling movement** and to the laws of manifested being by which is expressed in cosmic harmonies the phenomenon of the divine All-existence. The Jiva follows the cycle of its becoming **in the action of this divine Nature, *prakṛitiṁ māmikām*, *svāṁ prakṛitim*, the "own nature" of the Divine.** It becomes in the turns of her progression this or that personality; it follows always the curve of its own law of being as a manifestation of the divine Nature; **it returns out of her action into her immobility and silence in the lapse of the cycle. Ignorant, it is subject to her cyclic whirl, not master of itself, but dominated by her, *avaśaḥ prakṛiter vaśāt*;** only by return to the divine consciousness can it attain to mastery and freedom. (*see also IV-6*)

The Gita explains the ordinary imperfect action of the creature by its subjection to the mechanism of Prakriti and its limitation by the self-representations of Maya. These two terms are only complementary aspects of one and the same effective force of divine consciousness. Maya is not essentially illusion, — the element or appearance of illusion only enters in by the ignorance of the lower Prakriti, Maya of the three modes of Nature, — it is the divine consciousness in its power of various self-representation of its being, while Prakriti is the effective force of that consciousness which operates to work out each such self-representation according to its own law and fundamental idea, *svabhāva* and *svadharma*, in its own proper quality and particular force of working, *guṇa-karma*. **Leaning — pressing down upon my own Nature (Prakriti) I create (loose forth into various being) all this multitude of existences, all helplessly subject to the control of Nature.**

न च मां तानि कर्माणि निबध्नन्ति धनञ्जय ।
उदासीनवदासीनमसक्तं तेषु कर्मसु ।।९।।
मयाध्यक्षेण प्रकृतिः सूयते सचराचरम् ।
हेतुनानेन कौन्तेय जगद्विपरिवर्तते ।।१०।।

9-10. The Divine too follows the cycle, not as subject to it, but as its informing Spirit and guide, not with his whole being involved in it, but with his power of being accompanying and shaping it. **He is the presiding control of his own action of Nature, *adhyakṣa,* — not a spirit born in her, but the creative spirit who causes her to produce all that appears in the manifestation.** If in his power he accompanies her and causes all her workings, he is outside it too, **as if One seated above her universal action in the supracosmic mastery, *udāsīnavad āsīnaḥ,* not attached to her by any involving and mastering desire and not therefore bound by her works, because he infinitely exceeds them and precedes them, is the same before, during and after all their procession in the cycles of Time.** All their mutations make no difference to his immutable being. The silent self that pervades and supports the cosmos is not affected by its changes because, though supporting, it does not participate in them. This greatest supreme supracosmic Self also is not affected because it exceeds and eternally transcends them.

The knowledge of the philosopher is that of the true nature of mundane existence, the transience of outward things, the vanity of the world's differences and distinctions, the superiority of the inner calm, peace, light, self-dependence. It is an equality of philosophic indifference; it brings a high calm, but not the greater spiritual joy; it is an isolated freedom, a wisdom like that of the Lucretian sage high in his superiority upon the cliff-top whence he looks down on men tossed still upon the tempestuous waters from which he has escaped, — in the end something after all aloof and ineffective. The Gita admits the philosophic motive of indifference as a preliminary movement; but the indifference to which it finally arrives, if indeed that inadequate word can be at all applied, has nothing in it of the philosophic aloofness. **It is indeed a position as of one seated above, *udāsīnavat,*** but as the Divine is seated above, having no need at all in the world, yet he does works always and is present everywhere supporting, helping, guiding the labour of creatures. This equality is founded upon oneness with all beings. It brings in what is wanting to the philosophic equality; for its soul is the soul of peace, but also it is the soul of love. It sees all beings without exception in the Divine, it is one self with the Self of all existences and therefore it is in supreme sympathy with all of them. Without exception, *aśeṣeṇa*, not only with all that is good and fair and pleases; nothing and no one, however vile, fallen, criminal, repellent in appearance, can be excluded from this universal, this whole-souled sympathy and spiritual oneness. Here there is no room, not merely for hatred or anger or uncharitableness, but for aloofness, disdain or any petty pride of superiority. A divine compassion for the ignorance of the struggling mind, a divine will to pour forth on it all light and power and happiness there will be, indeed, for the apparent man; but for the divine Soul within him there will be more, there will be adoration and love. For from all, from the thief and the harlot and the outcaste as from the saint and the sage, the Beloved looks forth and cries to us, "This is I." "He who loves Me in all beings" (*VI- 31*), — what greater word of power for the utmost intensities and profundities of divine and universal love, has been uttered by any philosophy or any religion?

अवजानन्ति मां मूढा मानुषीं तनुमाश्रितम् ।
परं भावमजानन्तो मम भूतमहेश्वरम् ।।११।।
मोघाशा मोघकर्माणो मोघज्ञाना विचेतसः ।
राक्षसीमासुरीं चैव प्रकृतिं मोहिनीं श्रिताः ।।१२।।

11-12. But also since this action is the action of the divine Nature, *svā prakṛitiḥ*, and the divine Nature can never be separate from the Divine, in everything she creates the Godhead must be immanent. That is a relation which is not the whole truth of his being, but neither is it a truth which we can at all afford to ignore. **He is lodged in the human body. Those who ignore his presence, who despise because of its masks the divinity in the human form, are bewildered and befooled by the appearances of Nature and they cannot realise that there is the secret Godhead within,** whether conscious in humanity as in the Avatar or veiled by his Maya. **Deluded minds despise me lodged in the human body because they know not my supreme nature of being, Lord of all existences.** Those who know not the Divine lodged in the human body, are ignorant of it because they are grossly subject to this mechanism of Prakriti, helplessly subject to its mental limitations and acquiescent in them, **and dwell in an Asuric nature that deludes with desire and bewilders with egoism the will and the intelligence, *mohinīṁ prakṛitiṁ śritāḥ*.** For the Purushottama within is not readily manifest to any and every being; he conceals himself in a thick cloud of darkness or a bright cloud of light, **utterly he envelops and wraps himself in his Yoga-Maya, *nāhaṁ prakāśaḥ sarvasya yogamāyā-samāvṛitaḥ*.**

Mortal mind is bewildered by its ignorant reliance upon veils and appearances; it sees only the outward human body, human mind, human way of living and catches no liberating glimpse of the Divinity who is lodged in the creature. It ignores the divinity within itself and cannot see it in other men, and even though the Divine manifest himself in humanity as Avatar and

Vibhuti, it is still blind and ignores or despises the veiled Godhead, *avajānanti māṁ mūḍhā mānuṣīṁ tanum āśritam*. And if it ignores him in the living creature, still less can it see him in the objective world on which it looks out from its prison of separative ego through the barred windows of the finite mind. It does not see God in the universe. **All its** [the separative ego-consciousness] **hope, action, knowledge are vain things when judged by the divine and eternal standard,** for it shuts out the great hope, excludes the liberating action, banishes the illuminating knowledge. It is a false knowledge that sees the phenomenon but misses the truth of the phenomenon, a blind hope that chases after the transient but misses the eternal, a sterile action whose every profit is annulled by loss and amounts to a perennial labour of Sisyphus.

Those who are great-souled, who are not shut up in their idea of ego, who open themselves to the indwelling Divinity, know that the secret spirit in man which appears here bounded by the limited human nature, is the same ineffable splendour which we worship beyond as the supreme Godhead (*sl. 13*). They become aware of the highest status of him in which he is master and lord of all existences and yet see that in each existence he is still the supreme Deity and the indwelling Godhead. All the rest is a self-limitation for the manifesting of the variations of Nature in the cosmos. They see too that as it is his Nature which has become all that is in the universe, everything here is in its inner fact nothing but one Divine, all is Vasudeva, and **they worship him not only as the supreme Godhead beyond, but here in the world, in his oneness and in every separate being** (*sl. 15*). They see this truth and in this truth they live and act; **him they adore, live, serve** both as the Transcendent of things and as God in the world and as the Godhead in all that is, **serve him with works of sacrifice, seek him out by knowledge, see nothing else but him everywhere and lift their whole being to him both in its self and in all its inward and outward nature** (*sl. 34*). This they know to be the large and perfect way; for it is the way of the whole truth of the one supreme and universal and individual Godhead.

III — WORKS, DEVOTION AND KNOWLEDGE

This integral turning of the soul Godwards, *sarva-bhāvena*, bases royally the Gita's synthesis of knowledge and works and devotion. To know God thus integrally is to know him as One in the self and in all manifestation and beyond all manifestation, — and all this unitedly and at once. And yet even so to know him is not enough unless it is accompanied by an intense uplifting of the heart and soul Godwards, unless it kindles a one-pointed and at the same time all-embracing love, adoration, aspiration. Indeed the knowledge which is not companioned by an aspiration and vivified by an uplifting is no true knowledge, for it can be only an intellectual seeing and a barren cognitive endeavour. The vision of God brings infallibly the adoration and passionate seeking of the Divine, — a passion for the Divine in his self-existent being, but also for the Divine in ourselves and for the Divine in all that is. To know with the intellect is simply to understand and may be an effective starting-point, — or, too, it may not be, and it will not be if there is no sincerity in the knowledge, no urge towards inner realisation in the will, no power upon the soul, no call in the spirit: for that would mean that the brain has externally understood, but inwardly the soul has seen nothing. True knowledge is to know with the inner being, and when the inner being is touched by the light, then it arises to embrace that which is seen, it yearns to possess, it struggles to shape that in itself and itself to it, it labours to become one with the glory of its vision. Knowledge in this sense is an awakening to identity and, since the inner being realises itself by consciousness and delight, by love, by possession and oneness with whatever of itself it has seen, knowledge awakened must bring an overmastering impulse towards this true and only perfect realisation. Here that which is known is not an externalised object, but the divine Purusha, self and lord of all that we are. An all-seizing delight in him and a deep and moved love and adoration of him must be the inevitable result and is the very soul of this knowledge. And this adoration is no isolated seeking of the heart, but an offering of the whole existence. Therefore it must take also the form of a sacrifice; there is a giving of all our works to the Ishwara, there is a surrender of all our active inward and outward nature to the Godhead of our adoration in its every subjective and in its every objective movement. All our subjective workings move in him and they seek him, the Lord and Self, as the source and goal of their power and endeavour. All our objective workings move out towards him in the world and make him their object, initiate a service of God in the world of which the controlling power is the Divinity within us in whom we are one self with the universe and its creatures. For both world and self, Nature and the soul in her are enlightened by the consciousness of the One, are inner and outer bodies of the transcendent Purushottama. So comes a synthesis of mind and heart and will in the one self and spirit and with it the synthesis of knowledge, love and works in this integral union, this embracing God-realisation, this divine Yoga.

महात्मानस्तु मां पार्थ दैवीं प्रकृतिमाश्रिताः ।
भजन्त्यनन्यमनसो ज्ञात्वा भूतादिमव्ययम् ।।१३।।
सततं कीर्तयन्तो मां यतन्तश्च दृढव्रताः ।
नमस्यन्तश्च मां भक्त्या नित्ययुक्ता उपासते ।।१४।।

13-14. The great-souled who open themselves to the light and the largeness of the diviner nature of which man is capable, are alone on the path narrow in the beginning, inexpressibly wide in the end that leads to liberation and perfection (*see sl. 11/12*). The growth of the god in man is man's proper business; **the steadfast turning of this lower Asuric and Rakshasic into the divine nature** is the carefully hidden meaning of human life. As this growth increases, the veil falls and the soul comes to see the greater significance of action and the real truth of existence. The eye opens to the Godhead in man, to the Godhead in the world; **it sees inwardly and comes to know outwardly the infinite Spirit, the Imperishable from whom all existences originate** and who exists in all and by him and in him all exist always. Therefore when this vision, this knowledge seizes on the soul, **its whole life-aspiration becomes a surpassing love and fathomless adoration of the Divine and Infinite. The mind attaches itself singly to the eternal,** the spiritual, the living, the universal, the Real; it **values nothing but for its sake, it delights only in the all-blissful Purusha. All the word and all the thought become one hymning of the universal Greatness, Light, Beauty, Power and Truth that has revealed itself in its glory to the human spirit and a worship of the one supreme Soul and infinite Person. All the long stress of the inner self to break outward becomes a form now of spiritual endeavour and aspiration to possess the Divine in the soul and realise the Divine in the nature. All life becomes a constant Yoga and unification of that Divine and this human spirit. This is the manner of the integral devotion; it creates a single uplifting of our whole being and nature through sacrifice by the dedicated heart to the eternal Purushottama.**

ज्ञानयज्ञेन चाप्यन्ये यजन्तो मामुपासते ।
एकत्वेन पृथक्त्वेन बहुधा विश्वतोमुखम् ।।१५।।

15. Those who lay a predominant stress on knowledge, arrive to the same point by an always increasing, engrossing, enforcing power of the vision of the Divine on the soul and the nature. **Theirs is the sacrifice of knowledge and by an ineffable ecstasy of knowledge they come to the adoration of the Purushottama, *jñāna-yajñena yajanto mām upāsate*.** This is a comprehension filled with Bhakti, because it is integral in its instruments, integral in its objective. It is not a pursuit of the Supreme merely as an abstract unity or an indeterminable Absolute. It is a heart-felt seeking and seizing of the Supreme and the Universal, a pursuit of the Infinite in his infinity and of the Infinite in all that is finite, **a vision and embracing of the One in his oneness and of the One in all his several principles, his innumerable visages, forces, forms,** here, there, everywhere, timelessly and in time, multiply, multitudinously, in endless

aspects of his Godhead, in beings without number, **all his million universal faces fronting us in the world and its creatures, *ekatvena pṛithaktvena bahudhā viśvato-mukham*.** This knowledge becomes easily an adoration, a large devotion, a vast self-giving, an integral self-offering because it is the knowledge of a Spirit, the contact of a Being, the embrace of a supreme and universal Soul which claims all that we are even as it lavishes on us when we approach it all the treasures of its endless delight of existence.

अहं क्रतुरहं यज्ञः स्वधाहमहमौषधम् ।
मन्त्रोऽहमहमेवाज्यमहमग्निरहं हुतम् ।।१६।।

16. The way of works too turns into an adoration and a devotion of self-giving because it is an entire sacrifice of all our will and its activities to the one Purushottama. The outward Vedic rite is a powerful symbol, effective for a slighter though still a heavenward purpose; but the real sacrifice is that inner oblation in which **the Divine All becomes himself the ritual action, the sacrifice and every single circumstance of the sacrifice.** All the workings and forms of that inner rite are the self-ordinance and self-expression of his power in us mounting by our aspiration towards the source of its energies. **The Divine Inhabitant becomes himself the flame and the offering,** because the flame is the Godward will and that will is God himself within us. **The Divine Thinker becomes himself the sacred mantra;** it is the Light of his being that expresses itself in the thought directed Godward and is effective in the revealing word of splendour that enshrines the thought's secret and in the rhythm that repeats for man the rhythms of the Eternal.

पिताहमस्य जगतो माता धाता पितामहः ।
वेद्यं पवित्रमोङ्कार ऋक्साम यजुरेव च ।।१७।।

17. The illumining Godhead is himself the Veda and that which is made known by the Veda. He is both the knowledge and the object of the knowledge. The Rik, the Yajur, the Sama, the word of illumination, the word of power, the word of calm and harmonious attainment, are themselves the Brahman, the Godhead. **All word and thought are an outflowering of the great OM, — OM, the Word, the Eternal.** OM is the sovereign source, seed, womb of thing and idea, form and name, — it is itself, integrally, the supreme Intangible, the original Unity, the timeless Mystery self-existent above all manifestation in supernal being. This sacrifice is therefore at once works and adoration and knowledge.

To the soul that thus knows, adores, offers up all its workings in a great self-surrender of its being to the Eternal, God is all and all is the Godhead. **It knows God as the Father of this world** who nourishes and cherishes and watches over his children. **It knows God as the divine Mother** who holds us in her bosom, lavishes upon us the sweetness of her love and fills the universe with her forms of beauty. **It knows him as the first Creator** from whom has originated all that originates and creates in space and time and relation. **It knows him as the Master and ordainer** of all universal and of every individual dispensation.

गतिर्भर्ता प्रभुः साक्षी निवासः शरणं सुहृत् ।
प्रभवः प्रलयः स्थानं निधानं बीजमव्ययम् ।।१८।।

18. **God to the soul that sees is the path and God is the goal of his journey,** a path in which there is no self-losing and a goal to which his wisely guided steps are surely arriving at every moment. **He knows the Godhead as the master of his and all being, the upholder of his nature, the husband of the nature-soul, its lover and cherisher, the inner witness of all his thoughts and actions. God is his house and country, the refuge of his seekings and desires, the wise and close and benignant friend of all beings. All birth and status and destruction of apparent existences is to his vision and experience the One** who brings forward, maintains and withdraws his temporal self-manifestation in its system of perpetual recurrences. **He alone is the imperishable seed and origin of all that seem to be born and perish and their eternal resting-place in their non-manifestation.**

तपाम्यहमहं वर्षं निगृह्णाम्युत्सृजामि च ।
अमृतं चैव मृत्युश्च सदसच्चाहमर्जुन ।।१९।।

19. **It is he that burns in the heat of the sun and the flame; it is he who is the plenty of the rain and its withholding;** he is all this physical Nature and her workings. **Death is his mask and immortality is his self-revelation. All that we call existent is he and all that we look upon as non-existent** still is there secret in the Infinite and is part of the mysterious being of the Ineffable.

त्रैविद्या मां सोमपाः पूतपापा यज्ञैरिष्ट्वा स्वर्गतिं प्रार्थयन्ते ।
ते पुण्यमासाद्य सुरेन्द्रलोकमश्नन्ति दिव्यान्दिवि देवभोगान् ।।२०।।

20. Nothing but the highest knowledge and adoration, no other way than an entire self-giving and surrender to this Highest who is all, will bring us to the Highest. Other religion, other worship, other knowledge, other seeking has always its fruits, but these are transient and limited to the enjoyment of divine symbols and appearances. There are always open for our following according to the balance of our mentality an outer and an inmost knowledge, an outer and an inmost seeking. Outward religion is the worship of an outward deity and the pursuit of an external beatitude: **its devotees purify their conduct from sin and attain to an active ethical righteousness** in order to satisfy the fixed law, the Shastra, the external dispensation; **they perform the ceremonial symbol of the outer communion. But their object is to secure** after the mortal pleasure and pain of earthly life **the bliss of heavenly worlds,** a greater happiness than earth can give but still a personal and mundane enjoyment though in a larger world than the field of this limited and suffering terrestrial nature. **And to that to which they aspire, they attain by faith and right endeavour;** for material existence and earthly activities are not the whole scope of our personal becoming or the whole formula of the cosmos.

ते तं भुक्त्वा स्वर्गलोकं विशालं क्षीणे पुण्ये मर्त्यलोकं विशन्ति ।
एवं त्रयीधर्ममनुप्रपन्ना गतागतं कामकामा लभन्ते ।।२१।।

21. Other worlds there are of a larger felicity, *svargalokaṁ viśālam*. Thus the Vedic ritualist of old learned the exoteric sense of the triple Veda, purified himself from sin, drank the wine of communion with the gods and sought by sacrifice and good deeds the rewards of heaven. This firm belief in a Beyond and **this seeking of a diviner world** secures to the soul in its passing the strength **to attain to the joys of heaven** on which its faith and seeking were centred: **but the return to mortal existence imposes itself** because the true aim of that existence has not been found and realised.

अनन्याश्चिन्तयन्तो मां ये जनाः पर्युपासते ।
तेषां नित्याभियुक्तानां योगक्षेमं वहाम्यहम् ।।२२।।

22. Here and not elsewhere the highest Godhead has to be found, the soul's divine nature developed out of the imperfect physical human nature and through unity with God and man and universe the whole large truth of being discovered and lived and made visibly wonderful. That completes the long cycle of our becoming and admits us to a supreme result; that is the opportunity given to the soul by the human birth and, until that is accomplished, it cannot cease. The God-lover advances constantly towards this ultimate necessity of our birth in cosmos **through a concentrated love and adoration by which he makes the supreme and universal Divine the whole object of his living and the whole object of his thought and his seeing. To see nothing but the Divine, to be at every moment in union with him, to love him in all creatures and have the delight of him in all things** is the whole condition of his spiritual existence. His God-vision does not divorce him from life, nor does he miss anything of the fullness of life; **for God himself becomes the spontaneous bringer to him of every good and of all his inner and outer getting and having, *yoga-kṣemaṁ vahāmyaham.*** The joy of heaven and the joy of earth are only a small shadow of his possessions; for as he grows into the Divine, the Divine too flows out upon him with all the light, power and joy of an infinite existence.

येऽप्यन्यदेवता भक्ता यजन्ते श्रद्धयाऽन्विताः ।
तेऽपि मामेव कौन्तेय यजन्त्यविधिपूर्वकम् ।।२३।।
अहं हि सर्वयज्ञानां भोक्ता च प्रभुरेव च ।
न तु मामभिजानन्ति तत्त्वेनातश्च्यवन्ति ते ।।२४।।
यान्ति देवव्रता देवान् पितॄन्यान्ति पितृव्रताः ।
भूतानि यान्ति भूतेज्या यान्ति मद्याजिनोऽपि माम् ।।२५।।

23-25. Ordinary religion is a sacrifice to partial godheads other than the integral Divinity. The Gita takes its direct examples from the old Vedic religion on its exoteric side as it had then developed; it describes this outward worship as **a sacrifice to other godheads, *anya-devatāḥ*, to the gods, or to the divinised Ancestors, or to elemental powers and spirits, *devān, pitṛin, bhūtāni.*** Men consecrate their life and works ordinarily to partial powers or aspects of the divine Existence as they see or conceive them. **If they do this with faith, then their faith is justified; for the Divine accepts whatever symbol, form or conception of himself is present to the mind of the worshipper, *yāṁ yāṁ tanuṁ śraddhayā-arcati*, as it is said elsewhere, and meets him according to the faith that is in him.** All sincere religious belief and practice is really a seeking after the one supreme and universal Godhead; **for he always is the sole master of man's sacrifice and askesis and infinite enjoyer of his effort and aspiration. However small or low the form of the worship, however limited the idea of the godhead, however restricted the giving, the faith, the effort** to get behind the veil of one's own ego-worship and limitation by material Nature, it yet forms a thread of connection between the soul of man and the All-soul and there is a response. Still the response, the fruit of the adoration and offering is according to the knowledge, the faith and the work and cannot exceed their limitations and therefore from the point of view of the greater God-knowledge, which alone gives the entire truth of being and becoming, **this inferior offering is not given according to the true and highest law of the sacrifice. It is not founded on a knowledge of the supreme Godhead in his integral existence and the true principles of his self-manifestation, but attaches itself to external and partial appearances, *na mām abhijānanti tattvena.*** Therefore its sacrifice too is limited in its object, largely egoistic in its motive, partial and mistaken in its action and its giving, ***yajanti avidhi-pūrvakam.*** An entire seeing of the Divine is the condition of an entire conscious self-surrender; **the rest attains to things that are incomplete and partial, and has to fall back from them** and return to enlarge itself in a greater seeking and wider God-experience. But to follow after the supreme and universal Godhead alone and utterly is to attain to all knowledge and result which other ways acquire, while yet one is not limited by any aspect, though one finds the truth of him in all aspects. This movement embraces all forms of divine being on its way to the supreme Purushottama. **Those whose sacrifice is to the gods, to elemental spirits, reach the gods, reach the elemental spirits, but those whose sacrifice is to Me, to Me they come.** *(see also III-II-Intr.; VII-21/23)*

पत्रं पुष्पं फलं तोयं यो मे भक्त्या प्रयच्छति ।
तदहं भक्त्युपहृतमश्नामि प्रयतात्मनः ।।२६।।

26. Therefore the wise have always been unwilling to limit man's avenues towards God; they would not shut against his entry even the narrowest portal, the lowest and darkest postern, the humblest wicket-gate. Any name, any form, any symbol, any offering has been held to be sufficient if there is the consecration along with it; for the Divine knows himself in the heart of the seeker and accepts the sacrifice.

The worship given may take any shape from the dedication of a leaf or flower, a cup of water, a handful of rice, a loaf of bread, to consecration of all that we possess and the submission of all that we are. Whoever the recipient, whatever the gift, it is the Supreme, the Eternal in things, who receives and accepts it, even if it be rejected or ignored by the immediate recipient.

He who gives to me with a heart of adoration a leaf, a flower, a fruit or a cup of water, I take and enjoy that offering of his devotion; and it is not only any dedicated external gift that can be so offered with love and devotion, but all our thoughts, all our feelings and sensations, all our outward activities and their forms and objects can be such gifts to the Eternal. It is true that the special act or form of action has its importance, even a great importance, but it is the spirit in the act that is the essential factor; the spirit of which it is the symbol or materialised expression gives it its whole value and justifying significance.

यत्करोषि यदश्नासि यज्जुहोषि ददासि यत् ।
यत्तपस्यसि कौन्तेय तत्कुरुष्व मदर्पणम् ।।२७।।

27. This absolute self-giving, this one-minded surrender is the devotion which the Gita makes the crown of its synthesis. All action and effort are by this devotion turned into an offering to the supreme and universal Godhead. **Whatever thou doest, whatever thou enjoyest, whatever thou sacrificest, whatever thou givest, whatever energy of tapasya, of the soul's will or effort thou puttest forth, make it an offering unto Me.** Here the least, the slightest circumstance of life, the most insignificant gift out of oneself or what one has, the smallest action assumes a divine significance and it becomes an acceptable offering to the Godhead who makes it a means for his possession of the soul and life of the God-lover.

Limit not sacrifice to the giving up of earthly goods or the denial of some desires and yearnings, but let every thought and every work and every enjoyment be an offering to God within thee. Let thy steps walk in thy Lord, let thy sleep and waking be a sacrifice to Krishna.

शुभाशुभफलैरेवं मोक्ष्यसे कर्मबन्धनैः ।
संन्यासयोगयुक्तात्मा विमुक्तो मामुपैष्यसि ।।२८।।

28. The distinctions made by desire and ego then disappear. **As there is no straining after the good result of one's action, no shunning of unhappy result,** but all action and result are given up to the Supreme to whom all work and fruit in the world belong for ever, **there is no farther bondage.** For by an absolute self-giving all egoistic desire disappears from the heart and **there is a perfect union between the Divine and the individual soul through an inner renunciation of its separate living. The finite nature thus surrendered becomes a free channel of the Infinite; the soul** in its spiritual being, uplifted out of the ignorance and the limitation, **returns to its oneness with the Eternal [with Me].**

समोऽहं सर्वभूतेषु न मे द्वेष्योऽस्ति न प्रियः ।
ये भजन्ति तु मां भक्त्या मयि ते तेषु चाप्यहम् ।।२९।।

29. **The Divine Eternal is the inhabitant in all existences; he is equal in all and the equal friend, father, mother, creator, lover, supporter of all creatures. He is the enemy of none and he is the partial lover of none;** none has he cast out, none has he eternally condemned, none has he favoured by any despotism of arbitrary caprice: all at last equally come to him through their

circlings in the ignorance. **But it is only this perfect adoration that can make this indwelling of God in man and man in God a conscious thing and an engrossing and perfect union.** Love of the Highest and a total self-surrender are the straight and swift way to this divine oneness. **None is dear to him, none hated, to all he is equal in spirit; yet is the God-lover the special receiver of his grace,** because the relation he has created is different and the one impartial Lord of all yet meets each soul according to its way of approach to him.

अपि चेत्सुदुराचारो भजते मामनन्यभाक् ।
साधुरेव स मन्तव्यः सम्यग्व्यवसितो हि सः ॥३०॥

30. The equal Divine Presence in all of us makes no other preliminary condition, if once this integral self-giving has been made in faith and in sincerity and with a fundamental completeness. All have access to this gate, all can enter into this temple: our mundane distinctions disappear in the mansion of the All-lover. There the virtuous man is not preferred, nor the sinner shut out from the Presence; **together by this road the Brahmin pure of life and exact in the observance of the law and the outcaste born from a womb of sin and sorrow and rejected of men can travel** and find an equal and open access to the supreme liberation and the highest dwelling in the Eternal. **Man and woman find their equal right before God;** for the divine Spirit is no respecter of persons or of social distinctions and restrictions: all can go straight to him without intermediary or shackling condition. **If, says the divine Teacher, even a man of very evil conduct turns to me with a sole and entire love, he must be regarded as a saint, for the settled will of endeavour in him is a right and complete will.**

क्षिप्रं भवति धर्मात्मा शश्वच्छान्तिं निगच्छति ।
कौन्तेय प्रतिजानीहि न मे भक्तः प्रणश्यति ॥३१॥

31. **Swiftly he becomes a soul of righteousness and obtains eternal peace.** In other words, a will of entire self-giving opens wide all the gates of the spirit and brings in response an entire descent and self-giving of the Godhead to the human being, and that at once reshapes and assimilates everything in us to the law of the divine existence by a rapid transformation of the lower into the spiritual nature. The will of self-giving forces away by its power the veil between God and man; it annuls every error and annihilates every obstacle. Those who aspire in their human strength by effort of knowledge or effort of virtue or effort of laborious self-discipline, grow with much anxious

difficulty towards the Eternal; but when the soul gives up its ego and its works to the Divine, God himself comes to us and takes up our burden. **This is my word of promise, cries the voice of the Godhead to Arjuna, that he who loves me shall not perish, *pratijānīhi na me bhaktaḥ praṇaśyati.***

मां हि पार्थ व्यपाश्रित्य येऽपि स्युः पापयोनयः ।
स्त्रियो वैश्यास्तथा शूद्रास्तेऽपि यान्ति परां गतिम् ।।३२।।

32. Previous effort and preparation, **the purity and the holiness of the Brahmin, the enlightened strength of the king-sage great in works and knowledge** have their value, because they make it easier for the imperfect human creature to arrive at this wide vision and self-surrender; but even without this preparation **all who take refuge in the divine Lover of man, the Vaishya** once preoccupied with the narrowness of wealth-getting and the labour of production, **the Shudra** hampered by a thousand hard restrictions, **woman** shut in and stunted in her growth by the narrow circle society has drawn around her self-expansion, **those too**, *pāpa-yonayaḥ*, on whom their past Karma has imposed even the very worst of births, **the outcaste, the Pariah, the Chandala, find at once the gates of God opening before them.**

किं पुनर्ब्राह्मणाः पुण्या भक्ता राजर्षयस्तथा।
अनित्यमसुखं लोकमिमं प्राप्य भजस्व माम् ।।३३।।

33. **O soul that findest thyself in this transient and unhappy world, turn and put thy delight in Me, *anityam asukhaṁ lokam imaṁ prāpya bhajasva mām.*** The earthly world preoccupied with the dualities and bound to the immediate transient relations of the hour and the moment is for man, so long as he dwells here attached to these things and while he accepts the law they impose on him for the law of his life, a world of struggle, suffering and sorrow. The way to liberation is to turn from the outward to the inward, from the appearance created by the material life which lays its burden on the mind and imprisons it in the grooves of the life and the body to the divine Reality which waits to manifest itself through the freedom of the spirit. Love of the world, the mask, must change into the love of God, the Truth. Once this secret and inner Godhead is known and is embraced, the whole being and the whole life will undergo a sovereign uplifting and a marvellous transmutation.

Thou who hast come to this transient and unhappy world, love and turn to Me.

मन्मना भव मद्भक्तो मद्याजी मां नमस्कुरु ।
मामेवैष्यसि युक्त्वैवमात्मानं मत्परायणः ।।३४।।

34. To make the mind one with the divine consciousness, *man-manā bhava*, to make the whole of our emotional nature one love of God everywhere, *mad-bhaktaḥ*, to make all our works one sacrifice to the Lord of the worlds, *mad-yājī*, and all our worship and aspiration one adoration of him and self-surrender, *mām namaskuru*, to direct the whole self Godwards in an entire union, *yuktvā-evam ātmānaṁ matparāyaṇaḥ*, is the way to rise out of a mundane into a divine existence. This is the Gita's teaching of divine love and devotion, in which knowledge, works and the heart's longing become one in a supreme unification, a merging of all their divergences, an intertwining of all their threads, a high fusion, a wide identifying movement. (*see also XVIII-65*)

Chapter X

I — The Supreme Word of the Gita

We have now got to the inmost kernel of the Gita's Yoga, the whole living and breathing centre of its teaching. We can see now quite clearly that the ascent of the limited human soul when it withdraws from the ego and the lower nature into the immutable Self calm, silent and stable, was only a first step, an initial change. And now too we can see why the Gita from the first insisted on the Ishwara, the Godhead in the human form, who speaks always of himself, *aham*, *mām*, as of some great secret and omnipresent Being, lord of all the worlds and master of the human soul, one who is greater even than that immutable self-existence which is still and unmoved for ever and abides for ever untouched by the subjective and objective appearances of the natural universe.

All Yoga is a seeking after the Divine, a turn towards union with the Eternal. According to the adequacy of our perception of the Divine and the Eternal will be the way of the seeking, the depth and fullness of the union and the integrality of the realisation. Man, the mental being, approaches the Infinite through his finite mind and has to open some near gate of this finite upon that Infinite. And as he approaches it, so it receives him, *ye yathā māṁ prapadyante*.

Not by denying all relations, but through all relations is the Divine Infinite naturally approachable to man and most easily, widely, intimately seizable. There are a thousand relations by which the supreme Eternal is secretly in contact and union with our human existence and by all essential ways of our nature and of the world's nature, *sarva-bhāvena*, can that contact be made sensible and that union made real to our soul, heart, will, intelligence, spirit. Therefore is this other way natural and easy for man, *sukham āptum*. God does not make himself difficult of approach to us: only one thing is needed, one demand made on us, the single indomitable will to break through the veil of our ignorance and the whole, the persistent seeking of the mind and heart and life for that which is all the time near to it, within it, its own soul of being and spiritual essence and the secret of its personality and its impersonality, its self and its nature. This is our one difficulty; the rest the Master of our existence will himself see to and accomplish, *ahaṁ tvāṁ mokṣayiṣyāmi mā śucaḥ*.

He who pervades the world as the one unchanging self that supports all its mutations, is equally the Godhead in man, the Lord in the heart of every creature, the conscient Cause and Master of all our subjective becoming and all our inward-taking and outward-going objectivised action. The Ishwara of the Yogins is one with the Brahman of the seeker of knowledge, one supreme and universal Spirit, one supreme and universal Godhead. This Ishwara is not a reflection of the impersonal and indeterminable Brahman in illusive Maya: for from beyond all cosmos as well as within it he rules and is the Lord of the worlds and their creatures. He is Parabrahman who is Parameshwara, supreme Lord because he is the supreme Self and Spirit, and from his highest original existence he originates and governs the universe.

In the unrolling of this comprehensive vision of existence and super-existence the Yoga of the Gita finds its unified significance and unexampled amplitude. This supreme Godhead is the one unchanging imperishable Self in all that is. He is the Godhead in man who originates and directs all his workings. He is the Godhead whose divine nature, origin of all that we are, is thickly veiled by these lower natural derivations. This Godhead is one in all things that are, the self who lives in all and the self in whom all live and move. This Godhead is the origin of all that is here or elsewhere and by his Nature he has become all these innumerable existences, *abhūt sarvāṇi bhūtāni. Kasmai devāya haviṣā vidhema*, "To what Godhead shall we give all our life and activities as an offering?" This is that Godhead, this the Lord who claims our sacrifice. A passive relationless identity excludes the joy of adoration and devotion; but bhakti is the very soul and heart and summit of this richer, completer, more intimate union. This Godhead is the fulfilment of all relations, father, mother, lover, friend and refuge of the soul of every creature. He is the one supreme and universal Deva, Atman, Purusha, Brahman, Ishwara of the secret wisdom. He has manifested the world in himself in all these ways by his divine Yoga: its multitudinous existences are one in him and he is one in them in many aspects. To awaken to the revelation of him in all these ways together is man's side of the same divine Yoga.

श्रीभगवानुवाच
भूय एव महाबाहो शृणु मे परमं वचः ।
यत्तेऽहं प्रीयमाणाय वक्ष्यामि हितकाम्यया ।।१।।

1. *Krishna* — To make it perfectly and indisputably clear that this is the supreme and entire truth of his teaching, this the integral knowledge which he had promised to reveal, the divine Avatar declares, in a brief reiteration of the upshot of all that he has been saying, that this and no other is his supreme word, *paramaṁ vacaḥ*. **Again hearken to my supreme word, *bhūya eva śriṇu me paramaṁ vacaḥ*.** This supreme word of the Gita is, we find, first the explicit and unmistakable declaration that the highest worship and highest knowledge of the Eternal are the knowledge and the adoration of **him as the supreme and divine Origin of all that is in existence and the mighty Lord of the world and its peoples of whose being all things are the becomings.** It is, secondly, the declaration of **a unified knowledge and bhakti as the supreme Yoga;** that is the destined and the natural way given to man to arrive at union with the eternal Godhead. And to make more significant this definition of the way, to give an illuminating point to this highest importance of bhakti founded upon and opening to knowledge and made the basis and motive-power for divinely appointed works, the acceptance of it by the heart and mind of the disciple is put as a condition for the farther development by which the final command to action comes at last to be given to the human instrument, Arjuna. **I will speak this supreme word to thee, says the Godhead, from my will for thy soul's good, now that thy heart is taking delight in me, *te prīyamāṇāya vakṣyāmi*. For this delight of the heart in God is the whole constituent and essence of true bhakti, *bhajanti prītipūrvakam*.** As soon as the supreme word is given (*1-11*), Arjuna is made to utter his acceptance of it and to ask for a practical way of seeing God in all things in Nature (*12-18*), and from that question immediately and naturally there develops the vision of the Divine as the Spirit of the universe and there arises the tremendous command to the world-action.

न मे विदुः सुरगणाः प्रभवं न महर्षयः ।
अहमादिर्हि देवानां महर्षीणां च सर्वशः ।।२।।

2. The idea of the Divine on which the Gita insists as the secret of the whole mystery of existence, the knowledge that leads to liberation, is one that bridges the opposition between the cosmic procession in Time and a supracosmic eternity without denying either of them or taking anything from the reality of either. The Divine is the unborn Eternal who has no origin; there is and can be nothing before him from which he proceeds, because he is one and timeless and absolute. **Neither the gods nor the great Rishis know any birth of me.... He who knows me as the unborn without origin...** are the opening utterances of this supreme word. And it gives the high promise that this knowledge, not limiting, not intellectual, but pure and spiritual, — for the form and nature, if we can use such language, of this transcendental Being, his *svarūpa*, are necessarily unthinkable by the mind, *acintya-rūpa*, — **liberates mortal man from all confusion of ignorance and from all bondage of sin, suffering and evil, *yo vetti asammūḍhaḥ sa martyeṣu sarva-pāpaiḥ pramucyate*.**

The divine Transcendence is not a negation, nor is it an Absolute empty of all relation to the universe. It is a supreme positive, it is an absolute of all absolutes. All cosmic relations derive from this Supreme; all cosmic existences return to it and find in it alone their true and immeasurable existence. **For I am altogether and in every way the origin of the gods and the great Rishis.** The gods are the great undying Powers and immortal Personalities who consciously inform, constitute, preside over the subjective and objective forces of the cosmos. The gods are spiritual forms of the eternal and original Deity who descend from him into the many processes of the world. Multitudinous, universal, the gods weave out of the primary principles of being and its thousand complexities the whole web of this diversified existence of the One. All their own existence, nature, power, process proceeds in every way, in every principle, in its every strand from the truth of the transcendent Ineffable. Nothing is independently created here, nothing is caused self-sufficiently by these divine agents; everything finds its origin, cause, first spiritual reason for being and will to be in the absolute and supreme Godhead, *aham ādiḥ sarvaśaḥ*. Nothing in the universe has its real cause in the universe; all proceeds from this supernal Existence.

यो मामजमनादिं च वेत्ति लोकमहेश्वरम् ।
असम्मूढः स मर्त्येषु सर्वपापैः प्रमुच्यते ।।३।।

3. The Supreme who becomes all creation, yet infinitely transcends it, is not a will-less cause aloof from his creation. He is not an involuntary originator who disowns all responsibility for these results of his universal Power or casts them upon an illusive consciousness entirely different from his own or leaves them to a mechanical Law or to a Demiurge or to a Manichean conflict of Principles. He is not an aloof and indifferent Witness who waits impassively for all to abolish itself or return to its unmoved original principle. **He is the mighty lord of the worlds and peoples, *loka-maheśvara*,** and governs all not only from within but from above, from his supreme transcendence. Cosmos cannot be governed by a Power that does not transcend cosmos. A divine government implies the free mastery of an omnipotent Ruler and not an automatic force or mechanical law of determinative becoming limited by the apparent nature of the cosmos. An Absolute who has become all that is by his divine Nature, his effective power of Spirit, he governs all from his transcendence. He is intimately present within every creature and the cause, ruler, director of all cosmic happenings and yet is he far too great, mighty and infinite to be limited by his creation.

This character of the knowledge is emphasised in three separate verses of promise. **Whosoever knows me, says the Godhead, as the unborn who is without origin, mighty lord of the worlds and peoples, lives unbewildered among mortals and is delivered from all sin and evil.** (*see also 7, 8, 10, 11*)

बुद्धिर्ज्ञानमसम्मोहः क्षमा सत्यं दमः शमः ।
सुखं दुःखं भवोऽभावो भयं चाभयमेव च ।।४।।
अहिंसा समता तुष्टिस्तपो दानं यशोऽयशः ।
भवन्ति भावा भूतानां मत्त एव पृथग्विधाः ।।५।।

4-5. Here also all is from the supreme Godhead, a birth, a becoming, an evolution, *prabhava, bhāva, pravṛitti*, a process of development through action of Nature out of the Transcendent. ***Ahaṁ sarvasya prabhavo mattaḥ sarvaṁ pravartate*, I am the birth of everything and from me all proceeds into development of action and movement** (*sl. 8*). Not only is this true of all that we call good or praise and recognise as divine, all that is luminous, sattwic, ethical, peace-giving, spiritually joy-giving, **understanding and knowledge and freedom from the bewilderment of the Ignorance, forgiveness and truth and self government and calm of inner control, non-injuring and equality, contentment and austerity and giving.** It is true also of the oppositions that perplex the mortal mind and bring in ignorance and its bewilderment, **grief and pleasure, coming into being and destruction, fear and fearlessness, glory and ingloriousness,** with all the rest of the interplay of light and darkness, all the myriad mixed threads that quiver so painfully and yet with a constant stimulation through the entanglement of our nervous mind and its ignorant subjectivities. **All here in their separate diversities are subjective becomings of existences in the one great Becoming and they get their birth and being from Him who transcends them, *matta eva*.** The Transcendent knows and originates these things, but is not caught as in a web in that diversified knowledge and is not overcome by his creation. We must observe here the emphatic collocation of the three words from the verb *bhū*, to become, *bhavanti, bhāvāḥ, bhūtānām*. All existences are becomings of the Divine, *bhūtāni*; all subjective states and movements are his and their psychological becomings, *bhāvāḥ*. These even, our lesser subjective conditions and their apparent results no less than the highest spiritual states, are all becomings from the supreme Being, *bhavanti matta eva*. The Gita recognises and stresses the distinction between Being and becoming, but does not turn it into an opposition. For that would be to abrogate the universal oneness. The Godhead is one in his transcendence, one all-supporting Self of things, one in the unity of his cosmic nature. These three are one Godhead; all derives from him, all becomes from his being, all is eternal portion or temporal expression of the Eternal. In the Transcendence, in the Absolute, if we are to follow the Gita, we must look, not for a supreme negation of all things, but for the positive key of their mystery, the reconciling secret of their existence.

महर्षयः सप्त पूर्वे चत्वारो मनवस्तथा ।
मद्भावा मानसा जाता येषां लोक इमाः प्रजाः ।।६।।

6. **The great Rishis,** called here as in the Veda **the seven original Seers, *maharṣayaḥ sapta pūrve*, the seven Ancients of the world,** are intelligence-powers of that divine Wisdom which has evolved all things out of its own self-conscious infinitude, *prajñā purāṇī*, — developed them down the range of the seven principles of its own essence. These Rishis embody the all-upholding, all-illumining, all-manifesting seven Thoughts of the Veda, *sapta dhiyaḥ*. Along with these are coupled **the four eternal Manus, fathers of man,** — for the active nature of the Godhead is fourfold and humanity expresses this nature in its fourfold character. These also, as their name implies, are mental beings. Creators of all this life that depends on manifest or latent mind for its action, **from them are all these living creatures in the world; all are their children and offspring, *yeṣāṁ loka imāḥ prajāḥ*. And these great Rishis and these Manus are themselves perpetual mental becomings of the supreme Soul, *madbhāvā mānasā jātāḥ*,** and born out of his spiritual transcendence into cosmic Nature, — originators, but he the origin of all that originates in the universe. Spirit of all spirits, Soul of all souls, Mind of all mind, Life of all life, Substance of all form, this transcendent Absolute is no complete opposite of all we are, but, on the contrary, the originating and illuminating Absolute of all the principles and powers of our and the world's being and nature.

This transcendent Origin of our existence is not separated from us by any unbridgeable gulf and does not disown the creatures that derive from him or condemn them to be only the figments of an illusion. He is the Being, all are his becomings. He does not create out of a Void, out of a Nihil or out of an unsubstantial matrix of dream. Out of himself he creates, in himself he becomes; all are in his being and all is of his being. This truth admits and exceeds the pantheistic seeing of things. Vasudeva is all, *vāsudevaḥ sarvam*; but Vasudeva is all that appears in the cosmos because he is too all that does not appear in it, all that is never manifested. His being is in no way limited by his becoming; he is in no degree bound by this world of relations. Even in becoming all he is still a Transcendence; even in assuming finite forms he is always the Infinite. Nature, Prakriti, is in her essence his spiritual power, self-power, *ātma-śakti*; this spiritual self-power develops infinite primal qualities of becoming in the inwardness of things and turns them into an external surface of form and action. For in her essential, secret and divine order the spiritual truth of each and all comes first, a thing of her deep identities; their psychological truth of quality and nature is dependent on the spiritual for all in it that is authentic, it derives from the spirit; least in necessity, last in order the objective truth of form and action derives from inner quality of nature and depends on it for all these variable presentations of existence here in the external order. Or in other words, the objective fact is only an expression of a sum of soul factors and these go back always to a spiritual cause of their appearance. (*see also VII-19*)

एतां विभूतिं योगं च मम यो वेत्ति तत्त्वतः ।
सोऽविकम्पेन योगेन युज्यते नात्र संशयः ।।७।।

7. **Whosoever knows in its right principles this my pervading lordship and this my Yoga (the divine Yoga, *aiśvara yoga*, by which the Transcendent is one with all existences, even while more than them all, and dwells in them and contains them as becomings of his own Nature), unites himself to me by an untrembling Yoga.** The wisdom of the liberated man is not, in the view of the Gita, a consciousness of abstracted and unrelated impersonality, a do-nothing quietude. For the mind and soul of the liberated man are firmly settled in a constant sense, an integral feeling of **the pervasion of the world by the actuating and directing presence of the divine Master of the universe, *etāṁ vibhūtiṁ mama yo vetti*.** He is aware of his spirit's transcendence of the cosmic order, but he is aware also of **his oneness with it by the divine Yoga, *yogaṁ ca mama*.** And he sees each aspect of the transcendent, the cosmic and the individual existence in its right relation to the supreme Truth and puts all in their right place in the unity of the divine Yoga. He no longer sees each thing in its separateness, — the separate seeing that leaves all either unexplained or one-sided to the experiencing consciousness. **He becomes of like nature and law of being with the Divine, *sādharmyam āgataḥ*,** transcendent even in universality of spirit, universal even in the individuality of mind, life and body. **By this Yoga once perfected, undeviating and fixed, *avikampena yogena yujyate*,** he is able to take up whatever poise of nature, assume whatever human condition, do whatever world-action without any fall from his oneness with the divine Self, without any loss of his constant communion with the Master of existence, *sarvathā vartamāno'pi sa yogī mayi vartate.*

अहं सर्वस्य प्रभवो मत्तः सर्वं प्रवर्तते ।
इति मत्वा भजन्ते मां बुधा भावसमन्विताः ।।८।।

8. The wise hold me for the birth of each and all, hold each and all as developing from me its action and movement, and so holding they love and adore me. (*see also XVI-Intro.*)

मच्चित्ता मद्गतप्राणा बोधयन्तः परस्परम् ।
कथयन्तश्च मां नित्यं तुष्यन्ति च रमन्ति च ।।९।।

9. This knowledge translated into the affective, emotional, temperamental plane becomes a calm love and intense adoration of the original and transcendental Godhead above us, the ever-present Master of all things here, God in man, God in Nature. **It is at first a wisdom of the intelligence, the *buddhi*; but that is accompanied by a moved spiritualised state of the affective nature, *bhāva*, (*budhā bhāva-samanvitāḥ*).** This change of the heart and mind is the beginning of a total change of all the nature. A new inner birth and becoming prepares us for oneness with the supreme object of our love and adoration, *madbhāvāya.* **There is an intense delight of love** in the greatness and beauty and perfection of this divine Being now seen everywhere in the world and above it, *prīti.* That deeper ecstasy assumes the place of the scattered and external pleasure of the mind in existence or rather it draws all other delight into it and transforms by a marvellous alchemy the mind's and the heart's feelings and all sense movements. **The whole consciousness becomes full of the Godhead and replete with his answering consciousness; the whole life flows into one sea of bliss-experience. All the speech and thought of such God-lovers becomes a mutual utterance and understanding of the Divine. In that one joy is concentrated all the contentment of the being, all the play and pleasure of the nature.**

तेषां सततयुक्तानां भजतां प्रीतिपूर्वकम् ।
ददामि बुद्धियोगं तं येन मामुपयान्ति ते ।।१०।।

10. There is a continual union from moment to moment in the thought and memory, there is an unbroken continuity of the experience of oneness in the spirit. And from the moment that this inner state begins, even in the stage of imperfection, the Divine confirms it by the perfect Yoga of the will and intelligence. "And I give them the Yoga of the understanding by which they come to me",

तेषामेवानुकम्पार्थमहमज्ञानजं तमः ।
नाशयाम्यात्मभावस्थो ज्ञानदीपेन भास्वता ।।११।।

11. "and I destroy for them the darkness which is born of the ignorance". These results (*see also 3, 7, 8*) must arise inevitably from the very nature of the knowledge and from the very nature of the Yoga which converts that knowledge into spiritual growth and spiritual experience. **He uplifts the blazing lamp of knowledge within us, he destroys the ignorance of the separative mind and will, he stands revealed in the human spirit.** By the Yoga of the will and the intelligence founded on an illumined union of works and knowledge the transition was effected from our lower troubled mind-ranges to the immutable calm of the witnessing Soul above the active nature. But now by this greater yoga of the Buddhi founded on an illumined union of love and adoration with an all-comprehending knowledge the soul rises in a vast ecstasy to the whole transcendental truth of the absolute and all-originating Godhead. The Eternal is fulfilled in the individual spirit and individual nature; the individual spirit is exalted from birth in time to the infinitudes of the Eternal.

II — GOD IN POWER OF BECOMING

A very important step has been reached, a decisive statement of its metaphysical and psychological synthesis has been added to the development of the Gita's gospel of spiritual liberation and divine works. The Godhead has been revealed in thought to Arjuna; he has been made visible to the mind's search and the heart's seeing as the supreme and universal Being, the supernal and universal Person, the inward-dwelling Master of our existence for whom man's knowledge, will and adoration were seeking through the mists of the Ignorance. There remains only the vision of the multiple Virat Purusha to complete the revelation on one more of its many sides.

अर्जुन उवाच
परं ब्रह्म परं धाम पवित्रं परमं भवान् ।
पुरुषं शाश्वतं दिव्यमादिदेवमजं विभुम् ।।१२।।

12. *Arjuna* — Arjuna accepts the entire knowledge that has thus been given to him by the divine Teacher. His mind is already delivered from its doubts and seekings; his heart, turned now from the outward aspect of the world, from its baffling appearance to its supreme sense and origin and its inner realities, is already released from sorrow and affliction and touched with the ineffable gladness of a divine revelation. The language which he is made to use in voicing his acceptance is such as to emphasise and insist once again on the profound integrality of this knowledge and its all-embracing finality and fullness. **He accepts first the Avatar, the Godhead in man who is speaking to him as the supreme Brahman, as the supracosmic All and Absolute of existence in which the soul can dwell** when it rises out of this manifestation and this partial becoming to its source, ***paraṁ brahma, paraṁ dhāma.* He accepts him as the supreme purity of the ever free Existence** to which one arrives through the effacement of the ego in the self's immutable impersonality calm and still for ever, ***pavitraṁ paramam.* He accepts him next as the one Permanent, the eternal Soul, the divine Purusha, *puruṣaṁ śāśvataṁ divyam.* He acclaims in him the original Godhead, adores the Unborn who is the pervading, indwelling, self-extending master of all existence, *ādi-devam ajaṁ vibhum.***

आहुस्त्वामृषयः सर्वे देवर्षिर्नारदस्तथा ।
असितो देवलो व्यासः स्वयं चैव ब्रवीषि मे ।।१३।।

13. This is a secret wisdom which one must hear from the seers who have seen the face of this Truth, have heard its word and have become one with it in self and spirit. **All the Rishis say this of thee and the divine seer Narada, Asita, Devala, Vyasa.** Or else one must receive it from within by revelation and inspiration from the inner Godhead who lifts in us the blazing lamp of knowledge. ***svayam caiva bravīṣi me,* and thou thyself sayest it to me.** Once revealed, it has to be accepted by the assent of the mind, the consent of the will and the heart's delight and submission, the three elements of the complete mental faith, *śraddhā.*

सर्वमेतदृतं मन्ये यन्मां वदसि केशव ।
न हि ते भगवन्व्यक्तिं विदुर्देवा न दानवाः ।।१४।।

14. It is so that Arjuna has accepted it; **all this that thou sayest, my mind holds for the truth.** But still there will remain the need of that deeper possession in the very self of our being out from its most intimate psychic centre, the soul's demand for that inexpressible permanent spiritual realisation of which the mental is only a preliminary or a shadow and without which there cannot be a complete union with the Eternal.

The whole universe or even numberless universes cannot manifest him, cannot contain his ineffable light and infinite greatness. All other lesser God-knowledge has its truth only by dependence on the ever unmanifested and ineffable reality of the transcendent Godhead.

Arjuna accepts him therefore not only as that Wonderful who is beyond expression of any kind, for nothing is sufficient to manifest him, — **neither**

the Gods nor the Titans, O blessed Lord, know thy manifestation, ***na hi te bhagavan vyaktiṁ vidur devā na dānavāḥ,*** —

स्वयमेवात्मनात्मानं वेत्थ त्वं पुरुषोत्तम ।
भूतभावन भूतेश देवदेव जगत्पते ।।१५।।

15. **but as the lord of all existences and the one divine efficient cause of all their becoming, God of the gods from whom all godheads have sprung, master of the universe who manifests and governs it from above by the power of his supreme and his universal Nature,** ***bhūta-bhāvana bhūteśa deva-deva jagat-pate.*** He has accepted the truth with the adoration of his heart, the submission of his will and the understanding of his intelligence. He is already prepared to act as the divine instrument in this knowledge and with this self-surrender. But a desire for a deeper constant spiritual realisation has been awakened in his heart and will. This is a truth which is evident only to the supreme Soul in its own self-knowledge, — for, cries Arjuna, **thou alone, O Purushottama, knowest thyself by thyself,** ***ātmanā ātmānaṁ vettha.*** This is a knowledge that comes by spiritual identity and the unaided heart, will, intelligence of the natural man cannot arrive at it by their own motion and can only get at imperfect mental reflections that reveal less than they conceal and disfigure.

वक्तुमर्हस्यशेषेण दिव्या ह्यात्मविभूतयः ।
याभिर्विभूतिभिर्लोकानिमांस्त्वं व्याप्य तिष्ठसि ।।१६।।

16. And lastly Arjuna accepts him as that Vasudeva in and around us who is all things here by virtue of the world-pervading, all-inhabiting, all-constituting **master powers of his becoming,** ***vibhūtayaḥ,*** **"the sovereign powers of thy becoming by which thou standest pervading these worlds",** ***yābhir vibhūtibhir lokān imāṁs tvaṁ vyāpya tiṣṭhasi.*** Here constantly the assent of the understanding, the consent of the will and the heart's faith become difficult to a human mentality anchored always on phenomenon and appearance. At least some compelling indications are needed, some links and bridges, some supports to the difficult effort at oneness.

Arjuna, though he accepts the revelation of Vasudeva as all and though his heart is full of the delight of it, — for already he finds that it is delivering him from the perplexity and stumbling differentiations of his mind which was crying for a clue, a guiding truth amid the bewildering problems of a world of oppositions, and it is to his hearing the nectar of immortality, *amṛitam,*

— yet feels the need of such supports and indices. He feels that they are indispensable to overcome the difficulty of a complete and firm realisation; for how else can this knowledge be made a thing of the heart and life? He requires guiding indications, asks Krishna even for a complete and detailed enumeration of the sovereign powers of his becoming and desires that nothing shall be left out of the vision, nothing remain to baffle him. **Thou shouldst tell me, he says, of thy divine self-manifestations in thy sovereign power of becoming, *divyā ātma-vibhūtayaḥ*, all without exception, — *aśeṣeṇa*, nothing omitted, — thy Vibhutis by which thou pervadest these worlds and peoples.**

कथं विद्यामहं योगिंस्त्वां सदा परिचिन्तयन् ।
केषु केषु च भावेषु चिन्त्योऽसि भगवन्मया ।।१७।।

17. **How shall I know thee, O Yogin, by thinking of thee everywhere at all moments and in what pre-eminent becomings should I think of thee?**

विस्तरेणात्मनो योगं विभूतिं च जनार्दन ।
भूयः कथय तृप्तिर्हि शृण्वतो नास्ति मेऽमृतम् ।।१८।।

18. **This Yoga by which thou art one with all and one in all and all are becomings of thy being, all are pervading or pre-eminent or disguised powers of thy nature, tell me of it, he cries, in its detail and extent, and tell me ever more of it; it is nectar of immortality to me, and however much of it I hear, I am not satiated.** Here we get an indication in the Gita of something which the Gita itself does not bring out expressly, but which occurs frequently in the Upanishads and was developed later on by Vaishnavism and Shaktism in a greater intensity of vision, man's possible joy of the Divine in the world-existence, the universal Ananda, the play of the Mother, the sweetness and beauty of God's Lila.

श्रीभगवानुवाच
हन्त ते कथयिष्यामि दिव्या ह्यात्मविभूतयः ।
प्राधान्यतः कुरुश्रेष्ठ नास्त्यन्तो विस्तरस्य मे ।।१९।।

19. *Krishna* — The divine Teacher accedes to the request of the disciple, but with an initial reminder that a full reply is not possible. For God is infinite and his manifestation is infinite. The forms of his manifestation too are innumerable. Each form is a symbol of some divine power, *vibhūti*, concealed in it and to the seeing eye each finite carries in it its own revelation

of the infinite. **Yes, he says, I will tell thee of my divine Vibhutis, but only in some of my principal pre-eminences and as an indication and by the example of things in which thou canst most readily see the power of the Godhead, *prādhānyataḥ, uddeśataḥ*. For there is no end to the innumerable detail of the Godhead's self-extension in the universe, *nāsti-anto vistarasya me*.** This reminder begins the passage and is repeated at the end (*sl. 40*) in order to give it a greater and unmistakable emphasis. And then throughout the rest of the chapter (*sl. 21/38*) we get a summary description of these principal indications, these pre-eminent signs of the divine force present in the things and persons of the universe. *It seems at first as if they were given pell-mell, without any order, but still there is a certain principle in the enumeration, which, if it is once disengaged, can lead by a helpful guidance to the inner sense of the idea and its consequences.*[1] The chapter has been called the Vibhuti-Yoga, — an indispensable yoga. For while we must identify ourselves impartially with the universal divine Becoming in all its extension, its good and evil, perfection and imperfection, light and darkness, we must at the same time realise that there is an ascending evolutionary power in it, an increasing intensity of its revelation in things, a hierarchic secret something that carries us upward from the first concealing appearances through higher and higher forms towards the large ideal nature of the universal Godhead.

The world is only a partial manifestation of the Godhead, it is not itself that Divinity. The Godhead is infinitely greater than any natural manifestation can be. By his very infinity, by its absolute freedom he exists beyond all possibility of integral formulation in any scheme of worlds or extension of cosmic Nature, however wide, complex, endlessly varied this and every world may seem to us, — *nāsti-anto vistarasya me*, — however to our finite view infinite. Therefore beyond cosmos the eye of the liberated spirit will see the utter Divine. Cosmos he will see as a figure drawn from the Divinity who is beyond all figure, a constant minor term in the absolute existence. Every relative and finite he will see as a figure of the divine Absolute and Infinite, and both beyond all finites and through each finite he will arrive at that alone, see always that beyond each phenomenon and natural creature and relative action and every quality and every happening; looking at each of these things and beyond it, he will find in the Divinity its spiritual significance.

अहमात्मा गुडाकेश सर्वभूताशयस्थितः ।
अहमादिश्च मध्यं च भूतानामन्त एव च ।।२०।।

1. Editor's italics.

20. This summary enumeration begins with a statement of the primal principle that underlies all the power of this manifestation in the universe. It is this that **in every being and object God dwells concealed and discoverable; he is housed as in a crypt in the mind and heart of every thing and creature, an inner self in the core of its subjective and its objective becoming, one who is the beginning and middle and end of all that is, has been or will be.** For it is this inner divine Self hidden from the mind and heart which he inhabits, this luminous Inhabitant concealed from the view of the soul in Nature which he has put forth into Nature as his representative, who is all the time evolving the mutations of our personality in Time and our sensational existence in Space, — Time and Space that are the conceptual movement and extension of the Godhead in us. All is this self-seeing Soul, this self-representing Spirit.

All things are in fact and can be nothing but powers of his manifestation, vibhutis of this universal Soul and Spirit, Yoga of this great Yogin, self-creations of this marvellous self-Creator. **He is the unborn and the all-pervading Master of his own innumerable becomings in the universe, *ajo vibhuḥ*; all things are his powers and effectuations in his self-Nature, vibhutis. He is the origin of all they are, their beginning; he is their support in their ever-changing status, their middle; he is their end too, the culmination or the disintegration of each created thing in its cessation or its disappearance.** He brings them out from his consciousness and is hidden in them, he withdraws them into his consciousness and they are hidden in him for a time or for ever. What is apparent to us is only a power of becoming of the One: what disappears from our sense and vision is effect of that power of becoming of the One. All classes, genera, species, individuals are such vibhutis. But since it is through power in his becoming that he is apparent to us, he is especially apparent in whatever is of a pre-eminent value or seems to act with a powerful and pre-eminent force. And therefore in each kind of being we can see him most in those in whom the power of nature of that kind reaches its highest, its leading, its most effectively self-revealing manifestation. These are in a special sense Vibhutis. Yet the highest power and manifestation is only a very partial revelation of the Infinite; even the whole universe is informed by only one degree of his greatness, illumined by one ray of his splendour, glorious with a faint hint of his delight and beauty. This is in sum the gist of the enumeration, the result we carry away from it, the heart of its meaning.

आदित्यानामहं विष्णुर्ज्योतिषां रविरंशुमान् ।
मरीचिर्मरुतामस्मि नक्षत्राणामहं शशी ।।२१।।
वेदानां सामवेदोऽस्मि देवानामस्मि वासवः ।
इन्द्रियाणां मनश्चास्मि भूतानामस्मि चेतना ।।२२।।

रुद्राणां शङ्करश्चास्मि वित्तेशो यक्षरक्षसाम् ।
वसूनां पावकश्चास्मि मेरुः शिखरिणामहम् ।।२३।।
पुरोधसां च मुख्यं मां विद्धि पार्थ बृहस्पतिम् ।
सेनानीनामहं स्कन्दः सरसामस्मि सागरः ।।२४।।
महर्षीणां भृगुरहं गिरामस्म्येकमक्षरम् ।
यज्ञानां जपयज्ञोऽस्मि स्थावराणां हिमालयः ।।२५।।
अश्वत्थः सर्ववृक्षाणां देवर्षीणां च नारदः ।
गन्धर्वाणां चित्ररथः सिद्धानां कपिलो मुनिः ।।२६।।
उच्चैःश्रवसमश्वानां विद्धि माममृतोद्भवम् ।
ऐरावतं गजेन्द्राणां नराणां च नराधिपम् ।।२७।।
आयुधानामहं वज्रं धेनूनामस्मि कामधुक् ।
प्रजनश्चास्मि कन्दर्पः सर्पाणामस्मि वासुकिः ।।२८।।
अनन्तश्चास्मि नागानां वरुणो यादसामहम् ।
पितॄणामर्यमा चास्मि यमः संयमतामहम् ।।२९।।
प्रह्लादश्चास्मि दैत्यानां कालः कलयतामहम् ।
मृगाणां च मृगेन्द्रोऽहं वैनतेयश्च पक्षिणाम् ।।३०।।
पवनः पवतामस्मि रामः शस्त्रभृतामहम् ।
झषाणां मकरश्चास्मि स्रोतसामस्मि जाह्नवी ।।३१।।
सर्गाणामादिरन्तश्च मध्यं चैवाहमर्जुन ।
अध्यात्मविद्या विद्यानां वादः प्रवदतामहम् ।।३२।।
अक्षराणामकारोऽस्मि द्वन्द्वः सामासिकस्य च ।
अहमेवाक्षयः कालो धाताऽहं विश्वतोमुखः ।।३३।।
मृत्युः सर्वहरश्चाहमुद्भवश्च भविष्यताम् ।
कीर्तिः श्रीर्वाक्च नारीणां स्मृतिर्मेधा धृतिः क्षमा ।।३४।।
बृहत्साम तथा साम्नां गायत्री छन्दसामहम् ।
मासानां मार्गशीर्षोऽहमृतूनां कुसुमाकरः ।।३५।।
द्यूतं छलयतामस्मि तेजस्तेजस्विनामहम् ।
जयोऽस्मि व्यवसायोऽस्मि सत्त्वं सत्त्ववतामहम् ।।३६।।
वृष्णीनां वासुदेवोऽस्मि पाण्डवानां धनञ्जयः ।
मुनीनामप्यहं व्यासः कवीनामुशना कविः ।।३७।।
दण्डो दमयतामस्मि नीतिरस्मि जिगीषताम् ।
मौनं चैवास्मि गुह्यानां ज्ञानं ज्ञानवतामहम् ।।३८।।

21-38. God is imperishable, beginningless, unending Time; this is his most evident Power of becoming and the essence of the whole universal movement. ***Aham eva-akṣayaḥ kālaḥ.*** In that movement of Time and Becoming God appears to our conception or experience of him by the evidence of his works as **the divine Power who ordains and sets all things in their place in**

the movement. In his form of Space it is he who fronts us in every direction, million-bodied, myriad-minded, manifest in each existence; we see his faces on all sides of us. *Dhātā-aham viśvato-mukhaḥ*. For simultaneously in all these many million persons and things, *sarva-bhūteṣu*, there works the mystery of his self and thought and force and his divine genius of creation and his marvellous art of formation and his impeccable ordering of relations and possibilities and inevitable consequences. He appears to us too in the universe as the universal spirit of Destruction, who seems to create only to undo his creations in the end, — **I am all-snatching Death, *ahaṁ mṛityuḥ sarva-haraḥ*.** And yet his Power of becoming does not cease from its workings, for the force of rebirth and new creation ever keeps pace with the force of death and destruction, — **and I am too the birth of all that shall come into being.** The divine Self in things is the sustaining Spirit of the present, the withdrawing Spirit of the past, the creative Spirit of the future.

Then among all these living beings, cosmic godheads, superhuman and human and subhuman creatures, and amid all these qualities, powers and objects, the chief, the head, the greatest in quality of each class is a special power of the becoming of the Godhead. **I am, says the Godhead, Vishnu among the Adityas, Shiva among the Rudras, Indra among the gods, Prahlada among the Titans, Brihaspati the chief of the high priests of the world, Skanda the war-god, leader of the leaders of battle, Marichi among the Maruts, the lord of wealth among the Yakshas and Rakshasas, the serpent Ananta among the Nagas, Agni among the Vasus, Chitraratha among the Gandharvas, Kandarpa the love-God among the progenitors, Varuna among the peoples of the sea, Aryaman among the Fathers, Narada among the divine sages, Yama lord of the Law among those who maintain rule and law, among the powers of storm the Wind-God. At the other end of the scale I am the radiant sun among lights and splendours, the moon among the stars of night, the ocean among the flowing waters, Meru among the peaks of the world, Himalaya among the mountain-ranges, Ganges among the rivers, the divine thunderbolt among weapons. Among all plants and trees I am the Aswattha, among horses Indra's horse Uchchaihsravas, Airavata among the elephants, among the birds Garuda, Vasuki the snake-god among the serpents, Kamadhuk the cow of plenty among cattle, the alligator among fishes, the lion among the beasts of the forest. I am Margasirsha, first of the months; I am spring, the fairest of the seasons.**

In living beings, the Godhead tells Arjuna, I am consciousness by which they are aware of themselves and their surroundings. I am mind among the senses, mind by which they receive the impressions of objects and react upon them. I am man's qualities of mind and character and body and action; I am glory and speech and memory and intelligence and steadfastness and forgiveness, the energy of the energetic and the strength of the mighty. I am resolution and

perseverance and victory, I am the sattwic quality of the good, I am the gambling of the cunning; I am the mastery and power of all who rule and tame and vanquish and the policy of all who succeed and conquer; I am the silence of things secret, the knowledge of the knower, the logic of those who debate. I am the letter A among letters, the dual among compounds, the sacred syllable OM among words, the Gayatri among meters, the Sama-Veda among the Vedas and the great Sama among the mantras. I am Time the head of all reckoning to those who reckon and measure. I am spiritual knowledge among the many philosophies, arts and sciences. I am all the powers of the human being and all the energies of the universe and its creatures.

Those in whom my powers rise to the utmost heights of human attainment are myself always, my special Vibhutis. I am among men the king of men, the leader, the mighty man, the hero. I am Rama among warriors, Krishna among the Vrishnis, Arjuna among the Pandavas. The illumined Rishi is my Vibhuti; I am Bhrigu among the great Rishis. The great seer, the inspired poet who sees and reveals the truth by the light of the idea and sound of the word, is myself luminous in the mortal; I am Ushanas among the seer-poets. The great sage, thinker, philosopher is my power among men, my own vast intelligence; I am Vyasa among the sages. But, with whatever variety of degree in manifestation, all beings are in their own way and nature powers of the Godhead.

यच्चापि सर्वभूतानां बीजं तदहमर्जुन।
न तदस्ति विना यत्स्यान्मया भूतं चराचरम् ।।३९।।

39. Nothing moving or unmoving, animate or inanimate in the world can be without me. I am the divine seed of all existences and of that seed they are the branches and flowers; what is in the seed of self, that only they can develop in Nature.

नान्तोऽस्ति मम दिव्यानां विभूतीनां परन्तप ।
एष तूद्देशतः प्रोक्तो विभूतेर्विस्तरो मया ।।४०।।

40. There is no numbering or limit to my divine Vibhutis, *nānto'sti mama divyānām vibhūtīnām*; what I have spoken is nothing more than a summary development and I have given only the light of a few leading indications and a strong opening to endless verities.

यद्यद्विभूतिमत्सत्त्वं श्रीमदूर्जितमेव वा ।
तत्तदेवावगच्छ त्वं मम तेजोंऽशसम्भवम् ।।४१।।

41. Whatever beautiful and glorious creature thou seest in the world, whatever being is mighty and forceful among men and above man and below him, know to be a very splendour, light and energy of Me and born of a potent portion and intense power of my existence.

अथवा बहुनैतेन किं ज्ञातेन तवार्जुन ।
विष्टभ्याहमिदं कृत्स्नमेकांशेन स्थितो जगत् ।।४२।।

42. But what need is there of a multitude of details for this knowledge? Take it thus, that I am here in this world and everywhere, I am in all and I constitute all: there is nothing else than I, nothing without Me. I support this entire universe with a single degree of my illimitable power and an infinitesimal portion of my fathomless spirit; all these worlds are only sparks, hints, glintings of the I Am eternal and immeasurable.

The importance of this chapter of the Gita is very much greater than appears at first view or to an eye of prepossession which is looking into the text only for the creed of the last transcendence and the detached turning of the human soul away from the world to a distant Absolute. The message of the Gita is the gospel of the Divinity in man who by force of an increasing union unfolds himself out of the veil of the lower Nature, reveals to the human soul his cosmic spirit, reveals his absolute transcendences, reveals himself in man and in all beings. The potential outcome here of this union, this divine Yoga, man growing towards the Godhead, the Godhead manifest in the human soul and to the inner human vision, is our liberation from limited ego and our elevation to the higher nature of a divine humanity. For dwelling in this greater spiritual nature and not in the mortal weft, the tangled complexity of the three gunas, man, one with God by knowledge, love and will and the giving up of his whole being into the Godhead, is able indeed to rise to the absolute Transcendence, but also to act upon the world, no longer in ignorance, but in the right relation of the individual to the Supreme, in the truth of the Spirit, fulfilled in immortality, for God in the world and no longer for the ego. To call Arjuna to this action, to make him aware of the being and power that he is and of the Being and Power whose will acts through him, is the purpose of the embodied Godhead. To this end the divine Krishna is his charioteer; to this end there came upon him that great discouragement and deep dissatisfaction with the lesser human motives of his work; to substitute for them the larger spiritual motive this revelation is given to him in the supreme moment of the work to which he has been appointed. The vision of the World-Purusha and the divine command to action is the culminating point to which he was being led. That is already imminent; but without the knowledge now given to him through the Vibhuti-Yoga it would not bring with it its full meaning. Time in its creation and destruction must be seen by him as the figure of the Godhead in its steps, — steps that accomplish the cycles of the cosmos on whose spires of movement the divine spirit in the human body rises doing God's work in the world as his Vibhuti to the supreme transcendences. This knowledge has been given; the Time-figure of the Godhead is now to be revealed and from the million mouths of that figure will issue the command for the appointed action to the liberated Vibhuti.

Chapter XI

The Vision of the World-Spirit

I — TIME THE DESTROYER

अर्जुन उवाच
मदनुग्रहाय परमं गुह्यमध्यात्मसंज्ञितम् ।
यत्त्वयोक्तं वचस्तेन मोहोऽयं विगतो मम ।।१।।

1. *Arjuna* — The vision of the universal Purusha is one of the best known and most powerfully poetic passages in the Gita, but its place in the thought is not altogether on the surface. It is evidently intended for a poetic and revelatory symbol and we must see how it is brought in and for what purpose and discover to what it points in its significant aspects before we can capture its meaning. It is invited by Arjuna in his desire to see the living image, the visible greatness of the unseen Divine, the very embodiment of the Spirit and Power that governs the universe. **He has heard the highest spiritual secret of existence,** that all is from God and all is the Divine and in all things God dwells and is concealed and can be revealed in every finite appearance. **The illusion which so persistently holds man's sense and mind,** the idea that things at all exist in themselves or for themselves apart from God or that anything subject to Nature can be self-moved and self-guided, **has passed from him,** — that was the cause of his doubt and bewilderment and refusal of action.

भवाप्ययौ हि भूतानां श्रुतौ विस्तरशो मया ।
त्वत्तः कमलपत्राक्ष माहात्म्यमपि चाव्ययम् ।।२।।

2. **Now he knows what is the sense of the birth and passing away of existences. He knows that the imperishable greatness of the divine conscious Soul is the secret of all these appearances.** All is a Yoga of this great eternal Spirit in things and all happenings are the result and expression of that Yoga; all Nature is full of the secret Godhead and in labour to reveal him in her.

एवमेतद्यथात्थ त्वमात्मानं परमेश्वर ।
द्रष्टुमिच्छामि ते रूपमैश्वरं पुरुषोत्तम ।।३।।

3. **But he would see too the very form and body of this Godhead, if that be possible,** — the divine cosmic Form of That which is actually speaking to him through the veil of the human mind and body.

मन्यसे यदि तच्छक्यं मया द्रष्टुमिति प्रभो ।
योगेश्वर ततो मे त्वं दर्शयात्मानमव्ययम् ।।४।।

4. He has heard of his attributes and understood the steps and ways of his self-revelation; **but now he asks of this Master of the Yoga, *yogeśvaraḥ* (*mahā-yogeśvaro hariḥ,* in *śl. 9*) to discover his very imperishable Self to the eye of Yoga.** Not, evidently, the formless silence of his actionless immutability, but the Supreme from whom is all energy and action, of whom forms are the masks, who reveals his force in the Vibhuti, — the Master of works, the Master of knowledge and adoration, the Lord of Nature and all her creatures. For this greatest all-comprehending vision he is made to ask because it is so, from the Spirit revealed in the universe, that he must receive the command to his part in the world-action.

श्रीभगवानुवाच
पश्य मे पार्थ रूपाणि शतशोऽथ सहस्रशः ।
नानाविधानि दिव्यानि नानावर्णाकृतीनि च ।।५।।

5. *Krishna* — **Thou shalt see, replies the Avatar, my hundreds and thousands of divine forms, various in kind, various in shape and hue;**

पश्यादित्यान्वसून्रुद्रानश्विनौ मरुतस्तथा ।
बहून्यदृष्टपूर्वाणि पश्याश्चर्याणि भारत ।।६।।

6. **thou shalt see the Adityas and the Rudras and the Maruts and the Ashwins; thou shalt see many wonders that none has beheld;**

इहैकस्थं जगत्कृत्स्नं पश्याद्य सचराचरम् ।
मम देहे गुडाकेश यच्चान्यद्द्रष्टुमिच्छसि ।।७।।

7. thou shalt see today the whole world related and unified in my body and whatever else thou willest to behold.

न तु मां शक्यसे द्रष्टुमनेनैव स्वचक्षुषा ।
दिव्यं ददामि ते चक्षुः पश्य मे योगमैश्वरम् ।।८।।

8. What thou hast to see, he says, the human eye cannot grasp, — for the human eye can see only the outward appearances of things or make out of them separate symbol forms, each of them significant of only a few aspects of the eternal Mystery. **But there is a divine eye, an inmost seeing, by which the supreme Godhead in his Yoga can be beheld and that eye I now give to thee, *divyaṁ dadāmi te cakṣuḥ paśya me yogam aiśvaram.*** This then is the keynote, the central significance. It is the vision of the One in the many, the many in the One, — and all are the One. It is this vision that to the eye of the divine Yoga liberates, justifies, explains all that is and was and shall be. Once seen and held, it lays the shining axe of God at the root of all doubts and perplexities and annihilates all denials and oppositions. It is the vision that reconciles and unifies. If the soul can arrive at unity with the Godhead in this vision, — Arjuna has not yet done that, therefore we find that he has fear when he sees, — all even that is terrible in the world loses its terror. We see that it too is an aspect of the Godhead and once we have found his meaning in it, not looking at it by itself alone, we can accept the whole of existence with an all-embracing joy and a mighty courage, go forward with sure steps to the appointed work and envisage beyond it the supreme consummation. The soul admitted to the divine knowledge which beholds all things in one view, not with a divided, partial and therefore bewildered seeing, can make a new discovery of the world and all else that it wills to see, *yac cānyad draṣṭum icchasi*; it can move on the basis of this all-relating and all-unifying vision from revelation to completing revelation.

सञ्जय उवाच
एवमुक्त्वा ततो राजन्महायोगेश्वरो हरिः ।
दर्शयामास पार्थाय परमं रूपमैश्वरम् ।।९।।
अनेकवक्त्रनयनमनेकाद्भुतदर्शनम् ।
अनेकदिव्याभरणं दिव्यानेकोद्यतायुधम् ।।१०।।
दिव्यमाल्याम्बरधरं दिव्यगन्धानुलेपनम् ।
सर्वाश्चर्यमयं देवमनन्तं विश्वतोमुखम् ।।११।।
दिवि सूर्यसहस्रस्य भवेद्युगपदुत्थिता ।
यदि भाः सदृशी सा स्याद्भासस्तस्य महात्मनः ।।१२।।

तत्रैकस्थं जगत्कृत्स्नं प्रविभक्तमनेकधा ।
अपश्यद्देवदेवस्य शरीरे पाण्डवस्तदा ।।१३।।
ततः स विस्मयाविष्टो हृष्टरोमा धनञ्जयः ।
प्रणम्य शिरसा देवं कृताञ्जलिरभाषत ।।१४।।

9-14. *Sanjaya* — The supreme Form is then made visible. It is that of the infinite Godhead whose faces are everywhere and in whom are all the wonders of existence, who multiplies unendingly all the many marvellous revelations of his being, a world-wide Divinity seeing with innumerable eyes, speaking from innumerable mouths, armed for battle with numberless divine uplifted weapons, glorious with divine ornaments of beauty, robed in heavenly raiment of deity, lovely with garlands of divine flowers, fragrant with divine perfumes. Such is the light of this body of God as if a thousand suns had risen at once in heaven. The whole world multitudinously divided and yet unified is visible in the body of the God of Gods. Arjuna sees him, God magnificent and beautiful and terrible, the Lord of souls who has manifested in the glory and greatness of his spirit this wild and monstrous and orderly and wonderful and sweet and terrible world, and overcome with marvel and joy and fear he bows down and adores with words of awe and with clasped hands the tremendous vision.

अर्जुन उवाच
पश्यामि देवांस्तव देव देहे सर्वांस्तथा भूतविशेषसङ्घान् ।
ब्रह्माणमीशं कमलासनस्थमृषींश्च सर्वानुरगांश्च दिव्यान् ।।१५।।

15. *Arjuna* — I see, he cries, all the gods in thy body, O God, and different companies of beings, Brahma the creating lord seated in the Lotus, and the Rishis and the race of the divine Serpents.

अनेकबाहूदरवक्त्रनेत्रं पश्यामि त्वां सर्वतोऽनन्तरूपम् ।
नान्तं न मध्यं न पुनस्तवादिं पश्यामि विश्वेश्वर विश्वरूप ।।१६।।

16. I see numberless arms and bellies and eyes and faces, I see thy infinite forms on every side, but I see not thy end nor thy middle nor thy beginning, O Lord of the universe, O Form universal.

किरीटिनं गदिनं चक्रिणं च तेजोराशिं सर्वतो दीप्तिमन्तम् ।
पश्यामि त्वां दुर्निरीक्ष्यं समन्ताद्दीप्तानलार्कद्युतिमप्रमेयम् ।।१७।।

17. I see thee crowned and with thy mace and thy discus, hard to discern because thou art a luminous mass of energy on all sides of me, an encompassing blaze, a sun-bright fire-bright Immeasurable.

त्वमक्षरं परमं वेदितव्यं त्वमस्य विश्वस्य परं निधानम् ।
त्वमव्ययः शाश्वतधर्मगोप्ता सनातनस्त्वं पुरुषो मतो मे ।।१८।।

18. Thou art the supreme Immutable whom we have to know, thou art the high foundation and abode of the universe, thou art the imperishable guardian of the eternal laws, thou art the sempiternal soul of existence.

अनादिमध्यान्तमनन्तवीर्यमनन्तबाहुं शशिसूर्यनेत्रम् ।
पश्यामि त्वां दीप्तहुताशवक्त्रं स्वतेजसा विश्वमिदं तपन्तम् ।।१९।।

19. But in the greatness of this vision there is too the terrific image of the Destroyer. **This Immeasurable without end or middle or beginning is he in whom all things begin and exist and end. This Godhead who embraces the worlds with his numberless arms and destroys with his million hands, whose eyes are suns and moons, has a face of blazing fire and is ever burning up the whole universe with the flame of his energy.**

द्यावापृथिव्योरिदमन्तरं हि व्याप्तं त्वयैकेन दिशश्च सर्वाः ।
दृष्ट्वाद्भुतं रूपमुग्रं तवेदं लोकत्रयं प्रव्यथितं महात्मन् ।।२०।।

20. The form of him is fierce and marvellous and alone it fills all the regions and occupies the whole space between earth and heaven; when it is seen the three worlds are all in pain and suffer.

अमी हि त्वां सुरसङ्घा विशन्ति केचिद्भीताः प्राञ्जलयो गृणन्ति ।
स्वस्तीत्युक्त्वा महर्षिसिद्धसङ्घाः स्तुवन्ति त्वां स्तुतिभिः पुष्कलाभिः ।।२१।।
रुद्रादित्या वसवो ये च साध्या विश्वेऽश्विनौ मरुतश्चोष्मपाश्च ।
गन्धर्वयक्षासुरसिद्धसङ्घा वीक्षन्ते त्वां विस्मिताश्चैव सर्वे ।।२२।।
रूपं महत्ते बहुवक्त्रनेत्रं महाबाहो बहुबाहूरुपादम् ।
बहूदरं बहुदंष्ट्राकरालं दृष्ट्वा लोकाः प्रव्यथितास्तथाहम् ।।२३।।
नभःस्पृशं दीप्तमनेकवर्णं व्यात्ताननं दीप्तविशालनेत्रम् ।
दृष्ट्वा हि त्वां प्रव्यथितान्तरात्मा धृतिं न विन्दामि शमं च विष्णो ।।२४।।
दंष्ट्राकरालानि च ते मुखानि दृष्ट्वैव कालानलसन्निभानि ।
दिशो न जाने न लभे च शर्म प्रसीद देवेश जगन्निवास ।।२५।।

अमी च त्वां धृतराष्ट्रस्य पुत्राः सर्वे सहैवावनिपालसङ्घैः ।
भीष्मो द्रोणः सूतपुत्रस्तथासौ सहास्मदीयैरपि योधमुख्यैः ।।२६।।
वक्त्राणि ते त्वरमाणा विशन्ति दंष्ट्राकरालानि भयानकानि ।
केचिद्विलग्ना दशनान्तरेषु सन्दृश्यन्ते चूर्णितैरुत्तमाङ्गैः ।।२७।।
यथा नदीनां बहवोऽम्बुवेगाः समुद्रमेवाभिमुखा द्रवन्ति ।
तथा तवामी नरलोकवीरा विशन्ति वक्त्राण्यभिविज्वलन्ति ।।२८।।
यथा प्रदीप्तं ज्वलनं पतङ्गाः विशन्ति नाशाय समृद्धवेगाः ।
तथैव नाशाय विशन्ति लोकास्तवापि वक्त्राणि समृद्धवेगाः ।।२९।।
लेलिह्यसे ग्रसमानः समन्ताल्लोकान्समग्रान्वदनैर्ज्वलद्भिः ।
तेजोभिरापूर्य जगत्समग्रं भासस्तवोग्राः प्रतपन्ति विष्णो ।।३०।।

21-30. The companies of the gods enter it, afraid, adoring; the Rishis and the Siddhas crying "May there be peace and weal" praise it with many praises; the eyes of Gods and Titans and Giants are fixed on it in amazement. It has enormous burning eyes; it has mouths that gape to devour, terrible with many tusks of destruction; it has faces like the fires of Death and Time. The kings and the captains and the heroes on both sides of the world-battle are hastening into its tusked and terrible jaws and some are seen with crushed and bleeding heads caught between its teeth of power; the nations are rushing to destruction with helpless speed into its mouths of flame like many rivers hurrying in their course towards the ocean or like moths that cast themselves on a kindled fire. With those burning mouths the Form of Dread is licking all the regions around; the whole world is full of his burning energies and baked in the fierceness of his lustres. The world and its nations are shaken and in anguish with the terror of destruction and Arjuna shares in the trouble and panic around him; troubled and in pain is the soul within him and he finds no peace or gladness. He cries to the dreadful Godhead:

आख्याहि मे को भवानुग्ररूपो नमोऽस्तु ते देववर प्रसीद ।
विज्ञातुमिच्छामि भवन्तमाद्यं न हि प्रजानामि तव प्रवृत्तिम् ।।३१।।

31. Declare to me who thou art that wearest this form of fierceness. Salutation to thee, O thou great Godhead, turn thy heart to grace. I would know who thou art who wast from the beginning, for I know not the will of thy workings.

This last cry of Arjuna indicates the double intention in the vision. This is the figure of the supreme and universal Being, the Ancient of Days who is for ever, *sanātanam puruṣam purāṇam*, this is he who for ever creates, for Brahma the Creator is one of the Godheads seen in his body, he who keeps the world always in existence, for he is the guardian of the eternal laws, but who is always too destroying in order that he may new-create, who is Time, who is Death, who is Rudra the Dancer of the calm and awful dance, who is Kali with her garland of skulls trampling naked in battle and flecked with the blood of the slaughtered Titans, who is the cyclone and the fire and the earthquake and pain and famine and revolution and ruin and the swallowing ocean. And it is this last aspect of him which he puts forward at the moment. It is an aspect from which the mind in men willingly turns away and ostrich-like hides its head so that perchance, not seeing, it may not be seen by the Terrible. The weakness of the human heart wants only fair and comforting truths or in their absence pleasant fables; it will not have the truth in its entirety because there there is much that is not clear and pleasant and comfortable but hard to understand and harder to bear.

This world of our battle and labour is a fierce dangerous destructive devouring world in which life exists precariously and the soul and body of man move among enormous perils, a world in which by every step forward, whether we will it or no, something is crushed and broken, in which every breath of life is a breath too of death. To put away the responsibility for all that seems to us evil or terrible on the shoulders of a semi-omnipotent Devil, or to put it aside as part of Nature, making an unbridgeable opposition between world-nature and God-Nature, as if Nature were independent of God, or to throw the responsibility on man and his sins, as if he had a preponderant voice in the making of this world or could create anything against the will of God, are clumsily comfortable devices. We have to look courageously in the face of the reality and see that it is God and none else who has made this world in his being and that so he has made it. We have to see that Nature devouring her children, Time eating up the lives of creatures, Death universal and ineluctable and the violence of the Rudra forces in man and Nature are also the supreme Godhead in one of his cosmic figures. We have to see that God the bountiful and prodigal creator, God the helpful, strong and benignant preserver is also God the devourer and destroyer. The torment of the couch of pain and evil on which we are racked is his touch as much as happiness and sweetness and pleasure. It is only when we see with the eye of the complete union and feel this truth in the depths of our being that we can entirely discover behind that mask too the calm and beautiful face of the all-blissful Godhead and in this touch that tests our imperfection the touch of the friend and builder of the spirit in man. The discords of the worlds are God's discords and it is only by accepting and proceeding through them that we can arrive at the greater concords of his supreme harmony, the summits and thrilled vastnesses of his transcendent and his cosmic Ananda.

For why should it be thus that the All-spirit manifests himself in Nature? What is the significance of this creating and devouring flame that is mortal existence, this world-wide struggle, these constant disastrous revolutions, this labour and anguish and travail and perishing of creatures? He puts the ancient question and breathes the eternal prayer, **Declare to me who art thou..., for I know not the will of thy workings.**

श्रीभगवानुवाच
कालोऽस्मि लोकक्षयकृत्प्रवृद्धो लोकान्समाहर्तुमिह प्रवृत्तः ।
ऋतेऽपि त्वां न भविष्यन्ति सर्वे येऽवस्थिताः प्रत्यनीकेषु योधाः ।।३२।।

32. *Krishna* — Destruction, replies the Godhead, is the will of my workings with which I stand here on this field of Kurukshetra, the field of the working out of the Dharma, the field of human action, a world-wide destruction which has come in the process of the Time-Spirit. I have a foreseeing purpose which fulfils itself infallibly and no participation or abstention of any human being can prevent, alter or modify it; all is done by me already in my eternal eye of will before it can at all be done by man upon earth. I as Time have to destroy the old structures and to build up a new, mighty and splendid kingdom, *rājyam samṛiddham*. Thou as a human instrument of the divine Power and Wisdom hast in this struggle which thou canst not prevent to battle for the right and slay and conquer its opponents. Thou too, the human soul in Nature, hast to enjoy in Nature the fruit given by me, the empire of right and justice. Let this be sufficient for thee, — to be one with God in thy soul, to receive his command, to do his will, to see calmly a supreme purpose fulfilled in the world.

I am Time the waster of the peoples arisen and increased whose will in my workings is here to destroy the nations. Even without thee all these warriors shall be not, who are ranked in the opposing armies.

What then is the master man, the divine worker, the opened channel of the universal Will to do when he finds the World-Spirit turned towards some immense catastrophe, figured before his eyes as Time the destroyer arisen and increased for the destruction of the nations and himself put there in the forefront whether as a fighter with physical weapons or a leader and guide or an inspirer of men, as he cannot fail to be by the very force of his nature and the power within him, *svabhāvajena svena karmaṇā* (*XVIII-60*). To abstain, to sit silent, to protest by non-intervention? But abstention will not help, will not prevent the fulfilment of the destroying Will, but rather by the lacuna it creates increase confusion. **Even without thee, cries the Godhead, my will of destruction would still be accomplished, *ṛite'pi tvām*.** If Arjuna were to abstain or even if the battle of Kurukshetra were not to be fought, that evasion would only prolong and make worse the inevitable confusion, disorder, ruin that are coming. For these things are no accident, but an inevitable seed that has been sown and a harvest that must be reaped. They who have sown the wind, must reap the whirlwind. Nor indeed will his own nature allow him any real abstention, *prakṛitis tvāṁ niyokṣyati*. This the Teacher tells Arjuna at the close, "That which in thy egoism thou thinkest saying, I will not fight, vain is this thy resolve: Nature shall yoke thee to thy work. Bound by thy own action which is born of the law of thy being, what from delusion thou desirest not to do, that thou shalt do even perforce (*XVIII-59/60*)." Then to give another turn, to use some kind of soul force, spiritual method and power, not physical weapons? But that is only another form of the same action; the destruction will still take place, and the turn given too will be not what the individual ego, but what the World-Spirit wills.

तस्मात्त्वमुत्तिष्ठ यशो लभस्व जित्वा शत्रून्भुङक्ष्व राज्यं समृद्धम् ।
मयैवैते निहताः पूर्वमेव निमित्तमात्रं भव सव्यसाचिन् ।।३३।।

33. Therefore arise, get thee glory, conquer thy enemies and enjoy an opulent kingdom. By me and none other already even are they slain, do thou become the occasion only, O Savyasachin, *mayaivaite nihatāḥ purvam eva nimittamātraṁ bhava savyasācin.*

An entire surrender of the whole being to God is not merely a passive submission, but an active self-giving; not only a seeing and an accepting of the divine Will in all things, but a giving up of one's own will to be the instrument of the Master of works, and this not with the lesser idea of being a servant of God, but, eventually at least, of such a complete renunciation both of the consciousness and the works to him that our being becomes one with his being and the impersonalised nature only an instrument and nothing else. There is no assumption of personal will in the instrument; it is seen that all is already worked out in the omniscient prescience and omnipotent effective power of the universal Divine and that the egoism of men cannot alter the workings of that Will, *nimittamātraṁ bhava savyasācin*. This attitude must lead finally to an absolute union of the personal with the Divine Will and, with the growth of knowledge, bring about a faultless response of the instrument to the divine Power and Knowledge. A perfect, an absolute equality of self-surrender, the mentality a passive channel of the divine Light and Power, the active being a mightily effective instrument for its work in the world, will be the poise of this supreme union of the Transcendent, the universal and the individual.

द्रोणं च भीष्मं च जयद्रथं च कर्णं तथान्यानपि योधवीरान् ।
मया हतांस्त्वं जहि मा व्यथिष्ठा युध्यस्व जेतासि रणे सपत्नान् ।।३४।।

34. Slay, by me who are slain, Drona, Bhishma, Jayadratha, Karna, and other heroic fighters; be not pained and troubled. Fight, thou shalt conquer the adversary in the battle.

The fruit of the great and terrible work is promised and prophesied, not as a fruit hungered for by the individual, — for to that there is to be no attachment, — but as the result of the divine will, the glory and success of the thing to be done accomplished, the glory given by the Divine to himself in his Vibhuti. Thus is the final and compelling command to action given to the protagonist of the world-battle.

It is the Timeless manifest as Time and World-Spirit from whom the command to action proceeds. For certainly the Godhead when he says, "I am Time the Destroyer of beings," does not mean either that he is the Time-Spirit alone or that the whole essence of the Time-Spirit is destruction. But it is this which is the present will of his workings, *pravṛitti*. Destruction is always a simultaneous or alternate element which keeps pace with creation and it is by destroying and renewing that the Master of Life does his long work of preservation. More, destruction is the first condition of progress. Whoever prematurely attempts to get rid of this law of battle and destruction, strives vainly against the greater will of the World-Spirit. Whoever turns from it in the weakness of his lower members, as did Arjuna in the beginning, is showing not true virtue, but a want of spiritual courage to face the sterner truths of Nature and of action and existence. Man can only exceed the law of battle by discovering the greater law of his immortality. There are those who seek this where it always exists and must primarily be found, in the higher reaches of the pure spirit, and to find it turn away from a world governed by the law of Death. That is an individual solution which makes no difference to mankind and the world, or rather makes only this difference that they are deprived of so much spiritual power which might have helped them forward in the painful march of their evolution.

No real peace can be till the heart of man deserves peace; the law of Vishnu cannot prevail till the debt to Rudra is paid. To turn aside then and preach to a still unevolved mankind the law of love and oneness? Teachers of the law of love and oneness there must be, for by that way must come the ultimate salvation. But not till the Time-Spirit in man is ready, can the inner and ultimate prevail over the outer and immediate reality. Christ and Buddha have come and gone, but it is Rudra who still holds the world in the hollow of his hand. And meanwhile the fierce forward labour of mankind tormented and oppressed by the Powers that are profiteers of egoistic force and their servants cries for the sword of the Hero of the struggle and the word of its prophet.

The highest way appointed for him is to carry out the will of God without egoism, as the human occasion and instrument of that which he sees to be decreed, with the constant supporting memory of the Godhead in himself and man, *mām anusmaran*, and in whatever ways are appointed for him by the Lord of his Nature. *Nimitta-mātraṁ bhava savyasācin.* For God the Time-Spirit does not destroy for the sake of destruction, but to make the ways clear in the cyclic process for a greater rule and a progressing manifestation, *rājyaṁ samṛiddham*. Not appalled by the face of the Destroyer, he will see within it the eternal Spirit imperishable in all these perishing bodies and behind it the face of the Charioteer, the Leader of man, the Friend of all creatures, *suhṛidaṁ sarvabhūtānām*. This formidable World-Form once seen and acknowledged, it is to that reassuring truth that the rest of the chapter is directed; it discloses in the end a more intimate face and body of the Eternal.

II — THE DOUBLE ASPECT

सञ्जय उवाच
एतच्छ्रुत्वा वचनं केशवस्य कृताञ्जलिर्वेपमानः किरीटी ।
नमस्कृत्वा भूय एवाह कृष्णं सगद्गदं भीतभीतः प्रणम्य ।।३५।।

35. (*Untranslated*)

अर्जुन उवाच
स्थाने हृषीकेश तव प्रकीर्त्या जगत्प्रहृष्यत्यनुरज्यते च ।
रक्षांसि भीतानि दिशो द्रवन्ति सर्वे नमस्यन्ति च सिद्धसङ्घाः ।।३६।।

36. *Arjuna* — Even while the effects of the terrible aspect of this vision are still upon him, the first words uttered by Arjuna after the Godhead has spoken are eloquent of a greater uplifting and reassuring reality behind this face of death and this destruction. **Rightly and in good place, he cries, O Krishna, does the world rejoice and take pleasure in thy name, the Rakshasas are fleeing from thee in terror to all the quarters and the companies of the Siddhas bow down before thee in adoration.** From the first words there comes the suggestion that the hidden truth behind these terrifying forms is a reassuring, a heartening and delightful truth. There is something that makes the heart of the world to rejoice and take pleasure in the name and nearness of the Divine. It is the profound sense of that which makes us see in the dark face of Kali the face of the Mother and to perceive even in the midst of destruction the protecting arms of the Friend of creatures, in the midst of evil the

presence of a pure unalterable Benignity and in the midst of death the Master of Immortality. From the terror of the King of the divine action the Rakshasas, the fierce giant powers of darkness, flee destroyed, defeated and overpowered. But the Siddhas, but the complete and perfect who know and sing the names of the Immortal and live in the truth of his being, bow down before every form of Him and know what every form enshrines and signifies. Nothing has real need to fear except that which is to be destroyed, the evil, the ignorance, the veilers in Night, the Rakshasa powers. All the movement and action of Rudra the Terrible is towards perfection and divine light and completeness.

कस्माच्च ते न नमेरन्महात्मन् गरीयसे ब्रह्मणोऽप्यादिकर्त्रे ।
अनन्त देवेश जगन्निवास त्वमक्षरं सदसत्तत्परं यत् ॥३७॥

37. **How should they not do thee homage, O great Spirit? For thou art the original Creator and Doer of works and greater even than creative Brahma. O thou Infinite, O thou Lord of the gods, O thou abode of the universe, thou art the Immutable and thou art what is and is not and thou art that which is the Supreme.** For this Spirit, this Divine is only in outward form the Destroyer, Time who undoes all these finite forms: but in himself he is the Infinite, the Master of the cosmic Godheads, in whom the world and all its action are securely seated. He is the original and ever originating Creator, one greater than that figure of creative Power called Brahma which he shows to us in the form of things as one aspect of his trinity, creation chequered by a balance of preservation and destruction. The real divine creation is eternal; it is the Infinite manifested sempiternally in finite things, the Spirit who conceals and reveals himself for ever in his innumerable infinity of souls and in the wonder of their actions and in the beauty of their forms. He is the eternal Immutable; he is the dual appearance of the Is and Is-not, of the manifest and the never manifested, of things that were and seem to be no more, are and appear doomed to perish, shall be and shall pass. But what he is beyond all these is That, the Supreme, who holds all things mutable in the single eternity of a Time to which all is ever present. He possesses his immutable self in a timeless eternity of which Time and creation are an ever extending figure.

त्वमादिदेवः पुरुषः पुराणस्त्वमस्य विश्वस्य परं निधानम् ।
वेत्तासि वेद्यं च परं च धाम त्वया ततं विश्वमनन्तरूप ॥३८॥

38. **Thou art the ancient Soul and the first and original Godhead and the supreme resting-place of this All; thou art the knower and that which is**

to be known and the highest status; O infinite in form, by thee was extended the universe.

वायुर्यमोऽग्निर्वरुणः शशाङ्कः प्रजापतिस्त्वं प्रपितामहश्च ।
नमो नमस्तेऽस्तु सहस्रकृत्वः पुनश्च भूयोऽपि नमो नमस्ते ।।३९।।

39. Thou art Yama and Vayu and Agni and Soma and Varuna and Prajapati, father of creatures, and the great-grandsire. Salutation to thee a thousand times over and again and yet again salutation,

नमः पुरस्तादथ पृष्ठतस्ते नमोऽस्तु ते सर्वत एव सर्व ।
अनन्तवीर्यामितविक्रमस्त्वं सर्वं समाप्नोषि ततोऽसि सर्वः ।।४०।।

40. in front and behind and from every side, for thou art each and all that is. Infinite in might and immeasurable in strength of action thou pervadest all and art every one.

सखेति मत्वा प्रसभं यदुक्तं हे कृष्ण हे यादव हे सखेति ।
अजानता महिमानं तवेदं मया प्रमादात्प्रणयेन वापि ।।४१।।
यच्चावहासार्थमसत्कृतोऽसि विहारशय्यासनभोजनेषु ।
एकोऽथवाप्यच्युत तत्समक्षं तत्क्षामये त्वामहमप्रमेयम् ।।४२।।

41-42. And from that insistence the thought naturally turns to the presence of this one great Godhead in man. There the soul of the seer of the vision is impressed by three successive suggestions. First, it is borne in upon him that in the body of this son of Man who moved beside him as a transient creature upon earth, in this figure of mortal man was all the time something great, concealed, of tremendous significance, a Godhead, an Avatar, a universal Power, a One Reality, a supreme Transcendence. To this occult divinity he had been blind. **For whatsoever I have spoken to thee in rash vehemence, thinking of thee only as my human friend and companion, "O Krishna, O Yadava, O comrade", not knowing this thy greatness, in negligent error or in love, and for whatsoever disrespect was shown by me to thee in jest, on the couch and the seat and in the banquet, alone or in thy presence, I pray forgiveness from thee the immeasurable.**

Now only he sees the universal Spirit in the individual frame, the Divine embodied in humanity, the transcendent Inhabitant of this symbol of Nature. He has seen now only this tremendous, infinite, immeasurable Reality of all these apparent things, this boundless universal Form which so exceeds every individual form and yet of whom each individual thing is a house for his dwelling. For that great Reality is equal and infinite and the same in the individual and in the universe. And at first his blindness seems to him a sin against the Mightiness that was there. That and not the veiling outward humanity, *avajānan mānuṣīṁ tanum āśritam*, was what he should have seen with awe and with submission and veneration.

पितासि लोकस्य चराचरस्य त्वमस्य पूज्यश्च गुरुर्गरीयान् ।
न त्वत्समोऽस्त्यभ्यधिकः कुतोऽन्यो लोकत्रयेऽप्यप्रतिमप्रभाव ।।४३।।
तस्मात्प्रणम्य प्रणिधाय कायं प्रसादये त्वामहमीशमीड्यम् ।
पितेव पुत्रस्य सखेव सख्युः प्रियः प्रियायार्हसि देव सोढुम् ।।४४।।

43-44. But the second suggestion is that what was figured in the human manifestation and the human relation is also a reality which accompanies and mitigates for our mind the tremendous character of the universal vision. The transcendence and cosmic aspect have to be seen, for without that seeing the limitations of humanity cannot be exceeded. In that unifying oneness all has to be included. But by itself that would set too great a gulf between the transcendent spirit and this soul bound and circumscribed in an inferior Nature. The infinite presence in its unmitigated splendour would be too overwhelming for the separate littleness of the limited, individual and natural man. A link is needed by which he can see this universal Godhead in his own individual and natural being, close to him, not only omnipotently there to govern all he is by universal and immeasurable Power, but humanly figured to support and raise him to unity by an intimate individual relation. The adoration by which the finite creature bows down before the Infinite, receives all its sweetness and draws near to a closest truth of companionship and oneness when it deepens into the more intimate adoration which lives in the sense of the fatherhood of God, the friendhood of God, the attracting love between the Divine Spirit and our human soul and nature. For the Divine inhabits the human soul and body; he draws around him and wears like a robe the human mind and figure. He assumes the human relations which the soul affects in the mortal body and they find in God their own fullest sense and greatest realisation. **Thou art the Father of all this world of the moving and unmoving; thou art one to be worshipped and the most solemn object of veneration. None is equal to thee, how then another greater in all the three worlds, O incomparable in might? Therefore I bow down before thee and prostrate my body and I demand grace of thee the adorable Lord. As a father to his son, as a friend to his friend and comrade, as one dear with him he loves, so shouldst thou, O Godhead, bear with me.**

अदृष्टपूर्वं हृषितोऽस्मि दृष्ट्वा भयेन च प्रव्यथितं मनो मे ।
तदेव मे दर्शय देव रूपं प्रसीद देवेश जगन्निवास ।।४५।।
किरीटिनं गदिनं चक्रहस्तमिच्छामि त्वां द्रष्टुमहं तथैव ।
तेनैव रूपेण चतुर्भुजेन सहस्रबाहो भव विश्वमूर्ते ।।४६।।

45-46. And from this second suggestion a third immediately arises. The form of the transcendent and universal Being is to the strength of the liberated spirit a thing mighty, encouraging and fortifying, a source of power, an equalising, sublimating, all-justifying vision; but to the normal man it is overwhelming, appalling, incommunicable. The truth that reassures, even when known, is grasped with difficulty behind the formidable and mighty aspect of all-destructive Time and an incalculable Will and a vast immeasurable inextricable working. But there is too the gracious mediating form of divine Narayana, the God who is so close to man and in man, the Charioteer of the battle and the journey, with his four arms of helpful power, a humanised symbol of Godhead, not this million-armed universality. It is this mediating aspect which man must have for his support constantly before him. For it is this figure of Narayana which symbolises the truth that reassures. To this humanised embodied soul the end [of the universal workings] becomes here a union, a closeness, a constant companionship of man and God, man living in the world for God, God dwelling in man and turning to his own divine ends in him the enigmatic world-process. And beyond the end is a yet more wonderful oneness and inliving in the last transfigurations of the Eternal. **I have seen what never was seen before and I rejoice, but my mind is troubled with fear. O Godhead, show me that other form of thine. I would see thee even as before crowned and with thy mace and discus. Assume thy four-armed shape, O thousand-armed, O Form universal.**

श्रीभगवानुवाच
मया प्रसन्नेन तवार्जुनेदं रूपं परं दर्शितमात्मयोगात् ।
तेजोमयं विश्वमनन्तमाद्यं यन्मे त्वदन्येन न दृष्टपूर्वम् ।।४७।।

47. *Krishna* — First he [the Godhead] declares the incalculable significance of the other mighty Image which he is about to veil. **This that thou now seest is my supreme shape, my form of luminous energy, the universal, the original which none but thou amongst men has yet seen. I have shown it by my self-Yoga.** For it is an image of my very Self and Spirit, it is the very Supreme self-figured in cosmic existence and **the soul in perfect Yoga with me sees it without any trembling of the nervous parts or any bewilderment and**

confusion of the mind, because he descries not only what is terrible and overwhelming in its appearance, but also its high and reassuring significance.

न वेदयज्ञाध्ययनैर्न दानैर्न च क्रियाभिर्न तपोभिरुग्रैः ।
एवंरूपः शक्य अहं नृलोके द्रष्टुं त्वदन्येन कुरुप्रवीर ।।४८।।

48. It [the greater Form] cannot be won by Veda or austerities or gifts or sacrifice.

मा ते व्यथा मा च विमूढभावो दृष्ट्वा रूपं घोरमीदृङ्ममेदम् ।
व्यपेतभीः प्रीतमनाः पुनस्त्वं तदेव मे रूपमिदं प्रपश्य ।।४९।।

49. And thou also shouldst so envisage it without fear, without confusion of mind, without any sinking of the members.

सञ्जय उवाच
इत्यर्जुनं वासुदेवस्तथोक्त्वा स्वकं रूपं दर्शयामास भूयः ।
आश्वासयामास च भीतमेनं भूत्वा पुनः सौम्यवपुर्महात्मा ।।५०।।

50. *Sanjaya* — But since the lower nature in thee is not yet prepared to look upon it with that high strength and tranquillity, I will reassume again for thee my Narayana figure in which the human mind sees isolated and toned to its humanity the calm, helpfulness and delight of a friendly Godhead. **The Godhead in answer to Arjuna's prayer reassumes his own normal Narayana image, *svakaṁ rūpam*, the desired form of grace and love and sweetness and beauty.**

अर्जुन उवाच
दृष्ट्वेदं मानुषं रूपं तव सौम्यं जनार्दन ।
इदानीमस्मि संवृत्तः सचेताः प्रकृतिं गतः ।।५१।।

51. (*Untranslated*)

श्रीभगवानुवाच
सुदुर्दर्शमिदं रूपं दृष्टवानसि यन्मम ।
देवा अप्यस्य रूपस्य नित्यं दर्शनकाङ्क्षिणः ।।५२।।
नाहं वेदैर्न तपसा न दानेन न चेज्यया ।
शक्य एवंविधो द्रष्टुं दृष्टवानसि मां यथा ।।५३।।

भक्त्या त्वनन्यया शक्य अहमेवंविधोऽर्जुन ।
ज्ञातुं द्रष्टुं च तत्त्वेन प्रवेष्टुं च परन्तप ।।५४।।

52-54. *Krishna* — **The greater Form** — and this is repeated again after it has disappeared — **is only for the rare highest souls. The gods themselves ever desire to look upon it. It cannot be won by Veda or austerities or gifts or sacrifice, it can be seen, known, entered into only by that bhakti which regards, adores and loves Me alone in all things.**

But what then is the uniqueness of this Form by which it is lifted so far beyond cognizance that all the ordinary endeavour of human knowledge and even the inmost austerity of its spiritual effort are insufficient, unaided, to reach the vision? It is this that man can know by other means this or that exclusive aspect of the one existence, its individual, cosmic or world-excluding figures, but not this greatest reconciling Oneness of all the aspects of the Divinity in which at one and the same time and in one and the same vision all is manifested, all is exceeded and all is consummated. For here transcendent, universal and individual Godhead, Spirit and Nature, Infinite and finite, space and time and timelessness, Being and Becoming, all that we can strive to think and know of the Godhead, whether of the absolute or the manifested existence, are wonderfully revealed in an ineffable oneness. This vision can be reached only by the absolute adoration, the love, the intimate unity that crowns at their summit the fullness of works and knowledge. To know, to see, to enter into it, to be one with this supreme form of the Supreme becomes then possible, and it is that end which the Gita proposes for its Yoga.

मत्कर्मकृन्मत्परमो मद्भक्तः सङ्गवर्जितः ।
निर्वैरः सर्वभूतेषु यः स मामेति पाण्डव ।।५५।।

55. There is a supreme consciousness through which it is possible to enter into the glory of the Transcendent and contain in him the immutable Self and all mutable Becoming, — it is possible to be one with all, yet above all, to exceed world and yet embrace the whole nature at once of the cosmic and the supracosmic Godhead. This is difficult indeed for limited man imprisoned in his mind and body: but, says the Godhead, **be a doer of my works, accept me as the supreme being and object, *mat-paramaḥ*, become my bhakta, be free from attachment and without enmity to all existences; for such a man comes to me.** In other words superiority to the lower nature, unity with all creatures, oneness with the cosmic Godhead and the Transcendence, oneness of will with the Divine in works, absolute love for the One and for God in all, — this is the way to that absolute spiritual self-exceeding and that unimaginable transformation.

Chapter XII

The Way and the Bhakta

In the eleventh chapter of the Gita the original object of the teaching has been achieved and brought up to a certain completeness. The command to divine action done for the sake of the world and in union with the Spirit who dwells in it and in all its creatures and in whom all its working takes place, has been given and accepted by the Vibhuti. The disciple has been led away from the old poise of the normal man and the standards, motives, outlook, egoistic consciousness of his ignorance, away from all that had finally failed him in the hour of his spiritual crisis. The very action which on that standing he had rejected, the terrible function, the appalling labour, he has now been brought to admit and accept on a new inner basis.

But there is something more to be said in order to bring out all the meaning of the great spiritual change. The twelfth chapter leads up to this remaining knowledge and the last six that follow develop it to a grand final conclusion. This thing that remains still to be said turns upon the difference between the current Vedantic view of spiritual liberation and the larger comprehensive freedom which the teaching of the Gita opens to the spirit. In the way proposed by the Gita knowledge is indeed the indispensable foundation, but an integral knowledge. Impersonal integral works are the first indispensable means; but a deep and large love and adoration, to which a relationless Unmanifest, an aloof and immovable Brahman can return no answer, since these things ask for a relation and an intimate personal closeness, are the strongest and highest power for release and spiritual perfection and the immortal Ananda.

The liberation of the Gita is not a self-oblivious abolition of the soul's personal being in the absorption of the One, *sāyujya mukti*; it is all kinds of union at once. There is an entire unification with the supreme Godhead in essence of being and intimacy of consciousness and identity of bliss, *sāyujya*, — for one object of this Yoga is to become Brahman, *brahma-bhūta*. There is an eternal ecstatic dwelling in the highest existence of the Supreme, *sālokya*, — for it is said, "Thou shalt dwell in me," *nivasiṣyasi mayyeva*. There is an eternal love and adoration in a uniting nearness, there is an embrace of the liberated spirit by its divine Lover and the enveloping Self of its infinitudes, *sāmīpya*. There is an identity of the soul's liberated nature with the divine nature, *sādṛiśya mukti*, — for the perfection of the free spirit is to become even as the Divine, *madbhāvam āgataḥ*, and to be one with him in the law of its being and the law of its works and nature, *sādharmyam āgataḥ*. The orthodox Yoga of knowledge aims at a fathomless immergence in the one infinite existence, *sāyujya*; it looks upon that alone as the entire liberation. The Yoga of adoration envisages an eternal habitation or nearness as the greater release, *sālokya*, *sāmīpya*. The Yoga of works leads to oneness in power of being and nature, *sādṛiśya*. But the Gita envelops them all in its catholic integrality and fuses them all into one greatest and richest divine freedom and perfection.

अर्जुन उवाच
एवं सततयुक्ता ये भक्तास्त्वां पर्युपासते ।
ये चाप्यक्षरमव्यक्तं तेषां के योगवित्तमाः ॥१॥

1. *Arjuna* — Arjuna is made to raise the question of this difference. It must be remembered that the distinction between the impersonal immutable Akshara Purusha and the supreme Soul that is at once impersonality and divine Person and much more than either, — that this capital distinction implied in the later chapters and in the divine "I" of which Krishna has constantly spoken, *aham*, *mām*, has as yet not been quite expressly and definitely drawn. Arjuna has been enjoined first to sink his separate personality in the calm impersonality of the one eternal and immutable self, a teaching which agreed well with his previous notions and offered no difficulties. But now he is confronted with the vision of this greatest transcendent, this widest universal Godhead and commanded to seek oneness with him by knowledge and works and adoration. Therefore he asks the better to have a doubt cleared which might otherwise have arisen,

Those devotees who thus by a constant union seek after thee, *tvām*, and those who seek after the unmanifest Immutable, which of these have the greater knowledge of Yoga?

This recalls the distinction made in the beginning by such phrases as "In the self, then in me," *ātmani atho mayi*: Arjuna points the distinction, *tvām*, *akṣaram avyaktam*.

श्रीभगवानुवाच
मय्यावेश्य मनो ये मां नित्ययुक्ता उपासते ।
श्रद्धया परयोपेतास्ते मे युक्ततमा मताः ॥२॥

2. *Krishna* — To this question Krishna replies with an emphatic decisiveness. **Those who found their mind in Me and by constant union, possessed of a supreme faith, seek after Me, I hold to be the most perfectly in union of Yoga.** The supreme faith is that which sees God in all and to its eye the manifestation and the non-manifestation are one Godhead. The perfect union is that which meets the Divine at every moment, in every action and with all the integrality of the nature.

ये त्वक्षरमनिर्देश्यमव्यक्तं पर्युपासते ।
सर्वत्रगमचिन्त्यं च कूटस्थमचलं ध्रुवम् ।।३।।

3. **But those also who seek by a hard ascent after the indefinable unmanifest Immutable alone, arrive, says the Godhead, to Me.** For they are not mistaken in their aim, **but they follow a more difficult and a less complete and perfect path.** At the easiest, to reach the unmanifest Absolute they have to climb through the manifest Immutable here. This manifest Immutable is my own all-pervading impersonality and silence; **vast, unthinkable, the Summit Self, immobile, constant (*or,* the Permanent), omnipresent, it supports the action of personality but does not share in it.**

संनियम्येन्द्रियग्रामं सर्वत्र समबुद्धयः ।
ते प्राप्नुवन्ति मामेव सर्वभूतहिते रताः ।।४।।

4. It offers no hold to the mind; it can only be gained by a motionless spiritual impersonality and silence and those who follow after it alone have **to restrain altogether and even draw in completely the action of the mind and senses. But still by the equality of their understanding and by their seeing of one self in all things and by their tranquil benignancy of silent will for the good of all existences, *sarva-bhūta-hite ratāḥ*, they too meet me in all objects and creatures.** No less than those who unite themselves with the Divine in all ways of their existence, *sarva-bhāvena*, and enter largely and fully into the unthinkable living fountainhead of universal things, *divyaṁ puruṣam acintya-rūpam*, these seekers too who climb through this more difficult exclusive oneness towards a relationless unmanifest Absolute find in the end the same Eternal. **But this is a less direct and more arduous way;** it is not the full and natural movement of the spiritualised human nature.

क्लेशोऽधिकतरस्तेषामव्यक्तासक्तचेतसाम् ।
अव्यक्ता हि गतिर्दुःखं देहवद्भिरवाप्यते ।।५।।

5. The Yogin of exclusive knowledge imposes on himself a painful struggle with the manifold demands of his nature. The living way of the Gita finds out the most intense upward trend of all our being and by turning it Godwards uses knowledge, will, feeling and the instinct for perfection as so many puissant wings of a mounting liberation. **The unmanifest Brahman in its indefinable unity is a thing to which embodied souls can only arrive and that hardly by a constant mortification, a suffering of all the repressed members, a stern difficulty and anguish of the nature, *duḥkham avāpyate, kleśo 'dhikataras teṣām.*** The indefinable Oneness accepts all that climb to it, but offers no help of relation and gives no foothold to the climber. All has to be done by a severe austerity and a stern and lonely individual effort.

ये तु सर्वाणि कर्माणि मयि संन्यस्य मत्पराः ।
अनन्येनैव योगेन मां ध्यायन्त उपासते ।।६।।

6. How different is it for those who seek after the Purushottama in the way of the Gita! **When they meditate on him (*mām*) with a Yoga which sees none else, because it sees all to be Vasudeva, he meets them at every point, in every movement, at all times,** with innumerable forms and faces, holds up the lamp of knowledge within and floods with its divine and happy lustre the whole of existence. Illumined, they discern the supreme Spirit in every form and face, arrive at once through all Nature to the Lord of Nature, arrive through all beings to the Soul of all being, arrive through themselves to the Self of all that they are; incontinently they break through a hundred opening issues at once into that from which everything has its origin. **Here the actions are all given up to the supreme Master of action, *ye tu sarvāṇi karmāṇi mayi sannyasya matparāḥ*,** and he as the supreme Will meets the will of sacrifice, takes from it its burden and assumes to himself the charge of the works of the divine Nature in us.

तेषामहं समुद्धर्त्ता मृत्युसंसारसागरात् ।
भवामि नचिरात्पार्थ मय्यावेशितचेतसाम् ।।७।।

7. **And when too in the high passion of love the devotee of the divine Lover and Friend of man and of all creatures casts upon him (*mayi*) all his heart of consciousness and yearning of delight, then swiftly the Supreme (*aham*) comes to him as the saviour and deliverer and exalts him by a happy embrace of his mind and heart and body out of the waves of the sea of death in this mortal nature into the secure bosom of the Eternal.**

मय्येव मन आधत्स्व मयि बुद्धिं निवेशय ।
निवसिष्यसि मय्येव अत ऊर्ध्वं न संशयः ॥८॥

8. This then is the swiftest, largest and greatest way. **On me, says the Godhead to the soul of man, repose all thy mind and lodge all thy understanding in me:** I will lift them up bathed in the supernal blaze of the divine love and will and knowledge to myself from whom these things flow. **Doubt not that thou shalt dwell in me above this mortal existence, *nivasiṣyasi mayyeva*.**

अथ चित्तं समाधातुं न शक्नोषि मयि स्थिरम् ।
अभ्यासयोगेन ततो मामिच्छाप्तुं धनञ्जय ॥९॥

9. No doubt, on this way too there are difficulties; for there is the lower nature with its fierce or dull downward gravitation which resists and battles against the motion of ascent and clogs the wings of the exaltation and the upward rapture. The divine consciousness even when it has been found at first in a wonder of great moments or in calm and splendid durations, cannot at once be altogether held or called back at will; **there is felt often an inability to keep the personal consciousness fixed steadily in the Divine (*mayi*);** there are nights of long exile from the Light, there are hours or moments of revolt, doubt or failure. **But still by the practice of union and by constant repetition of the experience, *abhyāsa-yogena*, that highest spirit grows upon the being and takes permanent possession of the nature.**

अभ्यासेऽप्यसमर्थोऽसि मत्कर्मपरमो भव ।
मदर्थमपि कर्माणि कुर्वन्सिद्धिमवाप्स्यसि ॥१०॥

10. **Is this also found too difficult** because of the power and persistence of the outward-going movement of the mind? Then the way is simple, **to do all actions for the sake of the Lord of the action (*mad-artham*),** so that every outward-going movement of the mind shall be associated with the inner spiritual truth of the being and called back even in the very movement to the eternal reality and connected with its source. Then the presence of the Purushottama will grow upon the natural man, till he is filled with it and becomes a godhead and a spirit; **all life will become a constant remembering of God and perfection too will grow** and the unity of the whole existence of the human soul with the supreme Existence.

अथैतदप्यशक्तोऽसि कर्तुं मद्योगमाश्रितः ।
सर्वकर्मफलत्यागं ततः कुरु यतात्मवान् ॥११॥

11. But it may be that even this constant remembering of God and lifting up of our works to him is felt to be beyond the power of the limited mind, because in its forgetfulness it turns to the act and its outward object and will not remember to look within and lay our every movement on the divine altar of the Spirit. **Then the way is to control the lower self in the act and do works without desire of the fruit. All fruit has to be renounced,** to be given up to the Power that directs the work, and yet the work has to be done that is imposed by It on the nature.

श्रेयो हि ज्ञानमभ्यासाज्ज्ञानाद्ध्यानं विशिष्यते ।
ध्यानात्कर्मफलत्यागस्त्यागाच्छान्तिरनन्तरम् ।।१२।।

12. And here the Gita gives an ascending scale of potencies and assigns the palm of excellence to this Yoga of desireless action. ***Abhyāsa*, practice of a method, repetition of an effort and experience** is a great and powerful thing; **but better than this is knowledge,** the successful and luminous turning of the thought to the Truth behind things. **This thought-knowledge too is excelled by a silent complete concentration on the Truth** so that the consciousness shall eventually live in it and be always one with it. **But more powerful still is the giving up of the fruit of one's works,** because that immediately destroys all causes of disturbance **and brings and preserves automatically an inner calm and peace,** and calm and peace are the foundation on which all else becomes perfect and secure in possession by the tranquil spirit. Then the consciousness can be at ease, happily fix itself in the Divine and rise undisturbed to perfection. Then too knowledge, will and devotion can lift their pinnacles from a firm soil of solid calm into the ether of Eternity.

अद्वेष्टा सर्वभूतानां मैत्रः करुण एव च ।
निर्ममो निरहङ्कारः समदुःखसुखः क्षमी ।।१३।।

13. What then will be the divine nature, what will be the greater state of consciousness and being of the bhakta who has followed this way and turned to the adoration of the Eternal? The Gita in a number of verses rings the changes on its first insistent demand, on equality, on desirelessness, on freedom of spirit. This is to be the base always. Several formulas of this fundamental equal consciousness are given here. **First, an absence of egoism, of I-ness and my-ness, *nirmamo nirahaṅkāraḥ*.** The bhakta of the Purushottama is one who has a universal heart and mind which has broken down all the narrow walls of the ego. A universal love dwells in his heart, a universal compassion flows from it like an encompassing sea. He will have friendship and pity for all beings and hate for no living thing: for he is patient, long-suffering, enduring, a well of forgiveness.

सन्तुष्टः सततं योगी यतात्मा दृढनिश्चयः ।
मय्यर्पितमनोबुद्धिर्यो मद्भक्तः स मे प्रियः ।।१४।।

14. A desireless content is his, a tranquil equality to pleasure and pain, suffering and happiness, the steadfast control of self and the firm unshakable will and resolution of the Yogin and a love and devotion which gives up the whole mind and reason to the Lord (*mayi*), to the Master of his consciousness and knowledge.

यस्मान्नोद्विजते लोको लोकान्नोद्विजते च यः ।
हर्षामर्षभयोद्वेगैर्मुक्तो यः स च मे प्रियः ।।१५।।

15. Or, simply, he will be one who is freed from the troubled agitated lower nature and from its waves of joy and fear and anxiety and resentment and desire, a spirit of calm by whom the world is not afflicted or troubled, nor is he afflicted or troubled by the world, a soul of peace with whom all are at peace.

अनपेक्षः शुचिर्दक्ष उदासीनो गतव्यथः ।
सर्वारम्भपरित्यागी यो मद्भक्तः स मे प्रियः ।।१६।।

16. Or he will be one who has given up all desire and action to the Master of his being, one pure and still, indifferent to whatever comes, *udāsīnaḥ*, not pained or afflicted by any result or happening, one who has flung away from him all egoistic, personal and mental initiative whether of the inner or the outer act, *sarvārambha-parityāgī*, one who lets the divine will and divine knowledge flow through him undeflected by his own resolves, preferences and desires, and yet for that very reason is swift and skilful in all action of his nature, because this flawless unity with the supreme will, this pure instrumentation is the condition of the greatest skill in works.

यो न हृष्यति न द्वेष्टि न शोचति न काङ्क्षति ।
शुभाशुभपरित्यागी भक्तिमान्यः स मे प्रियः ।।१७।।

17. Again, he will be one who neither desires the pleasant and rejoices at its touch nor abhors the unpleasant and sorrows at its burden. He has abolished the distinction between fortunate and unfortunate happenings, because his devotion receives all things equally as good from the hands of his eternal Lover and Master.

समः शत्रौ च मित्रे च तथा मानापमानयोः ।
शीतोष्णसुखदुःखेषु समः सङ्गविवर्जितः ।।१८।।

18. The God-lover dear to God is a soul of wide equality, equal to friend and enemy, equal to honour and insult, pleasure and pain, praise and blame, grief and happiness, heat and cold, to all that troubles with opposite affections the normal nature. **He will have no attachment to person or thing, place or home;**

तुल्यनिन्दास्तुतिर्मौनी सन्तुष्टो येन केनचित् ।
अनिकेतः स्थिरमतिर्भक्तिमान्मे प्रियो नरः ।।१९।।

19. he will be content and well-satisfied with whatever surroundings, whatever relation men adopt to him, whatever station or fortune. He will keep a mind firm in all things, because it is constantly seated in the highest self and fixed for ever on the one divine object of his love and adoration Equality, desirelessness and freedom from the lower egoistic nature and its claims are always the one perfect foundation demanded by the Gita for the great liberation. And the crown of this equality is love founded on knowledge, fulfilled in instrumental action, extended to all things and beings, a vast absorbing and all-containing love for the divine Self who is Creator and Master of the universe, *suhṛidaṁ sarva-bhūtānāṁ sarva-loka-maheśvaram*.

ये तु धर्म्यामृतमिदं यथोक्तं पर्युपासते ।
श्रद्दधाना मत्परमा भक्तास्तेऽतीव मे प्रियाः ।।२०।।

20. This is the foundation, the condition, the means by which the supreme spiritual perfection is to be won, and those who have it in any way **are all dear to me, says the Godhead, *bhaktimān me priyaḥ*. But exceedingly dear, *atīva me priyāḥ*, are those souls nearest to the Godhead whose love of** me is completed by the still wider and greatest perfection of which I have just shown to you the way and the process. **These are the bhaktas who make Me, the Purushottama, their one supreme aim, *mat-paramāḥ*, and follow out**

with a perfect faith and exactitude the immortalising Dharma described in this teaching.

Dharma in the language of the Gita means the innate law of the being and its works and an action proceeding from and determined by the inner nature, *svabhāva-niyataṁ karma*. The immortal Dharma is one; it is that of the highest spiritual divine consciousness and its powers, *parā prakṛitiḥ*. The one liberating unifying consciousness and power of the Eternal has to become the infinite source of our action, its mould, determinant and exemplar. To rise out of our lower personal egoism, to enter into the impersonal and equal calm of the immutable eternal all-pervading Akshara Purusha, to aspire from that calm by a perfect self-surrender of all one's nature and existence to that which is other and higher than the Akshara, is the first necessity of this Yoga. In the strength of that aspiration one can rise to the immortal Dharma. There, made one in being, consciousness and divine bliss with the greatest Uttama Purusha, made one with his supreme dynamic nature-force, *svā prakṛitiḥ*, the liberated spirit can know infinitely, love illimitably, act unfalteringly in the authentic power of a highest immortality and a perfect freedom. The rest of the Gita is written to throw a fuller light on this immortal Dharma.

CHAPTER XIII

The Field and its Knower

The Gita in its last six chapters, in order to found on a clear and complete knowledge the way of the soul's rising out of the lower into the divine nature, restates in another form the enlightenment the Teacher has already imparted to Arjuna. Essentially it is the same knowledge, but details and relations are now made prominent and assigned their entire significance, thoughts and truths brought out in their full value that were alluded to only in passing or generally stated in the light of another purpose. Thus in the first six chapters the knowledge necessary for the distinction between the immutable self and the soul veiled in nature was accorded an entire prominence. The references to the supreme Self and Purusha were summary and not at all explicit; it was assumed in order to justify works in the world and it was affirmed to be the Master of being, but there was otherwise nothing to show what it was and its relations to the rest were not even hinted at, much less developed. The remaining chapters are devoted to the bringing out of this suppressed knowledge in a conspicuous light and strong pre-eminence. It is to the Lord, the Ishwara, it is to the distinction of the higher and the lower nature and to the vision of the all-originating and all-constituting Godhead in Nature, it is to the One in all beings that prominence has been assigned in the next six Adhyayas (VII-XII) in order to found a root-unity of works and love with knowledge. But now it is necessary to bring out more definitely the precise relations between the supreme Purusha, the immutable self, the Jiva and Prakriti in her action and her gunas. Arjuna is therefore made to put a question which shall evoke a clearer elucidation of these still ill-lighted matters.

अर्जुन उवाच
प्रकृतिं पुरुषं चैव क्षेत्रं क्षेत्रज्ञमेव च ।
एतद्वेदितुमिच्छामि ज्ञानं ज्ञेयं च केशव ।।१।।

1. *Arjuna* — **He asks to learn of the Purusha and the Prakriti; he inquires of the field of being and the knower of the field and of knowledge and the object of knowledge.** Here is contained the sum of all the knowledge of self

and the world that is still needed if the soul is to throw off its natural ignorance and staying its steps on a right use of knowledge, of life, of works and of its own relations with the Divine in these things ascend into unity of being with the eternal Spirit of existence.

Action being admitted, a divine action done with self-knowledge as the instrument of the divine Will in the cosmos being accepted as perfectly consistent with the Brahmic status and an indispensable part of the Godward movement, that action being uplifted inwardly as a sacrifice with adoration to the Highest, how does this way practically affect the great object of spiritual life, the rising from the lower into the higher nature, from mortal into immortal being? All life, all works are a transaction between the soul and Nature. What is the original character of that transaction? what does it become at its spiritual culminating point? to what perfection does it lead the soul that gets free from its lower and external motives and grows inwardly into the very highest poise of the Spirit and deepest motive-force of the works of its energy in the universe?

We have to see now more in detail what farther considerations this change of being involves and especially what is the difference between these two natures and how our action and our soul-status are affected by the liberation. For that purpose the Gita enters largely into certain details of the highest knowledge which it had hitherto kept in the background. Especially it dwells on the relation between Being and becoming, Soul and Nature, the action of the three gunas, the highest liberation, the largest fullest self-giving of the human soul to the Divine Spirit. There is in all that it says in these closing six chapters (XIII-XVIII) much of the greatest importance, but it is the last thought with which it closes that is of supreme interest; for in it we shall find the central idea of its teaching, its great word to the soul of man, its highest message.

श्रीभगवानुवाच
इदं शरीरं कौन्तेय क्षेत्रमित्यभिधीयते ।
एतद्यो वेत्ति तं प्राहुः क्षेत्रज्ञ इति तद्विदः ।।२।।

2. *Krishna* — First, the whole of existence must be regarded as a field of the soul's construction and action in the midst of Nature. **The Gita explains the *kṣetram*, field, by saying that it is this body which is called the field of the spirit, and in this body there is someone who takes cognizance of the field, *kṣetra-jña*, the knower of Nature.** It is evident, however, from the definitions that succeed that it is not the physical body alone which is the field, but all too that the body supports, the working of nature, the mentality, the natural

action of the objectivity and subjectivity of our being. This wider body too is only the individual field; there is a larger, a universal, a world-body, a world-field of the same Knower. For in each embodied creature there is this one Knower.

क्षेत्रज्ञं चापि मां विद्धि सर्वक्षेत्रेषु भारत ।
क्षेत्रक्षेत्रज्ञयोर्ज्ञानं यत्तज्ज्ञानं मतं मम ।।३।।

3. There is something beyond to be known, *jñeyam*, and it is when the knower of the field turns from the field itself to learn of himself within it and of all that is behind its appearances that real knowledge begins, *jñānam*, — the true knowledge of the field no less than of the knower. That turning inward alone delivers from ignorance. For the farther we go inward, the more we seize on greater and fuller realities of things and grasp the complete truth both of God and the soul and of the world and its movements. **Therefore, says the divine Teacher, it is the knowledge at once of the field and its knower, *kṣetra-kṣetrajñayor jñānam*, a united and even unified self-knowledge and world-knowledge, which is the real illumination and the only wisdom.** For both soul and nature are the Brahman, but the true truth of the world of Nature can only be discovered by the liberated sage who possesses also the truth of the spirit. One Brahman, one reality in Self and Nature is the object of all knowledge.

तत्क्षेत्रं यच्च यादृक्च यद्विकारि यतश्च यत् ।
स च यो यत्प्रभावश्च तत्समासेन मे शृणु ।।४।।

4. **The Gita proceeds to state the character, nature, source, deformations, powers of this sensible embodiment of our being. We see then that it is the whole working of the lower Prakriti that is meant by the *kṣetra*. That totality is the field of action of the embodied spirit here within us, the field of which it takes cognizance.**

ऋषिभिर्बहुधा गीतं छन्दोभिर्विविधैः पृथक् ।
ब्रह्मसूत्रपदैश्चैव हेतुमद्भिर्विनिश्चितैः ।।५।।

5. For a varied and detailed knowledge of all this world of Nature in its essential action as seen from the spiritual view-point **we are referred to the verses of the ancient seers, the seers of the Veda and Upanishads, in which we get the inspired and intuitive account of these creations of the**

Spirit, and to the Brahma Sutras which will give us the rational and philosophic analysis.

महाभूतान्यहङ्कारो बुद्धिरव्यक्तमेव च ।
इन्द्रियाणि दशैकं च पञ्च चेन्द्रियगोचराः ।।६।।

6. The Gita contents itself with a brief practical statement of the lower nature of our being in the terms of the Sankhya thinkers. **First there is the indiscriminate unmanifest Energy; out of that has come the objective evolution of the five elemental states of matter [ether, air, fire, water and earth]; as also the subjective evolution of the senses, intelligence and ego; there are too five objects of the senses,** or rather five different ways of sense cognizance of the world, powers evolved by the universal energy in order to deal with all the forms of things she has created from the five elemental states assumed by her original objective substance, — organic relations by which the ego endowed with intelligence and sense acts on the formations of the cosmos: this is the constitution of the kshetra.

इच्छा द्वेषः सुखं दुःखं सङ्घातश्चेतना धृतिः ।
एतत्क्षेत्रं समासेन सविकारमुदाहृतम् ।।७।।

7. **Then there is a general consciousness** that first informs and then illumines the Energy in its works; **there is a faculty of that consciousness by which the Energy holds together the relations of objects; there is too a continuity, a persistence of the subjective and objective relations of our consciousness with its objects.** These are the necessary powers of the field; all these are common and universal powers at once of the mental, vital and physical Nature. **Pleasure and pain, liking and disliking are the principal deformations of the kshetra.** These dualities are the positive and negative terms in which the ego soul of the lower nature enjoys the universe. All these things taken together constitute the fundamental character of our first transactions with the world of Nature, but it is evidently not the whole description of our being; it is our actuality but not the limit of our possibilities.

अमानित्वमदम्भित्वमहिंसा क्षान्तिरार्जवम् ।
आचार्योपासनं शौचं स्थैर्यमात्मविनिग्रहः ।।८।।

8. **The Gita then tells us what is the spiritual knowledge or rather it tells us what are the conditions of knowledge,** the marks, the signs of the man

whose soul is turned towards the inner wisdom. First, there comes a certain moral condition, a sattwic government of the natural being. **There is fixed in him a total absence of wordly pride and arrogance, a candid soul, a tolerant, long-suffering and benignant heart, purity of mind and body, tranquil firmness and steadfastness, self-control and a masterful government of the lower nature and the heart's worship given to the Teacher,** whether to the divine Teacher within or to the human Master in whom the divine Wisdom is embodied, — for that is the sense of the reverence given to the Guru.

इन्द्रियार्थेषु वैराग्यमनहङ्कार एव च ।
जन्ममृत्युजराव्याधिदुःखदोषानुदर्शनम् ।।९।।
असक्तिरनभिष्वङ्गः पुत्रदारगृहादिषु ।
नित्यं च समचित्तत्वमिष्टानिष्टोपपत्तिषु ।।१०।।

9-10. Then there is a nobler and freer attitude towards the outward world, an attitude of perfect detachment and equality, **a firm removal of the natural being's attraction to the objects of the senses and a radical freedom from the claims of that constant clamorous ego-sense, ego-idea, ego-motive** which tyrannises over the normal man. **There is no longer any clinging to the attachment and absorption of family and home. There is instead of these vital and animal movements an unattached will and sense and intelligence, a keen perception of the defective nature of the ordinary life of physical man with its aimless and painful subjection to birth and death and disease and age, a constant equalness to all pleasant or unpleasant happenings,** — for the soul is seated within and impervious to the shocks of external events, —

मयि चानन्ययोगेन भक्तिरव्यभिचारिणी ।
विविक्तदेशसेवित्वमरतिर्जनसंसदि ।।११।।
अध्यात्मज्ञाननित्यत्वं तत्त्वज्ञानार्थदर्शनम् ।
एतज्ज्ञानमिति प्रोक्तमज्ञानं यदतोऽन्यथा ।।१२।।

11-12. and a meditative mind turned towards solitude and away from the vain noise of crowds and the assemblies of men. Finally, there is a strong turn within towards the things that really matter, a philosophic perception of the true sense and large principles of existence, a tranquil continuity of inner spiritual knowledge and light, (knowledge of the Self and Nature, — the knowledge, *tattvajñāna*, of those essential principles of Being, those essential modes of self-existence on which the absolute Divine has based its self-manifestation) **the Yoga of an unswerving devotion, love of God, the heart's deep and constant adoration of the universal and eternal Presence.**

ज्ञेयं यत्तत्प्रवक्ष्यामि यज्ज्ञात्वामृतमश्नुते ।
अनादिमत्परं ब्रह्म न सत्तन्नासदुच्यते ।।१३।।

13. The one object to which the mind of spiritual knowledge must be turned is the Eternal by fixity in whom the soul clouded here and swathed in the mists of Nature recovers and enjoys its native and original consciousness of immortality and transcendence. To be fixed on the transient, to be limited in the phenomenon is to accept mortality; the constant truth in things that perish is that in them which is inward and immutable. The soul when it allows itself to be tyrannised over by the appearances of Nature, misses itself and goes whirling about in the cycle of the births and deaths of its bodies. There, passionately following without end the mutations of personality and its interests, it cannot draw back to the possession of its impersonal and unborn self-existence. To be able to do that is to find oneself and get back to one's true being, that which assumes these births but does not perish with the perishing of its forms. To enjoy the eternity to which birth and life are only outward circumstances, is the soul's true immortality and transcendence. **That Eternal or that Eternity is the Brahman.** Brahman is That which is transcendent and That which is universal: it is the free spirit who supports in front the play of soul with nature and assures behind their imperishable oneness; it is at once the mutable and the immutable, the All that is the One. **In his highest supracosmic status Brahman is a transcendent Eternity without origin or change far above the phenomenal oppositions of existence and non-existence [*sat* and *asat*], persistence and transience between which the outward world moves.**

सर्वतः पाणिपादं तत्सर्वतोऽक्षिशिरोमुखम् ।
सर्वतः श्रुतिमल्लोके सर्वमावृत्य तिष्ठति ।।१४।।

14. But once seen in the substance and light of this eternity, the world also becomes other than it seems to the mind and senses; for then we see the universe no longer as a whirl of mind and life and matter or a mass of the determinations of energy and substance, but as no other than this eternal Brahman. **A spirit who immeasurably fills and surrounds all this movement with himself** — for indeed the movement too is himself — and who throws on all that is finite the splendour of his garment of infinity, **a bodiless and million-bodied spirit whose hands of strength and feet of swiftness are on every side of us, whose heads and eyes and faces are those innumerable visages which we see wherever we turn, whose ear is everywhere** listening to the silence of eternity and the music of the worlds, **is the universal Being in whose embrace we live.**

सर्वेन्द्रियगुणाभासं सर्वेन्द्रियविवर्जितम् ।
असक्तं सर्वभृच्चैव निर्गुणं गुणभोक्तृ च ।।१५।।

15. All relations of Soul and Nature are circumstances in the eternity of Brahman; **sense and quality, their reflectors and constituents, are this supreme Soul's devices for the presentation of the workings that his own energy in things constantly liberates into movement. He is himself beyond the limitation of the senses,** sees all things but not with the physical eye, hears all things but not with the physical ear, is aware of all things but not with the limiting mind — mind which represents but cannot truly know. **Not determined by any qualities, he possesses and determines in his substance all qualities and enjoys this qualitative action of his own Nature, *nirguṇaṁ guṇa-bhoktṛi*. He is attached to nothing, bound by nothing, fixed to nothing that he does; calm, he supports in a large and immortal freedom all the action and movement and passion of his universal Shakti, *asaktaṁ sarva-bhṛt*.**

बहिरन्तश्च भूतानामचरं चरमेव च ।
सूक्ष्मत्वात्तदविज्ञेयं दूरस्थं चान्तिके च तत् ।।१६।।

16. **He becomes all that is in the universe; that which is in us is he and all that we experience outside ourselves is he. The inward and the outward, the far and the near, the moving and the unmoving, all this he is at once. He is the subtlety of the subtle which is beyond our knowledge,** even as he is the density of force and substance which offers itself to the grasp of our minds.

अविभक्तं च भूतेषु विभक्तमिव च स्थितम् ।
भूतभर्तृ च तज्ज्ञेयं ग्रसिष्णु प्रभविष्णु च ।।१७।।

17. **He is indivisible and the One, but seems to divide himself in forms and creatures and appears as all these separate existences, *avibhaktaṁ ca bhūteṣu vibhaktam iva ca sthitam*.**

The One is the eternal unity of the Many differentiating and undifferentiating itself in the cosmos. This means that cosmos and individual are manifestations of a transcendent Self who is indivisible being although he seems to be divided or distributed; but he is not really divided or distributed but indivisibly present everywhere. Therefore all is in each and each is in all and all is in God and God in all.

All things can get back in him, can return in the Spirit to the indivisible unity of their self-existence. **All is eternally born from him, upborne in his eternity, taken eternally back into his oneness.**

The co-existence of the Infinite and the finite, which is the very nature of universal being, is not a juxtaposition or mutual inclusion of two opposites, but as natural and inevitable as the relation of the principle of Light and Fire with the suns. The finite is a frontal aspect and a self-determination of the Infinite; no finite can exist in itself and by itself, it exists by the Infinite and because it is of one essence with the Infinite. For by the Infinite we do not mean solely an illimitable self-extension in Space and Time, but something that is also spaceless and timeless, a self-existent Indefinable and Illimitable which can express itself in the infinitesimal as well as in the vast, in a second of time, in a point of space, in a passing circumstance. The finite is looked upon as a division of the Indivisible, but there is no such thing; for this division is only apparent; there is a demarcation, but no real separation is possible. When we see with the inner vision and sense and not with the physical eye a tree or other object, what we become aware of is an infinite one Reality constituting the tree or object, pervading its every atom and molecule, forming them out of itself, building the whole nature, process of becoming, operation of indwelling energy; all of these are itself, are this infinite, this Reality: we see it extending indivisibly and uniting all objects so that none is really separate from it or quite separate from other objects. **"It stands undivided in beings and yet as if divided."** Thus each object is that Infinite and one in essential being with all other objects that are also forms and names — powers, numens — of the Infinite.

ज्योतिषामपि तज्ज्योतिस्तमसः परमुच्यते ।
ज्ञानं ज्ञेयं ज्ञानगम्यं हृदि सर्वस्य विष्ठितम् ।।१८।।

18. He is the light of all lights and luminous beyond all the darkness of our ignorance. He is knowledge and the object of knowledge. The spiritual supramental knowledge that floods the illumined mind and transfigures it is this spirit manifesting itself in light to the force-obscured soul which he has put forth into the action of Nature. **This eternal Light is in the heart of every being; it is he who is the secret knower of the field, *kṣetra-jña*, and presides as the Lord in the heart of things over this province and over all these kingdoms of his manifested becoming and action.**

इति क्षेत्रं तथा ज्ञानं ज्ञेयं चोक्तं समासतः ।
मद्भक्त एतद्विज्ञाय मद्भावायोपपद्यते ।।१९।।

19. That is the supreme status of the soul, *parā gatiḥ* (*sl. 29*), **that is**

the divine being and nature, *madbhāva*, and whoever arrives at spiritual knowledge, rises to that supreme immortality of the Eternal.

प्रकृतिं पुरुषं चैव विद्ध्यनादी उभावपि ।
विकारांश्च गुणांश्चैव विद्धि प्रकृतिसम्भवान् ।।२०।।

20. The Soul and Nature are only two aspects of the eternal Brahman, an apparent duality which founds the operations of his universal existence. **The Soul is without origin and eternal, Nature too is without origin and eternal; but the modes of Nature and the lower forms she assumes to our conscious experience have an origin in the transactions of these two entities.**

कार्यकरणकर्तृत्वे हेतुः प्रकृतिरुच्यते ।
पुरुषः सुखदुःखानां भोक्तृत्वे हेतुरुच्यते ।।२१।।

21. **They come from her, wear by her the outward chain of cause and effect, doing and the results of doing,** force and its workings, all that is here transient and mutable. Constantly they change and the soul and Nature seem to change with them, but in themselves these two powers are eternal and always the same. **Nature creates and acts, the Soul enjoys her creation and action;** but in this inferior form of her action she turns this enjoyment into the obscure and petty figures of **pain and pleasure.**

पुरुषः प्रकृतिस्थो हि भुङ्क्ते प्रकृतिजान्गुणान् ।
कारणं गुणसङ्गोऽस्य सदसद्योनिजन्मसु ।।२२।।

22. **Forcibly the soul, the individual Purusha, is attracted by her qualitative workings and this attraction of her qualities draws him constantly to births of all kinds in which he enjoys the variation and vicissitudes, the good and evil of birth in Nature.** But this is only the outward experience of the soul mutable in conception by identification with mutable Nature.

उपद्रष्टानुमन्ता च भर्ता भोक्ता महेश्वरः ।
परमात्मेति चाप्युक्तो देहेऽस्मिन्पुरुषः परः ।।२३।।

23. **Seated in this body is her and our Divinity, the supreme Self, Paramatman, the supreme Soul, the mighty Lord of Nature, who watches her action, *upadraṣṭā* (or *sākṣī*), sanctions her operations, *anumantā*, upholds all**

she does, *bhartā*, commands her manifold creation, *maheśvaraḥ*, enjoys with his universal delight this play of her figures of his own being, *bhoktā*.

य एवं वेत्ति पुरुषं प्रकृतिं च गुणैः सह ।
सर्वथा वर्तमानोऽपि न स भूयोऽभिजायते ॥२४॥

24. That is the self-knowledge to which we have to accustom our mentality before we can truly know ourselves as an eternal portion of the Eternal. Once that is fixed, no matter how the soul in us may comport itself outwardly in its transactions with Nature, whatever it may seem to do or however it may seem to assume this or that figure of personality and active force and embodied ego, it is in itself free, no longer bound to birth because one through impersonality of self with the inner unborn spirit of existence. That impersonality is our union with the supreme egoless I of all that is in cosmos.

ध्यानेनात्मनि पश्यन्ति केचिदात्मानमात्मना ।
अन्ये सांख्येन योगेन कर्मयोगेन चापरे ॥२५॥

25. This knowledge comes by an inner meditation through which the eternal self becomes apparent to us in our own self-existence, *ātmani paśyanti kecid ātmānam ātmanā*; there must be some direct seeing by the soul of the Soul or Self everywhere in its own delivered force of vision, — the direct vision of Indian aspiration, — not the sensuous or the imaginative or the intellectual or the vital insistence, but a greater Potency using and surmounting them, the Soul's own delivered self-vision in all things and delight of its own greatness and light and beauty. Or it comes by the Yoga of the Sankhyas, the separation of the soul from nature. Or it comes by the Yoga of works in which the personal will is dissolved through the opening up of our mind and heart and all our active forces to the Lord who assumes to himself the whole of our works in nature.

अन्ये त्वेवमजानन्तः श्रुत्वान्येभ्य उपासते ।
तेऽपि चातितरन्त्येव मृत्युं श्रुतिपरायणाः ॥२६॥

26. The spiritual knowledge may be awakened by the urging of the spirit within us, its call to this or that Yoga, this or that way of oneness. Or it may come to us by hearing of the truth from others and the moulding of the

mind into the sense of that to which it listens with faith and concentration. But however arrived at, it carries us beyond death to immortality.

यावत्सञ्जायते किञ्चित्सत्त्वं स्थावरजङ्गमम् ।
क्षेत्रक्षेत्रज्ञसंयोगात्तद्विद्धि भरतर्षभ ।।२७।।
समं सर्वेषु भूतेषु तिष्ठन्तं परमेश्वरम् ।
विनश्यत्स्वविनश्यन्तं यः पश्यति स पश्यति ।।२८।।

27-28. All life, all works are a transaction between the soul and Nature (*see sl. 1*). Knowledge shows us high above the mutable transactions of the soul with the mortality of nature our highest Self as the supreme Lord of her actions, one and equal in all objects and creatures, not born in the taking up of a body, not subject to death in the perishing of all these bodies. That is the true seeing, the seeing of that in us which is eternal and immortal.

समं पश्यन्हि सर्वत्र समवस्थितमीश्वरम् ।
न हिनस्त्यात्मनात्मानं ततो याति परां गतिम् ।।२९।।

29. As we perceive more and more this equal spirit in all things, we pass into that equality of the spirit; as we dwell more and more in this universal being, we become ourselves universal beings; as we grow more and more aware of this eternal, we put on our own eternity and are for ever. We identify ourselves with the eternity of the self and no longer with the limitation and distress of our mental and physical ignorance. **We do not injure ourselves** by casting our being into the hands of desire and passions. (*see also sl. 19*)

प्रकृत्यैव च कर्माणि क्रियमाणानि सर्वशः ।
यः पश्यति तथात्मानमकर्तारं स पश्यति ।।३०।।

30. Then we see that all our works are an evolution and operation of Nature and our real self not the executive doer, but the free witness and lord and unattached enjoyer of the action. If then a man casts from him the idea of himself as the doer or of the works as his, if, as the Gita enjoins, he fixes himself in the view of himself as the inactive non-doer, *ātmānam akartāraṁ*, and all action as not his own but Nature's, as the play of her gunas, will not a like result follow?

यदा भूतपृथग्भावमेकस्थमनुपश्यति ।
तत एव च विस्तारं ब्रह्म सम्पद्यते तदा ।।३१।।

31. All this surface of cosmic movement is a diverse becoming of natural existences in the one eternal Being, all is extended, manifested, rolled out by the universal Energy from the seeds of her Idea deep in his existence.

अनादित्वान्निर्गुणत्वात्परमात्मायमव्ययः ।
शरीरस्थोऽपि कौन्तेय न करोति न लिप्यते ।।३२।।

32. But the spirit even though it takes up and enjoys her workings in this body of ours is not affected by its mortality because it is eternal beyond birth and death, **is not limited by the personalities which it multiply assumes in her because it is the one supreme** self of all these personalities, **is not changed by the mutations of quality because it is itself undetermined by quality, does not act even in action,** ***kartāram api akartāram,*** because it supports natural action in a perfect spiritual freedom from its effects, **is the originator indeed of all activities, but in no way changed or affected by the play of its Nature.**

यथा सर्वगतं सौक्ष्म्यादाकाशं नोपलिप्यते ।
सर्वत्रावस्थितो देहे तथात्मा नोपलिप्यते ।।३३।।

33. As the all-pervading ether is not affected or changed by the multiple forms it assumes, but remains always the same pure subtle original substance, even so this spirit when it has done and become all possible things, remains through it all the same pure immutable subtle infinite essence.

यथा प्रकाशयत्येकः कृत्स्नं लोकमिमं रविः ।
क्षेत्रं क्षेत्री तथा कृत्स्नं प्रकाशयति भारत ।।३४।।

34. This Brahman, this eternal and spiritual knower of the field of his own natural becoming, this Nature, his perpetual energy, which converts herself into that field, this immortality of the soul in mortal nature, — these things together make the whole reality of our existence. **The spirit within, when we turn to it, illumines the entire field of Nature with its own truth in all the splendour of its rays.**

क्षेत्रक्षेत्रज्ञयोरेवमन्तरं ज्ञानचक्षुषा ।
भूतप्रकृतिमोक्षं च ये विदुर्यान्ति ते परम् ।।३५।।

35. In the light of that sun of knowledge the eye of knowledge opens in us and we live in that truth and no longer in this ignorance. Then we perceive that our limitation to our present mental and physical nature was an error of the darkness, **then we are liberated from the law of the lower Prakriti, the law of the mind and body, then we attain to the supreme nature of the spirit.** That splendid and lofty change is the last, the divine and infinite becoming, the putting off of mortal nature, the putting on of an immortal existence.

Chapter XIV

Above the Gunas

The distinctions between the Soul and Nature and especially the distinction between the embodied soul subjected to the action of Nature by its enjoyment of her gunas, qualities or modes and the Supreme Soul which dwells enjoying the gunas, but not subject because it is itself beyond them, are the basis on which the Gita rests its whole idea of the liberated being made one in the conscious law of its existence with the Divine. That liberation, that oneness, that putting on of the divine nature, *sādharmya*, it declares to be the very essence of spiritual freedom and the whole significance of immortality. This supreme importance assigned to *sādharmya* is a capital point in the teaching of the Gita.

To be immortal was never held in the ancient spiritual teaching to consist merely in a personal survival of the death of the body: all beings are immortal in that sense and it is only the forms that perish. The souls that do not arrive at liberation, live through the returning aeons. Pralaya, the end of a cycle of aeons, is the temporary disintegration of a universal form of existence and of all the individual forms which move in its rounds, but that is only a momentary pause, a silent interval followed by an outburst of new creation, reintegration and reconstruction in which they reappear and recover the impetus of their progression. Our physical death is also a pralaya, — the Gita will presently use the word in the sense of this death, *pralayaṁ yāti deha-bhṛit*, "the soul bearing the body comes to a pralaya," to a disintegration of that form of matter with which its ignorance identified its being and which now dissolves into the natural elements. But the soul itself persists and after an interval resumes in a new body formed from those elements its rounds of birth in the cycle.

To be immortal in the deeper sense is something different from this survival of death and this constant recurrence. Immortality is that supreme status in which the Spirit knows itself to be superior to death and birth, not conditioned by the nature of its manifestation, infinite, imperishable, immutably eternal, — immortal, because never being born it never dies. The divine Purushottama, who is the supreme Lord and supreme Brahman, possesses for ever this immortal eternity and is not affected by his taking up a body or by his continuous assumption of cosmic forms and powers because he exists always in this self-knowledge. His very nature is to be unchangeably conscious of his own eternity. Liberation, immortality is to live in this unchangeably conscious eternal being of the Purushottama.[1] But to arrive here at this greater spiritual immortality the embodied soul must cease to live according to the law of the lower nature; it must put on the law of the Divine's supreme way of existence which is in fact the real law of its own eternal essence. In the spiritual evolution of its becoming, no less than in its secret original being, it must grow into the likeness of the Divine.

श्रीभगवानुवाच
परं भूयः प्रवक्ष्यामि ज्ञानानां ज्ञानमुत्तमम् ।
यज्ज्ञात्वा मुनयः सर्वे परां सिद्धिमितो गताः ॥१॥
इदं ज्ञानमुपाश्रित्य मम साधर्म्यमागताः ।
सर्गेऽपि नोपजायन्ते प्रलये न व्यथन्ति च ॥२॥

1-2. *Krishna* — To get back to self-knowledge and to the knowledge of the real as distinct from the apparent relations of the soul with Nature, to know God and ourselves and the world with a spiritual and no longer with a physical or externalised experience, through the deepest truth of the inner soul-consciousness and not through the misleading phenomenal significances of the sense-mind and the outward understanding, is an indispensable means of this perfection. Perfection cannot come without self-knowledge and God-knowledge and a spiritual attitude towards our natural existence, and that is why the ancient wisdom laid so much stress on salvation by knowledge, — not an intellectual cognizance of things, but a growing of man the mental being into a greater spiritual consciousness. The soul's salvation cannot come without the soul's perfection, without its growing into the divine nature. Divine works are effective for salvation because they lead us towards this perfection and to a knowledge of self and nature and God by a growing unity with the inner Master of our existence. Divine love is effective because by it we grow into the likeness of the sole and supreme object of

1. Mark that nowhere in the Gita is there any indication that dissolution of the individual spiritual being into the unmanifest, indefinable or absolute Brahman, *avyaktam anirdeśyam*, is the true meaning or condition of immortality or the true aim of Yoga. On the contrary it describes immortality later on as an indwelling in the Ishwara in his supreme status, *mayi nivasiṣyasi*, *paraṁ dhāma*, and here as *sādharmya*, *parāṁ siddhim*, a supreme perfection, a becoming of one law of being and nature with the Supreme, persistent still in existence and conscious of the universal movement but above it, as all the sages still exist, *munayaḥ sarve*, not bound to birth in the creation, not troubled by the dissolution of the cycles.

our adoration and call down the answering love of the Highest to flood us with the light of his knowledge and the uplifting power and purity of his eternal spirit. Therefore, says the Gita, **this is the supreme knowledge and the highest of all knowings because it leads to the highest perfection and spiritual status, *paraṁ siddhim*, and brings the soul to likeness with the Divine, *sādharmya*. It is the eternal wisdom, the great spiritual experience by which all the sages attained to that highest perfection, grew into one law of being with the Supreme and live for ever in his eternity, not born in the creation, not troubled by the anguish of the universal dissolution.** This perfection, then, this *sādharmya* is the way of immortality and the indispensable condition without which the soul cannot consciously live in the Eternal.

मम योनिर्महद्ब्रह्म तस्मिन्गर्भं दधाम्यहम् ।
सम्भवः सर्वभूतानां ततो भवति भारत ।।३।।
सर्वयोनिषु कौन्तेय मूर्तयः सम्भवन्ति याः ।
तासां ब्रह्म महद्योनिरहं बीजप्रदः पिता ।।४।।

3-4. The soul of man could not grow into the likeness of the Divine, if it were not in its secret essence imperishably one with the Divine and part and parcel of his divinity: it could not be or become immortal if it were merely a creature of mental, vital and physical Nature. All existence is a manifestation of the divine Existence and that which is within us is spirit of the eternal Spirit. We have come indeed into the lower material nature and are under its influence, but we have come there from the supreme spiritual nature: this inferior imperfect status is our apparent, but that our real being. **The Eternal puts all this movement forth as his self-creation. He is at once the Father and Mother of the universe; the substance of the infinite Idea, *vijñāna*, the Mahat Brahman, is the womb into which he casts the seed of his self-conception.** As the Over-Soul he casts the seed; as the Mother, the Nature-Soul, the Energy filled with his conscious power, he receives it into this infinite substance of being made pregnant with his illimitable, yet self-limiting Idea. He receives into this Vast of self-conception and develops there the divine embryo into mental and physical form of existence born from the original act of conceptive creation. **All we see springs from that act of creation;** but that which is born here is only finite idea and form of the unborn and infinite.

सत्त्वं रजस्तम इति गुणाः प्रकृतिसम्भवाः ।
निबध्नन्ति महाबाहो देहे देहिनमव्ययम् ।।५।।

5. What is it that gets the soul into the appearance of birth and death and bondage, — for this is patent that it is only an appearance? It is a subordinate act or state of consciousness, it is a self-oblivious identification with the modes of Nature in the limited workings of this lower motivity and with this self-wrapped ego-bounded knot of action of the mind, life and body. To rise above the modes of Nature, to be *traiguṇyātīta*, is indispensable, if we are to get back into our fully conscious being away from the obsessing power of the lower action and to put on the free nature of the spirit and its eternal immortality. That condition of the *sādharmya* is what the Gita next proceeds to develop. It has now to indicate what are these modes, these gunas, how they bind the soul and keep it back from spiritual freedom and what is meant by rising above the modes of Nature.

The modes of Nature are all qualitative in their essence and are called for that reason its gunas or qualities. In any spiritual conception of the universe this must be so, because the connecting medium between spirit and matter must be psyche or soul power and the primary action psychological and qualitative, not physical and quantitative; for quality is the immaterial, the more spiritual element in all the action of the universal Energy, her prior dynamics. The predominance of physical Science has accustomed us to a different view of Nature, because there the first thing that strikes us is the importance of the quantitative aspect of her workings and her dependence for the creation of forms on quantitative combinations and dispositions. And yet even there the discovery that matter is rather substance or act of energy than energy a motive power of self-existent material substance or an inherent power acting in matter has led to some revival of an older reading of universal Nature.

The whole qualitative action of Nature, so infinitely intricate in its detail and variety, is figured as cast into the mould of three general modes of quality everywhere present, intertwined, almost inextricable, *sattva*, *rajas*, *tamas*. These modes are described in the Gita only by their psychological action in man.

On their psychological side the three qualities may be defined, tamas as Nature's power of nescience, rajas as her power of active seeking ignorance enlightened by desire and impulsion, sattwa as her power of possessing and harmonising knowledge.

The three qualities are a triple power which by their interaction determine the character and disposition and through that and its various motions the actions of the natural man. But this triple power is at the same time a triple cord of bondage. **The three gunas born of Prakriti, says the Gita, bind in the body the imperishable dweller in the body.** In a certain sense we can see at once that there must be this bondage in following the action of the gunas;

for they are all limited by their finite of quality and operation and cause limitation.

तत्र सत्त्वं निर्मलत्वात्प्रकाशकमनामयम् ।
सुखसङ्गेन बध्नाति ज्ञानसङ्गेन चानघ ।।६।।

6. The Gita applies this generalised analysis of the universal Energy to the psychological nature of man in relation to his bondage to Prakriti and the realisation of spiritual freedom. **Sattwa, it tells us, is by the purity of its quality a cause of light and illumination and by virtue of that purity it produces no disease or morbidity or suffering in the nature. Sattwa binds by attachment to knowledge and attachment to happiness.**

रजो रागात्मकं विद्धि तृष्णासङ्गसमुद्भवम् ।
तन्निबध्नाति कौन्तेय कर्मसङ्गेन देहिनम् ।।७।।

7. **Rajas, again, has for its essence attraction of liking and longing. Rajas is a child of the attachment of the soul to the desire of objects; it is born from the nature's thirst for an unpossessed satisfaction. Rajas binds the embodied spirit by attachment to works.**

तमस्त्वज्ञानजं विद्धि मोहनं सर्वदेहिनाम् ।
प्रमादालस्यनिद्राभिस्तन्निबध्नाति भारत ।।८।।

8. **Tamas, finally, is born of inertia and ignorance and its fruit too is inertia and ignorance. It is the darkness of tamas which obscures knowledge and causes all confusion and delusion. Tamas binds by negligence and indolence and sleep.**

सत्त्वं सुखे सञ्जयति रजः कर्मणि भारत ।
ज्ञानमावृत्य तु तमः प्रमादे सञ्जयत्युत ।।९।।

9. But there is the question, how does our infinite and imperishable spirit, even involved in Nature, come thus to confine itself to the lower action of Prakriti and undergo this bondage and how is it not, like the supreme spirit of which it is a portion, free in its infinity even while enjoying the self-limitations of its active evolution? The reason, says the Gita, is our

attachment to the gunas and to the result of their workings. **Sattwa attaches to happiness, rajas attaches to action, tamas covers up the knowledge and attaches to negligence of error and inaction.** In other words, the soul by attachment to the enjoyment of the gunas and their results concentrates its consciousness on the lower and outward action of life, mind and body in Nature, imprisons itself in the form of these things and becomes oblivious of its own greater consciousness behind in the spirit, unaware of the free power and scope of the liberating Purusha.

रजस्तमश्चाभिभूय सत्त्वं भवति भारत ।
रजः सत्त्वं तमश्चैव तमः सत्त्वं रजस्तथा ।।१०।।

10. These three qualities of Nature are evidently present and active in all human beings and none can be said to be quite devoid of one and another or free from any one of the three; none is cast in the mould of one guna to the exclusion of the others. But these qualities are not constant in any man in the quantitative action of their force or in the combination of their elements. **Now one leads, now another increases and predominates, and each subjects us to its characteristic action and consequences.**

सर्वद्वारेषु देहेऽस्मिन्प्रकाश उपजायते ।
ज्ञानं यदा तदा विद्याद्विवृद्धं सत्त्वमित्युत ।।११।।

11. **When into all the doors in the body there comes a flooding of light,** as if the doors and windows of a closed house were opened to sunshine, **a light of understanding, perception and knowledge,** — when the intelligence is alert and illumined, the senses quickened, the whole mentality satisfied and full of brightness and the nervous being calmed and filled with an illumined ease and clarity, *prasāda*, **one should understand that there has been a great increase and uprising of the sattwic guna in the nature.**

लोभः प्रवृत्तिरारम्भः कर्मणामशमः स्पृहा ।
रजस्येतानि जायन्ते विवृद्धे भरतर्षभ ।।१२।।

12. **Rajas is full of unrest and fever and lust and greed and excitement, a thing of seeking impulsions, and all this mounts in us when the middle guna increases. It is the force of desire which motives all ordinary personal initiative of action, *ārambha*, and all that movement of stir and seeking and propulsion in our nature which is the impetus towards action and works, *pravṛitti*.**

Rajas, then, is evidently the kinetic force in the modes of Nature. Its fruit is the lust of action, but also grief, pain, all kinds of suffering; for it has no right possession of its object — desire in fact implies non-possession.

अप्रकाशोऽप्रवृत्तिश्च प्रमादो मोह एव च ।
तमस्येतानि जायन्ते विवृद्धे कुरुनन्दन ।।१३।।

13. Tamas is the opposite of sattwa, for the essence of sattwa is enlightenment, *prakāśa*, and the essence of tamas is absence of light, nescience, *aprakāśa*. But tamas brings incapacity and negligence of action as well as the incapacity and negligence of error, inattention and misunderstanding or non-understanding; indolence, languor and sleep belong to this guna. Therefore it is the opposite too of rajas; for the essence of rajas is movement and impulsion and kinesis, *pravṛitti*, but the essence of tamas is inertia, *apravṛitti*. Tamas is inertia of nescience and inertia of inaction, a double negative.

यदा सत्त्वे प्रवृद्धे तु प्रलयं याति देहभृत् ।
तदोत्तमविदां लोकानमलान्प्रतिपद्यते ।।१४।।

14. (*Untranslated*)

रजसि प्रलयं गत्वा कर्मसङ्गिषु जायते ।
तथा प्रलीनस्तमसि मूढयोनिषु जायते ।।१५।।

15. (*Untranslated*)

कर्मणः सुकृतस्याहुः सात्त्विकं निर्मलं फलम् ।
रजसस्तु फलं दुःखमज्ञानं तमसः फलम् ।।१६।।

16. Evidently, in order to be liberated and perfect we must get back from these things, away from the gunas and above them and return to the power of that free spiritual consciousness above Nature. But this would seem to imply a cessation of all doing, since all natural action is done by the gunas, by Nature through her modes. The soul cannot act by itself, it can only act through Nature and her modes. And yet the Gita, while it demands freedom from the modes, insists upon the necessity of action. Here comes in the importance of its insistence on the abandonment of the fruits; for it is the desire of the fruits which is the most potent cause of the soul's bondage and by abandoning it the soul can be free in action. Ignorance is the result of tamasic action, pain the consequence of rajasic works, pain of reaction, disappointment, dissatisfaction or transience. But of works rightly done the fruit is pure and sattwic, the inner result is knowledge and happiness.

सत्त्वात्सञ्जायते ज्ञानं रजसो लोभ एव च ।
प्रमादमोहौ तमसो भवतोऽज्ञानमेव च ।।१७।।

17. (*Untranslated*)

ऊर्ध्वं गच्छन्ति सत्त्वस्था मध्ये तिष्ठन्ति राजसाः ।
जघन्यगुणवृत्तिस्था अधो गच्छन्ति तामसाः ।।१८।।

18. (*Untranslated*)

नान्यं गुणेभ्यः कर्तारं यदा द्रष्टानुपश्यति ।
गुणेभ्यश्च परं वेत्ति मद्भावं सोऽधिगच्छति ।।१९।।

19. But, even if one is free from any clinging to the fruit, there may be an attachment to the work itself. And here evidently the resource is in that other injunction of the Gita, to give up the action itself to the Lord of works and be only a desireless and equal-minded instrument of his will. **To see that the modes of Nature are the whole agency and cause of our works and to know and turn to that which is supreme above the gunas, is the way to rise above the lower nature. Only so can we attain to the movement and status of the Divine, *madbhāva*.**

गुणानेतानतीत्य त्रीन्देही देहसमुद्भवान् ।
जन्ममृत्युजरादुःखैर्विमुक्तोऽमृतमश्नुते ।।२०।।

20. Then lifted beyond the three gunas and free from subjection to birth and death and their concomitants, decay, old age and suffering, the liberated soul shall enjoy in the end the immortality of its self-existence and all that is eternal.

अर्जुन उवाच
कैर्लिङ्गैस्त्रीन्गुणानेतानतीतो भवति प्रभो ।
किमाचारः कथं चैतांस्त्रीन्गुणानतिवर्तते ।।२१।।

21. *Arjuna* — **But what are the signs of such a man, what his action and how is he said even in action to be above the three gunas?**

श्रीभगवानुवाच
प्रकाशं च प्रवृत्तिं च मोहमेव च पाण्डव ।
न द्वेष्टि सम्प्रवृत्तानि न निवृत्तानि काङ्क्षति ।।२२।।

22. *Krishna* — The sign is that equality of which I have so constantly spoken. **Sattwa, rajas or tamas may rise or cease in his outer mentality and his physical movements with their results of enlightenment, of impulsion to works or of inaction and the clouding over of the mental and nervous being, but he does not rejoice when this comes or that ceases, nor on the other hand does he abhor or shrink from the operation or the cessation of these things.**

उदासीनवदासीनो गुणैर्यो न विचाल्यते ।
गुणा वर्तन्त इत्येव योऽवतिष्ठति नेङ्गते ।।२३।।

23. **He has seated himself in the conscious light of another principle than the nature of the gunas and that greater consciousness remains steadfast in him, above these powers and unshaken by their motions, *udāsīnavad-āsīnaḥ*,** like the sun above clouds to one who has risen into a higher atmosphere. **He from that height sees that it is the gunas that are in process of action and that their storm and calm are not himself but only a movement of Prakriti; his self is immovable above** and his spirit does not participate in that shifting mutability of things unstable. This is the impersonality of the Brahmic status; for that higher principle, that greater wide high-seated consciousness, *kūṭastha*, is the immutable Brahman.

समदुःखसुखः स्वस्थः समलोष्टाश्मकाञ्चनः ।
तुल्यप्रियाप्रियो धीरस्तुल्यनिन्दात्मसंस्तुतिः ।।२४।।
मानापमानयोस्तुल्यस्तुल्यो मित्रारिपक्षयोः ।
सर्वारम्भपरित्यागी गुणातीतः स उच्यते ।।२५।।

24-25. **The sign is that inwardly he regards happiness and suffering alike, gold and mud and stone as of equal value and that to him the pleasant and the unpleasant, praise and blame, honour and insult, the faction of his friends and the faction of his enemies are equal things. He is steadfast in a wise imperturbable and immutable inner calm and quietude. He initiates no action,**

***sarvārambha-parityāgī*, but leaves all works to be done by the gunas of Nature, *guṇātītaḥ*.**

मां च योऽव्यभिचारेण भक्तियोगेन सेवते ।
स गुणान्समतीत्यैतान्ब्रह्मभूयाय कल्पते ।।२६।।

26. But still there is evidently here a double status, there is a scission of the being between two opposites; a liberated spirit in the immutable Self or Brahman watches the action of an unliberated mutable Nature, — Akshara and Kshara. Is there no greater status, no principle of more absolute perfection, or is this division the highest consciousness possible in the body, and is the end of Yoga to drop the mutable nature and the gunas born of the embodiment in Nature and disappear into the impersonality and everlasting peace of the Brahman? Is that *laya* or dissolution of the individual Purusha the greatest liberation? There is, it would seem, something else; for the Gita says at the close, always returning to this one final note, **He also who loves and strives after Me with an undeviating love and adoration, passes beyond the three gunas and he too is prepared for becoming the Brahman, *brahma-bhūyāya*.**

ब्रह्मणो हि प्रतिष्ठाहममृतस्याव्ययस्य च ।
शाश्वतस्य च धर्मस्य सुखस्यैकान्तिकस्य च ।।२७।।

27. **This "I" is the Purushottama who is the foundation of the silent Brahman and of immortality and imperishable spiritual existence and of the eternal dharma and of an utter bliss of happiness.** There is a status then which is greater than the peace of the Akshara as it watches unmoved the strife of the gunas. There is a highest spiritual experience and foundation above the immutability of the Brahman, there is an eternal dharma greater than the rajasic impulsion to works, *pravṛitti*, there is an absolute delight which is untouched by rajasic suffering and beyond the sattwic happiness, and these things are found and possessed by dwelling in the being and power of the Purushottama. But since it is acquired by bhakti, its status must be that divine delight, Ananda, in which is experienced the union of utter love[1] and possessing oneness, the crown of bhakti. And to rise into that Ananda, into that imperishable oneness must be the completion of spiritual perfection and the fulfilment of the eternal immortalising dharma.

1. *niratiśaya-premāspadatvam ānandatattvam.*

Chapter XV

The Three Purushas

श्रीभगवानुवाच
ऊर्ध्वमूलमधःशाखमश्वत्थं प्राहुरव्ययम् ।
छन्दांसि यस्य पर्णानि यस्तं वेद स वेदवित् ।।१।।
अधश्चोर्ध्वं प्रसृतास्तस्य शाखा गुणप्रवृद्धा विषयप्रवालाः ।
अधश्च मूलान्यनुसन्ततानि कर्मानुबन्धीनि मनुष्यलोके ।।२।।
न रूपमस्येह तथोपलभ्यते नान्तो न चादिर्न च सम्प्रतिष्ठा ।
अश्वत्थमेनं सुविरूढमूलमसङ्गशस्त्रेण दृढेन छित्त्वा ।।३।।
ततः पदं तत्परिमार्गितव्यं यस्मिन्गता न निवर्तन्ति भूयः ।
तमेव चाद्यं पुरुषं प्रपद्ये यतः प्रवृत्तिः प्रसृता पुराणी ।।४।।

1-4. *Krishna* — First there comes a description of cosmic existence in the Vedantic image of the aswattha tree. This tree of cosmic existence has no beginning and no end, *nānto na cādiḥ*, in space or in time; for it is eternal and imperishable, *avyaya*. The real form of it cannot be perceived by us in this material world of man's embodiment, nor has it any apparent lasting foundation here; it is an infinite movement and its foundation is above in the supreme of the Infinite. Its principle is the ancient sempiternal urge to action, *pravṛitti*, which for ever proceeds without beginning or end from the original Soul of all existence. Therefore its original source is above, beyond Time in the Eternal, but its branches stretch down below and it extends and plunges its other roots, well-fixed and clinging roots of attachment and desire with their consequences of more and more desire and an endlessly developing action, plunges them downward here into the world of men. The hymns of the Veda are compared to its leaves and the man who knows this tree of the cosmos is the Veda-knower. The branches of this cosmic tree extend both below and above, below in the material, above in the supraphysical planes; they grow by the gunas of Nature, for the triple guna is all the subject of the Vedas, *traiguṇya-viṣayā vedāḥ*. The Vedic rhythms, *chandāṁsi*, are the leaves and the sensible objects of desire supremely gained by a right doing of sacrifice are the constant budding of the foliage. Man, therefore, so long as he enjoys the play of the gunas and is attached to desire, is held in the coils of Pravritti, in the movement of birth and action and is unable to get back to his supreme spiritual infinitudes. **This was perceived by the sages. To achieve liberation they followed the path of Nivritti or cessation from the original urge to action,** and the consummation of this way is the cessation of birth itself and a transcendent status in the highest supracosmic reach of the Eternal. **But for this purpose it is necessary to cut these long-fixed roots of desire by the strong sword of detachment and then to seek for that highest goal whence, once having reached it, there is no compulsion of return to mortal life.**

निर्मानमोहा जितसङ्गदोषा अध्यात्मनित्या विनिवृत्तकामाः ।
द्वन्द्वैर्विमुक्ताः सुखदुःखसंज्ञैर्गच्छन्त्यमूढाः पदमव्ययं तत् ॥५॥

5. To be free from the bewilderment of this lower Maya, without egoism, the great fault of attachment conquered, all desires stilled, the duality of joy and grief cast away, always to be fixed in wide equality, always to be firm in a pure spiritual consciousness, these are the steps of the way to that supreme Infinite, *padam avyayam*.

न तद्भासयते सूर्यो न शशाङ्को न पावकः ।
यद्गत्वा न निवर्तन्ते तद्धाम परमं मम ॥६॥

6. There we find the timeless being which is not illumined by sun or moon or fire, but is itself the light of the presence of the eternal Purusha. "I turn away, says the Vedantic verse, to seek that original Soul alone and to reach him in the great passage." That is the highest status of the Purushottama, his supracosmic existence, *tad dhāma paramaṁ mama*. But it would seem that this can be attained very well, best even, pre-eminently, directly, by the quiescence of Sannyasa. Its appointed path would seem to be the way of the Akshara, a complete renunciation of works and life, an ascetic seclusion, an ascetic inaction. Where is the room here, or at least where is the call, the necessity, for the command to action, and what has all this to do with the maintenance of the cosmic existence, *loka-saṅgraha*, the slaughter of Kurukshetra, the ways of the Spirit in Time, the vision of the million-bodied Lord and his high-voiced bidding, "Arise, slay the foe, enjoy a wealthy kingdom"? And what then is this soul in Nature? — This spirit, too, this Kshara, this enjoyer of our mutable existence is the Purushottama, it is he in his eternal multiplicity, that is the Gita's answer.

ममैवांशो जीवलोके जीवभूतः सनातनः ।
मनःषष्ठानीन्द्रियाणि प्रकृतिस्थानि कर्षति ॥७॥

7. **It is an eternal portion of me, *mamaivāṁśaḥ sanātanaḥ*, that becomes the Jiva in a world of Jivas, *jīva-loke jīva-bhūtaḥ*.** This is an epithet, a statement of immense bearing and consequence. For it means that each soul, each being in its spiritual reality is the very Divine, however partial its actual manifestation of him in Nature. And it means too, if words have any sense, that each manifesting spirit, each of the many, is an eternal individual, an eternal unborn and undying power of the one Existence. **We call this manifesting spirit the Jiva, because it appears here as if a living creature in a world of living creatures,** and we speak of this spirit in man as the human soul and think of it in the terms of humanity only. But in truth it is something greater than its present appearance and not bound to its humanity: it was a lesser manifestation than the human in its past, it can become something much greater than mental man in its future. And when this soul rises above all ignorant limitation, then it puts on its divine nature of which its humanity is only a temporary veil, a thing of partial and incomplete significance. The individual spirit exists and ever existed beyond in the Eternal, for it is itself everlasting, *sanātana*. This much is clear that there is an eternal, a real and not only an illusive principle of multiplicity in the spiritual being of the one divine Existence.

शरीरं यदवाप्नोति यच्चाप्युत्क्रामतीश्वरः ।
गृहीत्वैतानि संयाति वायुर्गन्धानिवाशयात् ।।८।।

8. This eternal individual is not other than or in any way really separate from the Divine Purusha. **It is the Lord himself, the Ishwara** who by virtue of the eternal multiplicity of his oneness — is not all existence a rendering of that truth of the Infinite? — exists for ever as the immortal soul within us **and has taken up this body and goes forth from the transient framework when it is cast away to disappear into the elements of Nature. He brings in with him and cultivates for the enjoyment of the objects of mind and sense** (*sl.* 9) **the subjective powers of Prakriti, mind and the five senses** (*sl.* 7), **and in his going forth too he goes taking them as the wind takes the perfumes from a vase.** But the identity of the Lord and the soul in mutable Nature is hidden from us by outward appearance and lost in the crowding mobile deceptions of that Nature. And those who allow themselves to be governed by the figures of Nature, the figure of humanity or any other form, will never see it, but will ignore and despise the Divine lodged in the human body.

श्रोत्रं चक्षुः स्पर्शनं च रसनं घ्राणमेव च ।
अधिष्ठाय मनश्चायं विषयानुपसेवते ।।९।।

उत्क्रामन्तं स्थितं वापि भुञ्जानं वा गुणान्वितम् ।
विमूढा नानुपश्यन्ति पश्यन्ति ज्ञानचक्षुषः ।।१०।।

9-10. Their ignorance cannot perceive him in his coming in and his going forth or in his staying and enjoying and assumption of quality, but sees only what is there visible to the mind and senses, not the greater truth which can only be glimpsed by the eye of knowledge.

यतन्तो योगिनश्चैनं पश्यन्त्यात्मन्यवस्थितम् ।
यतन्तोऽप्यकृतात्मानो नैनं पश्यन्त्यचेतसः ।।११।।

11. Never can they have sight of him, even if they strive to do so, until they learn to put away the limitations of the outward consciousness and build in themselves their spiritual being, create for it, as it were, a form in their nature. **Man, to know himself, must be *kṛitātmā*, formed and complete in the spiritual mould, enlightened in the spiritual vision. The Yogins who have this eye of knowledge, see the Divine Being we are in their own endless reality, their own eternity of spirit. Illumined, they see the Lord in themselves and are deliv**ered from the crude material limitation, from the form of mental personality, from the transient life formulation: they dwell immortal in the truth of the self and spirit.

यदादित्यगतं तेजो जगद्भासयतेऽखिलम् ।
यच्चन्द्रमसि यच्चाग्नौ तत्तेजो विद्धि मामकम् ।।१२।।

12. But they see him too not only in themselves, but in all the cosmos. **In the light of the sun that illumines all this world they witness the light of the Godhead which is in us; the light in the moon and in fire is the light of the Divine.**

गामाविश्य च भूतानि धारयाम्यहमोजसा ।
पुष्णामि चौषधीः सर्वाः सोमो भूत्वा रसात्मकः ।।१३।।

13. It is the Divine who has entered into this form of earth and is the spirit of its material force and sustains by his might these multitudes. The Divine is the godhead of Soma who by the *rasa*, the sap in the Earth-mother, nourishes the plants and trees that clothe her surface.

अहं वैश्वानरो भूत्वा प्राणिनां देहमाश्रितः ।
प्राणापानसमायुक्तः पचाम्यन्नं चतुर्विधम् ।।१४।।

14. The Divine and no other is the flame of life that sustains the physical body of living creatures and turns its food into sustenance of their vital force.

सर्वस्य चाहं हृदि सन्निविष्टो मत्तः स्मृतिर्ज्ञानमपोहनं च ।
वेदैश्च सर्वैरहमेव वेद्यो वेदान्तकृद्वेदविदेव चाहम् ।।१५।।

15. He is lodged in the heart of every breathing thing; from him are memory and knowledge and the debates of the reason. He is that which is known by all the Vedas and by all forms of knowing; he is the knower of Veda and the maker of Vedanta. In other words, the Divine is at once the Soul of matter and the Soul of life and the Soul of mind as well as the Soul of the supramental light that is beyond mind and its limited reasoning intelligence. (*see also II-52/53*)

द्वाविमौ पुरुषौ लोके क्षरश्चाक्षर एव च ।
क्षरः सर्वाणि भूतानि कूटस्थोऽक्षर उच्यते ।।१६।।

16. "There is the immutable and impersonal spiritual being (Purusha), says Krishna, and there is the mutable and personal spiritual being."

The doctrine of the Gita from the beginning to the end converges on all its lines and through all the flexibility of its turns towards one central thought. This central thought is the idea of a triple consciousness, three and yet one, present in the whole scale of existence.

There is a spirit here at work in the world that is one in innumerable appearances. It is the developer of birth and action, the moving power of life, the inhabiting and associating consciousness in the myriad mutabilities of Nature; it is the constituting reality of all this stir in Time and Space; it is itself Time and Space and Circumstance. It is this multitude of souls in the worlds; it is the gods and men and creatures and things and forces and qualities and quantities and powers and presences. It is Nature, which is power of the Spirit, and objects, which are its phenomena of name and idea and form, and existences, who are portions and births and becomings of this single self-existent spiritual entity, the One, the Eternal. It is the Kshara, the universal Soul, the spirit in the mutability of cosmic phenomenon and becoming, one with the Immutable and the Supreme.

Then there is another spirit of whom we become aware and who is none of these things, but self and self only. This Spirit is eternal, always the same, never changed or affected by manifestation, the one, the stable, a self-existence undivided and not even seemingly divided by the divisions of things and powers in Nature, inactive in her action, immobile in her motion. It is the Self of all and yet unmoved, indifferent, intangible. This spirit is timeless, though we see it in Time; it is unextended in space, though we see it as if pervading space. We become aware of it in proportion as we draw back from out inward, or look behind the action and motion for something that is eternal and stable, or get away from time and its creation to the uncreated, away from phenomenon to being, from the personal to impersonality, from becoming to unalterable self-existence. This is the Akshara, the immutable in the mutable, the immobile in the mobile, the imperishable in things perishable. Or rather, since there is only an appearance of pervasion, it is the immutable, immobile and imperishable in which proceeds all the mobility of mutable and perishable things.

The Kshara spirit visible to us as all natural existence and the totality of all existences moves and acts pervadingly in the immobile and eternal Akshara. This mobile Power of Self acts in that fundamental stability of Self. These two then are the two spirits we see in the world; one emerges in front in its action, the other remains behind it steadfast in that perpetual silence from which the action comes and in which all actions cease and disappear into timeless being, Nirvana. ***Dvāvi mau puruṣau loke kṣaraś cākṣara eva ca.***

The difficulty which baffles our intelligence is that these two seem to be irreconcilable opposites with no real nexus between them or any transition from the one to the other except by an intolerant movement of separation. The Kshara acts, or at least motives action, separately in the Akshara; the Akshara stands apart, self-centred, separate in its inactivity from the Kshara. But after all the final experience is that of a unity of all beings which is not merely a community of experience, a common subjection to one force of Nature, but a oneness in the spirit, a vast identity of conscious being beyond all this endless variety of determination, behind all this apparent separativism of relative existence. The Gita takes its stand in that highest spiritual experience. It affirms with a strong insistence that the Akshara is the one self of all these many souls, and it is therefore evident that these two spirits are a dual status of one eternal and universal existence.

But this greater knowledge and experience, however true and however powerful in its appeal to our highest seeing, has still to get rid of a very real and pressing difficulty, a practical as well as a logical contradiction which seems at first sight to persist up to the highest heights of spiritual experience. The Eternal is other than this mobile subjective and objective experience, there is a greater consciousness, *na idaṁ yad upāsate* (Kena Up.): and yet at the same time all this is the Eternal, all this is the perennial self-seeing of the Self, *sarvaṁ khalu-idaṁ brahma, ayam ātmā brahma* (Chhandogya Up., Mandukya Up.), "Verily all this that is is the Brahman, and the Self is the Brahman." The Eternal has become all existences, *ātmā abhūt sarvāṇi-bhūtāni* (Isha Up.); as the Swetaswatara puts it, "Thou art this boy and yonder girl and that old man walking supported on his staff," even as in the Gita the Divine says that he is Krishna and Arjuna and Vyasa and Ushanas, and the lion and the aswattha tree, and consciousness and intelligence and all qualities and the self of all creatures. But how are these two the same, when they seem not only so opposite in nature, but so difficult to unify in experience? The Gita insists that we can and should, while we live, be conscious in the self and its silence and yet act with power in the world of Nature. And it gives the example of the Divine himself who is not bound by necessity of birth, but free, superior to the cosmos, and yet abides eternally in action, *varta eva ca karmaṇi*. Therefore it is by putting on a likeness of the divine nature in its completeness that the unity of this double experience becomes entirely possible.

उत्तमः पुरुषस्त्वन्यः परमात्मेत्युदाहृतः ।
यो लोकत्रयमाविश्य बिभर्त्यव्यय ईश्वरः ।।१७।।

17. **"But there is too another Highest, *uttamaḥ puruṣa*, called the supreme self, Paramatman, he who has entered into this whole world and upbears it, the Lord, the imperishable."**

But what is the principle of that oneness? The Gita finds it in its supreme vision of the Purushottama; for that is the type, according to its doctrine, of the complete and the highest experience, it is the knowledge of the whole-knowers, *kṛitsna-vidaḥ*. The Akshara is *para*, supreme in relation to the elements and action of cosmic Nature. It is the immutable Self of all, and the immutable Self of all is the Purushottama. The Akshara is he in the freedom of his self-existence unaffected by the action of his own power in Nature, not impinged on by the urge of his own becoming, undisturbed by the play of his own qualities. But this is only one aspect though a great aspect of the integral knowledge. The Purushottama is at the same time greater than the Akshara, because he is more than this immutability and he is not limited even by the highest eternal status of his being, *paraṁ dhāma*. Still, it is through whatever is immutable and eternal in us that we arrive at that highest status from which there is no returning to birth. But when pursued through the Akshara alone, this attempt at liberation becomes the seeking of the Indefinable, a thing hard for our nature embodied as we are here in

The Indefinable, to which the Akshara, the pure intangible self here in us rises in its separative urge, is some supreme Unmanifest, *paro avyaktaḥ*, and that highest unmanifest Akshara is still the Purushottama. Therefore, the Gita has said, those also who follow after the Indefinable, come to me, the eternal Godhead. But yet is he more even than a highest unmanifest Akshara, more than any negative Absolute, *neti neti*, because he is to be known also as the supreme Purusha who extends this whole universe in his own existence. He is a supreme mysterious All, an ineffable positive Absolute of all things here.

He is the Lord in the Kshara, Purushottama not only there, but here in the heart of every creature, Ishwara. And there too even in his highest eternal status, *paro avyaktaḥ*, he is the supreme Lord, Parameshwara, no aloof and unrelated Indefinable, but the origin and father and mother and first foundation and eternal abode of self and cosmos and Master of all existences and enjoyer of askesis and sacrifice. It is by knowing him at once in the Akshara and the Kshara, it is by knowing him as the Unborn who partially manifests himself in all birth and even himself descends as the constant Avatar, it is by knowing him in his entirety, *samagraṁ mām*, that the soul is easily released from the appearances of the lower Nature and returns by a vast sudden growth and broad immeasurable ascension into the divine being and supreme Nature. For the truth of the Kshara too is a truth of the Purushottama. The Purushottama is in the heart of every creature and is manifested in his countless Vibhutis; the Purushottama is the cosmic spirit in Time and it is he that gives the command to the divine action of the liberated human spirit. He is both Akshara and Kshara, and yet he is other because he is more and greater than either of these opposites. ***Uttamaḥ puruṣas tvanyaḥ paramātmā-iti-udāhṛitaḥ, yo lokatrayam āviśya bibharti-avyaya īśvaraḥ.***

But other than these two is that highest spirit called the supreme Self, who enters the three worlds and upbears them, the imperishable Lord. This verse is the keyword of the Gita's reconciliation of these two apparently opposite aspect of our existence.

The idea of the Purushottama has been prepared, alluded to, adumbrated, assumed even from the beginning, but it is only now in the fifteenth chapter that it is expressly stated and the distinction illuminated by a name. And it is instructive to see how it is immediately approached and developed. To ascend into the divine nature, we have been told, one must first fix oneself in a perfect spiritual equality and rise above the lower nature of the three gunas. Thus transcending the lower Prakriti we fix ourselves in the impersonality, the imperturbable superiority to all action, the purity from all definition and limitation by quality which is one side of the manifested nature of the Purushottama, his manifestation as the eternity and unity of the Self, the

Akshara. But there is also an ineffable eternal multiplicity of the Purushottama, a highest truest truth behind the primal mystery of soul manifestation. The Infinite has an eternal power, an unbeginning and unending action of his divine Nature, and in that action the miracle of soul personality emerges from a play of apparently impersonal forces, *prakṛitir jīvabhūtā*. This is possible because personality too is a character of the Divine and finds in the Infinite its highest spiritual truth and meaning. But the Person in the Infinite is something exalted, universal and transcendent, immortal and divine. That mystery of the supreme Person is the secret of love and devotion. The spiritual person, *puruṣa*, the eternal soul in us offers itself and all it has and is to the eternal Divine, the supreme Person and Godhead of whom it is a portion, *aṁśa*. Having so stated this double requisite, equality in the one self, adoration of the one Lord, at first separately as if they were two different ways of arriving at the Brahmic status, *brahmabhūyayā*, the Gita proceeds now to unite the personal and the impersonal in the Purushottama and to define their relations. For the object of the Gita is to get rid of exclusions and separative exaggerations and fuse these two sides of knowledge and spiritual experience into a single and perfect way to the supreme perfection.

यस्मात्क्षरमतीतोऽहमक्षरादपि चोत्तमः ।
अतोऽस्मि लोके वेदे च प्रथितः पुरुषोत्तमः ॥१८॥

18. "I am this Purushottama who am beyond the mutable and am greater and higher even than the immutable."

Thus the Divine is manifest in a double soul of his mystery, a twofold power, *dvāv imau puruṣau*; he supports at once the spirit of mutable things that is all these existences, *kṣaraḥ sarvāṇi bhūtāni*, and the immutable spirit that stands above them in his imperturbable immobility of eternal silence and calm, *kuṭṭastho'kṣaraḥ*. And it is by the force of the Divine in them that the mind and heart and will of man are so powerfully drawn in different directions by these two spirits as if by opposing and incompatible attractions one insistent to annul the other. But the Divine is neither wholly the Kshara, nor wholly the Akshara. **He is greater than the immutable Self and he is much greater than the Soul of mutable things.** If he is capable of being both at once, it is because he is other than they, *anyaḥ*, **the Purushottama above all cosmos and yet extended in the world and extended in the Veda, in self-knowledge and in cosmic experience.** (*see also II-52/53*)

यो मामेवमसम्मूढो जानाति पुरुषोत्तमम् ।
स सर्वविद्भजति मां सर्वभावेन भारत ॥१९॥

19. And whoever thus knows and sees him as the Purushottama, is no longer bewildered whether by the world-appearance or by the separate attraction of these two apparent contraries. These at first confront each other here in him as a positive of the cosmic action and as its negative in the Self who has no part in an action that belongs or seems to belong entirely to the ignorance of Nature. Or again they challenge his consciousness as a positive of pure, indeterminable, stable, eternal self-existence and as its negative of a world of elusive determinations and relations, ideas and forms, perpetual unstable becoming and the creating and uncreating tangle of action and evolution, birth and death, appearance and disappearance. He embraces and escapes them, overcomes their opposition **and becomes all-knowing, *sarva-vid*, a whole-knower.** He sees the entire sense both of the self and of things; he restores the integral reality of the Divine, *samagraṁ mām*; he unites the Kshara and the Akshara in the Purushottama. **He loves, worships, cleaves to and adores the supreme Self of his and all existence,** the one Lord of his and all energies, the close and far-off Eternal in and beyond the world. **And he does this too with no single side or portion of himself,** exclusive spiritualised mind, blinding light of the heart intense but divorced from largeness, or sole aspiration of the will in works, **but in all the perfectly illumined ways of his being and his becoming, his soul and his nature, *sarva-bhāvena*.**

"He who has knowledge of me as the Purushottama, adores me (has bhakti for me, *bhajati*), with all-knowledge and in every way of his natural being."

The Divine meets us in many aspects and to each of them knowledge is the key, so that by knowledge we enter into and possess the infinite and divine in every way of his being, and receive him into us and are possessed by him in every way of ours.

इति गुह्यतमं शास्त्रमिदमुक्तं मयानघ ।
एतद्बुद्ध्वा बुद्धिमान्स्यात्कृतकृत्यश्च भारत ।।२०।।

20. And is that not too after all the real Adwaita which makes no least scission in the one eternal Existence? This utmost undividing Monism sees the one as the one even in the multiplicities of Nature, in all aspects, as much in the reality of self and of cosmos as in that greatest reality of the supracosmic which is the source of self and the truth of the cosmos and is not bound either by any affirmation of universal becoming or by any universal or absolute negation. That at least is the Adwaita of the Gita. **This is the most secret Shastra, *guhyatamaṁ śāstram*, says the Teacher to Arjuna; this is the supreme teaching and science which leads us into the heart of the highest mystery**

of existence. Absolutely to know it, to seize it in knowledge and feeling and force and experience **is to be perfected in the transformed understanding, divinely satisfied in heart and successful in the supreme sense and objective of all will and action and works, *kṛita-kṛityaḥ*.** It is the way to be immortal, to rise towards the highest divine nature and to assume the eternal Dharma.

The development of the idea of the Gita has reached a point at which one question alone remains for solution, — the question of our nature bound and defective and how it is to effect, not only in principle but in all its movements, its evolution from the lower to the higher being and from the law of its present action to the immortal Dharma. The difficulty is one which is implied in certain of the positions laid down in the Gita, but has to be brought out into greater prominence than it gets there and to be put into a clearer shape before our intelligence. The Gita proceeded on a psychological knowledge which was familiar to the mind of the time, and in the steps of its thought it was well able to abridge its transitions, to take much for granted and to leave many things unexpressed which we need to have put strongly into light and made precise to us. Its teaching sets out at the beginning to propose a new source and level for our action in the world; that was the starting-point and that motives also the conclusion. Its initial object was not precisely to propose a way of liberation, *mokṣa*, but rather to show the compatibility of works with the soul's effort towards liberation and of spiritual freedom itself when once attained with continued action in the world, *muktasya karma*. Incidentally, a synthetic Yoga or psychological method of arriving at spiritual liberation and perfection has been developed and certain metaphysical affirmations have been put forward, certain truths of our being and nature on which the validity of this Yoga reposes. But the original preoccupation remains throughout, the original difficulty and problem, how Arjuna, dislodged by a strong revulsion of thought and feeling from the established natural and rational foundations and standards of action, is to find a new and satisfying spiritual norm of works, or how he is to live in the truth of the Spirit — since he can no longer act according to the partial truths of the customary reason and nature of man — and yet to do his appointed work on the battlefield of Kurukshetra. To live inwardly calm, detached, silent in the silence of the impersonal and universal Self and yet do dynamically the works of dynamic Nature, and more largely, to be one with the Eternal within us and to do all the will of the Eternal in the world expressed through a sublimated force, a divine height of the personal nature uplifted, liberated, universalised, made one with God-nature, — this is the Gita's solution.

The Gita has said that not the cessation of works, but renunciation of desire is the better way; it has spoken of the action of the liberated man, *muktasya karma*. It has even insisted on doing all actions, *sarvāṇi karmāṇi*, *kṛitsna-karma-kṛit*; it has said that in whatever way the perfected Yogin lives and acts, he lives and acts in God. This can only be, if the nature also in its dynamics and workings becomes divine, a power imperturbable, intangible, inviolate, pure and untroubled by the reactions of the inferior Prakriti. How and by what steps is this most difficult transformation to be effected? What is this last secret of the soul's perfection? what the principle or the process of this transmutation of our human and earthly nature?

CHAPTER XVI

Deva and Asura

The practical difficulty of the change from the ignorant and shackled normal nature of man to the dynamic freedom of a divine and spiritual being will be apparent if we ask ourselves, more narrowly, how the transition can be effected from the fettered embarrassed functioning of the three qualities to the infinite action of the liberated man who is no longer subject to the gunas. The transition is indispensable; for it is clearly laid down that he must be above or else without the three gunas, *triguṇātīta*, *nistraiguṇya*. On the other hand it is no less clearly laid down that in every natural existence here on earth the three gunas are there in their inextricable working and it is even said that all action of man or creature or force is merely the action of these three modes upon each other, *guṇā guṇeṣu vartante*. To act is to be subject to the three qualities of Nature; to be beyond these conditions of her working is to be silent in the Spirit. But the Gita has said that the liberated Yogin is delivered from the guna reactions and whatever he does, however he lives, moves and acts in God, in the power of his freedom and immortality, in the law of the supreme eternal Infinite, *sarvathā vartamāno'pi sa yogī mayi vartate*. There seems here to be a contradiction, an impasse.

What moves the world is not really the modes of Prakriti, — these are only the lower aspect, the mechanism of our normal nature. The real motive power is a divine spiritual Will which uses at present these inferior conditions, but is itself not limited, not dominated, not mechanised, as is the human will, by the gunas. No doubt, since these modes are so universal in their action, they must proceed from something inherent in the power of the Spirit; there must be powers in the divine Will-force from which these aspects of Prakriti have their origin. For everything in the lower normal nature is derived from the higher spiritual power of being of the Purushottama, *mattaḥ pravartate*; it does not come into being *de novo* and without a spiritual cause. Something in the essential power of the spirit there must be from which the sattwic light and satisfaction, the rajasic kinesis, the tamasic inertia of our nature are derivations and of which they are the imperfect or degraded forms.

For what is behind this troubled kinesis of the cosmos with all its clash and struggle? What is it that when it touches the mind, when it puts on mental values, creates the reactions of desire, striving, straining, error of will, sorrow, sin, pain? It is a will of the spirit in movement, it is a large divine will in action, it is a power, *tapas*, *cit-śakti*, of the free and infinite conscious Godhead which has no desire because it exercises a universal possession and a spontaneous Ananda of its movements. The soul that lives in God acts by this spiritual will.

And again what is behind the inertia of Nature, behind this Tamas? This Tamas is an obscurity which mistranslates into inaction of power and inaction of knowledge the Spirit's eternal principle of calm and repose, *śama*, — the repose which the Divine never loses even while he acts, the eternal repose which supports his integral action of knowledge and the force of his creative will. The peace of the Godhead is not a disintegration of energy or a vacant inertia. The Eternal does not need to sleep or rest. The Godhead is calm and at rest in the midst of his action. The liberated soul enters into this calm and participates in the eternal repose of the spirit.

And so too beyond the inferior light and happiness of that purest quality of Nature, Sattwa, the power that makes for assimilation and equivalence, right knowledge and right dealing, fine harmony, firm balance, right law of action, right possession and brings so full a satisfaction to the mind, beyond this highest thing in the normal nature, there is at its high and distant source a greater light and bliss free in the free spirit. That is a luminous spiritual and in its native action a direct supramental force of knowledge, *jyotiḥ*, not our modified and derivative mental light, *prakāśa*. That light is full of a luminous spiritual will and there is no gulf or disparateness between its knowledge and its action. That delight is not our paler mental happiness, *sukham*, but a profound concentrated intense self-existent bliss extended to all that our being does, envisages, creates, a fixed divine rapture, Ananda. The liberated soul participates more and more profoundly in this light and bliss and grows the more perfectly into it, the more integrally it unites itself with the Divine. And while among the gunas of the lower Nature there is a necessary disequilibrium, a shifting inconstancy of measures and a perpetual struggle for domination, the greater light and bliss, calm, will of kinesis of the Spirit do not exclude each other, are not at war, are not even merely in equilibrium, but each an aspect of the two others and in their fullness all are inseparable and one.[1]

1. The account given here of the supreme spiritual and supramental forms of highest Nature action corresponding to the gunas is not derived from the Gita, but introduced from spiritual experience. The Gita does not describe in any detail the action of the highest Nature, *rahasyam uttamam*; it leaves that for the seeker to discover by his own spiritual experience. It only points out the nature of the high sattwic temperament and action through which this supreme mystery has to be reached and insists at the same time on the overpassing of Sattwa and transcendence of the three gunas.

We see then that action is possible without the subjection of the soul to the normal degraded functioning of the modes of Nature. When we grow into the spirit, this dharma or inferior law of Nature is replaced by the immortal dharma of the spirit; there is the experience of a free immortal action, a divine illimitable knowledge, a transcendent power, an unfathomable repose. But still there remains the question of the transition; for there must be a transition, a proceeding by steps, since nothing in God's workings in this world is done by an abrupt action without procedure or basis. We have the thing we seek in us, but we have in practice to evolve it out of the inferior forms of our nature.[1] Therefore in the action of the modes itself there must be some means, some leverage, some *point d'appui*, by which we can effect this transformation. The Gita finds it in the full development of the sattwic guna till that in its potent expansion reaches a point at which it can go beyond itself and disappear into its source. The reason is evident, because sattwa is a power of light and happiness, a force that makes for calm and knowledge, and at its highest point it can arrive at a certain reflection, almost a mental identity with the spiritual light and bliss from which it derives. The sattwic quality is a first mediator between the higher and the lower nature. It must indeed at a certain point transform or escape from itself and break up and dissolve into its source; its conditioned derivative seeking light and carefully constructed action must change into the free direct dynamics and spontaneous light of the spirit. To develop sattwa till it becomes full of spiritual light and calm and happiness is the first condition of this preparatory discipline of the nature.

श्रीभगवानुवाच
अभयं सत्त्वसंशुद्धिर्ज्ञानयोगव्यवस्थितिः ।
दानं दमश्च यज्ञश्च स्वाध्यायस्तप आर्जवम् ।।१।।
अहिंसा सत्यमक्रोधस्त्यागः शान्तिरपैशुनम् ।
दया भूतेष्वलोलुप्त्वं मार्दवं ह्रीरचापलम् ।।२।।
तेजः क्षमा धृतिः शौचमद्रोहो नातिमानिता ।
भवन्ति सम्पदं दैवीमभिजातस्य भारत ।।३।।
दम्भो दर्पोऽभिमानश्च क्रोधः पारुष्यमेव च ।
अज्ञानं चाभिजातस्य पार्थ सम्पदमासुरीम् ।।४।।

1. This is from the point of view of our nature ascending upwards by self-conquest, effort and discipline. There must also intervene more and more a descent of the divine Light, Presence and Power into the being to transform it; otherwise the change at the point of culmination and beyond it cannot take place. That is why there comes in as the last movement the necessity of an absolute self-surrender.

1-4. *Krishna* — That, we shall find, is the whole intention of the remaining chapters of the Gita. But first it prefaces the consideration of this enlightening movement by a distinction between two kinds of being, the Deva and the Asura; for the Deva is capable of a high self-transforming sattwic action, the Asura incapable. We actually see that men, at least men above a certain level, fall very largely into two classes, those who have a dominant force of sattwic nature turned towards knowledge, self-control, beneficence, perfection and those who have a dominant force of rajasic nature turned towards egoistic greatness, satisfaction of desire, the indulgence of their own strong will and personality which they seek to impose on the world, not for the service of man or God, but for their own pride, glory and pleasure. These are the human representatives of the Devas and Danavas or Asuras, the Gods and the Titans.

The Deva nature is distinguished by an acme of the sattwic habits and qualities; self-control, sacrifice, the religious habit, cleanness and purity, candour and straightforwardness, truth, calm and self-denial, compassion to all beings, modesty, gentleness, forgivingness, patience, steadfastness, a deep sweet and serious freedom from all restlessness, levity and inconstancy are its native attributes. The Asuric qualities, wrath, greed, cunning, treachery, wilful doing of injury to others, pride and arrogance and excessive self-esteem have no place in its composition. But its gentleness and self-denial and self-control are free too from all weakness: it has energy and soul force, strong resolution, the fearlessness of the soul that lives in the right and according to the truth as well as its harmlessness, *tejaḥ, abhayam, dhṛitih, ahiṁsā, satyam*. The whole being, the whole temperament is integrally pure; there is a seeking for knowledge and a calm and fixed abiding in knowledge. This is the wealth, the plenitude of the man born into the Deva nature.

दैवी सम्पद्विमोक्षाय निबन्धायासुरी मता ।
मा शुचः सम्पदं दैवीमभिजातोऽसि पाण्डव ॥५॥

5. Arjuna, says the Teacher, is of the Deva nature. He need not grieve with the thought that by acceptance of battle and slaughter he will be yielding to the impulses of the Asura. The action on which all turns, the battle which Arjuna has to fight with the incarnate Godhead as his charioteer at the bidding of the Master of the world in the form of the Time-Spirit, is a struggle to establish the kingdom of the Dharma, the empire of Truth, Right and Justice. **He himself is born in the Deva kind;** he has developed in himself the sattwic being, until he has now come to a point at which he is capable of a high transformation and liberation from the *traiguṇya* and therefore even from the sattwic nature. The distinction between the Deva and the Asura is not comprehensive of all humanity, not rigidly applicable to all its individuals, neither is it sharp and definite in all stages of the moral or spiritual history of the race or in all phases of the individual evolution. For here what is in question is a certain culmination in the evolution of the qualitative nature. On one side there can be a sublimation of the sattwic quality, the culmination or manifestation of the unborn Deva, on the other a sublimation of the rajasic turn of the soul in nature, the entire birth of the Asura. **The one leads towards that movement of liberation on which the Gita is about to lay stress;** it makes possible a high self-exceeding of the sattwa quality and a transformation into the likeness of the divine being, *vimokṣāya*. **The other leads away from that universal potentiality and precipitates towards an exaggeration of our bondage to the ego.** This is the point of the distinction.

द्वौ भूतसर्गौ लोकेऽस्मिन्दैव आसुर एव च ।
दैवो विस्तरशः प्रोक्त आसुरं पार्थ मे शृणु ॥६॥

6. **When it is said that there are two creations of beings in this material world, Deva and Asura,** it is not meant that human souls are so created by God from the beginning each with its own inevitable career in Nature, nor is it meant that there is a rigid spiritual predestination and those rejected from the beginning by the Divine are blinded by him so that they may be thrust down to eternal perdition and the impurity of Hell. All souls are eternal portions of the Divine, the Asura as well as the Deva, all can come to salvation: even the greatest sinner can turn to the Divine.

But the evolution of the soul in Nature is an adventure of which Swabhava and the Karma governed by the swabhava are ever the chief powers; and if an excess in the manifestation of the swabhava, the self-becoming of the soul, turns the law of being to the perverse side, if the rajasic qualities are given the upper hand, then the trend of Karma and its results necessarily culminate in the highest exaggeration of the perversities of the lower nature. The man, if he does not stop short and abandon his way of error, has eventually the Asura full-born in him, and once he has taken that enormous turn away from the Light and Truth, he can no more reverse the fatal speed of his course because of the very immensity of the misused divine power in him until he has plumbed the depths to which it falls, found bottom and seen where the way has led him, the power exhausted and misspent, himself down in the lowest state of the soul nature, which is Hell. Only when he understands and turns to the Light, does that other truth of the Gita come in, that even the greatest sinner, the most impure and violent evil-doer is saved the moment he turns to adore and follow after the Godhead within him. Then, simply by that turn, he gets very soon into the sattwic way which leads to perfection and freedom.

प्रवृत्तिं च निवृत्तिं च जना न विदुरासुराः ।
न शौचं नापि चाचारो न सत्यं तेषु विद्यते ।।७।।

7. The Asuric nature has too its wealth, its plenitude of force, but it is of a very different, a powerful and evil kind. **Asuric men have no true knowledge of the way of action or the way of abstention, the fulfilling or the holding in of the nature. Truth is not in them, nor clean doing, nor faithful observance.**

असत्यमप्रतिष्ठं ते जगदाहुरनीश्वरम् ।
अपरस्परसम्भूतं किमन्यत्कामहैतुकम् ।।८।।

8. They see naturally in the world nothing but a huge play of the satisfaction of self; **theirs is a world with Desire for its cause and seed and governing force and law, a world of Chance, a world devoid of just relation and linked Karma, a world without God, not true, not founded in Truth.** Whatever better intellectual or higher religious dogma they may possess, this alone is the true creed of their mind and will in action; they follow always the cult of Desire and Ego.

एतां दृष्टिमवष्टभ्य नष्टात्मानोऽल्पबुद्धयः ।
प्रभवन्त्युग्रकर्माणः क्षयाय जगतोऽहिताः ।।९।।

9. **On that way of seeing life they lean in reality and by its falsehood they ruin their souls and their reason. The Asuric man becomes the centre or instrument of a fierce, Titanic, violent action, a power of destruction in the world, a fount of injury and evil.**

काममाश्रित्य दुष्पूरं दम्भमानमदान्विताः ।
मोहाद्गृहीत्वासद्ग्राहान्प्रवर्तन्तेऽशुचिव्रताः ।।१०।।

10. **Arrogant, full of self-esteem and the drunkenness of their pride, these misguided souls delude themselves, persist in false and obstinate aims and pursue the fixed impure resolution of their longings.**

चिन्तामपरिमेयां च प्रलयान्तामुपाश्रिताः ।
कामोपभोगपरमा एतावदिति निश्चिताः ।।११।।

11. They imagine that desire and enjoyment are all the aim of life and in their inordinate and insatiable pursuit of it they are the prey of a devouring, a measurelessly unceasing care and thought and endeavour and anxiety till the moment of their death.

आशापाशशतैर्बद्धाः कामक्रोधपरायणाः ।
ईहन्ते कामभोगार्थमन्यायेनार्थसञ्चयान् ।।१२।।

12. Bound by a hundred bonds, devoured by wrath and lust, unweariedly occupied in amassing unjust gains which may serve their enjoyment and the satisfaction of their craving,

इदमद्य मया लब्धमिमं प्राप्स्ये मनोरथम् ।
इदमस्तीदमपि मे भविष्यति पुनर्धनम् ।।१३।।

13. always they think, "Today I have gained this object of desire, tomorrow I shall have that other; today I have so much wealth, more I will get tomorrow.

असौ मया हतः शत्रुर्हनिष्ये चापरानपि ।
ईश्वरोऽहमहं भोगी सिद्धोऽहं बलवान्सुखी ।।१४।।

14. I have killed this my enemy, the rest too I will kill. I am a lord and king of men, I am perfect, accomplished, strong, happy, fortunate, a privileged enjoyer of the world;

आढ्योऽभिजनवानस्मि कोऽन्योऽस्ति सदृशो मया ।
यक्ष्ये दास्यामि मोदिष्य इत्यज्ञानविमोहिताः ।।१५।।

15. I am wealthy, I am of high birth; who is there like unto me? I will sacrifice, I will give, I will enjoy."

अनेकचित्तविभ्रान्ता मोहजालसमावृताः ।
प्रसक्ताः कामभोगेषु पतन्ति नरकेऽशुचौ ।।१६।।

16. Thus occupied by many egoistic ideas, deluded, doing works, but doing them wrongly, acting mightily, but for themselves, for desire, for enjoyment, not for God in themselves and God in man, they fall into the unclean hell of their own evil.

आत्मसम्भाविताः स्तब्धा धनमानमदान्विताः ।
यजन्ते नामयज्ञैस्ते दम्भेनाविधिपूर्वकम् ।।१७।।

17. They sacrifice and give, but from a self-regarding ostentation, from vanity and with a stiff and foolish pride, — and not in the true order, *avidhi-pūrvakam.*

अहङ्कारं बलं दर्पं कामं क्रोधं च संश्रिताः ।
मामात्मपरदेहेषु प्रद्विषन्तोऽभ्यसूयकाः ।।१८।।

18. In the egoism of their strength and power, in the violence of their wrath and arrogance they hate, despise and belittle the God hidden in themselves and the God in man.

तानहं द्विषतः क्रूरान्संसारेषु नराधमान् ।
क्षिपाम्यजस्रमशुभानासुरीष्वेव योनिषु ।।१९।।

19. And because they have this proud hatred and contempt of good and of God, because they are cruel and evil, the Divine casts them down continually into more and more Asuric births.

आसुरीं योनिमापन्ना मूढा जन्मनि जन्मनि ।
मामप्राप्यैव कौन्तेय ततो यान्त्यधमां गतिम् ।।२०।।

20. Not seeking him, they find him not, and at last, losing the way to him altogether, sink down into the lowest status of soul-nature, *adhamāṁ gatim.*

त्रिविधं नरकस्येदं द्वारं नाशनमात्मनः ।
कामः क्रोधस्तथा लोभस्तस्मादेतत्त्रयं त्यजेत् ।।२१।।

21. The Asuric Prakriti is the rajasic at its height; it leads to the slavery of the soul in Nature, to desire, wrath and greed, the three powers of the

rajasic ego, and these are the threefold doors of Hell, the Hell into which the natural being falls when it indulges the impurity and evil and error of its lower or perverted instincts.

एतैर्विमुक्तः कौन्तेय तमोद्वारैस्त्रिभिर्नरः ।
आचरत्यात्मनः श्रेयस्ततो याति परां गतिम् ।।२२।।

22. **These three are again the doors of a great darkness,** they fold back into tamas, the characteristic power of the original Ignorance; for the unbridled force of the rajasic nature, when exhausted, falls back into the weakness, collapse, darkness, incapacity of the worst tamasic soul-status. **To escape from this downfall one must get rid of these three evil forces and turn to the light of the sattwic quality, live by the right, in the true relations, according to the Truth and the Law; then one follows one's own higher good and arrives at the highest soul-status.**

यः शास्त्रविधिमुत्सृज्य वर्तते कामकारतः ।
न स सिद्धिमवाप्नोति न सुखं न परां गतिम् ।।२३।।

23. To follow the law of desire is not the true rule of our nature; there is a higher and juster standard of its works. The human race has always been seeking for this just and high Law and whatever it has discovered is embodied in its Shastra, its rule of science and knowledge, rule of ethics, rule of religion, rule of best social living, rule of one's right relations with man and God and Nature. Shastra does not mean a mass of customs, some good, some bad, unintelligently followed by the customary routine mind of the tamasic man. Shastra is the knowledge and teaching laid down by intuition, experience and wisdom, the science and art and ethic of life, the best standards available to the race. **The half-awakened man who leaves the observance of its rule to follow the guidance of his instincts and desires, can get pleasure but not happiness; for the inner happiness can only come by right living. He cannot move to perfection, cannot acquire the highest spiritual status.** The law of instinct and desire seems to come first in the animal world, but the manhood of man grows by the pursuit of truth and religion and knowledge and a right life.

तस्माच्छास्त्रं प्रमाणं ते कार्याकार्यव्यवस्थितौ ।
ज्ञात्वा शास्त्रविधानोक्तं कर्म कर्तुमिहार्हसि ।।२४।।

24. **The Shastra, the recognised Right that he has set up to govern his lower members by his reason and intelligent will, must therefore first be observed and made the authority for conduct and works and for what should or should not be done,** till the instinctive desire nature is schooled and abated and put down by the habit of self-control and man is ready first for a freer intelligent self-guidance and then for the highest supreme law and supreme liberty of the spiritual nature.

For the Shastra in its ordinary aspect is not that spiritual law, although at its loftiest point, when it becomes a science and art of spiritual living, Adhyatma-shastra, — the Gita itself describes its own teaching as the highest and most secret Shastra, — it formulates a rule of the self-transcendence of the sattwic nature and develops the discipline which leads to spiritual transmutation. Yet all Shastra is built on a number of preparatory conditions, dharmas; it is a means, not an end. The supreme end is the freedom of the spirit when abandoning all dharmas the soul turns to God for its sole law of action, acts straight from the divine will and lives in the freedom of the divine nature, not in the Law, but in the Spirit. This is the development of the teaching which is prepared by the next question of Arjuna.

CHAPTER XVII

The Gunas, Faith and Works

अर्जुन उवाच
ये शास्त्रविधिमुत्सृज्य यजन्ते श्रद्धयान्विताः ।
तेषां निष्ठा तु का कृष्ण सत्त्वमाहो रजस्तमः ।।१।।

1. *Arjuna* — **When men sacrifice to God or the gods with faith, *śraddhā,* but abandon the rule of the Shastra, what is that concentrated will of devotion in them, *niṣṭhā,* which gives them this faith and moves them to this kind of action? Is it sattwa, rajas or tamas?** to which strand of our nature does it belong?

The Gita has made a distinction between action according to the license of personal desire and action done according to the Shastra. We must understand by the latter the recognised science and art of life which is the outcome of mankind's collective living, its culture, religion, science, its progressive discovery of the best rule of life, — but mankind still walking in the ignorance and proceeding in a half light towards knowledge. The action controlled by Shastra is an outcome of intellectual, ethical, aesthetic, social and religious culture; it embodies an attempt at a certain right living, harmony and right order and is evidently an effort, more or less advanced according to circumstances, of the sattwic element in man to overtop, regulate and control or guide, where it must be admitted, his rajasic and tamasic egoism. It is the means to a step in advance, and therefore mankind must first proceed through it and make this Shastra its law of action rather than obey the impulsion of its personal desires. This is a general rule which humanity has always recognised wherever it has arrived at any kind of established and developed society; it has an idea of an order, a law, a standard of its perfection, something other than the guidance of its desires or the crude direction of its raw impulses. This greater rule the individual finds usually outside himself in some more or less fixed outcome of the experience and wisdom of the race, which he accepts, to which his mind and the leading parts of his being give their assent or sanction and which he tries to make his own by living it in his mind, will and action. And this assent of the being, its conscious acceptance and will to believe and realise, may be called by the name which the Gita gives to it, his faith, *śraddhā.*

The religion, the philosophy, the ethical law, the social idea, the cultural idea in which I put my faith, gives me a law for my nature and its works, an idea of relative right or an idea of relative or absolute perfection, and in proportion as I have a sincerity and completeness of faith in it and an intensity of will to live according to that faith, I can become what it proposes to me, I can shape myself into an image of that right or an exemplar of that perfection.

But we see also that there is a freer tendency in man other than the leading of his desires and other than his will to accept the Law, the fixed idea, the safe governing rule of the Shastra. The individual frequently enough, the community at any moment of its life is seen to turn away from the Shastra, becomes impatient of it, loses that form of its will and faith and goes in search of another law which it is now more disposed to accept as the right rule of living and regard as a more vital or higher truth of existence. This may happen when the established Shastra ceases to be a living thing and degenerates or stiffens into a mass of customs and conventions. Or it may come because it is found that the Shastra is imperfect or no longer useful for the progress demanded; a new truth, a more perfect law of living has become imperative. If that does not exist, it has to be discovered by the effort of the race or by some great and illumined individual mind who embodies the desire and seeking of the race. But this practically means that there is an ideal, an eternal Dharma which religion, philosophy, ethics and all other powers in man that strive after truth and perfection are constantly endeavouring to embody in new statements of the science and art of the inner and outer life, a new Shastra. And the human search does not stop there, but leaves these formulations too, goes back to some past truth it had rejected or breaks forward to some new truth and power, but is always in search of the same thing, the law of its perfection, its rule of right living, its complete, highest and essential self and nature.

This movement begins with the individual, who is no longer satisfied with the law because he finds that it no longer corresponds to his ideal and largest or intensest experience of himself and existence and therefore he can no longer bring to it the will to believe and practise. It does not correspond to his inner way of being, it is not to him *sat*, the thing that truly is, the right, the highest or best or real good; it is not the truth and law of his or of all being. The Shastra is something impersonal to the individual, and that gives it its authority over the narrow personal law of his members; but at the same time it is personal to the collectivity and is the outcome of its experience, its culture or its nature. It is not in all its form and spirit the ideal rule of fulfilment of the Self or the eternal law of the Master of our nature. And the individual may have gone beyond the collectivity and be ready for a greater truth, a wider walk, a deeper intention of the Life-Spirit.

And even if the Shastra is still a living thing and the best rule for the human average, the exceptional man, spiritual, inwardly developed, is not bound by that standard. He is called upon to go beyond the fixed line of the Shastra. For this is a rule for the guidance, control and relative perfection of the normal imperfect man and he has to go on to a more absolute perfection: this is a system of fixed dharmas and he has to learn to live in the liberty of the Spirit.

श्रीभगवानुवाच
त्रिविधा भवति श्रद्धा देहिनां सा स्वभावजा ।
सात्त्विकी राजसी चैव तामसी चेति तां शृणु ।।२।।

2. *Krishna* — **The answer of the Gita first states the principle that the faith in us is of a triple kind like all things in Nature and varies according to the dominating quality of our nature.**

But what then shall be the secure base of an action which departs both from the guidance of desire and from the normal law? The law, the Shastra has behind it all the authority of long established rule, old successful sanctions and a secure past experience. But this new movement is of the nature of a powerful adventure into the unknown or partly known, a daring development and a new conquest, and what then is the clue to be followed, the guiding light on which it can depend or its strong basis in our being? The answer is that the clue and support is to be found in man's *śraddhā*, his faith, his will to believe, to live what he sees or thinks to be the truth of himself and of existence. In other words this movement is man's appeal to himself or to something potent and compelling in himself or in universal existence for the discovery of his truth, his law of living, his way to fullness and perfection. And everything depends on the nature of his faith, the thing in himself or in the universal Soul — of which he is a portion or manifestation — to which he directs it and on how near he gets by it to his real self and the Self or true being of the universe.

In all effort at self-finding these possibilities are there [tamasic, rajasic or sattwic and its culmination and transcendence]; they are the conditions of this spiritual adventure.

The perfect faith is an assent of the whole being to the truth seen by it or offered to its acceptance, and its central working is a faith of the soul in its own will to be and attain and become and its idea of self and things and its knowledge, of which the belief of the intellect, the heart's consent and the desire of the life mind to possess and realise are the outward figures. This *śraddhā* — the English word faith is inadequate to express it — is in reality an influence from the supreme Spirit and its light a message from our supramental being which is calling the lower nature to rise out of its petty present to a great self-becoming and self-exceeding. Faith is the reflex in the lower consciousness of a Truth or real Idea yet unrealised in the manifestation. It is this self-certainty of the Idea which is meant by the Gita when it says, "Whatever is a man's faith or the sure Idea in him, that he becomes."

सत्त्वानुरूपा सर्वस्य श्रद्धा भवति भारत ।
श्रद्धामयोऽयं पुरुषो यो यच्छ्रद्धः स एव सः ।।३।।

3. **The faith of each man takes the shape, hue, quality given to it by his stuff of being, his constituting temperament, his innate power of existence, *sattvānurūpā sarvasya śraddhā*.** And then there comes a remarkable line in which the Gita tells us that, **This Purusha, this soul in man, is, as it were, made of *śraddhā*, a faith, a will to be, a belief in itself and existence, and whatever is that will, faith or constituting belief in him, he is that and that is he, *śraddhā-mayo 'yaṁ puruṣo yo yacchraddhaḥ sa eva saḥ*.**

If we look into this pregnant saying a little closely, we shall find that this single line contains implied in its few forceful words almost the whole theory of the modern gospel of pragmatism. For if a man or the soul in a man consists of the faith which is in him, taken in this deeper sense, then it follows that the truth which he sees and wills to live is for him the truth of his being, the truth of himself that he has created or is creating and there can be for him no other real truth. This truth is a thing of his inner and outer action, a thing of his becoming, of the soul's dynamics, not of that in him which never changes. He is what he is today by some past will of his nature sustained and continued by a present will to know, to believe and to be in his intelligence and vital force, and whatever new turn is taken by this will and faith active in his very substance, that he will tend to become in the future. We create our own truth of existence in our own action of mind and life, which is another way of saying that we create our own selves, are our own makers.

But very obviously this is only one aspect of the truth, and all one-aspected statements are suspect to the thinker. Truth is not merely whatever our own personality is or creates; that is only the truth of our becoming, one point or line of emphasis in a movement of widest volume. Beyond our personality there is, first, a universal being as well as a universal becoming of which ours is a little movement; and beyond that too there is the eternal Being out of which all becoming derives and to which it owes its potentialities, elements, original and final motives.

There is in the highest superconscience a highest truth and dharma of immortality, a greatest divine way of being, a way of the eternal and infinite. That eternal way of existence and divine manner of being exists already in the eternity of the Purushottama, but we are now attempting to create it here too in our becoming by Yoga; our endeavour is to become the Divine, to be as He, *mad-bhāva*. That also depends on *śraddhā*. It is by an act of our conscious substance and a belief in its truth, an inmost will to live it or be it that we come by it; but this does not mean that it does not already exist beyond us. Though it may not exist for our outward mind until we see and create ourselves anew into it, it is still there in the Eternal and we may say even that it is already there in our own secret self; for in us also, in our depths the Purushottama always is. Our growing into that, our creation of it is his and its manifestation in us. All creation indeed since it proceeds from the conscious substance of the Eternal, is a manifestation of him and proceeds by a faith, acceptance, will to be in the originating consciousness, Chit-Shakti.

We are concerned at present, however, not with the metaphysical issue, but with the relation of this will or faith in our being to our possibility of growth into the perfection of the divine nature. This power, this *śraddhā* is in any case our basis. When we live, when we are and do according to our desires, and when we try to be, to live and to do according to the Shastra, or to some ideal or novel conception of truth of our own finding or our own individual acceptance, or to the divine nature, — that is a persistent act of *śraddhā* which may be dominated by any one of these three qualities that constantly govern our every thought, will, feeling and act. But all and any of these things implies some kinesis or displacement of nature, all supppose an inner or outer or ordinarily both an inner and an outer action. And what then will be the character of this action?

यजन्ते सात्त्विका देवान्यक्षरक्षांसि राजसाः ।
प्रेतान्भूतगणांश्चान्ये यजन्ते तामसा जनाः ।।४।।

4. [*see below, before (13)*][1]

अशास्त्रविहितं घोरं तप्यन्ते ये तपो जनाः ।
दम्भाहङ्कारसंयुक्ताः कामरागबलान्विताः ।।५।।

1. For understanding in the present and the next chapters the change of order of the English translation of a few *slokas*, kindly refer to the end of the first paragraph — in italics — of *slokas* 11-13.

In both these chapters, the use of italics and bold typeface for a few English words is by the editor. (*Editor's note*)

कर्षयन्तः शरीरस्थं भूतग्राममचेतसः ।
मां चैवान्तःशरीरस्थं तान्विद्ध्यासुरनिश्चयान् ।।६।।

5-6. *[see below, after (18)]*

आहारस्त्वपि सर्वस्य त्रिविधो भवति प्रियः ।
यज्ञस्तपस्तथा दानं तेषां भेदमिमं शृणु ।।७।।

7. The Gita states three main elements of the work we have to do, *kartavyaṁ karma*, and these three are *sacrifice* (*4, 11-13*), ***giving*** (*20-22*) **and *askesis*** (5-6, 14-19). All dynamic action may be reduced in its essential parts to these three elements. For all dynamic action, all kinesis of the nature involves a voluntary or an involuntary tapasya or askesis, an energism and concentration of our forces or capacities or of some capacity which helps us to achieve, to acquire or to become something, *tapas*. All action involves a giving of what we are or have, an expenditure which is the price of that achievement, acquisition or becoming, *dāna*. All action involves too a sacrifice to elemental or to universal powers or to the supreme Master of our works. The question is whether our sacrifice, giving and askesis are tamasic, rajasic or sattwic in nature. **For everything here, including physical things, partakes of this triple character. Our food, for example, the Gita tells us, is either sattwic, rajasic or tamasic according to its character and effect on the body.**

आयुःसत्त्वबलारोग्यसुखप्रीतिविवर्धनाः ।
रस्याः स्निग्धाः स्थिरा हृद्या आहाराः सात्त्विकप्रियाः ।।८।।

8. The sattwic temperament in the mental and physical body turns naturally to the things that increase the life, increase the inner and outer strength, nourish at once the mental, vital and physical force and increase the pleasure and satisfaction and happy condition of mind and life and body, all that is succulent and soft and firm and satisfying.

कट्वम्ललवणात्युष्णतीक्ष्णरूक्षविदाहिनः ।
आहारा राजसस्येष्टा दुःखशोकामयप्रदाः ।।९।।

9. The rajasic temperament prefers naturally food that is violently sour, pungent, hot, acrid, rough and strong and burning, the aliments that increase ill-health and the distempers of the mind and body.

यातयामं गतरसं पूति पर्युषितं च यत् ।
उच्छिष्टमपि चामेध्यं भोजनं तामसप्रियम् ।।१०।।

10. The tamasic temperament takes a perverse pleasure in cold, impure, stale, rotten or tasteless food or even accepts like the animals the remnants half-eaten by others.

अफलाकाङ्क्षिभिर्यज्ञो विधिदृष्टो य इज्यते ।
यष्टव्यमेवेति मनः समाधाय स सात्त्विकः ।।११।।
अभिसन्धाय तु फलं दम्भार्थमपि चैव यत् ।
इज्यते भरतश्रेष्ठ तं यज्ञं विद्धि राजसम् ।।१२।।
विधिहीनमसृष्टान्नं मन्त्रहीनमदक्षिणम् ।
श्रद्धाविरहितं यज्ञं तामसं परिचक्षते ।।१३।।

11-13. All-pervading is the principle of the three gunas. The gunas apply at the other end in the same way to the things of the mind and spirit, to ***sacrifice, giving*** and ***askesis***, and the Gita distinguishes under each of these three heads between the three kinds in the customary terms of these things. *And it will be convenient to take them in the reverse order, from tamas to sattwa, since we are considering how we go upward out of our lower nature through a certain sattwic culmination and self-exceeding to a divine nature and action beyond the three gunas.*[1]

(4) The *tamasic* man does not offer his *sacrifice* to the gods, but to inferior elemental powers or to those grosser spirits behind the veil who feed upon his works and dominate his life with their darkness. **The *rajasic* man offers his *sacrifice* to lower godheads or to perverse powers, the Yakshas, the keepers of wealth, or to the Asuric and the Rakshasic forces. The *sattwic sacrifice* is offered to the gods without any reservation;** it is acceptable to the divine powers by whom — for they are his masks and personalities — the Master of existence governs the universe. It is carried out as a fixed dharma, and it is offered as a sacrifice or service to the gods, to some partial power or aspect of the Divine manifested in ourselves or in the universe.

(13) The *tamasic sacrifice* is work which is done without faith, without, that is to say, any full conscious idea and acceptance and will towards the thing Nature yet compels us to execute. It is done mechanically, because the act of living demands it, because it comes in our way. And it is apt to be done

1. Editor's italics.

carelessly, perfunctorily, in the wrong way. **It will not be performed by the *vidhi* or right rule of the Shastra. There will be no giving of food in the sacrifice. The work will be done without the dakshina, the much-needed giving or self-giving. It will be done without the mantra,** without the dedicating thought which is the sacred body of our will and knowledge lifted upwards to the godheads we serve by our sacrifice.

(12) **[The *sacrifice* of the *rajasic* man] may be performed outwardly according to the Shastra, but its motive is ostentation, pride or a strong lust after the fruit of his action, a vehement demand for the reward of his works.** It is the inner state, motive and direction which give their value to our works, and not merely the apparent outer direction, the divine names we may call to sanction them or even the sincere intellectual belief which seems to justify us in the performance. **Wherever there is a dominating egoism in our acts, there our work becomes a rajasic sacrifice.**

(11) **The true *sattwic sacrifice* is dictated by the effective truth, executed according to the *vidhi*,** the right principle, the exact method and rule, the just rhythm and law of our works, their true functioning, their dharma. **It is executed with a mind concentrated and fixed on the idea of the thing to be done as a true sacrifice imposed on us by the divine law that governs our life and therefore performed out of a high inner obligation or imperative truth and without desire for the personal fruit,** — the more impersonal the motive of the action and the temperament of the force put out in it, the more sattwic is its nature. The culmination of the sattwic action is the high last sacrifice offered by us to the supreme Divine in his integral being and with a seeking for the Purushottama or with the vision of Vasudeva in all that is, the action done impersonally, universally, for the good of the world, for the fulfilment of the divine will in the universe. That culmination leads to its own transcending, to the immortal Dharma. For then comes a freedom in which there is no personal action at all, no sattwic rule of dharma, no limitation of Shastra. There is no sacrifice, — unless we can say that the Master of sacrifice is offering the works of his energy in the Jiva to himself in his own cosmic form. This is the supreme self-surpassing state arrived at by the action that is sacrifice, this the perfection of the soul that has come to its full consciousness in the divine nature.

देवद्विजगुरुप्राज्ञपूजनं शौचमार्जवम् ।
ब्रह्मचर्यमहिंसा च शारीरं तप उच्यते ।।१४।।
अनुद्वेगकरं वाक्यं सत्यं प्रियहितं च यत् ।
स्वाध्यायाभ्यसनं चैव वाङ्मयं तप उच्यते ।।१५।।

मनःप्रसादः सौम्यत्वं मौनमात्मविनिग्रहः ।
भावसंशुद्धिरित्येतत्तपो मानसमुच्यते ।।१६।।

14-16. *[see below, after (17)]*

श्रद्धया परया तप्तं तपस्तत्त्रिविधं नरैः ।
अफलाकाङ्क्षिभिर्युक्तैः सात्त्विकं परिचक्षते ।।१७।।
सत्कारमानपूजार्थं तपो दम्भेन चैव यत् ।
क्रियते तदिह प्रोक्तं राजसं चलमध्रुवम् ।।१८।।
मूढग्राहेणात्मनो यत्पीडया क्रियते तपः ।
परस्योत्सादनार्थं वा तत्तामसमुदाहृतम् ।।१९।।

17-19. (19) *Tamasic tapasya* is that which is pursued under a clouded and deluded idea, performed with effort and suffering imposed on oneself or else with a concentration of the energy in a will to do hurt to others.

(18) *Rajasic* energisms of *askesis* are those which are undertaken to get honour and worship from men, for the sake of personal distinction and outward glory and greatness. This kind of askesis is devoted to fleeting particular objects; it is a thing without fixed and helpful principle, an energy bound up with changeful and passing occasion and itself of that nature.

(5-6) If any kind of arrogance or pride or any great strength of violent self-will or desire enters into the askesis or if it drives some violent, lawless or terrible action contrary to the Shastra, opposed to the right rule of life and works and afflicting to oneself and to others, or if it is of the nature of self-torture and hurts the mental, vital and physical elements or violates the God within us who is seated in the inner subtle body, then too it is an unwise, an Asuric, a rajasic or rajaso-tamasic tapasya.

(17) *Sattwic tapasya* is that which is done with a highest enlightened faith, with no desire for any external or narrowly personal fruit in the action. It is of the character of self-discipline and asks for self-control and a harmonising of one's nature.

(14) The Gita describes three kinds of sattwic askesis. First comes the physical, the askesis of the outward act: worship and reverence of those deserving reverence, cleanness of the person, the action and the life, candid dealing, sexual purity and avoidance of killing and injury to others.

(15) Next is askesis of speech, and that consists in the study of Scripture, kind, true and beneficient speech and a careful avoidance of words that may cause fear, sorrow and trouble to others.

(16) Finally there is the askesis of mental and moral perfection, and that means the purifying of the whole temperament, gentleness and a clear and calm gladness of mind, self-control and silence. At that lofty point of its greater culmination the ethical is already passing away into the spiritual type and character. And this culmination too can be made to transcend itself, can be raised into a higher and freer light, can pass away into the settled godlike energy of the supreme nature. And what will remain then will be the spirit's immaculate Tapas, a highest will and luminous force in all the members acting in a wide and solid calm and a deep and pure spiritual delight, Ananda. There will then be no farther need of askesis, no tapasya, because all is naturally and easily divine, all is that Tapas.

दातव्यमिति यद्दानं दीयतेऽनुपकारिणे ।
देशे काले च पात्रे च तद्दानं सात्त्विकं स्मृतम् ।।२०।।
यत्तु प्रत्युपकारार्थं फलमुद्दिश्य वा पुनः ।
दीयते च परिक्लिष्टं तद्दानं राजसं स्मृतम् ।।२१।।
अदेशकाले यद्दानमपात्रेभ्यश्च दीयते ।
असत्कृतमवज्ञातं तत्तामसमुदाहृतम् ।।२२।।

20-22. **(22) The *tamasic gift* is offered ignorantly with no consideration of the right conditions of time, place and object;** it is a foolish, inconsiderate and in reality a self-regarding movement, an ungenerous and ignoble generosity, the gift offered without sympathy or true liberality, **without regard for the feelings of the recipient and despised by him even in the acceptance.**

(21) The *rajasic* kind of *giving* is that which is done with regret, unwillingness or violence to oneself or with a personal and egoistic object or in the hope of a return of some kind from whatever quarter or a corresponding or greater benefit to oneself from the receiver.

(20) The *sattwic* way of *giving* is to bestow with right reason and goodwill and sympathy in the right conditions of time and place and on the right recipient who is worthy or to whom the gift can be really helpful. Its act is performed for the sake of the giving and the beneficence, without any view to a benefit already done or yet to be done to oneself by the receiver of the benefit and without any personal object in the action. The culmination of the sattwic way of *dāna* will bring into the action an increasing element of that wide self-giving to others and to the world and to God, *ātma-dāna*, *ātma-samarpaṇa*, which is the high consecration of the sacrifice of works enjoined by the Gita. And the transcendence in the divine nature will be a greatest completeness of self-offering founded on the largest meaning of existence. All this manifold universe comes into birth and is constantly maintained by God's giving of himself and his powers and the lavish outflow of his self and spirit into all these existences; universal being, says the Veda, is the sacrifice of the Purusha. All the action of the perfected soul will be even such a constant divine giving of itself and its powers, an outflowing of the knowledge, light, strength, love, joy, helpful shakti which it possesses in the Divine and by his influence and effluence on all around it according to their capacity of reception or on all this world and its creatures. That will be the complete result of the complete self-giving of the soul to the Master of our existence.

ॐ तत्सदिति निर्देशो ब्रह्मणस्त्रिविधः स्मृतः ।
ब्राह्मणास्तेन वेदाश्च यज्ञाश्च विहिताः पुरा ।।२३।।

23. The Gita closes this chapter with what seems at first sight a recondite utterance. **The formula OM, Tat, Sat, is, it says, the triple definition of the Brahman, by whom the Brahmanas, the Vedas and sacrifices were created of old and in it resides all their significance.** Tat, That, indicates the Absolute. Sat indicates the supreme and universal existence in its principle. OM is the symbol of the triple Brahman, the outward-looking, the inward or subtle and the superconscient causal Purusha. Each letter A, U, M, indicates one of these three in ascending order and the syllable as a whole brings out the fourth state, Turiya, which rises to the Absolute.

तस्मादोमित्युदाहृत्य यज्ञदानतपःक्रियाः ।
प्रवर्तन्ते विधानोक्ताः सततं ब्रह्मवादिनाम् ।।२४।।

24. Om is the initiating syllable pronounced at the outset as a benedictory prelude and sanction to all act of sacrifice, all act of giving and all act of askesis; it is a reminder that our work should be made an expression of the triple Divine in our inner being and turned towards him in the idea and motive.

तदित्यनभिसन्धाय फलं यज्ञतपःक्रियाः ।
दानक्रियाश्च विविधाः क्रियन्ते मोक्षकाङ्क्षिभिः ।।२५।।

25. **The seekers of liberation do these actions without desire of fruit and only with the idea, feeling, Ananda of the absolute Divine (Tat) behind their nature.** It is that which they seek by this purity and impersonality in their works, this high desirelessness, this vast emptiness of ego and plenitude of Spirit.

सद्भावे साधुभावे च सदित्येतत्प्रयुज्यते ।
प्रशस्ते कर्मणि तथा सच्छब्दः पार्थ युज्यते ।।२६।।

26. **Sat means good and it means existence. Both these things, the principle of good and the principle of reality, must be there behind all the three kinds of action. All good works are Sat, for they prepare the soul for the higher reality of our being.**

यज्ञे तपसि दाने च स्थितिः सदिति चोच्यते ।
कर्म चैव तदर्थीयं सदित्येवाभिधीयते ।।२७।।

27. **All firm abiding in sacrifice, giving and askesis and all works done with that central view, as sacrifice, as giving, as askesis, are Sat, for they build the basis for the highest truth of our spirit.**

अश्रद्धया हुतं दत्तं तपस्तप्तं कृतं च यत् ।
असदित्युच्यते पार्थ न च तत्प्रेत्य नो इह ।।२८।।

28. **And because *śraddhā* is the central principle of our existence, any of these things done without *śraddhā* is a falsity and has no true meaning or true substance on earth or beyond, no reality *(asat)*, no power to endure or create in life here or after the mortal life in greater regions of our conscious spirit.** The soul's faith, not a mere intellectual belief, but its concordant will to know, to see, to believe and to do and be according to its vision and knowledge, is that which determines by its power the measure of our possibilities of becoming, and it is this faith and will turned in all our inner and outer self, nature and action towards all that is highest, most divine, most real and eternal that will enable us to reach the supreme perfection.

CHAPTER XVIII

I — The Gunas, Mind and Works

The Gita has not yet completed its analysis of action in the light of this fundamental idea of the three gunas and the transcendence of them by a self-exceeding culmination of the highest sattwic discipline. Faith, *śraddhā*, the will to believe and to be, know, live and enact the Truth that we have seen is the principal factor, the indispensable force behind the growth of the soul by works into its full spiritual stature. But there are also the mental powers, the instruments and the conditions which help to constitute the momentum, direction and character of the activity and are therefore of importance for a full understanding of this psychological discipline. We have to follow the Gita in its brief descriptions; for these are secondary things, but yet each of great consequence in its own place and for its own purpose. It is their action cast in the type of the gunas that we have to bring out from the brief descriptions in the text.

अर्जुन उवाच
संन्यासस्य महाबाहो तत्त्वमिच्छामि वेदितुम् ।
त्यागस्य च हृषीकेश पृथक्केशिनिषूदन ।।१।।

1. *Arjuna* — This part of the subject is introduced by **a last question of Arjuna regarding the principle of Sannyasa and the principle of Tyaga and their difference.** The frequent harping, the reiterated emphasis of the Gita on this crucial distinction has been amply justified by the subsequent history of the later Indian mind, its constant confusion of these two very different things and its strong bent towards belittling any activity of the kind taught by the Gita as at best only a preliminary to the supreme inaction of Sannyasa. As a matter of fact, when people talk of Tyaga, of renunciation, it is always the physical renunciation of the world which they understand by the word or at least on which they lay emphasis, while the Gita takes absolutely the opposite view that the real Tyaga has action and living in the world as its basis and not a flight to the monastery, the cave or the hill-top. The real Tyaga is action with a renunciation of desire and that too is the real Sannyasa. Not the

renunciation of work in the world, not any outward asceticism or any ostentation of a visible giving up of enjoyment, but a renunciation, a leaving, *tyāga*, of vital desire and ego, a total laying aside, *sannyāsa*, of the separate personal life of the desire soul and ego-governed mind and rajasic vital nature.

श्रीभगवानुवाच
काम्यानां कर्मणां न्यासं संन्यासं कवयो विदुः ।
सर्वकर्मफलत्यागं प्राहुस्त्यागं विचक्षणाः ।।२।।

2. *Krishna* — **More conventionally taken, Sannyasa in the standing terminology of the sages means the physical depositing or laying aside of desirable actions: Tyaga — this is the Gita's distinction — is the name given by the wise to a mental and spiritual renunciation, an entire abandonment of all attached clinging to the fruit of our works, to the action itself or to its personal initiation or rajasic impulse.** In that sense Tyaga, not Sannyasa, is the better way. It is not the desirable actions that must be laid aside, but the desire which gives them that character has to be put away from us.

त्याज्यं दोषवदित्येके कर्म प्राहुर्मनीषिणः ।
यज्ञदानतपःकर्म न त्याज्यमिति चापरे ।।३।।

3. The question still arises, what works are to be done? Those even who stand for a final physical renunciation are not at one in this difficult matter. **Some would have it that all works must be excised from our life,** as if that were possible. But it is not possible so long as we are in the body and alive. **The more liberal and comprehensive solution was evidently to continue the three most sattwic activities, sacrifice, giving and askesis. And these certainly are to be done.**

निश्चयं शृणु मे तत्र त्यागे भरतसत्तम ।
त्यागो हि पुरुषव्याघ्र त्रिविधः सम्प्रकीर्तितः ।।४।।

4. (*Untranslated*)

यज्ञदानतपःकर्म न त्याज्यं कार्यमेव तत् ।
यज्ञो दानं तपश्चैव पावनानि मनीषिणाम् ।।५।।

5. **Krishna insists that these three things ought not to be renounced at all but ought altogether to be done, for they are the work before us, *kartavyaṁ***

***karma*, and they purify the wise.** In other words these acts constitute the means of our perfection. But at the same time they may be done unwisely or less wisely by the unwise.

एतान्यपि तु कर्माणि सङ्गं त्यक्त्वा फलानि च ।
कर्तव्यानीति मे पार्थ निश्चितं मतमुत्तमम् ॥६॥

6. The fruit of the action may come in the dispensation of the Master of works, **but there is to be no egoistic demand for that as a reward and condition of doing works. Or the fruit may not at all come and still the work has to be performed as the thing to be done, *kartavyaṁ karma*, the thing which the Master within demands of us.** The success, the failure are in his hands and he will regulate them according to his omniscient will and inscrutable purpose. Action, all action has indeed to be given up in the end, not physically by abstention, by immobility, by inertia, but spiritually to the Master of our being by whose power alone can any action be accomplished. There has to be a renunciation of the false idea of ourselves as the doer; for in reality it is the universal Shakti that works through our personality and our ego. The spiritual transference of all our works to the Master and his Shakti is the real Sannyasa in the teaching of the Gita.

नियतस्य तु संन्यासः कर्मणो नोपपद्यते ।
मोहात्तस्य परित्यागस्तामसः परिकीर्तितः ॥७॥

7. But more generally, and understanding these three things in their widest sense, **it is the rightly regulated action, *niyataṁ karma*, that has to be done,** action regulated by the Shastra, the science and art of right knowledge, right works, right living, or regulated by the essential nature, *svabhāva-niyataṁ karma*, or, finally and best of all, regulated by the will of the Divine within and above us. The last is the true and only action of the liberated man, *muktasya karma*. **To renounce these works is not a right movement — the Gita lays that down plainly and trenchantly in the end, *niyatasya tu sannyāsaḥ karmaṇo nopapadyate*.** To **renounce them from an ignorant confidence in the sufficiency of that withdrawal for the true liberation is a tamasic renunciation.** The gunas follow us, we see, into the renunciation of works as well as into works. **A renunciation with attachment to inaction, *saṅgo akarmaṇi*, would be equally a tamasic withdrawal.**

दुःखमित्येव यत्कर्म कायक्लेशभयात्त्यजेत् ।
स कृत्वा राजसं त्यागं नैव त्यागफलं लभेत् ॥८॥

8. **And to give them up because they bring sorrow or are a trouble to the flesh and a weariness to the mind or in the feeling that all is vanity and vexation of spirit, is a rajasic renunciation and does not bring the high spiritual fruit;** that too is not the true Tyaga. It is a result of intellectual pessimism or vital weariness, it has its roots in ego. No freedom can come from a renunciation governed by this self-regarding principle.

कार्यमित्येव यत्कर्म नियतं क्रियतेऽर्जुन ।
सङ्गं त्यक्त्वा फलं चैव स त्यागः सात्त्विको मतः ॥९॥

9. **The sattwic principle of renunciation is to withdraw not from action, but from the personal demand, the ego factor behind it. It is to do works not dictated by desire but by the law of right living or by the essential nature,** its knowledge, its ideal, its faith in itself and the Truth it sees, its *śraddhā*. Or else, on a higher spiritual plane, **they are dictated by the will of the Master and done with the mind in Yoga, without any personal attachment either to the action or to the fruit of the action.**

न द्वेष्ट्यकुशलं कर्म कुशले नानुषज्जते ।
त्यागी सत्त्वसमाविष्टो मेधावी छिन्नसंशयः ॥१०॥

10. There must be a complete renunciation of all desire and of all self-regarding egoistic choice and impulse and finally of that much subtler egoism of the will which either says, "The work is mine, I am the doer," or even, "The work is God's, but I am the doer." **There must be no attachment to pleasant, desirable, lucrative or successful work and no doing of it because it has that nature;** but that kind of work too has to be done, — done totally, selflessly, with the assent of the spirit, — when it is the action demanded from above and from within us, *kartavyaṁ karma*. **There must be no aversion to unpleasant, undesirable or ungratifying action or work that brings or is likely to bring with it suffering, danger, harsh conditions, inauspicious consequences;** for that too has to be accepted, totally, selflessly, with a deep understanding of its need and meaning, when it is the work that should be done, *kartavyaṁ karma*. **The wise man puts away the shrinkings and hesitations of the desire-soul and the doubts of the ordinary human intelligence,** that measure by little personal, conventional or otherwise limited standards. He follows in the light of the full sattwic mind and with the power of an inner renunciation.

न हि देहभृता शक्यं त्यक्तुं कर्माण्यशेषतः ।
यस्तु कर्मफलत्यागी स त्यागीत्यभिधीयते ।।११।।

11. He will not do action for the sake of any personal result or for any reward in this life or with any attachment to success, profit or consequence: neither will his works be undertaken for the sake of a fruit in the invisible hereafter or ask for a reward in other births or in worlds beyond us, the prizes for which the half-baked religious mind hungers. The liberated worker who has given up his works by the inner sannyasa to a greater Power is free from Karma. Action he will do, for some kind of action, less or more, small or great, is inevitable, natural, right for the embodied soul, — action is part of the divine law of living, it is the high dynamics of the spirit. The essence of renunciation, the true Tyaga, the true Sannyasa is not any rule of thumb of inaction but a disinterested soul, a selfless mind, the transition from ego to the free impersonal and spiritual nature. The spirit of this inner renunciation is the first mental condition of the highest culminating sattwic discipline.

अनिष्टमिष्टं मिश्रं च त्रिविधं कर्मणः फलम् ।
भवत्यत्यागिनां प्रेत्य न तु संन्यासिनां क्वचित् ।।१२।।

12. The three kinds of result, pleasant, unpleasant and mixed, in this or other worlds, in this or another life are for the slaves of desire and ego; these things do not cling to the free spirit.

पञ्चैतानि महाबाहो कारणानि निबोध मे ।
सांख्ये कृतान्ते प्रोक्तानि सिद्धये सर्वकर्मणाम् ।।१३।।

13. The Gita then speaks of the five causes (*kāraṇa*), or indispensable requisites for the accomplishment of works as laid down by the Sankhya.

अधिष्ठानं तथा कर्ता करणं च पृथग्विधम् ।
विविधाश्च पृथक्चेष्टा दैवं चैवात्र पञ्चमम् ।।१४।।

14. These five are, first, the frame of body, life and mind which are the basis or standing-ground of the soul in Nature, *adhiṣṭhāna*; next, the doer, *kartā*, third, the various instrumentation of Nature, *karaṇa*, fourth, the many kinds of effort which make up the force of action, *ceṣṭāḥ*, and last, Fate, *daivam*, that is to say, the influence of the Power or powers other than the human

factors, other than the visible mechanism of Nature, that stand behind these and modify the work and dispose its fruits in the steps of act and consequence.

शरीरवाङ्मनोभिर्यत्कर्म प्रारभते नरः ।
न्याय्यं वा विपरीतं वा पञ्चैते तस्य हेतवः ।।१५।।

15. **These five elements make up among them all the efficient causes, *kāraṇa*, that determine the shaping and outcome of whatever work man undertakes with mind and speech and body.**

तत्रैवं सति कर्तारमात्मानं केवलं तु यः ।
पश्यत्यकृतबुद्धित्वान्न स पश्यति दुर्मतिः ।।१६।।

16. **The doer is ordinarily supposed to be our surface personal ego, but that is the false idea of the understanding that has not arrived at knowledge. The ego is the ostensible doer,** but the ego and its will are creations and instruments of Nature with which **the ignorant understanding wrongly identifies our self** and they are not the only determinants even of human action, much less of its turn and consequence. When we are liberated from ego, **our real self behind comes forward, impersonal and universal, and it sees in its self-vision of unity with the universal Spirit universal Nature as the doer of the work and the Divine Will behind as the Master of universal Nature.**

यस्य नाहंकृतो भावो बुद्धिर्यस्य न लिप्यते ।
हत्वापि स इमांल्लोकान्न हन्ति न निबध्यते ।।१७।।

17. **But once we live in this greater knowledge, the character and consequences of the work can make no difference to the freedom of the spirit.** The work may be outwardly a terrible action like this great battle and slaughter of Kurukshetra; but **although the liberated man takes his part in the struggle and though he slay all these peoples, he slays no man and he is not bound by his work,** because the work is that of the Master of the Worlds and it is he who has already slain in his hidden omnipotent will all these armies. This work of destruction was needed that humanity might move forward to another creation and a new purpose, might get rid as in a fire of its past karma of unrighteousness and oppression and injustice and move towards a kingdom of the Dharma. **[He is free from] this poor, trepidant, braggart egoistic condition of consciousness, *ahaṅkṛita bhāva*, the crippling narrowness of this little**

helpless separative personality according to whose viewpoint we ordinarily think and act, feel and respond to the touches of existence. **The liberated man does all his appointed work as the living instrument one in spirit with the universal Spirit.** And knowing that all this must be and looking beyond the outward appearance he acts not for self but for God and man and the human and cosmic order, not in fact himself acting, but conscious of the presence and power of the divine Force in his deeds and their issue. He knows that the supreme Shakti is doing in his mental, vital and physical body, *adhiṣṭhāna*, as the sole doer the thing appointed by a Fate which is in truth not Fate, not a mechanical dispensation but the wise and all-seeing Will that is at work behind human Karma.

ज्ञानं ज्ञेयं परिज्ञाता त्रिविधा कर्मचोदना ।
करणं कर्म कर्तेति त्रिविधः कर्मसंग्रहः ॥१८॥
ज्ञानं कर्म च कर्ता च त्रिधैव गुणभेदतः ।
प्रोच्यते गुणसंख्याने यथावच्छृणु तान्यपि ॥१९॥

18-19[1]**.** It is clear then that the **work** is not the sole thing that matters; the knowledge in which we do works makes an immense spiritual difference. **There are three things, says the Gita, which go to constitute the mental impulsion to works, and they are the *knowledge* in our will, the object of knowledge and the knower; and into the knowledge there comes always the working of the three gunas. It is this element of the gunas that makes all the difference to our view of the thing known and to the spirit in which the knower does his work.**

There are again three things, the *doer*, the instrument and the work done, that hold the action together and make it possible. And here again it is the difference of the gunas that determines the character of each of these elements.

सर्वभूतेषु येनैकं भावमव्ययमीक्षते ।
अविभक्तं विभक्तेषु तज्ज्ञानं विद्धि सात्त्विकम् ॥२०॥
पृथक्त्वेन तु यज्ज्ञानं नानाभावान्पृथग्विधान् ।
वेत्ति सर्वेषु भूतेषु तज्ज्ञानं विद्धि राजसम् ॥२१॥
यत्तु कृत्स्नवदेकस्मिन्कार्ये सक्तमहैतुकम् ।
अतत्त्वार्थवदल्पं च तत्तामसमुदाहृतम् ॥२२॥

1. See footnote at XVII-4 (Editor's note).

20-22. (22) The *tamasic* ignorant *knowledge* is a small and narrow, a lazy or dully obstinate way of looking at things which has no eye for the real nature of the world or of the thing done or its field or the act or its conditions. The tamasic mind does not look for real cause and effect, but absorbs itself in one movement or one routine with an obstinate attachment to it, can see nothing but the little section of personal activity before its eyes and does not know in fact what it is doing but blindly lets natural impulsion work out through its deed results of which it has no conception, foresight or comprehending intelligence.

(21) The *rajasic knowledge* is that which sees the multiplicity of things only in their separateness and variety of operation in all these existences and is unable to discover a true principle of unity or rightly coordinate its will and action, but follows the bent of ego and desire.

(20) The *sattwic knowledge* on the contrary sees existence as one indivisible whole in all these divisions, one imperishable being in all becomings. At the highest top of knowledge this seeing becomes the knowledge of the one spirit in the world, one in all these many existences, of the one Master of all works, of the forces of cosmos as expressions of the Godhead and of the work itself as the operation of his supreme will and wisdom in man and his life and essential nature.

नियतं सङ्गरहितमरागद्वेषतः कृतम् ।
अफलप्रेप्सुना कर्म यत्तत्सात्त्विकमुच्यते ।।२३।।
यत्तु कामेप्सुना कर्म साहङ्कारेण वा पुनः ।
क्रियते बहुलायासं तद्राजसमुदाहृतम् ।।२४।।
अनुबन्धं क्षयं हिंसामनवेक्ष्य च पौरुषम् ।
मोहादारभ्यते कर्म यत्तत्तामसमुच्यते ।।२५।।

23-25. (25) *Tamasic action* is that done with a confused, deluded and ignorant mind, in mechanical obedience to the instincts, impulsions and unseeing ideas, without regarding the strength or capacity or the waste and loss of blind misapplied effort or the antecedent and consequence and right conditions of the impulse, effort or labour.

(24) *Rajasic action* is that which a man undertakes under the dominion of desire, with his eyes fixed on the work and its hoped-for fruit and nothing else, or with an egoistic sense of his own personality in the action, and it is done with

inordinate effort, with a passionate labour, with a great heaving and straining of the personal will to get at the object of its desire.

(23) ***Sattwic action* is that which a man does calmly in the clear light of reason and knowledge and with an impersonal sense of right or duty or the demand of an ideal, as the thing that ought to be done whatever may be the result to himself in this world or another, a work performed without attachment, without liking or disliking for its spur or its drag.** At the line of culmination of sattwa it will be transformed and become a highest impersonal action dictated by the spirit within us and no longer by the intelligence, an action moved by the highest law of the nature, free from the lower ego.

मुक्तसङ्गोऽनहंवादी धृत्युत्साहसमन्वितः ।
सिद्ध्यसिद्ध्योर्निर्विकारः कर्ता सात्त्विक उच्यते ।।२६।।
रागी कर्मफलप्रेप्सुर्लुब्धो हिंसात्मकोऽशुचिः ।
हर्षशोकान्वितः कर्ता राजसः परिकीर्तितः ।।२७।।
अयुक्तः प्राकृतः स्तब्धः शठो नैष्कृतिकोऽलसः ।
विषादी दीर्घसूत्री च कर्ता तामस उच्यते ।।२८।।

26-28. (28) **The *tamasic doer* of action is one who does not put himself really into the work, but acts with a mechanical mind,** or obeys the most vulgar thought of the herd, follows the common routine or is wedded to a blind error and prejudice. **He is obstinate in stupidity, stubborn in error and takes a foolish pride in his ignorant doing; a narrow and evasive cunning replaces true intelligence;** he has a stupid and insolent contempt for those with whom he has to deal, especially for wiser men and his betters. **A dull laziness, slowness, procrastination, looseness, want of vigour or of sincerity mark his action. The tamasic man is ordinarily slow to act, dilatory in his steps, easily depressed,** ready soon to give up his task if it taxes his strength, his diligence or his patience.

(27) **The *rajasic doer* of action on the contrary is one eagerly attached to the work, bent on its rapid completion, passionately desirous of fruit and reward and consequence, greedy of heart, impure of mind, often violent and cruel and brutal in the means he uses;** he cares little whom he injures or how much he injures others so long as he gets what he wants, satisfies his passions and will, vindicates the claims of his ego. **He is full of an incontinent joy in success and bitterly grieved and stricken by failure.**

(26) **The *sattwic doer* is free from all this attachment, this egoism, this violent strength or passionate weakness; his is a mind and will unelated by suc-**

cess, undepressed by failure, full of a fixed impersonal resolution, a calm rectitude of zeal or a high and pure and selfless enthusiasm in the work that has to be done. At and beyond the culmination of sattwa this resolution, zeal, enthusiasm become the spontaneous working of the spiritual Tapas and at last a highest soul-force, the direct God-Power, the mighty and steadfast movement of a divine energy in the human instrument, the self-assured steps of the Seer-will, the gnostic intelligence and with it the wide delight of the free spirit in the works of the liberated nature.

बुद्धेर्भेदं धृतेश्चैव गुणतस्त्रिविधं शृणु ।
प्रोच्यमानमशेषेण पृथक्त्वेन धनञ्जय ।।२९।।

29. **The *reason* armed with the intelligent will works in man in whatever manner or measure he may possess these human gifts and it is accordingly right or perverted, clouded or luminous, narrow and small or large and wide like the mind of its possessor.** It is the understanding power of his nature, *buddhi*, that chooses the work for him or, more often, approves and sets its sanction on one or other among the many suggestions of his complex instincts, impulsions, ideas and desires. It is that which determines for him what is right or wrong, to be done or not to be done, Dharma or Adharma. **And the *persistence of the will, dhriti,* is that continuous force of mental Nature which sustains the work and gives it consistence and persistence. Here again there is the incidence of the gunas.**

प्रवृत्तिं च निवृत्तिं च कार्याकार्ये भयाभये ।
बन्धं मोक्षं च या वेत्ति बुद्धिः सा पार्थ सात्त्विकी ।।३०।।
यया धर्ममधर्मं च कार्यं चाकार्यमेव च ।
अयथावत्प्रजानाति बुद्धिः सा पार्थ राजसी ।।३१।।
अधर्मं धर्ममिति या मन्यते तमसावृता ।
सर्वार्थान्विपरीतांश्च बुद्धिः सा पार्थ तामसी ।।३२।।
धृत्या यया धारयते मनःप्राणेन्द्रियक्रियाः ।
योगेनाव्यभिचारिण्या धृतिः सा पार्थ सात्त्विकी ।।३३।।
यया तु धर्मकामार्थान्धृत्या धारयतेऽर्जुन ।
प्रसङ्गेन फलाकाङ्क्षी धृतिः सा पार्थ राजसी ।।३४।।
यया स्वप्नं भयं शोकं विषादं मदमेव च ।
न विमुञ्चति दुर्मेधा धृतिः सा पार्थ तामसी ।।३५।।

30-35. **(32) The *tamasic reason* is a false, ignorant and darkened instrument which chains us to see all things in a dull and wrong light, a cloud of** misconceptions, a stupid ignoring of the values of things and people. This reason calls light darkness and darkness light, takes what is not the true law and upholds it as the law, persists in the thing which ought not to be done and holds it up to us as the one right thing to be done. Its ignorance is invincible,

(35) and its *persistence of will* is a persistence in the satisfaction and dull pride of its ignorance. That is on its side of blind action; but it is pursued also by a heavy stress of inertia and impotence, a persistence in dullness and sleep, an aversion to mental change and progress, a dwelling on the fears and pains and depressions of mind which deter us in our path or keep us to base, weak and cowardly ways. Timidity, shirking, evasion, indolence, the justification by the mind of its fears and false doubts and cautions and refusals of duty and its lapses and turnings from the call of our higher nature, a safe following of the line of least resistance so that there may be the least trouble and effort and peril in the winning of the fruit of our labour, — rather no fruit or poor result, it says, than a great and noble toil or a perilous and exacting endeavour and adventure, — these are characteristics of the *tamasic* will and intelligence.

(31) The *rajasic understanding*, when it does not knowingly choose error and evil for the sake of the error and evil, can make distinctions between right and wrong, between what should or should not be done, but not rightly, rather with a pulling awry of their true measures and a constant distortion of values. And this is because its reason and will are a reason of the ego and a will of desire, and these powers misrepresent and distort the truth and the right to serve their own egoistic purpose. It is only when we are free from ego and desire and look steadily with a calm, pure, disinterested mind concerned only with the truth and its sequences that we can hope to see things rightly and in their just values.

(34) But the *rajasic will* fixes its persistent attention on the satisfaction of its own attached clingings and desires in its pursuit of interest and pleasure and of what it thinks or chooses to think right and justice, Dharma. Always it is apt to put on these things the construction which will most flatter and justify its desires and to uphold as right or legitimate the means which will best help it to get the coveted fruits of its work and endeavour. That is the cause of three-fourths of the falsehood and misconduct of the human reason and will. Rajas with its vehement hold on the vital ego is the great sinner and positive misleader.

(30) The *sattwic understanding* sees in its right place, right form, right measure the movement of the world, the law of action and the law of abstention from action, the thing that is to be done and the thing that is not to be done, what

is safe for the soul and what is dangerous, what is to be feared and shunned and what is to be embraced by the will, what binds the spirit of man and what sets it free.

(33) These are the things that it follows or avoids by the *persistence of its conscious will* according to the degree of its light and the stage of evolution it has reached in its upward ascent to the highest self and Spirit. The culmination of this sattwic intelligence is found by a high persistence of the aspiring buddhi when it is settled on what is beyond the ordinary reason and mental will, pointed to the summits, **turned to a steady control of the senses and the life and a union by Yoga with man's highest Self, the universal Divine, the transcendent Spirit.** It is there that arriving through the sattwic guna one can pass beyond the gunas, can climb beyond the limitations of the mind and its will and intelligence and sattwa itself disappear into that which is above the gunas and beyond this instrumental nature. Arrived upon that summit we can leave the Highest to guide Nature in our members in the free spontaneity of a divine action. All these lower conditions, laws, dharmas cease to have any hold on us; the Infinite acts in the liberated man and there is no law but the immortal truth and right of the free spirit, no Karma, no kind of bondage.

सुखं त्विदानीं त्रिविधं शृणु मे भरतर्षभ ।
अभ्यासाद्रमते यत्र दुःखान्तं च निगच्छति ।।३६।।
यत्तदग्रे विषमिव परिणामेऽमृतोपमम् ।
तत्सुखं सात्त्विकं प्रोक्तमात्मबुद्धिप्रसादजम् ।।३७।।
विषयेन्द्रियसंयोगाद्यत्तदग्रेऽमृतोपमम् ।
परिणामे विषमिव तत्सुखं राजसं स्मृतम् ।।३८।।
यदग्रे चानुबन्धे च सुखं मोहनमात्मनः ।
निद्रालस्यप्रमादोत्थं तत्तामसमुदाहृतम् ।।३९।।

36-39. Harmony and order are the characteristic qualities of the sattwic mind and temperament, quiet happiness, a clear and calm content and an inner ease and peace. Happiness is indeed the one thing which is openly or indirectly the universal pursuit of our human nature, — happiness or its suggestion or some counterfeit of it, some pleasure, some enjoyment, some satisfaction of the mind, *the will*, the passions or the body. **But there are various kinds of *happiness* or pleasure according to the guna which dominates in our nature.**

(39) Thus the *tamasic* mind can remain well-pleased in its indolence and inertia, its stupor and sleep, its blindness and its error. Nature has armed it with

the privilege of a smug satisfaction in its stupidity and ignorance, its dim lights of the cave, its inert contentment, its petty or base joys and its vulgar pleasures. **Delusion is the beginning of this satisfaction and delusion is its consequence;** but still there is given a dull, a by no means admirable but a sufficient pleasure in his delusions to the dweller in the cave. **There is a tamasic happiness founded in inertia and ignorance.**

(38) **The mind of the *rajasic* man drinks of a more fiery and intoxicating cup; the keen, mobile, active pleasure of the senses and the body and the sense-entangled or fierily kinetic will and intelligence are to him all the joy of life and the very significance of living. This joy is nectar to the lips at the first touch, but there is a secret poison in the bottom of the cup and after it the bitterness of disappointment, satiety, fatigue, revolt, disgust, sin, suffering, loss, transience.** And it must be so because these pleasures in their external figure are not the things which the spirit in us truly demands from life; there is something behind and beyond the transience of the form, something that is lasting, satisfying, self-sufficient.

(37) **What the *sattwic* nature seeks, therefore, is the satisfaction of the higher mind and the spirit and when it once gets this large object of its quest, there comes in a clear, pure happiness of the soul, a state of fullness, an abiding ease and peace.** This happiness does not depend on outward things, but on ourselves alone and on the flowering of what is best and most inward within us.

(36) **But it is not at first our normal possession; it has to be conquered by self-discipline, a labour of the soul, a high and arduous endeavour. At first this means much loss of habitual pleasure, much suffering and struggle, a poison born of the churning of our nature, a painful conflict of forces,** much revolt and opposition to the change due to the ill-will of the members or the insistence of vital movements, **but in the end the nectar of immortality rises in the place of this bitterness and as we climb to the higher spiritual nature we come to the end of sorrow, the euthanasia of grief and pain.** That is the surpassing happiness which descends upon us at the point or line of culmination of the sattwic discipline.

The self-exceeding of the sattwic nature comes when we get beyond the great but still inferior sattwic pleasure, beyond the pleasures of mental knowledge and virtue and peace to the eternal calm of the self and the spiritual ecstasy of the divine oneness. That spiritual joy is no longer the sattwic happiness, *sukham*, but the absolute Ananda. Ananda is the secret delight from which all things are born, by which all is sustained in existence and to which all can rise in the spiritual culmination. Only then can it be possessed when the liberated man, free from ego and its desires, lives at last one with his highest self, one with all beings and one with God in an absolute bliss of the spirit.

II — SWABHAVA AND SWADHARMA

There is still an incidental question of great importance in the old Indian system of culture and on which we have had some passing pronouncements already by the Gita and which now falls into its proper place. All men can eventually arrive by spiritual evolution to this strong discipline, this large perfection, this highest spiritual state. But while the general rule of mind and action is the same for all men, we see too that there is a constant law of variation and each individual acts not only according to the common laws of the human spirit, mind, will, life, but according to his own nature; each man fulfils different functions or follows a different bent according to the rule of his own circumstances, capacities, turn, character, powers. What place is to be assigned to this variation, this individual rule of nature in the spiritual discipline?

The Gita has laid some stress on this point and even assigned to it a great preliminary importance. At the very start it has spoken of the nature, rule and function of the Kshatriya as Arjuna's own law of action, *svadharma* (*II-31*); it has proceeded to lay it down with a striking emphasis (*in III-35*). This swadharma is of four general kinds formulated outwardly in the action of the four orders of the old Indian social culture, *cātur-varṇya*. That system corresponds, says the Gita, to a divine law, it "was created by me according to the divisions of the gunas and works" (*IV-13*), — created from the beginning by the Master of existence. In other words, there are four distinct orders of the active nature, or four fundamental types of the soul in nature, *svabhāva*, and the work and proper function of each human being corresponds to his type of nature. This is now finally explained in preciser detail.

न तदस्ति पृथिव्यां वा दिवि देवेषु वा पुनः ।
सत्त्वं प्रकृतिजैर्मुक्तं यदेभिः स्यात्त्रिभिर्गुणैः ।।४०।।

40. At present all our activities are determined in their trend and shape by the nature, and this Nature here is the nature of the three gunas, *prakṛiti-jaiḥ tribhir-guṇaiḥ*, and in all natural being and in all natural activities there is

the triple guna. In fact the mental, the vital, the physical existence are all subject to the limitations of quality, all are governed by its determinations.

ब्राह्मणक्षत्रियविशां शूद्राणां च परन्तप।
कर्माणि प्रविभक्तानि स्वभावप्रभवैर्गुणैः ॥४१॥

41. The works of Brahmins, Kshatriyas, Vaishyas and Sudras are divided according to the qualities, *guṇas*, born of their own inner nature, spiritual temperament, essential character, *svabhāva-prabhavair guṇaiḥ*.

What precisely is the intention of the Gita? These verses (*41-48*) and the earlier pronouncements of the Gita on the same subject (*see also IV-13*) have been seized upon in current controversies on the caste question and interpreted by some as a sanction of the present system, used by others as a denial of the hereditary basis of caste. In point of fact the verses in the Gita have no bearing on the existing caste system, because this is a very different thing from the ancient social ideal of *caturvarṇa*, the four clear-cut orders of the Aryan community, and in no way corresponds with the description of the Gita. The Gita's words refer to the ancient system of *caturvarṇa*, as it existed or was supposed to exist in its ideal purity.

The ancient system of the four orders had a triple aspect; it took a social and economic, a cultural and a spiritual appearance. On the economic side it recognised four functions of the social man in the community, the religious and intellectual, the political, the economic and the servile functions. There are thus four kinds of works, the work of religious ministration, letters, learning and knowledge, the work of government, politics, administration and war, the work of production, wealth-making and exchange, the work of hired labour and service. An endeavour was made to found and stabilise the whole arrangement of society on the partition of these four functions among four clearly marked classes. This system was not peculiar to India, but was with certain differences the dominating feature of a stage of social evolution in other ancient or mediaeval societies. The four functions are still inherent in the life of all normal communities, but the clear divisions no longer exist anywhere. The old system everywhere broke down and gave place to a more fluid order or, as in India, to a confused and complex social rigidity and economic immobility degenerating towards a chaos of castes. Along with this economic division there existed the association of a cultural idea which gave to each class its religious custom, its law of honour, ethical rule, suitable education and training, type of character, family ideal and discipline. Finally, wherever this system existed, it was given more or less a religious sanction and in India a profounder spiritual use and significance. This spiritual significance is the real kernel of the teaching of the Gita.

The Gita found this system in existence and its ideal in possession of the Indian mind and it recognised and accepted both the ideal and system and its religious sanction. **The fourfold order was created by me, says Krishna, according to the divisions of quality and active function, *cāturvarṇyaṁ mayā sṛiṣṭam guṇa-karma-vibhāgaśaḥ*** (*IV-13*). On the mere strength of this phrase it cannot altogether be concluded that the Gita regarded this system as an eternal and universal social order. Still we may understand from the phrase that the fourfold function of social man was considered as normally inherent in the psychological and economic needs of every community and therefore a dispensation of the Spirit that expresses itself in the human corporate and individual existence. But what then should be the natural basis and form of practice of these functions? The practical basis in ancient times came to be the hereditary principle. A man's social function and position were no doubt determined originally, as they are still in freer, less closely ordered communities by environment, occasion, birth and capacity; but as there set in a more fixed stratification, his rank came practically to be regulated by birth mainly or alone and in the later system of caste birth came to be the sole rule of status. The son of a Brahmin is always a Brahmin in status, though he may have nothing of the typical Brahmin qualities or character.

This was an inevitable evolution, because the external signs are the only ones which are easily and conveniently determinable and birth was the most handy and manageable in an increasingly mechanised, complex and conventional social order. The ancient lawgivers, while recognising the hereditary practice, insisted that quality, character and capacity were the one sound and real basis and that without them the hereditary social status became an unspiritual falsehood because it had lost its true significance. The Gita too, as always, founds its thought on the inner significance. It speaks indeed in one verse of **the work born with a man, *saha-jaṁ karma*** (*sl. 48*); but this does not in itself imply a hereditary basis. According to the Indian theory of rebirth, which the Gita recognises, a man's inborn nature and course of life are essentially determined by his own past lives, are the self-development already effected by his past actions and mental and spiritual evolution and cannot depend solely on the material factor of his ancestry, parentage, physical birth, which can only be of subordinate moment, one effective sign perhaps, but not the dominant principle. The word *sahaja* means that which is born with us, whatever is natural, inborn, innate; its equivalent in all other passages is *svabhāvaja*.

What matters most in my life, is not my heredity; that only gives me my opportunity or my obstacle, my good or my bad material. What matters supremely is what I make of my heredity and not what my heredity makes of me. The past of the world, bygone humanity, my ancestors are there in me; but still I myself am the artist of my self, my life, my actions. And there is the present of the world, of humanity, there are my contemporaries as well as my ancestors; the life of my environment too enters into me, offers me a new material, shapes me by its influence, lays its direct or its indirect touch on my being. But here again the individual comes in subtly and centrally as the decisive power. What is supremely important is what I make of all this surrounding and invading present and not what it makes of me.

The work or function of a man is determined by his qualities, *karma* is determined by *guṇa*; it is the work born of his Swabhava, *svabhāva-jaṁ karma*, and regulated by his Swabhava, *svabhāva-niyataṁ karma*. This emphasis on an inner quality and spirit which finds expression in work, function and action is the whole sense of the Gita's idea of Karma. And from this emphasis on the inner truth and not on the outer form arises the spiritual significance and power which the Gita assigns to the following of the Swadharma. That is the really important bearing of the passage. In fact it lays very little stress on the external rule and a very great stress on the internal law which the Varna system attempted to put into regulated outward practice. And it is on the individual and spiritual value of this law and not on its communal and economic or other social and cultural importance that the eye of the thought is fixed in this passage. The Gita accepts the theory of the four orders of men, but gives to it a profound turn, an inner, subjective and universal meaning, a spiritual sense and direction. What the Gita is concerned with is not the validity of the Aryan social order, but the relation of a man's outward life to his inward being, the evolution of his action from his soul and inner law of nature.

शमो दमस्तपः शौचं क्षान्तिरार्जवमेव च ।
ज्ञानं विज्ञानमास्तिक्यं ब्रह्मकर्म स्वभावजम् ।।४२।।

42. And we see in fact that the Gita itself indicates very clearly its intention when it describes the work of the Brahmin and the Kshatriya not in terms of external function, not defined as learning, priest-work and letters or government, war and politics, but entirely in terms of internal character. The language reads a little curiously to our ear. **Calm, self-control, askesis, purity, long-suffering, candour, knowledge, acceptance and practice of spiritual truth are the work of the Brahmin, born of his swabhava.** [These things] would not ordinarily be described as a man's function, work or life occupation. Yet this is precisely what the Gita means and says, — that these things, their development, their expression in conduct, their power to cast into form the law of the sattwic nature are the real work of the Brahmin: learning, religious ministration and the other outer functions are only its most suitable field, a favourable means of this inner development, its appropriate self-expression, its way of fixing itself into firmness of type and externalised solidity of character.

शौर्यं तेजो धृतिर्दाक्ष्यं युद्धे चाप्यपलायनम् ।
दानमीश्वरभावश्च क्षात्रं कर्म स्वभावजम् ।।४३।।

43. War, government, politics, leadership and rule are a similar field and means for the Kshatriya; but his real work is the development, the expression in conduct, the power to cast into form and dynamic rhythm of movement the law of the active battling royal or warrior spirit. **Heroism, high spirit, resolution, ability, not fleeing in the battle, giving, lordship, *īśvara-bhāva*, the temperament of the ruler and leader are the natural work of the Kshatriya.**

कृषिगौरक्ष्यवाणिज्यं वैश्यकर्म स्वभावजम् ।
परिचर्यात्मकं कर्म शूद्रस्यापि स्वभावजम् ।।४४।।

44. **Agriculture, cattle-keeping, trade inclusive of the labour of the craftsman and the artisan are the natural work of the Vaishya. All work of the character of service falls within the natural function of the Shudra.** The work of the Vaishya and Shudra is expressed in terms of external function, and this opposite turn may have some significance. For the temperament moved to production and wealth-getting or limited in the circle of labour and service, the mercantile and the servile mind, are usually turned outward, more occupied with the external values of their work than its power for character, and this disposition is not so favourable to a sattwic or spiritual action of the nature. That too is the reason why a commercial and industrial age or a society preoccupied with the idea of work and labour creates around it an atmosphere more favourable to the material than the spiritual life, more adapted to vital efficiency than to the subtler perfection of the high-reaching mind and spirit. Nevertheless, this kind of nature too and its functions have their inner significance, their spiritual value and can be made a means and power for perfection. As has been said elsewhere (*IX-32*), not alone the Brahmin with his ideal of spirituality, ethical purity and knowledge and the Kshatriya with his ideal of nobility, chivalry and high character, but the wealth-seeking Vaishya, the toil-imprisoned Shudra, woman with her

narrow circumscribed and subject life, the very outcaste born from a womb of sin, *pāpayonayaḥ*, can by this road rise at once towards the highest inner greatness and spiritual freedom, towards perfection, towards the liberation and fulfilment of the divine element in the human being.

स्वे स्वे कर्मण्यभिरतः संसिद्धिं लभते नरः ।
स्वकर्मनिरतः सिद्धिं यथा विन्दति तच्छृणु ।।४५।।
यतः प्रवृत्तिर्भूतानां येन सर्वमिदं ततम् ।
स्वकर्मणा तमभ्यर्च्य सिद्धिं विन्दति मानवः ।।४६।।

45-46. A man who devotes himself to his own natural work in life acquires spiritual perfection, not indeed by the mere act itself, but if he does it with right knowledge and the right motive, if he can make it a worship of the Spirit of this creation and dedicate it sincerely to the Master of the universe from whom is all impulse to action, *yataḥ pravṛittir-bhūtānāṁ yena sarvam idaṁ tatam.* All labour, all action and function, whatever it be, can be consecrated by this dedication of works, can convert the life into a self-offering to the Godhead within and without us and is itself converted into a means of spiritual perfection.

Three propositions suggest themselves and may be taken as implicit in all that the Gita says in this passage. First, all action must be determined from within because each man has in him something his own, some characteristic principle and inborn power of his nature. That is the efficient power of his spirit, that creates the dynamic form of his soul in nature. Next, there are broadly four types of nature each with its characteristic function and ideal rule of work and character and the type indicates the man's proper field and should trace for him his just circle of function in his outer social existence. Finally, whatever work a man does, if done according to the law of his being, the truth of his nature, can be turned Godwards and made an effective means of spiritual liberation and perfection. Whatever a man's work and function in life, he can, if it is determined from within or if he is allowed to make it a self-expression of his nature, turn it into a means of growth and of a greater inner perfection. And whatever it be, if he performs his natural function in the right spirit, if he enlightens it by the ideal mind, if he turns its action to the uses of the Godhead within, serves with it the Spirit manifested in the universe or makes it a conscious instrumentation for the purposes of the Divine in humanity, he can transmute it into a means towards the highest spiritual perfection and freedom.

The Gita's philosophy of life and works is that all proceeds from the Divine Existence, the transcendent and universal Spirit. All is a veiled manifestation of the Godhead, Vasudeva, *yataḥ pravṛittir bhūtānāṁ yena sarvam idaṁ tatam,* and to unveil the Immortal within and in the world, to dwell in unity with the Soul of the universe, to rise in consciousness, knowledge, will, love, spiritual delight to oneness with the supreme Godhead, to live in the highest spiritual nature with the individual and natural being delivered from shortcoming and ignorance and made a conscious instrument for the works of the divine Shakti is the perfection of which humanity is capable and the condition of immortality and freedom. But how is this possible? The answer is that all this natural action, however now enveloped in a veiled and contrary working, still contains the principle of its own evolving freedom and perfection. A Godhead is seated in the heart of every man and is the Lord of this mysterious action of Nature. And though this Spirit of the universe, this One who is all, seems to be turning us on the wheel of the world as if mounted on a machine by the force of Maya, shaping us in our ignorance as the potter shapes a pot, as the weaver a fabric, by some skilful mechanical principle, yet is this spirit our own greatest self and it is according to the Real Idea, the truth of ourselves, that which is growing in us and finding always new and more adequate forms in birth after birth, in our animal and human and divine life, in that which we were, that which we are, that which we shall be, — it is in accordance with this inner soul-truth that, as our opened eyes will discover, we are progressively shaped by this spirit within us in its all-wise omnipotence. This machinery of ego, this tangled complexity of the three gunas, mind, body, life, is only the outward imperfect form taken by a higher spiritual Force in me which pursues through its vicissitudes the progressive self-expression of the divine reality and greatness I am secretly in spirit and shall overtly become in nature. This action contains in itself the principle of its own success, the principle of the Swabhava and Swadharma.

The Jiva is in self-expression a portion of the Purushottama. He represents in Nature the power of the supreme Spirit, he is in his personality that Power; he brings out in an individual existence the potentialities of the Soul of the universe. This Jiva itself is spirit and not the natural ego; the spirit and not the form of ego is our reality and inner soul principle. The spiritual Nature which has become this multiple personality in the universe, *parā prakṛitir jīva-bhūtā*, is the basic stuff of our existence: all the rest is lower derivation and outer formation from a highest hidden activity of the spirit. And in Nature each of us has a principle and will of our own becoming; each soul is a force of self-consciousness that formulates an idea of the Divine in it and guides by that its action and evolution, its progressive self-finding, its constant varying self-expression, its apparently uncertain but secretly inevitable growth to fullness. That is our Swabhava, our own real nature; that is our truth of being which is finding now only a constant partial expression in our various becoming in the world. The law of action determined by this Swabhava is our right law of self-shaping, function, working, our Swadharma.

This principle obtains throughout cosmos; there is everywhere the one Power at work, one common universal Nature, but in each grade, form, energy, genus, species, individual creature she follows out a major Idea and minor ideas and principles of constant and complex variation that found both the permanent dharma of each and its temporary dharmas. These fix for it the law of its being in becoming, the curve of its birth and persistence and change, the force of its self-preservation and self-increasing, the lines of its stable and evolving self-expression and self-finding, the rules of its relations to all the rest of the expression of the Self in the universe. To follow the law of its being, Swadharma, to develop the idea in its being, Swabhava, is its ground of safety, its right walk and procedure.

श्रेयान्स्वधर्मो विगुणः परधर्मात्स्वनुष्ठितात् ।
स्वभावनियतं कर्म कुर्वन्नाप्नोति किल्बिषम् ।।४७।।

47. **But a work not naturally one's own, even though it may be well performed, may look better from the outside** when judged by an external and mechanical standard or may lead to more success in life, is still inferior as a means of subjective growth precisely because it has an external motive and a mechanical impulsion. **One's own natural work is better, even if it looks from some other point of view defective. One does not incur sin or stain when one acts in the true spirit of the work and in agreement with the law of one's own nature.** Imperfect capacity and effect in the work that is meant for thee is better than an artificial competency and a borrowed perfection. (*see also III-35*)

सहजं कर्म कौन्तेय सदोषमपि न त्यजेत् ।
सर्वारम्भा हि दोषेण धूमेनाग्निरिवावृताः ।।४८।।

48. **All action in the three gunas is imperfect, all human work is subject to fault, defect or limitation; but that should not make us abandon our own proper work and natural function. Action should be rightly regulated action, *niyataṁ karma*, but intrinsically one's own, evolved from within, in harmony with the truth of one's being, regulated by the Swabhava, *svabhāva-niyataṁ karma*.**

The Gita's injunction is to worship the Divine by our own work, *svakarmaṇā*; our offering must be the works determined by our own law of being and nature. **For from the Divine all movement of creation and impulse to act originates and by him all this universe is extended and for the holding together of the worlds he presides over and shapes all action through the Swabhava** (*sl. 46*). To worship him with our inner and outer activities, to make our whole life a sacrifice of works to the Highest is to prepare ourselves to become one with him in all our will and substance and nature. Our work should be according to the truth within us, it should not be an accommodation with outward and artificial standards: it must be a living and sincere expression of the soul and its inborn powers. For to follow out the living inmost truth of this soul in our present nature will help us eventually to arrive at the immortal truth of the same soul in the now superconscious supreme nature. There we can live in oneness with God and our true self and all beings and, perfected, become a faultless instrument of divine action [*the bow of the divine Archer*] in the freedom of the immortal Dharma.

III — TOWARDS THE SUPREME SECRET

All that rests [for the Teacher] to do is to put into decisive phrase and penetrating formula the one last word, the heart itself of the message, the very core of his gospel. And we find that this decisive, last and crowning word is not merely the essence of what has been already said on the matter, not merely a concentrated description of the needed self-discipline, the Sadhana, and of that greater spiritual consciousness which is to be the result of all its effort and askesis; it sweeps out, as it were, yet farther, breaks down every limit and rule, canon and formula and opens into a wide and illimitable spiritual truth with an infinite potentiality of significance. And that is a sign of the profundity, the wide reach, the greatness of spirit of the Gita's teaching. An ordinary religious teaching or philosophical doctrine is well enough satisfied to seize on certain great and vital aspects of truth and turn them into utilisable dogma and instruction, method and practice for the guidance of man in his inner life and the law and form of his action; it does not go farther, it does not open doors out of the circle of its own system, does not lead us out into some widest freedom and unimprisoned largeness. This limitation is useful and indeed for a time indispensable. Man bounded by his mind and will has need of a law and rule, a fixed system, a definite practice selective of his thought and action; he asks for the single unmistakable hewn path hedged, fixed and secure to the tread, for the limited horizons, for the enclosed resting-places. It is only the strong and few who can move through freedom to freedom. And yet in the end the free soul ought to have an issue out of the forms and systems in which the mind finds its account and takes its limited pleasure. To exceed our ladder of ascent, not to stop short even on the topmost stair but move untrammelled and at large in the wideness of the spirit is a release important for our perfection; the spirit's absolute liberty is our perfect status. And this is how the Gita leads us: it lays down a firm and sure but very large way of ascent, a great Dharma, and then it takes us out beyond all that is laid down, beyond all dharmas, into infinitely open spaces, divulges to us the hope, lets us into the secret of an absolute perfection founded in an absolute spiritual liberty, and that secret, *guhyatamam*, is the substance of what it calls its supreme word, that the hidden thing, the inmost knowledge.

असक्तबुद्धिः सर्वत्र जितात्मा विगतस्पृहः ।
नैष्कर्म्यसिद्धिं परमां संन्यासेनाधिगच्छति ।।४९।।

49. And first the Gita restates the body of its message. It summarises the whole outline and essence in the short space of fifteen verses. Here it is evidently intended to extract what the Gita itself considers to be the central sense of its own teaching. The statement sets out from the original starting-point of the thought in the book, the enigma of human action, the apparently insuperable difficulty of living in the highest self and spirit while yet we continue to do the works of the world.

And therefore in the first five of these verses the Gita so phrases its statement that it shall be applicable to both the way of the inner and the way of the outer renunciation. How, while absorbed and continually forced outward by the engrossing call of its active nature, is [the soul] to get back to its real self and spiritual existence? The ascetic renunciation and the way of the Gita are both agreed that it must first of all renounce this absorption, must cast from it the external solicitation of outward things and separate silent self from active nature; it must identify itself with the immobile Spirit and live in the silence. It must arrive at an inner inactivity, *naiṣkarmya*. It is therefore this saving inner passivity that the Gita puts here as the first object of its Yoga, the first necessary perfection in it or Siddhi.

An understanding without attachment in all things, a soul self-conquered and empty of desire, man attains by renunciation a supreme perfection of *naiṣkarmya*.

The principle [of that which is called in Indian philosophy self and impersonal Brahman] is an infinite and an impersonal existence one and the same in all: and, since this impersonal existence is without ego, without conditioning quality, without desire, need or stimulus, it is immobile and immutable; eternally the same, it regards and supports but does not share or initiate the action of the universe. The soul when it throws itself out into active Nature is the Gita's Kshara, its mobile or mutable Purusha; the same soul gathered back into pure silent self and essential spirit is the Gita's Akshara, immobile or immutable Purusha.

What is called becoming Brahman, *brahma-bhūya*, is to put off the lower mental, vital, physical existence and to put on the pure spiritual being. This can best be done by the intelligence and will, *buddhi*, our present topmost principle. It has to turn away from the things of the lower existence and first and foremost from its effective knot of desire, from our attachment to the objects pursued by the mind and the senses. **One must become an understanding unattached in all things, *asakta-buddhiḥ sarvatra*. Then all desire passes away from the soul in its silence; it is free from all longings, *vigata-spṛihaḥ*. That brings with it or it makes possible the subjection of our lower and the possession of our higher self, a possession dependent on complete self-mastery, secured by a radical victory and conquest over our mobile nature, *jitātmā*. And all this amounts to an absolute inner renunciation of the desire of things, *sannyāsa*. The one thing needed is a complete inner quietism and that is all the Gita's sense of *naiṣkarmya*.**

That inactivity and divorce of self from Nature are not the whole truth of our spiritual release. Self and Nature are in the end one thing; a total and perfect spirituality makes us one with all the Divine in self and in nature. In fact this becoming Brahman, this assumption into the self of eternal silence, *brahma-bhūya*, is not all our objective, but only the necessary immense base for a still greater and more marvellous divine becoming, *mad-bhāva*. And to get to that greatest spiritual perfection we have indeed to be immobile in the self, silent in all our members, but also to act in the power, Shakti, Prakriti, the true and high force of the Spirit. And if we ask how a simultaneity of what seem to be two opposites is possible, the answer is that that is the very nature of a complete spiritual being; always it has this double poise of the Infinite.

सिद्धिं प्राप्तो यथा ब्रह्म तथाप्नोति निबोध मे ।
समासेनैव कौन्तेय निष्ठा ज्ञानस्य या परा ।।५०।।

50. A completest inner quietism once admitted as our necessary means towards living in the pure impersonal self, the question how practically it brings about that result is the next issue that arises. **How, having attained this perfection, one thus attains to the Brahman, hear from me, O son of Kunti, — that which is the supreme concentrated direction of the knowledge, *niṣṭhā*.** The knowledge meant here is the Yoga of the Sankhyas, — the Yoga

of pure knowledge accepted by the Gita, so far as it is one with its own Yoga which includes also the way of works of the Yogins. But all mention of works is kept back for the moment. For by Brahman here is meant at first the silent, the impersonal, the immutable. The Brahman indeed is both for the Upanishads and the Gita all that is and lives and moves; it is not solely an impersonal Infinite or an unthinkable and incommunicable Absolute, *acintyam avyavahāryam*. "All this is Brahman" says the Upanishad, "All this is Vasudeva" says the Gita, — **the supreme Brahman is all that moves or is stable.** It is only when we lose our limited ego personality in the impersonality of the self that we arrive at the calm and free oneness by which we can possess a true unity with the universal power of the Divine in his world movement. Impersonality is a denial of limitation and division, and the cult of impersonality is a natural condition of true being, an indispensable preliminary of true knowledge and therefore a first requisite of true action. It is very clear that we cannot become one self with all or one with the universal Spirit and his vast self-knowledge, his complex will and his widespread world-purpose by insisting on our limited personality of ego; for that divides us from others and it makes us bound and self-centred in our view and in our will to action. To be one with all and with the Divine and his will in the cosmos we must become at first impersonal and free from our ego and its claims and from the ego's way of seeing ourselves and the world and others. And we cannot do this if there is not something in our being other than the personality, other than the ego, an impersonal self one with all existences. To lose ego and be this impersonal self, to become this impersonal Brahman in our consciousness is therefore the first movement of this Yoga.

बुद्ध्या विशुद्धया युक्तो धृत्यात्मानं नियम्य च ।
शब्दादीन्विषयांस्त्यक्त्वा रागद्वेषौ व्युदस्य च ।।५१।।

51. How then is this to be done? **First, says the Gita, through a union of our purified intelligence with the pure spiritual substance in us by the Yoga of the buddhi, *buddhyā viśuddhayā yuktaḥ*.** This spiritual turning of the buddhi from the outward and downward to the inward and upward look is the essence of the Yoga of knowledge. **The purified understanding has to control the whole being, *ātmānaṁ niyamya*; it must draw us away from attachment to the outward-going desires of the lower nature by a firm and a steady will, *dhṛityā*, which in its concentration faces entirely towards the impersonality of the pure spirit. The senses must abandon their objects, the mind must cast away the liking and disliking which these objects excite in it,** — for the impersonal self has no desires and repulsions.

विविक्तसेवी लघ्वाशी यतवाक्कायमानसः ।
ध्यानयोगपरो नित्यं वैराग्यं समुपाश्रितः ।।५२।।

52. **An entire control has to be acquired over the mind, speech and body; the whole of our being must become indifferent, unaffected by these things, equal to all outward touches and to their inward reactions and responses. There has to be a complete cessation of desire and attachment, *vairāgya*; a strong resort to impersonal solitude, a constant union with the inmost self by meditation is demanded of the seeker.**

अहङ्कारं बलं दर्पं कामं क्रोधं परिग्रहम् ।
विमुच्य निर्ममः शान्तो ब्रह्मभूयाय कल्पते ।।५३।।

53. And yet the object of this austere discipline is not to be self-centred in some supreme egoistic seclusion and tranquillity; the object is to get rid of all ego. **One must put away utterly first the rajasic kind of egoism, egoistic strength and violence, arrogance, desire, wrath, the sense and instinct of possession, the urge of the passions, the strong lusts of life.** But afterwards must be discarded egoism of all kinds, even of the most sattwic type; **for the aim is to make soul and mind and life free in the end from all imprisoning I-ness and my-ness, *nirmama*.** For the pure impersonal self which, unshaken, supports the universe has no egoism and makes no demand on thing or person; **it is calm and luminously impassive and silently regards all things and persons with an equal and impartial eye** of self-knowledge and world-knowledge. Then clearly it is by living inwardly in a similar or identical impersonality that **the soul within, released from the siege of things, can best become capable of oneness with the immutable Brahman, *brahma-bhūyāya kalpate*.**

This first pursuit of impersonality as enjoined by the Gita brings with it evidently a certain completest inner quietism. And yet there is a limit imposed to prevent the inner quietism from deepening into refusal of action and a physical withdrawal. **The renunciation of their objects by the senses, *viśayāṁs tyaktvā*, is to be of the nature of Tyaga;** it must be a giving up of all sensuous attachment, *rasa*, not a refusal of the intrinsic necessary activity of the senses. One must move among surrounding things and act on the objects of the sense-field with a pure, true and intense, a simple and absolute operation of the senses for their utility to the spirit in divine action, *kevalair indriyaiś-caran*, and not at all for the fulfilment of desire. **There is to be *vairāgya*,** not in the common significance of disgust of life or distaste for the world action, but **renunciation of *rāga*, as also of its opposite, *dveṣa*. There must be a withdrawal from all mental and vital liking as from all mental and vital disliking whatso-**

ever. And this is asked not for extinction, but in order that there may be a perfect enabling equality. **A continual resort to meditation, *dhyāna-yoga-paro nityam*, is the firm means by which the soul of man can realise its self of Power and its self of silence.** And yet there must be no abandonment of the active life for a life of pure meditation; action must always be done as a sacrifice to the supreme Spirit. This movement of recoil [in the Gita's path of Tyaga] is a preparation for the turning of our whole life and existence and of all action into an integral oneness with the serene and immeasurable being, consciousness and will of the Divine, and it preludes and makes possible a vast and total passing upward of the soul out of the lower ego to the inexpressible perfection of the supreme spiritual nature, *parā prakṛitiḥ*.

ब्रह्मभूतः प्रसन्नात्मा न शोचति न काङ्क्षति ।
समः सर्वेषु भूतेषु मद्भक्तिं लभते पराम् ।।५४।।

54. This decisive departure of the Gita's thought is indicated in the next two verses, of which the first runs with a significant sequence, **When one has become the Brahman, when one neither grieves nor desires, when one is equal to all beings, then one gets the supreme love and devotion to Me, *mad-bhaktiṁ labhate parām*.** But in the narrow path of knowledge bhakti, devotion to the personal Godhead, can be only an inferior and preliminary movement; the end, the climax is the disappearance of personality in a featureless oneness with the impersonal Brahman in which there can be no place for bhakti: for there is none to be adored and none to adore; **all else is lost in the silent immobile identity of the Jiva with the Atman, *brahma-bhūtaḥ prasannātmā*.** Here there is given to us something yet higher than the Impersonal, — here there is the supreme Self who is the supreme Ishwara, here there is the supreme Soul and its supreme nature, here there is the Purushottama who is beyond the personal and impersonal and reconciles them on his eternal heights. All Nature becomes the power of the one Divine and all action his action through the individual as channel and instrument. The One who eternally becomes the Many, the Many who in their apparent division are still eternally one, the Highest who displays in us this secret and mystery of existence, not dispersed by his multiplicity, not limited by his oneness, — this is the integral knowledge, this is the reconciling experience which makes one capable of liberated action, *muktasya karma*.

भक्त्या मामभिजानाति यावान्यश्चास्मि तत्त्वतः ।
ततो मां तत्त्वतो ज्ञात्वा विशते तदनन्तरम् ।।५५।।

55. **This knowledge comes, says the Gita, by a highest bhakti.** It is attained when the mind exceeds itself by a supramental and high spiritual seeing of things and when the heart too rises in unison beyond our more ignorant mental forms of love and devotion to a love that is calm and deep and luminous with widest knowledge, to a supreme delight in God and an illimitable adoration, the unperturbed ecstasy, the spiritual Ananda. **When the soul has lost its separative personality, when it has become the Brahman,** it is then that it can live in the true Person and can attain to the supreme revealing bhakti for the Purushottama and **can come to know him utterly by the power of its profound bhakti, its heart's knowledge, *bhaktyā mām abhijānāti*.** That is the integral knowledge, when the heart's fathomless vision completes the mind's absolute experience, — *samagraṁ māṁ jñātvā*. **He comes to know Me, says the Gita, who and how much I am and in all the reality and principles of my being, *yāvān yaś cāsmi tattvataḥ*.**

The soul of the liberated man thus enters by a reconciling knowledge, penetrates by a perfect simultaneous delight of the transcendent Divine, of the Divine in the individual and of the Divine in the universe into the Purushottama, *māṁ viśate tad-anantaram*. He becomes one with him in his self-knowledge and self-experience, one with him in his being and consciousness and will and world-knowledge and world-impulse, one with him in the universe and in his unity with all creatures in the universe and one with him beyond world and individual in the transcendence of the eternal Infinite, *śāśvataṁ padam avyayam*. This is the culmination of the supreme bhakti that is at the core of the supreme knowledge.

**सर्वकर्माण्यपि सदा कुर्वाणो मद्व्यपाश्रयः ।
मत्प्रसादादवाप्नोति शाश्वतं पदमव्ययम् ।।५६।।**

56. And it then becomes evident how action continual and unceasing and of all kinds without diminution or abandonment of any part of the activities of life can be not only quite consistent with a supreme spiritual experience, but as forceful a means of reaching this highest spiritual condition as bhakti or knowledge. Nothing can be more positive than the Gita's statement in this matter. **And by doing also all actions always lodged in Me he attains by my grace the eternal and imperishable status.**

Thus these eight verses are a brief, but still a comprehensive indication of the whole essential idea, the entire central method, all the kernel of the complete Yoga of the Gita.

IV — THE SUPREME SECRET

The essence of the teaching and the Yoga has thus been given to the disciple on the field of his work and battle and the divine Teacher now proceeds to apply it to his action, but in a way that makes it applicable to all action. Attached to a crucial example, spoken to the protagonist of Kurukshetra, the words bear a much wider significance and are a universal rule for all who are ready to ascend above the ordinary mentality and to live and act in the highest spiritual consciousness. To break out of ego and personal mind and see everything in the wideness of the self and spirit, to know God and adore him in his integral truth and in all his aspects, to surrender all oneself to the transcendent Soul of nature and existence, to possess and be possessed by the divine consciousness, to be one with the One in universality of love and delight and will and knowledge, one in him with all beings, to do works as an adoration and a sacrifice on the divine foundation of a world in which all is God and in the divine status of a liberated spirit, is the sense of the Gita's Yoga.

These are lines (57-62) that carry in them the innermost heart of this Yoga and lead to its crowning experience and we must understand them in their innermost spirit and in the whole vastness of that high summit of experience. The words express the most complete, intimate and living relation possible between God and man; they are instinct with the concentrated force of religious feeling that springs from the human being's absolute adoration, his upward surrender of his whole existence, his unreserved and perfect self-giving to the transcendent and universal Divinity from whom he comes and in whom he lives. It is no abstract Absolute of the philosopher, no indifferent impersonal Presence or ineffable Silence intolerant of all relations to whom this complete surrender of all our works can be made. It is a Master of our works, a Friend and Lover of our soul, an intimate Spirit of our life, an indwelling and overdwelling Lord of all our personal and impersonal self and nature who alone can utter to us this near and moving message. And yet this is not the common relation established by the religions between man living in his sattwic or other ego-mind and some personal form and aspect of the Deity, *iṣṭa-deva*. Here there is something wider that passes beyond the mind and its limits and its dharmas. It is something deeper than the mind that offers and something greater than the Ishta-deva that receives the surrender.

That which surrenders here is the Jiva, the essential soul, the original central and spiritual being of man, the individual Purusha. It is the Jiva delivered from the limiting and ignorant ego-sense who knows himself not as a separate personality but as an eternal portion and power and soul-becoming of the Divine, *aṁśa-sanātana*. It is this central spiritual being in us who thus enters into a perfect and closely real relation of delight and union with the origin and continent and governing Self and Power of our existence. And he who receives our surrender is no limited Deity but the Purushottama, the one eternal Godhead, the one supreme Soul of all that is and of all Nature, the original transcendent Spirit of existence. An immutable impersonal self-existence is his first obvious spiritual self-presentation to the experience of our liberated knowledge, the first sign of his presence, the first touch and impression of his substance. A universal and transcendent infinite Person or Purusha is the mysterious hidden secret of his very being, unthinkable in form of mind, *acintya-rūpa*, but very near and present to the powers of our consciousness, emotion, will and knowledge. It is He, ineffable Absolute but also Friend and Lord and Enlightener and Lover, who is the object of this most complete devotion and approach and this most intimate inner becoming and surrender. This union, this relation is a thing lifted beyond the forms and laws of the limiting mind, too high for all these inferior dharmas; it is a truth of our self and spirit. And yet or rather therefore, because it is the truth of our self and spirit, the truth of its oneness with that Spirit from which all comes and by it and as its derivations and suggestions all exists and travails, it is not a negation but a fulfilment of all that mind and life point to and bear in them as their secret and unaccomplished significance. Thus it is not by a nirvana, an exclusion and negating extinction of all that we are here, but by a nirvana, an exclusion and negating extinction of ignorance and ego and a consequent ineffable fulfilment of our knowledge and will and heart's aspiration, an uplifted and limitless living of them in the Divine, in the Eternal, *nivasiṣyasi mayyeva*, a transfigurement and transference of all our consciousness to a greater inner status that there comes this supreme perfection and release in the spirit.

चेतसा सर्वकर्माणि मयि संन्यस्य मत्परः ।
बुद्धियोगमुपाश्रित्य मच्चित्तः सततं भव ।।५७।।

57. The mystery of our being implies necessarily a similar supreme mystery of the being of the Purushottama, *rahasyam uttamam*. It is not an exclusive impersonality of the Absolute that is the highest secret. This highest secret is the miracle of a supreme Person and apparent vast Impersonal that are one, an immutable transcendent Self of all things and a Spirit that manifests itself here at the very foundation of cosmos as an infinite and multiple personality acting everywhere, — a Self and Spirit revealed to our last, closest, profoundest experience as an illimitable Being who accepts us and takes

us to him, not into a blank of featureless existence, but most positively, deeply, wonderfully into all Himself and in all the ways of his and our conscious existence.

Therefore, says the Teacher, devoting all thyself to me, giving up in thy conscious mind all thy actions into Me, resorting to Yoga of the will and intelligence be always one in heart and consciousness with Me.

It is not the austerity of knowledge alone that can help us; there is room and infinite room for the heart's love and aspiration illumined and uplifted by knowledge, a more mystically clear, a greater calmly passionate knowledge. It is by the perpetual unified closeness of our heart-consciousness, mind-consciousness, all consciousness, *satatam̐ maccittaḥ*, that we get the widest, the deepest, the most integral experience of our oneness with the Eternal. A nearest oneness in all the being, profoundly individual in a divine passion even in the midst of universality, even at the top of transcendence is here enjoined on the human soul as its way to reach the Highest and its way to possess the perfection and the divine consciousness to which it is called by its nature as a spirit. The intelligence and will have to turn the whole existence in all its parts to the Ishwara, to the divine Self and Master of that whole existence, *buddhi-yogam upāśritya*. The heart has to cast all other emotion into the delight of oneness with him and the love of Him in all creatures. The sense spiritualised has to see and hear and feel him everywhere. The life has to be utterly his life in the Jiva. All the actions have to proceed from his sole power and sole initiation in the will, knowledge, organs of action, senses, vital parts, body, *cetasā sarva-karmāṇi mayi sannyasya mat-paraḥ*.

मच्चित्तः सर्वदुर्गाणि मत्प्रसादात्तरिष्यसि ।
अथ चेत्त्वमहङ्कारान्न श्रोष्यसि विनङ्क्ष्यसि ।।५८।।

58. If thou art that (one in heart and consciousness with Me) at all times, then by my grace thou shalt pass safe through all difficult and perilous passages; but if from egoism thou hear not, thou shalt fall into perdition.

The refusal of Arjuna to persevere in his divinely appointed work proceeded from the ego-sense in him, *ahaṅkāra*. The spiritual consequences will be infinitely worse now than before, now that a higher truth and a greater way and spirit of action have been revealed to him, if yet persisting in his egoism he perseveres in a vain and impossible refusal.

यदहङ्कारमाश्रित्य न योत्स्य इति मन्यसे ।
मिथ्यैष व्यवसायस्ते प्रकृतिस्त्वां नियोक्ष्यति ।।५९।।

59. Vain is this thy resolve, that in thy egoism thou thinkest, saying "I will not fight"; thy nature shall yoke thee to thy work, *prakṛitis-tvāṁ niyokṣyati*.

For it is a vain resolution, a futile recoil, since it springs only from a temporary failure of strength, a strong but passing deviation from the principle of energy of his inmost character, and is not the true will and way of his nature. If now he casts down his arms, he will yet be compelled by that nature to resume them when he sees the battle and slaughter go on without him. And in this return there will be no spiritual virtue. It will be his nature working through a restoration of the characteristic ideas and feelings of the ego mind that will compel him to annul his refusal. But whatever the direction, this continued subjection to the ego will mean a worse, a more fatal spiritual refusal, a perdition, *vinaṣṭi*; for it will be a definite falling away from a greater truth of his being than that which he has followed in the ignorance of the lower nature. He has been admitted to a higher consciousness, a new self-realisation, he has been shown the possibility of a divine instead of an egoistic action; the gates have been opened before him of a divine and spiritual in place of a merely intellectual, emotional, sensuous and vital life. He is called to be no longer a great blind instrument, but a conscious soul and an enlightened power and vessel of the Godhead. For there is this possibility within us: there is open to us even at our human highest this consummation and transcendence.

स्वभावजेन कौन्तेय निबद्धः स्वेन कर्मणा ।
कर्तुं नेच्छसि यन्मोहात् करिष्यस्यवशोऽपि तत् ॥६०॥

60. What from delusion thou desirest not to do, that helplessly thou shalt do bound by thy own work born of thy swabhava, *svabhāva-jena svena karmaṇā* (by the very force of his nature and the power within him). (*see also XI-32*)

ईश्वरः सर्वभूतानां हृद्देशेऽर्जुन तिष्ठति ।
भ्रामयन्सर्वभूतानि यन्त्रारूढानि मायया ॥६१॥

61. The Lord is stationed in the heart of all existences, O Arjuna, and turns them all round and round mounted on a machine by his Maya.

It is only when [man] is in possession of his real self and spirit that his nature can become a conscious instrument and enlightened power of the godhead. For then, when we enter into that inmost self of our existence, we come to know that in us and in all is the one Spirit and Godhead whom all Nature serves and manifests and we ourselves are soul of this Soul, spirit of this Spirit, our body his delegated image, our life a movement of the rhythm of his life, our mind a sheath of his consciousness, our senses his instruments, our emotions and sensations the seekings of his delight of being, our actions a means of his purpose. **It is the Lord seated in the heart of every creature, *īśvaraḥ sarva-bhūtānāṁ hṛiddeśe'rjuna tiṣṭhati*, who has been turning us in all our inner and outer action during the ignorance as if mounted on a machine on the wheel of this Maya of the lower Nature, *yantrā-rūḍhāni māyayā*.** And whether obscure in the Ignorance or luminous in the Knowledge, it is for him in us and him in the world that we have our existence. To live consciously and integrally in this knowledge and this truth is to escape from ego and break out of Maya.

तमेव शरणं गच्छ सर्वभावेन भारत ।
तत्प्रसादात्परां शान्तिं स्थानं प्राप्स्यसि शाश्वतम् ।।६२।।

62. In him take refuge in every way of thy being and by his grace thou shalt come to the supreme peace and the eternal status.

All other highest dharmas are only a preparation for this Dharma, and all Yoga is only a means by which we can come first to some kind of union and finally, if we have the full light, to an integral union with the Master and supreme Soul and Self of our existence. **The greatest Yoga is to take refuge from all the perplexities and difficulties of our nature with this indwelling Lord of all Nature, to turn to him with our whole being,** with the life and body and sense and mind and heart and understanding, with our whole dedicated knowledge and will and action, ***sarva-bhāvena*, in every way of our conscious self and our instrumental nature.** And when we can at all times and entirely do this, then the divine Light and Love and Power takes hold of us, fills both self and instruments and leads us safe through all the doubts and difficulties and perplexities and perils that beset our soul and our life, **leads us to a supreme peace and the spiritual freedom of our immortal and eternal status, *parāṁ śāntim, sthānaṁ śāśvatam*.**

इति ते ज्ञानमाख्यातं गुह्याद्गुह्यतरं मया ।
विमृश्यैतदशेषेण यथेच्छसि तथा कुरु ।।६३।।
सर्वगुह्यतमं भूयः शृणु मे परमं वचः ।
इष्टोऽसि मे दृढमिति ततो वक्ष्यामि ते हितम् ।।६४।।

63-64. So have I expounded to thee a knowledge more secret, *guhyataram*, than that which is hidden, *guhyāt*. Further hear the most secret, *guhyatamam*, the supreme word that I shall speak to thee.

For after giving out all the laws, the dharmas, and the deepest essence of its Yoga, after saying that beyond all the first secrets revealed to the mind of man by the transforming light of spiritual knowledge, *guhyāt*, this is a still deeper more secret truth, *guhyataram*, the Gita suddenly declares that there is yet a supreme word that it has to speak, *paramaṁ vacaḥ*, and a most secret truth of all, *sarva-guhyatamam*. **This secret of secrets the Teacher will tell to Arjuna as his highest good because he is the chosen and beloved soul, *iṣṭa*.** For evidently, as had already been declared by the Upanishad, it is only the rare soul chosen by the Spirit for the revelation of his very body, *tanuṁ svām*,[1] who can be admitted to this mystery, because **he alone is near enough in heart and mind and life to the Godhead to respond truly to it in all his being and to make it a living practice; *yathecchasi tathā kuru*.**

मन्मना भव मद्भक्तो मद्याजी मां नमस्कुरु ।
मामेवैष्यसि सत्यं ते प्रतिजाने प्रियोऽसि मे ॥६५॥
सर्वधर्मान्परित्यज्य मामेकं शरणं व्रज ।
अहं त्वा सर्वपापेभ्यो मोक्षयिष्यामि मा शुचः ॥६६॥

65-66. The last, the closing supreme word of the Gita expressing the highest mystery is spoken in two brief, direct and simple slokas and these are left without farther comment or enlargement to sink into the mind and reveal their own fullness of meaning in the soul's experience. For it is alone this inner incessantly extending experience that can make evident the infinite deal of meaning with which are for ever pregnant these words in themselves apparently so slight and simple. And we feel, as they are being uttered, that it was this for which the soul of the disciple was being prepared all the time and the rest was only an enlightening and enabling discipline and doctrine. Thus runs this secret of secrets, the highest most direct message of the Ishwara.

Become my-minded, my lover and adorer, a sacrificer to me, bow thyself to me, to me thou shalt come, this is my pledge and promise to thee, for dear art thou to me.

Abandon all dharmas and take refuge in me alone. I will deliver thee from all sin and evil, do not grieve.

The Gita throughout has been insisting on a great and well-built discipline of Yoga, a large and clearly traced philosophical system; and now suddenly it seems to break out of its own structure and says to the human

1. *yamevaiṣa vṛiṇute tena labhyas-tasyaiṣa ātmā vivṛinute tanum svām.* "Only by him whom this Being chooses can He be won; to him this Self unveils His own body".

Compare in *The Synthesis of Yoga* (I-1-§2): "He who chooses the Infinite, has been chosen by the Infinite." (*Editor's note*)

soul, "Abandon all dharmas, give thyself to the Divine alone, to the supreme Godhead above and around and within thee: that is all that thou needest, that is the truest and greatest way, that is the real deliverance."

"All this personal effort and self-discipline will not in the end be needed, all following and limitation of rule and dharma can at last be thrown away as hampering encumbrances if thou canst make a complete surrender to Me, depend alone on the Spirit and Godhead within thee and all things and trust to his sole guidance. I am here with thee in thy chariot of battle revealed as the Master of Existence within and without thee and I repeat the absolute assurance, the infallible promise that I will lead thee to myself through and beyond all sorrow and evil. Whatever difficulties and perplexities arise, be sure of this that I am leading thee to a complete divine life in the universal and an immortal existence in the transcendent Spirit."

The secret thing, *guhyam*, that all deep spiritual knowledge reveals to us, mirrored in various teachings and justified in the soul's experience, is for the Gita the secret of the spiritual self hidden within us of which mind and external Nature are only manifestations or figures. It is the secret of the constant relations between soul and Nature, Purusha and Prakriti, the secret of an indwelling Godhead who is the lord of all existence and veiled from us in its forms and movements. These are the truths taught in many ways by Vedanta and Sankhya and Yoga and synthetised in the earlier chapters of the Gita.

The more secret thing, *guhyataram*, developed by the Gita is the profound reconciling truth of the divine Purushottama, at once self and Purusha, supreme Brahman and a sole, intimate, mysterious, ineffable Godhead. This deeper mystery is founded on the secret of the supreme spiritual Prakriti and of the Jiva, an eternal portion of the Divine in that eternal and this manifested Nature and of one spirit and essence with him in his immutable self-existence. This profounder knowledge escapes from the elementary distinction of spiritual experience between the Beyond and what is here. For the Transcendent beyond the worlds is at the same time Vasudeva who is all things in all worlds; he is the Lord standing in the heart of every creature and the self of all existences and the origin and supernal meaning of everything that he has put forth in his Prakriti.

And now there comes the supreme word and most secret thing of all, *guhyatamam*, that the Spirit and Godhead is an Infinite free from all dharmas and though he conducts the world according to fixed laws and leads man through his dharmas of ignorance and knowledge, sin and virtue, right and wrong, liking and disliking and indifference, pleasure and pain, joy and sorrow and the rejection of these opposites, through his physical and vital, intellectual, emotional, ethical and spiritual forms and rules and standards, yet the Spirit and Godhead transcends all these things, and if we too can cast away all dependence on dharmas, surrender ourselves to this free and eternal Spirit and, taking care only to keep ourselves absolutely and exclusively open to him, trust to the light and power and delight of the Divine in us and, unafraid and ungrieving, accept only his guidance, then that is the truest, the greatest release and that brings the absolute and inevitable perfection of our self and nature. This is the way offered to the chosen of the Spirit, — to those only in whom he takes the greatest delight because they are nearest to him and most capable of oneness and of being even as he, freely consenting and concordant with Nature in her highest power and movement, universal in soul consciousness, transcendent in the spirit.

For a time comes in spiritual development when we become aware that all our effort and action are only our mental and vital reactions to the silent and secret insistence of a greater Presence in and around us. It is borne in upon us that all our Yoga, our aspiration and our endeavour are imperfect or narrow forms. Our ideas and experiences and efforts are mental images only of greatest things which would be done more perfectly, directly, freely, largely, more in harmony with the universal and eternal will by that Power itself in us if we could only put ourselves passively as instruments in the hands of a supreme and absolute strength and wisdom. That Power is not separate from us; it is our own self one with the self of all others and at the same time a transcendent Being and an immanent Person. Our existence, our action taken up into this greatest Existence would be the vast movement of an Infinity and an intimate ineffable Presence; it would be the constant spontaneity of formation and expression in us of this deep universal self and this transcendent Spirit. The Gita indicates that in order that that may wholly be, the surrender must be without reservations; our Yoga, our life, our state of inner being must be determined freely by this living Infinite, not predetermined by our mind's insistence on this or that dharma or any dharma. The divine Master of the Yoga, *yogeśvaraḥ kṛiṣṇaḥ*, will then himself take up our Yoga and raise us to our utmost possible perfection, vast and comprehensive, to the mind incalculable.

There is nothing really binding or permanent in man's knowledge-structures or his life-structures; but still he cannot but create standards of thought, knowledge, personality, life, conduct and, more or less consciously and completely, base his existence on them or, at least, try his best to frame his life in the ideative cadre of his chosen or accepted dharmas. In the passage to the spiritual life the supreme ideal held up is, on the contrary, not law, but liberty in the spirit; the spirit breaks through all formulas to find its self and, if it has still to be concerned with expression, it must arrive at the liberty of a free and true instead of an artificial expression, a true and spontaneous spiritual order. “Abandon all dharmas, all standards and rules of being and action, and take refuge in Me alone,” is the summit rule of the highest existence held up by the Divine Being to the seeker.

इदं ते नातपस्काय नाभक्ताय कदाचन ।
न चाशुश्रूषवे वाच्यं न च मां योऽभ्यसूयति ।।६७।।
य इमं परमं गुह्यं मद्भक्तेष्वभिधास्यति ।
भक्तिं मयि परां कृत्वा मामेवैष्यत्यसंशयः ।।६८।।
न च तस्मान्मनुष्येषु कश्चिन्मे प्रियकृत्तमः ।
भविता न च मे तस्मादन्यः प्रियतरो भुवि ।।६९।।
अध्येष्यते च य इमं धर्म्यं संवादमावयोः ।
ज्ञानयज्ञेन तेनाहमिष्टः स्यामिति मे मतिः ।।७०।।
श्रद्धावाननसूयश्च शृणुयादपि यो नरः ।
सोऽपि मुक्तः शुभांल्लोकान्प्राप्नुयात्पुण्यकर्मणाम् ।।७१।।
कच्चिदेतच्छ्रुतं पार्थ त्वयैकाग्रेण चेतसा ।
कच्चिदज्ञानसम्मोहः प्रनष्टस्ते धनञ्जय ।।७२।।

67-72. (*Untranslated*)

अर्जुन उवाच
नष्टो मोहः स्मृतिर्लब्धा त्वत्प्रसादान्मयाच्युत ।
स्थितोऽस्मि गतसन्देहः करिष्ये वचनं तव ।।७३।।

73. *Arjuna* — The whole Yoga is revealed, the great word of the teaching is given, and Arjuna the chosen human soul is once more turned, no longer in his egoistic mind but in this greatest self-knowledge, to the divine action. The Vibhuti is ready for the divine life in the human, his conscious spirit for the works of the liberated soul, *muktasya karma*. **Destroyed is the illusion of the mind; the soul's memory of its self and its truth concealed so long by the misleading shows and forms of our life has returned to it and become its normal consciousness: all doubt and perplexity gone, it can turn to the execution of the command and do faithfully whatever work for God and the world** may be appointed and apportioned to it by the Master of our being, the Spirit and Godhead self-fulfilled in Time and universe.

सञ्जय उवाच
इत्यहं वासुदेवस्य पार्थस्य च महात्मनः ।
संवादमिमश्रौषमद्भुतं रोमहर्षणम् ।।७४।।

व्यासप्रसादाच्छ्रुतवानेतद्गुह्यमहं परम् ।
योगं योगेश्वरात्कृष्णात्साक्षात्कथयतः स्वयम् ।।७५।।
राजन्संस्मृत्य संस्मृत्य संवादमिमद्भुतम् ।
केशवार्जुनयोः पुण्यं हृष्यामि च मुहुर्मुहुः ।।७६।।
तच्च संस्मृत्य संस्मृत्य रूपमत्यद्भुतं हरेः ।
विस्मयो मे महान् राजन्हृष्यामि च पुनः पुनः ।।७७।।
यत्र योगेश्वरः कृष्णो यत्र पार्थो धनुर्धरः ।
तत्र श्रीर्विजयो भूतिर्ध्रुवा नीतिर्मतिर्मम ।।७८।।

74-78. (*Untranslated*)

THE MESSAGE OF THE GITA

The call of the Gita is to the individual who has become capable of a complete spiritual existence; but for the rest of the race it prescribes only a gradual advance, to be wisely effected by following out faithfully with more and more of intelligence and moral purpose and with a final turn to spirituality the law of their nature.

The Supreme, the all-conscious Self, the Godhead, the Infinite is not solely a spiritual existence remote and ineffable; he is here in the universe at once hidden and expressed through man and the gods and through all beings and in all that is. And it is by finding him not only in some immutable silence but in the world and its beings and in all self and in all Nature, it is by raising to an integral as well as to a highest union with him all the activities of the intelligence, the heart, the will, the life that man can solve at once his inner riddle of Self and God and the outer problem of his active human existence. Made Godlike, God-becoming, he can enjoy the infinite breadth of a supreme spiritual consciousness that is reached through works no less than through love and knowledge. Immortal and free he can continue his human action from that highest level and transmute it into a supreme and all-embracing divine activity, — that indeed is the ultimate crown and significance here of all works and living and sacrifice and the world's endeavour.

This highest message is first for those who have the strength to follow after it, the master men, the great spirits, the God-knowers, God-doers, God-lovers who can live in God and for God and do their work joyfully for him in the world, a divine work uplifted above the restless darkness of the human mind and the false limitations of the ego. At the same time, and here we get the gleam of a larger promise which we may even extend to the hope of a collective turn towards perfection, — for if there is hope for man, why should there not be hope for mankind? — the Gita declares that all can if they will, even to the lowest and sinfullest among men, enter into the path of this Yoga. And if there is a true self-surrender and an absolute unegoistic faith in the indwelling Divinity, success is certain in this path. The decisive turn is needed; there must be an abiding belief in the Spirit, a sincere and insistent will to live in the Divine, to be in self one with him and in Nature — where too we are an eternal portion of his being — one with his greater spiritual Nature, God-possessed in all our members and Godlike.

It will be sufficient to close with a formulation of the living message the Gita still brings for man the eternal seeker and discoverer to guide him through the present circuits and the possible steeper ascent of his life up to the luminous heights of his spirit.

"The secret of action," so we might summarise the message of the Gita, the word of its divine Teacher, "is one with the secret of all life and existence. Existence is not merely a machinery of Nature, a wheel of law in which the soul is entangled for a moment or for ages; it is a constant manifestation of the Spirit. Life is not for the sake of life alone, but for God, and the living soul of man is an eternal portion of the Godhead. Action is for self-finding, for self-fulfilment, for self-realisation and not only for its own external and apparent fruits of the moment or the future. There is an inner law and meaning of all things dependent on the supreme as well as the manifested nature of the self; the true truth of works lies there and can be represented only incidentally, imperfectly and disguised by ignorance in the outer appearances of the mind and its action. The supreme, the faultless largest law of action is therefore to find out the truth of your own highest and inmost existence and live in it and not to follow any outer standard and dharma. All life and action must be till then an imperfection, a difficulty, a struggle and a problem. It is only by discovering your true self and living according to its true truth, its real reality that the problem can be finally solved, the difficulty and struggle overpassed and your doings perfected in the security of the discovered self and spirit turn into a divinely authentic action. Know then your self; know your true self to be God and one with the self of all others; know your soul to be a portion of God. Live in what you know; live in the self, live in your supreme spiritual nature, be united with God and Godlike. Offer, first, all your actions as a sacrifice to the Highest and the One in you and to the Highest and the One in the world; deliver last all you are and do into his hands for the supreme and universal spirit to do through you his own will and works in the world. This is the solution that I present to you and in the end you will find that there is no other."

Appendix

Self-Surrender in Works

THE WAY OF THE GITA

The greatest gospel of spiritual works ever yet given to the race, the most perfect system of Karmayoga known to man in the past, is to be found in the Bhagavad Gita. In that famous episode of the Mahabharata the great basic lines of Karmayoga are laid down for all time with an incomparable mastery and the infallible eye of an assured experience. It is true that the path alone, as the ancients saw it, is worked out fully; the perfect fulfilment, the highest secret is hinted rather than developed; it is kept back as an unexpressed part of a supreme mystery. There are obvious reasons for this reticence; for the fulfilment is in any case a matter of experience and no teaching can express it. It cannot be described in a way that can really be understood by a mind that has not the effulgent transmuting experience. And for the soul that has passed the shining portals and stands in the blaze of the inner light, all mental and verbal description is as poor as it is superfluous, inadequate and an impertinence. All divine consummations have perforce to be figured by us in the inept and deceptive terms of a language which was made to fit the normal experience of mental man; so expressed, they can be rightly understood only by those who already know, and, knowing, are able to give these poor external terms a changed, inner and transfigured sense. As the Vedic Rishis insisted in the beginning, the words of the supreme wisdom are expressive only to those who are already of the wise. The Gita at its cryptic close may seem by its silence to stop short of that solution for which we are seeking; it pauses at the borders of the highest spiritual mind and does not cross them into the splendours of the supramental Light. And yet its secret of dynamic, and not only static, identity with the inner Presence, its highest mystery of absolute surrender to the Divine Guide, Lord and Inhabitant of our nature, is the central secret. This surrender is the indispensable means of the supramental change and, again, it is through the supramental change that the dynamic identity becomes possible.

(*The Synthesis of Yoga*)

II

The difficult abstractive method of self-negation, however it may draw to it some exceptional natures, cannot satisfy universally the embodied soul in man, because it does not give an outlet to all the straining of his complex nature towards the perfect Eternal. Not only his abstracting contemplative intellect but his yearning heart, his active will, his positive mind in search of some Truth to which his existence and the existence of the world is a manifold key, have their straining towards the Eternal and Infinite and seek to find in it their divine Source and the justification of their being and their nature. From this need arise the religions of love and works, whose strength is that they satisfy and lead Godwards the most active and developed powers of our humanity, — for only by starting from these can knowledge be effective.

But the weakness of the kinetic and the emotional religions is that they are too much absorbed in some divine Personality and in the divine values of the finite. And, even when they have a conception of the infinite Godhead, they do not give us the full satisfaction of knowledge because they do not follow it out into its most ultimate and supernal tendencies. These religions fall short of a complete absorption in the Eternal and the perfect union by identity, — and yet to that identity in some other way, if not in the abstractive, since there all oneness has its basis, the spirit that is in man must one day arrive. On the other hand, the weakness of a contemplative quietistic spirituality is that it arrives at this result by two absolute abstractions and in the end it turns into a nothing or a fiction the human soul whose aspiration was yet all the time the whole sense of this attempt at union; for without the soul and its aspiration liberation and union could have no meaning. The little that this way of thinking recognises of his other powers of existence, it relegates to an inferior preliminary action which never arrives at any full or satisfying realisation in the Eternal and Infinite. Yet these things too which it restricts unduly, the potent will, the strong yearning of love, the positive light and all-embracing intuition of the conscious mental being are from the Divine, represent essential powers of him and must have some justification in their Source and some dynamic way of self-fulfilment in him. No God-knowledge can be integral, perfect or universally satisfying which leaves unfulfilled their absolute claim, no wisdom utterly wise which in its intolerant asceticism of search negates or in the pride of pure knowledge belittles the spiritual reality behind these ways of the Godhead.

The greatness of the central thought of the Gita in which all its threads are gathered up and united, consists in the synthetic value of a conception which recognises the whole nature of the soul of man in the universe and validates by a large and wise unification its many-sided need of the supreme and infinite Truth, Power, Love, Being to which our humanity turns in its search for perfection and immortality and some highest joy and power and peace. There is a strong and wide endeavour towards a comprehensive spiritual view of God and man and universal existence. Not indeed that everything without any exception is seized in these eighteen chapters, no spiritual problem left for solution; but still so large a scheme is laid out that we have only to fill in, to develop, to modify, to stress, to follow out points, to work out hint and illuminate adumbration in order to find a clue to any further claim of our intelligence and need of our spirit. The Gita itself does not evolve any quite novel solution out of its own questionings. To arrive at the comprehensiveness at which it aims, it goes back behind the great philosophical systems to the original Vedanta of the Upanishads; for there we have the widest and profoundest extant synthetic vision of spirit and man and cosmos. But what is in the Upanishads undeveloped to the intelligence because wrapped up in a luminous kernel of intuitive vision and symbolic utterance, the Gita brings out in the light of a later intellectual thinking and distinctive experience.

(*Essays on the Gita*)

III

All philosophy is concerned with the relations between two things, the fundamental truth of existence and the forms in which existence presents itself to our experience. The deepest experience shows that the fundamental truth is truth of the Spirit; the other is the truth of life, truth of form and shaping force and living idea and action. Our view is that the antinomy created between them is an unreal one. Spirit being the fundamental truth of existence, life can be only its manifestation; Spirit must be not only the origin of life but its basis, its pervading reality and its highest and total result. But the forms of life as they appear to us are at once its disguises and its instruments of self-manifestation. Man has to grow in knowledge till they cease to be disguises and grow in spiritual power and quality till they become in him its perfect instruments. To grow into the fullness of the divine is the true law of human life and to shape his earthly existence into its image is the meaning of his evolution. This is the fundamental tenet of the philosophy of the *Arya*.

The Gita we are treating as a powerful application of truth of spirit to the largest and most difficult part of the truth of life, to action, and a way by which action can lead us to birth into the Spirit and can be harmonised with the spiritual life.

(*Essays in Philosophy and Yoga*)

IV

The Gita was *not* meant by the writer to be an allegory — you can say, if you like, that now we should dismiss the ancient war element by interpreting it as if it were an allegory. The Gita is yoga, spiritual truth applied to the external life and action — but it may be *any* action and not necessarily an action *resembling* that of the Gita. The *principle* of the spiritual consciousness applied to action has to be kept — the particular example used by the Gita may be treated as a thing belonging to a past world.

*

The Gita cannot be described as exclusively a gospel of love. What it sets forth is a Yoga of knowledge, devotion and works based on a spiritual consciousness and realisation of oneness with the Divine and of the oneness of all beings in the Divine. Bhakti, devotion and love of God carrying with it unity with all beings and love for all beings is given a high place but always in connection with knowledge and works.

*

I may say however, that I do not regard business as something evil or tainted, any more than it is so regarded in ancient spiritual India. Even if I myself had had the command to do business as I had the command to do politics I would have done it without the least spiritual or moral compunction. All depends on the spirit in which a thing is done, the principles on which it is built and the use to which it is turned. I have done politics and the most violent kind of revolutionary politics, *ghoraṁ karma*, and I have supported war and sent men to it, even though politics is not always or often a very clean occupation nor can war be called a spiritual line of action. But Krishna calls upon Arjuna to carry on war of the most terrible kind and by his example encourage men to do every kind of human work, *sarvakarmāṇi*. Do you contend that Krishna was an unspiritual man and that his advice to Arjuna was mistaken or wrong in principle? Krishna goes further and declares that a man by doing in the right way and in the right spirit the work dictated to him by his fundamental nature, temperament and capacity and according to his and its dharma can move towards the Divine. He validates the function and dharma of the Vaishya as well as of the Brahmin and Kshatriya. It is in his view quite possible for a man to do business and make money and earn profits and yet be a spiritual man, practise Yoga, have an inner life. The Gita is constantly justifying works as a means of spiritual salvation and enjoining a Yoga of works as well as of

Bhakti and Knowledge. Krishna, however, superimposes a higher law also that work must be done without desire, without attachment to any fruit or reward, without any egoistic attitude or motive, as an offering or sacrifice to the Divine. This is the traditional Indian attitude towards these things, that all work can be done if it is done according to the dharma and, if it is rightly done, it does not prevent the approach to the Divine or the access to spiritual knowledge and the spiritual life.

There is the way of spiritual self-mastery and the way of spiritual self-giving and surrender to the Divine, abandoning ego and desire even in the midst of action or of any kind of work or all kinds of work demanded from us by the Divine. If it were not so, there would not have been great spiritual men like Janaka or Vidura in India and even there would have been no Krishna or else Krishna would have been not the Lord of Brindavan and Mathura and Dwaraka or a prince and warrior or the charioteer of Kurukshetra, but only one more great anchorite. The Indian scriptures and Indian tradition, in the Mahabharata and elsewhere, make room both for the spirituality of the renunciation of life and for the spiritual life of action. One cannot say that one only is the Indian tradition and that the acceptance of life and works of all kinds, *sarvakarmāṅi*, is un-Indian, European or Western and unspiritual.

*

It is not a fact that the Gita gives the whole base of Sri Aurobindo's message; for the Gita seems to admit the cessation of birth in the world as the ultimate aim or at least the ultimate culmination of Yoga; it does not bring forward the idea of spiritual evolution or the idea of the higher planes and the supramental Truth-Consciousness and the bringing down of that consciousness as the means of the complete transformation of earthly life.

(*Letters on Yoga*)

Index

This index is not comprehensive, but contains only the important words and phrases used in the text. For frequently used words (e.g. God, Purusha), only the important references are given. Sanskrit words are listed under their commonly used form (e.g. *śraddhā*); variations (e.g. *śraddhām*) are listed under the common form.

B

H

I

U

V

Postscript from the Editor

In a letter of 1946, Sri Aurobindo wrote:

> Our yoga is not identical with the yoga of the Gita although it contains all that is essential in the Gita's yoga. In our yoga we begin with the idea, the will, the aspiration of the complete surrender; but at the same time we have to reject the lower nature, deliver our consciousness from it, deliver the self involved in the lower nature by the self rising to freedom in the higher nature. If we do not do this double movement, we are in danger of making a tamasic and therefore unreal surrender, making no effort, no tapas and therefore no progress; or else we may make a rajasic surrender not to the Divine but to some self-made false idea or image of the Divine which masks our rajasic ego or something still worse.

In another letter he remarked:

> I may say that the way of the Gita is itself a part of the yoga here and those who have followed it, to begin with or as a first stage, have a stronger basis than others for this yoga.

The purpose of the present book is to show, in Sri Aurobindo's words and following the order of the *slokas* of the Bhagavad Gita, what the Yoga of the Gita is and how it can become a strong basis for the practice of Sri Aurobindo's Integral Yoga. It is meant to serve as an introduction to the Gita and to Sri Aurobindo's commentary on it, *Essays on the Gita*, which contains his all-embracing vision of the Gita's Yoga and of the way beyond it.

In the course of our research we found that Sri Aurobindo has actually translated nearly all 700 *slokas* of the Gita. Most of those translations appear in his *Essays*, but some occur in *The Synthesis of Yoga, The Life Divine*, and various articles and essays published recently under the titles *Essays Divine and Human* and *Essays in Philosophy and Yoga*. A translation he made around 1902 contains an early rendering of the first six chapters of the Gita.

Our main task consisted in extracting those renderings from their various sources and weaving them together in the order of the Gita's *slokas*;

that is the reason why these *slokas* are not presented here in the ordinary way, with the four *padas* arranged on two or three consecutive lines.

Sri Aurobindo did not translate a score of *slokas*, including the last twelve of the final chapter, and about a score of *padas;* many of them are phrases such as "This I will now declare to thee", and "There is no doubt about that". In those rare cases, we chose not to translate them ourselves: a blank has been left beneath the Sanskrit text.

The length of the translated *slokas* varies considerably because Sri Aurobindo elaborated some of his renderings in order to better bring out their significance. The deeper truth of the *slokas* is here revealed, and with all their implications, suggestions and allusions brought to light, they become more penetrating, more vibrant and alive in us; and sometimes they open us to vistas beyond.

This book also contains explanatory passages from *Essays on the Gita,* dealing with the great ideas, theories and systems prevailing at the time. These concepts include *caturvarna* and the caste system, Sannyasa and Tyaga, Sankhya Yoga and Vedanta, Avatarhood, the theory of sacrifice, the determinism of Nature and free will, the reconciliation of Spirit and Nature and the reconciliation of works and spiritual living. These and other aspects of the Gita's teaching are often alluded to merely by a single word or *pada,* yet they underlie the fundamental message of this great Scripture and sustain its whole structure. These explanatory passages help to introduce the reader to the relevant portion of the teaching; some of them form a link with the preceding portion, others indicate the foundation upon which some new aspect rests, show the direction in which it is leading or place it in its context.

In a few cases (*slokas* VII.8-11, X.21-38, XI.9-14, 24-30, XVII.4-22 and XVIII.18-39), Sri Aurobindo did not follow the order of the Sanskrit text. In this book, the normal sequence of the Sanskrit *slokas* has been maintained, but the English translation of them follows the order of Sri Aurobindo's translation.

In a letter to a disciple, Sri Aurobindo mentioned that he had not translate the Gita. Indeed, the present work is not a translation, strictly speaking, in the sense that it is not merely a word-by-word rendering of the text. It is the Gita *after* Sri Aurobindo, the Gita as it has been *seen* and realised by him, and given to us so that we may discover and follow our own path of self-discovery and self-perfection.

We feel that there is truly an urgent need for the Yoga of the Gita, and for a vision beyond it. This Yoga is set forth amidst a gigantic panorama, a colossal internecine war, a giant destruction of all the values, whether domestic, social, ethical or religious, of the past. A dejected Arjuna is admonished and then encouraged by his Charioteer Sri Krishna, who urges him to fight for the Dharma, the true spiritual Law, and perform all his actions as an offering to the Lord. On this battlefield of Life, the Divine Teacher reveals to his beloved friend and disciple the glorious vision of Time and the World-Spirit and, at the end, the supreme mystery of our existence.

In the first chapter of his *Essays*, Sri Aurobindo writes:

> We of the coming day stand at the head of a new age of development which must lead to a new and larger synthesis.... We do not belong to the past dawns, but to the noons of the future.

Sri Aurobindo has stressed both the need and the possibility of breaking down the barriers of the past in order to prepare for the new age that is to come. The seeker of the Integral Yoga should always look for something else beyond, something more, something new in this continuous and endless ascent of "the hill of Yoga" towards the highest secret of "the ever unmanifest mystery of the Supreme". As the Vedic Rishis expressed it:

> *yat sanoh sanum aruhat*
> *bhuri aspasta kartvam*
>
> As one ascends from peak to peak
> there is made clear the much that has still to be done.

This great Vedic cry has been echoed and amplified by Sri Krishna in Chapter X of the Gita:

> *nastyanto vistarasya me*
> *nanto'sti mama divyanam vibhutinam parantapa*
>
> There is no end to my divine manifestations, O Parantapa,
> and I have revealed to you only a small part of My infinite Splendour.

Galeran d'Esterno